THE CHILKAT DANCING BLANKET

THE CHILKAT DANCING BLANKET

BY CHERYL SAMUEL

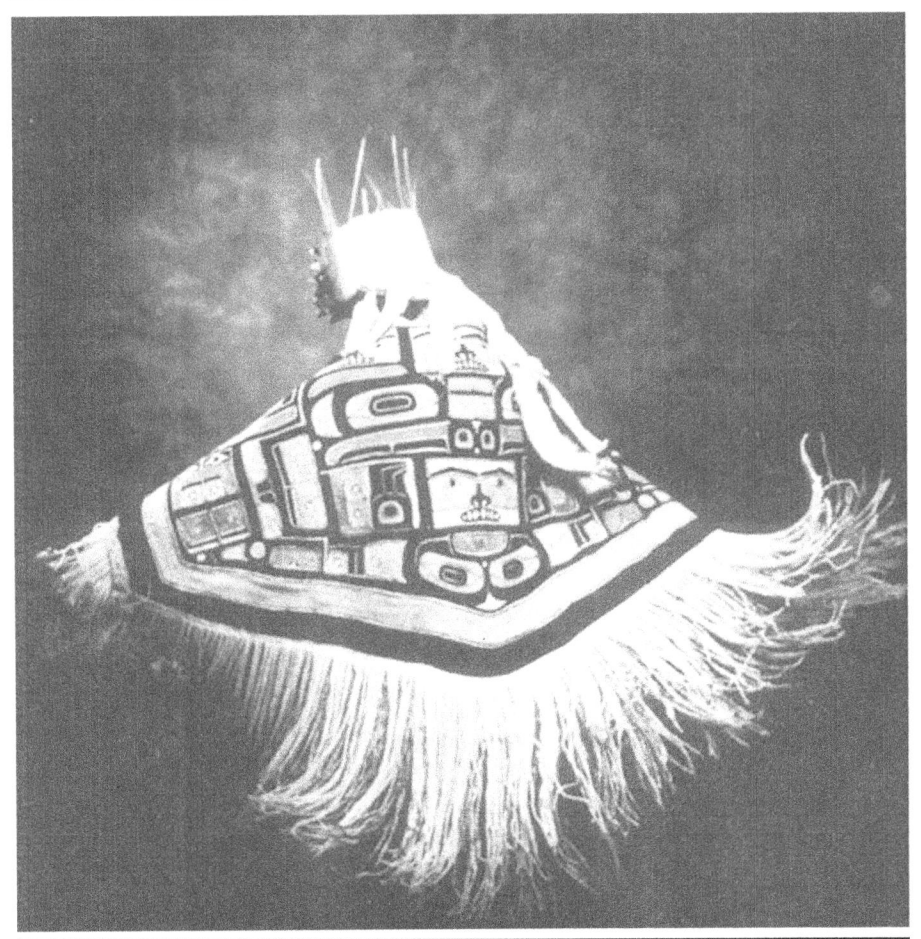

ILLUSTRATED BY SARA PORTER

UNIVERSITY OF OKLAHOMA PRESS : NORMAN

Edited by Marlene Leamon
Designed by Judy Petry

Illustrations are by Sara Porter except those by Duane Pasco—
    figures 27, 29, 31, 442, 443, 445, 448-50, 456, 458-60, 464.

Map drawn by Dean Samuel
Map insert courtesy of University of Washington Press

The author wishes to express special appreciation to the British
Columbia Provincial Museum, Victoria, British Columbia for its
cooperation and assistance. Photographs are by the author (noted
by "CS" in corresponding captions) or are reprinted by permission
of museums except those by the following.
    Sara Porter—figures 3 and 339
    Edgar Samuel—figures 44-49, 51-52, 54, and C
    Chris Sherman—figure 25
    Jorgen Svendsen—cover photo, part heading photos, and
        figures 14 and 439
    Art Thompson—figure 440

Cover: *Tony Hunt, a well-known Kwagulth artist, wears his Dancing
Blanket while performing a Headdress Dance. (Jorgen Svendsen)*

Library of Congress Cataloging-in-Publication Data

Samuel, Cheryl, 1944—
    The Chilkat dancing blanket.

    Bibliography: p. 226.
    Includes index.
    1. Chilkat Indians—Textile industry and fabrics. 2. Indians Of
North America—Northwest coast of North America—Textile
industry and fabrics. 3. Hand weaving—Northwest coast of North
America. 4. Indian craft. I. Title.
E99.C552S25   746.9'7'08997   82–5824
ISBN 978-0-8061-2299-1 (paper)   AACR2

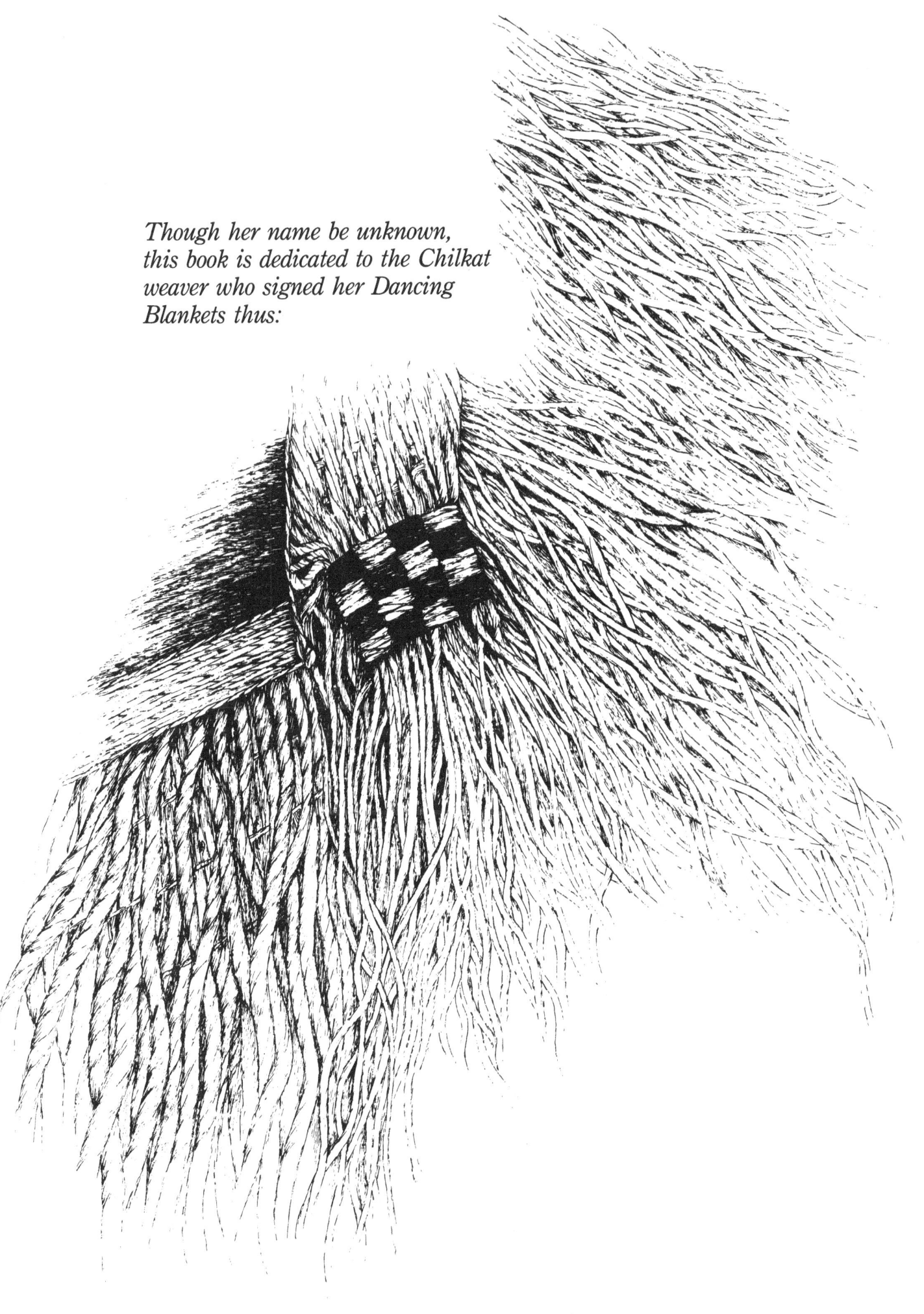

Though her name be unknown, this book is dedicated to the Chilkat weaver who signed her Dancing Blankets thus:

C O N T E N T S

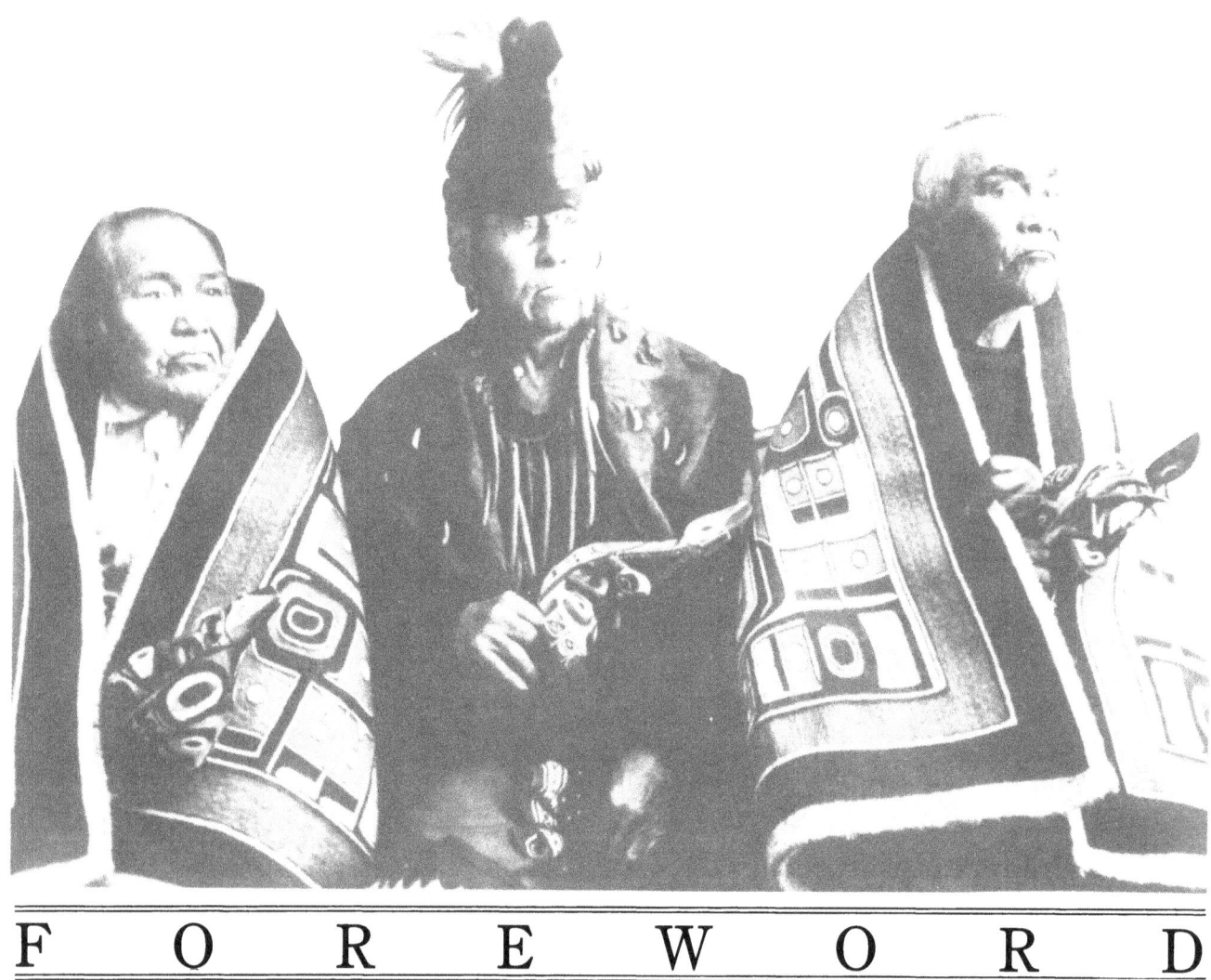

F O R E W O R D

There is a mysterious and beautiful textile which can be seen
hanging in exhibit cases or shelved in the dark recesses of museum
storerooms. It may rest, out of sight, in an Indian chest on the
Northwest Coast and appear, as it was meant to, around the shoulders
of a dancing chief celebrating the heritage from which it came. We
have called this rich tapestry robe the Chilkat Blanket, after the
people who made it in historic times. Of all the treasures born of this
opulent society, the Chilkat Blanket expresses most graphically ideas
of nobility and prestigious display.

Yet this textile, as we know it, was not seen by the first European
explorers who came to the Northwest Coast in the closing years of the
eighteenth century. It was just then being perfected, out of the joining

of an ancient tradition of *twining* with mountain goat wool and cedar bark and the *painting* of awesome creatures of mythology on wooden chests and screens. By the early years of the nineteenth century, skillful, innovative weavers had solved the difficult problems of rendering broad black formline designs in woolen twining, producing the classic Chilkat Dancing Blanket as we know it.

The literature on the Chilkat weaving tradition is very meager. The major work has been George T. Emmons' 1907 study, *The Chilkat Blanket,* with an accompanying analysis of blanket designs by Franz Boas. Although a pioneering and useful work, it is at best a general description. In 1950 Philip Drucker published some tantalizing notes on blanket weaving in his *Culture Element Distributions: Northwest Coast* and in 1955 Joanne Hirabayashi published an article, "The Chilkat Weaving Complex," which is an analysis of the characteristics of blankets based on those in the collection of the Washington State Museum. Beyond these few, the Chilkat Blanket appears in print only in brief descriptions, almost all based on Emmons' study.

My own interest in the blankets has been a long-standing one, and I have experimented with weaving. I believe that there is no understanding of an art tradition quite like that which comes from firsthand personal experience with its materials, tools, and methods. There were others experimenting with Chilkat techniques in the early 1950s, among them Richard Conn, now Curator of Native Arts at the Denver Art Museum. And in 1965, another dedicated admirer of the Dancing Blanket, Doris Kyber-Gruber, completed her first blanket. Independent of other experimenters, she had solved for herself the intricate puzzles of the weave. About this same time, I had the opportunity to visit in Alaska one of the last Tlingit weavers, Mrs. Jennie Thlunaut, who had been Drucker's informant, and who clarified some puzzling details. Since then, others have experimented with weaving, and two of them, Dorica Jackson and Jeannie Stewart, have completed blankets. In recent years, a number of blankets in the Chilkat style have been woven by Kwakiutl women in British Columbia, notably the late Mrs. Mungo Martin; but they utilize very different techniques from those of traditional Chilkat Blankets.

Nearly a decade ago, during this period of experimentation, a young weaver named Cheryl came to see me at the Burke Museum. She wanted to find out about Chilkat weaving. The existing literature had not answered her questions, and peering at blankets in museum cases had been little more satisfying. Cheryl spent a lot of time with the museum's blankets, and later with many others from different collections, patiently examining them, experimenting, and deciphering their most cryptic secrets. There is a Tlingit tale, one of the many surrounding the beginning of this weaving complex, that tells of Chilkat weavers laboriously unraveling a blanket obtained from the Tsimshian in order to understand the techniques involved in reproducing it. Cheryl Samuel has repeated their accomplishment. She has "unraveled" the complexities of the Dancing Blanket and laid it out before our eyes. Her analysis leaves me in awe of her achievement and of the marvelous Dancing Blanket which is her subject.

Bill Holm
Curator, Northwest Coast Indian Art
Thomas Burke Memorial Washington State Museum
January 1982

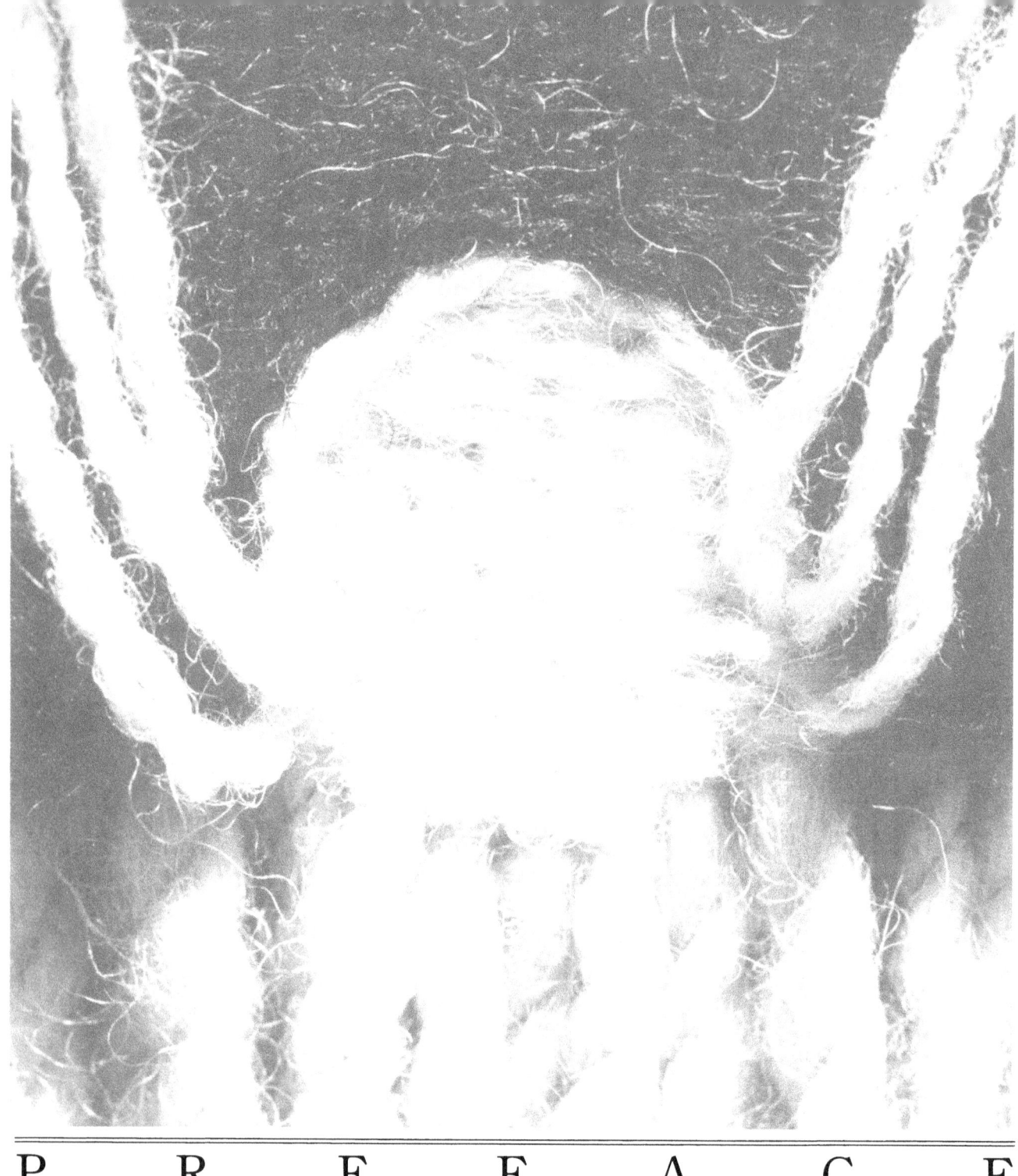

P R E F A C E

2. A circle (CS)

A circle of hands...a circle of stones...a fairy ring...Within the magic line of a circle a tremendous energy flows and this energy tapped me when I first asked, "how can I weave a perfect circle?" There were so many answers: tapestry techniques, knotting techniques, lace techniques, and still none of them seemed *perfect*. Then I heard Bill Holm speak about the weaving of the Chilkat women; I saw *perfect circles*.

The story of the Dancing Blanket is one of tradition and technique. For me, it has been an odyssey of learning, from the first glimpse I had of a Dancing Blanket to the knowledge my daughter Alena can now share with me; she has spun far more warp yarns than I have. The adventure began a decade ago, when the energy of that small circle caught me in its sphere. I wished to unravel its mysteries;

what I did not know then was that it would lead me into a world of drama and dancing birds; of music, museums, and manuscripts; of firelight, feasts, and friends.

How were these circles woven? I turned first to Bill Holm, his notes, and his immense knowledge, and to Lieutenant Emmons and his invaluable monograph. Eventually, I met with three women in my home to share what I thought I knew. We laugh together now at our beginnings. Eyes twinkle when we recall the first time we boiled "old" urine *in* the kitchen. We would look at a strand of blue-grey yarn and see the Chilkat blue-green, so desperate were we to know the secret of the dye. The things we did! A fish and berry diet for a month, just in case. . . Children's urine? The kindergarten teacher phoning home: "I don't know what to do with your child, she just keeps saying, 'Quick, I need a cup for my mama's dying.' "

There was never a chance to unravel a weaving. They are too precious, too few, too coveted. Ironic, now, that Katie Pasco has this chance regularly as she restores old blankets to new use. But we could not do it then, so it just took hours of looking and thinking and trying. Eventually, I gained enough understanding to know what questions to ask. Bill Holm taught me that unless you can duplicate a technique, you can never really claim you know how it is done. This proved itself true repeatedly. For six years we *knew* that all the horizontal outlines were three-strand twining which changed to braiding when they traveled vertically. Our corners were not quite square, but we assumed that this was due to inexperience. Then Dr. Rozaire told me how to distinguish between twining and braiding on a completed piece: the outlines on the Dancing Blankets were entirely braided. It seems strange, now, that we made that mistake, but the mental blocks which precede discovery are mysteriously enormous.

At times I have felt a desire to explode these traditional techniques into the modern world, or even to better them. Fortunately, the native weavers have saved me from gross arrogance. Whenever I thought I knew more, or best, and attempted to improve on a technique, I was humbled. Again and again, the traditional perfection of rhythms passed on from generation to generation proved more efficient, more beautiful, more enduring than anything I could "invent." My respect for traditional knowledge has become immense.

I wish I could travel back a hundred years to a time when women wove the Dancing Blankets with such skill and dexterity. Still unanswered questions would be resolved. Indeed, some of what I set forth here would be changed; it is inevitable. The vast majority of the information in this volume does come, not from written sources but from the Dancing Blankets themselves, and, by extension, from the women who wove them. A grant from the National Museums of Canada made possible a trip through major museum collections in the United States, Canada, and Europe. I spent hours with the Dancing Blankets, absorbing the wisdom of the weavers. For the most part, collection data is incomplete or nonexistent. If there seems a lack of historical documentation in this book, it is because this information *is* lacking. I must leave it to another to answer questions relating to the dates or the tribal origins of particular Dancing Blankets.

There is always more to learn. As contemporary weavers master these techniques, perhaps the combination of this beginning and the knowledge to come will result once more in the perfection of one of the most controlled, yet freest, forms of tapestry weaving ever developed.

The Dawn of the Dancing Blanket

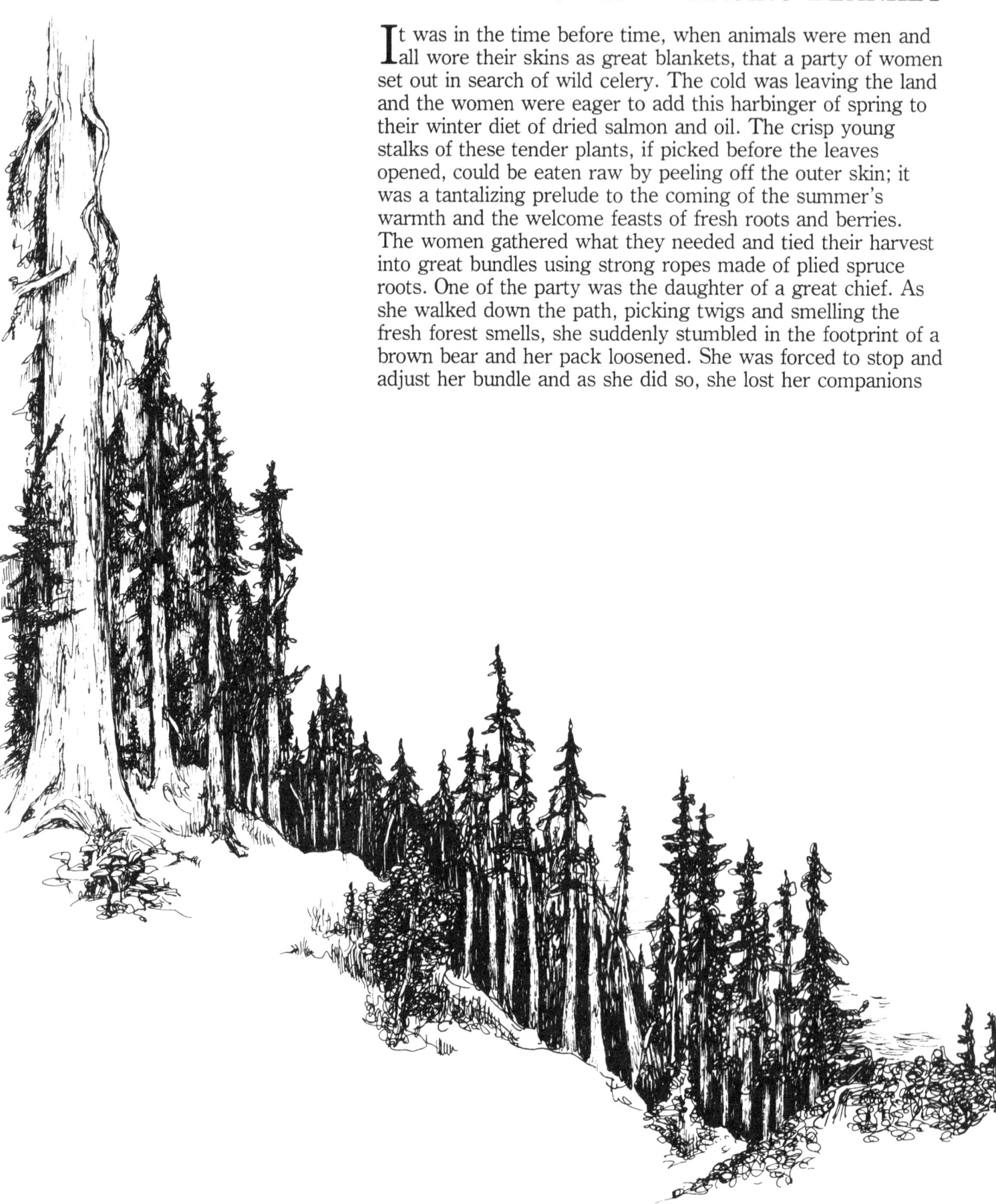

It was in the time before time, when animals were men and all wore their skins as great blankets, that a party of women set out in search of wild celery. The cold was leaving the land and the women were eager to add this harbinger of spring to their winter diet of dried salmon and oil. The crisp young stalks of these tender plants, if picked before the leaves opened, could be eaten raw by peeling off the outer skin; it was a tantalizing prelude to the coming of the summer's warmth and the welcome feasts of fresh roots and berries. The women gathered what they needed and tied their harvest into great bundles using strong ropes made of plied spruce roots. One of the party was the daughter of a great chief. As she walked down the path, picking twigs and smelling the fresh forest smells, she suddenly stumbled in the footprint of a brown bear and her pack loosened. She was forced to stop and adjust her bundle and as she did so, she lost her companions in the distance. Angrily, she mumbled abuses at the Bear family. When her pack was well settled she started after her friends, going slowly and cautiously in the coming dusk.

The twilight came on. The woods stilled in preparation for the night's hunt. Little birds came to rest in the great boughs and the wind hushed. Raven's wings pounded overhead as he flew to join the darkness. As the light lowered, the girl was suddenly aware of footsteps behind her. A handsome youth appeared and whispered soft words in her ear, persuading her to follow him to his home and become his wife. She was gladdened by his comforting words and went with him.

Deep in the forest they reached a village of the Bear family. Echoes of her disgruntled words beat in her ears and she trembled at the thought of the trickery to which she had fallen victim. Her daring suitor was of the Bear clan.

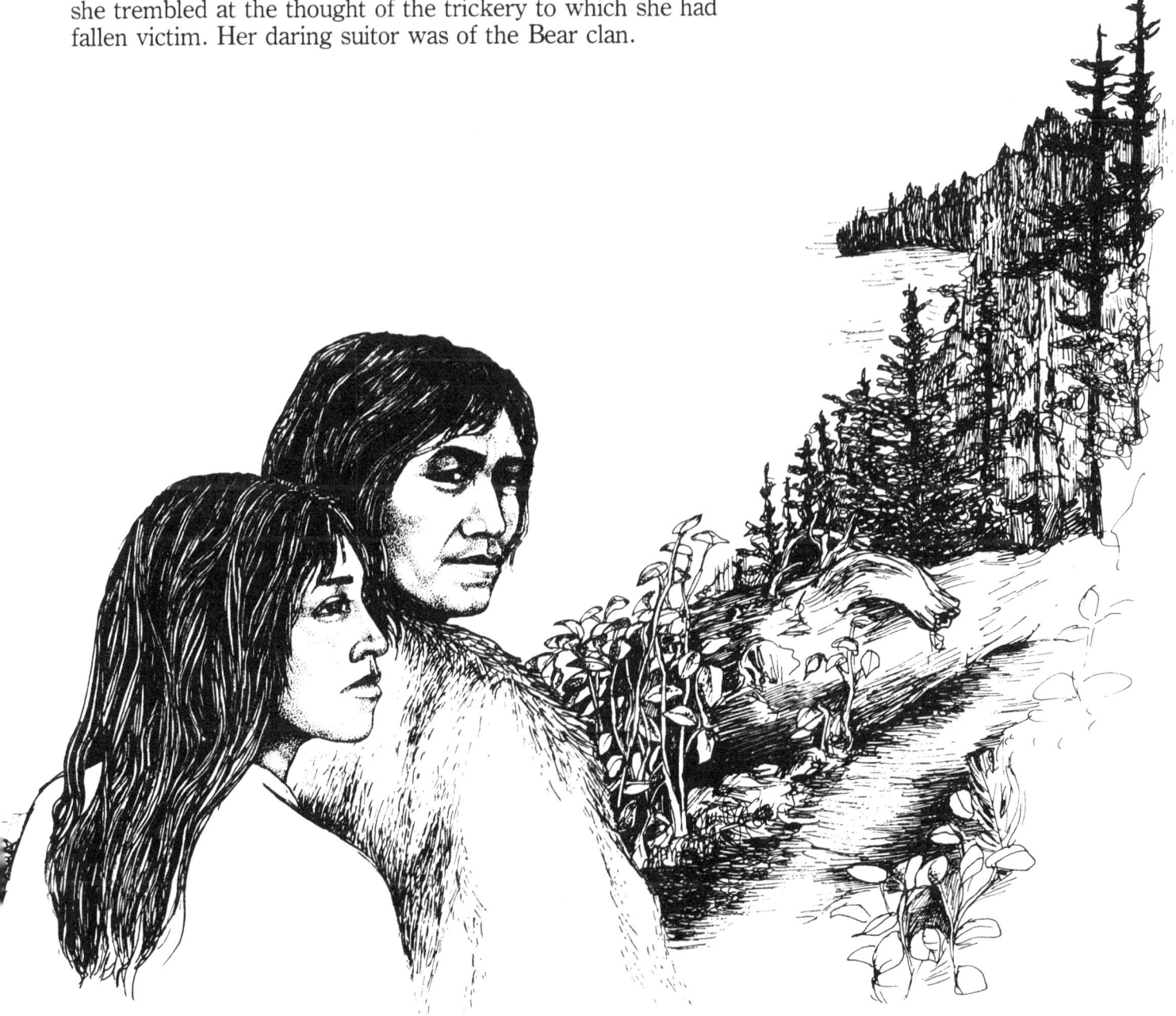

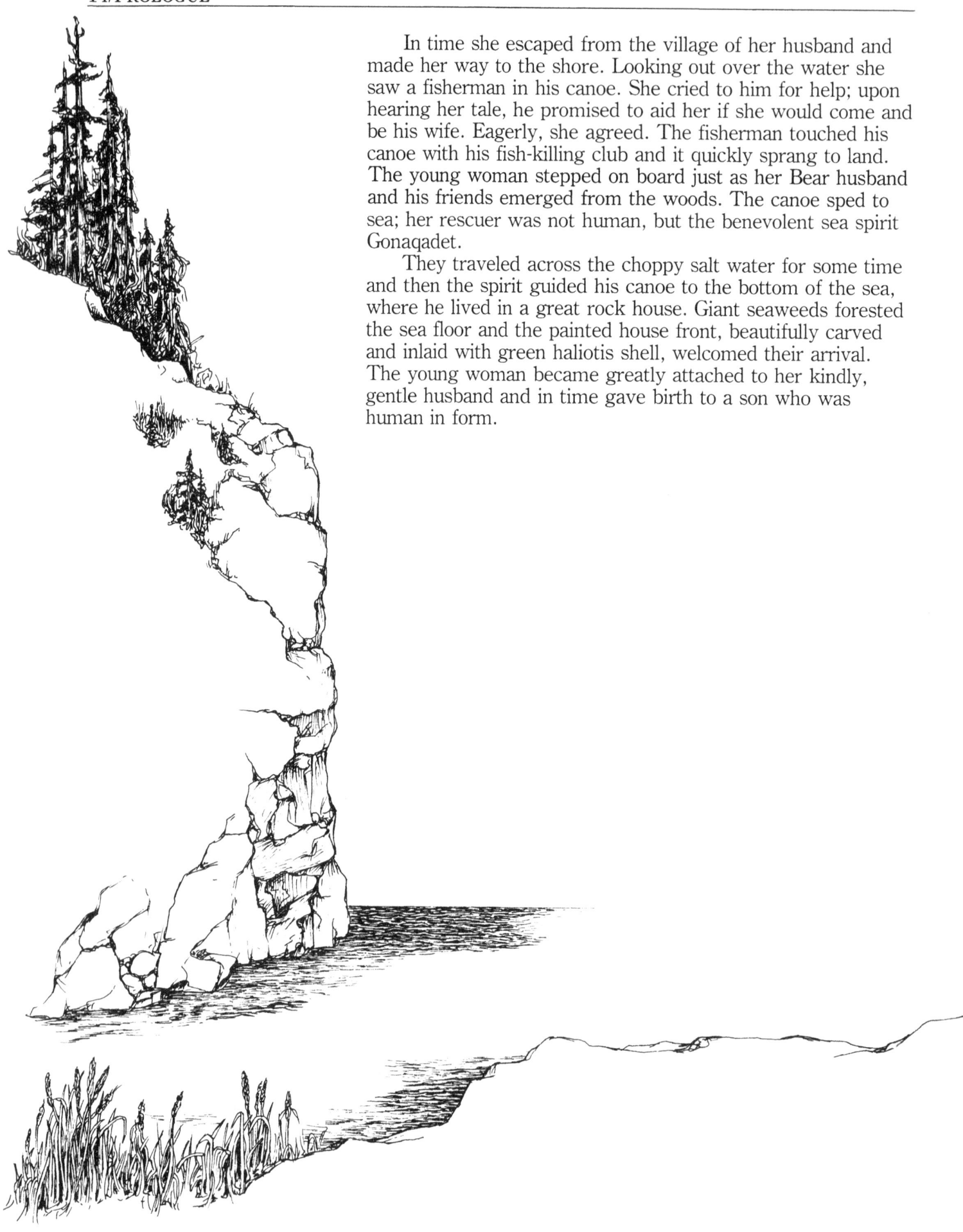

In time she escaped from the village of her husband and made her way to the shore. Looking out over the water she saw a fisherman in his canoe. She cried to him for help; upon hearing her tale, he promised to aid her if she would come and be his wife. Eagerly, she agreed. The fisherman touched his canoe with his fish-killing club and it quickly sprang to land. The young woman stepped on board just as her Bear husband and his friends emerged from the woods. The canoe sped to sea; her rescuer was not human, but the benevolent sea spirit Gonaqadet.

They traveled across the choppy salt water for some time and then the spirit guided his canoe to the bottom of the sea, where he lived in a great rock house. Giant seaweeds forested the sea floor and the painted house front, beautifully carved and inlaid with green haliotis shell, welcomed their arrival. The young woman became greatly attached to her kindly, gentle husband and in time gave birth to a son who was human in form.

When the boy was old enough to begin his training for manhood, she asked her husband to let her travel to the land so that she could put him in the care of her brother. He agreed to her plan on the condition that she promise not to forget him. She and the boy made the long journey back to the land and went to live in the house of her brother. While the boy grew and learned the arts of hunting and of fishing, of making tools and of carving, of singing, of dancing and of all the many things a boy needed to know to live in the world of men, Gonaqadet's wife began to weave. She created a magnificent ceremonial robe into which she wove the story of her meeting with her husband and their courtship. When her son had reached the age of manhood, she left the land and returned to her home under the sea, presenting her husband with the robe she had woven. This was the origin of the first Dancing Blanket.

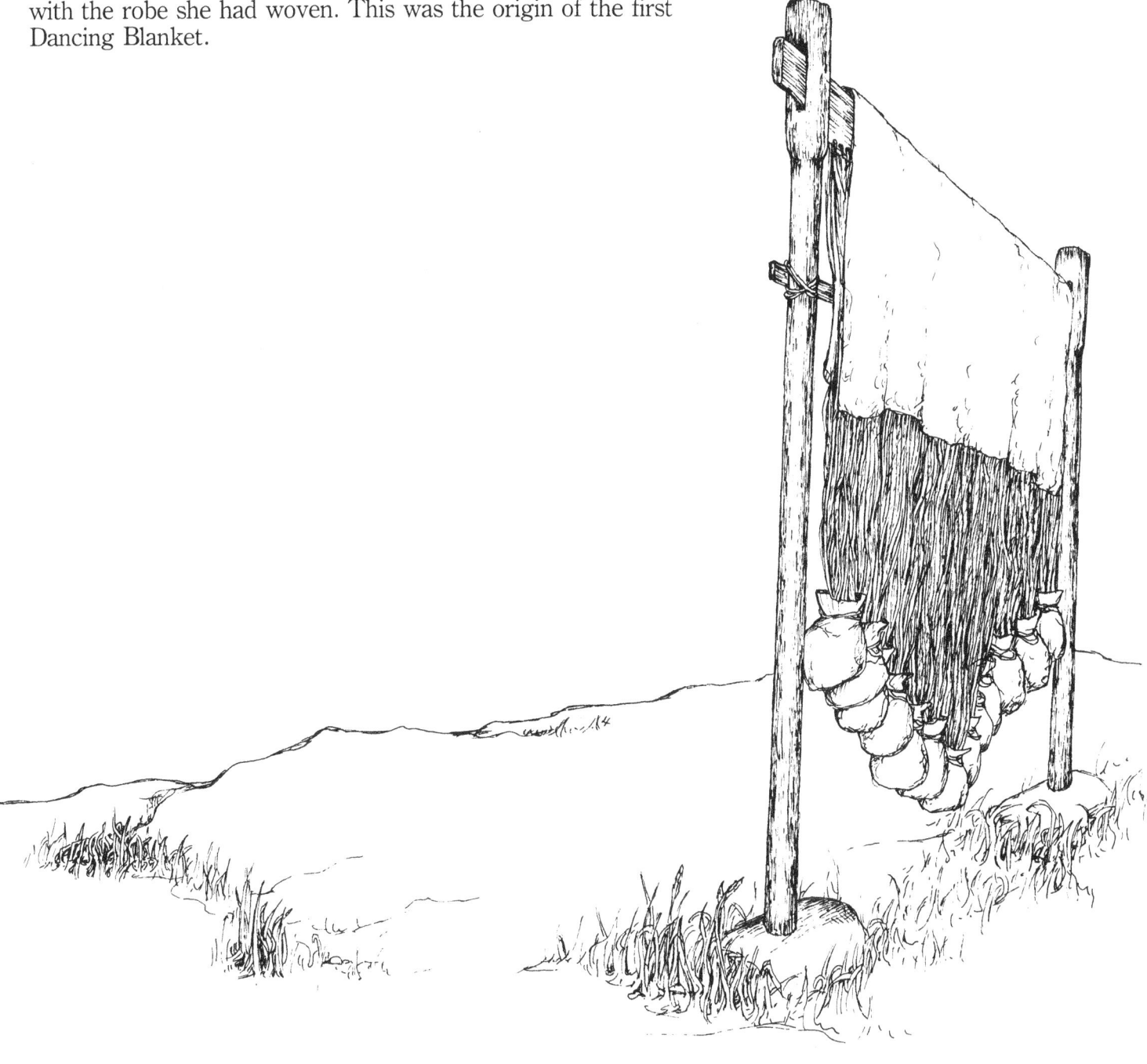

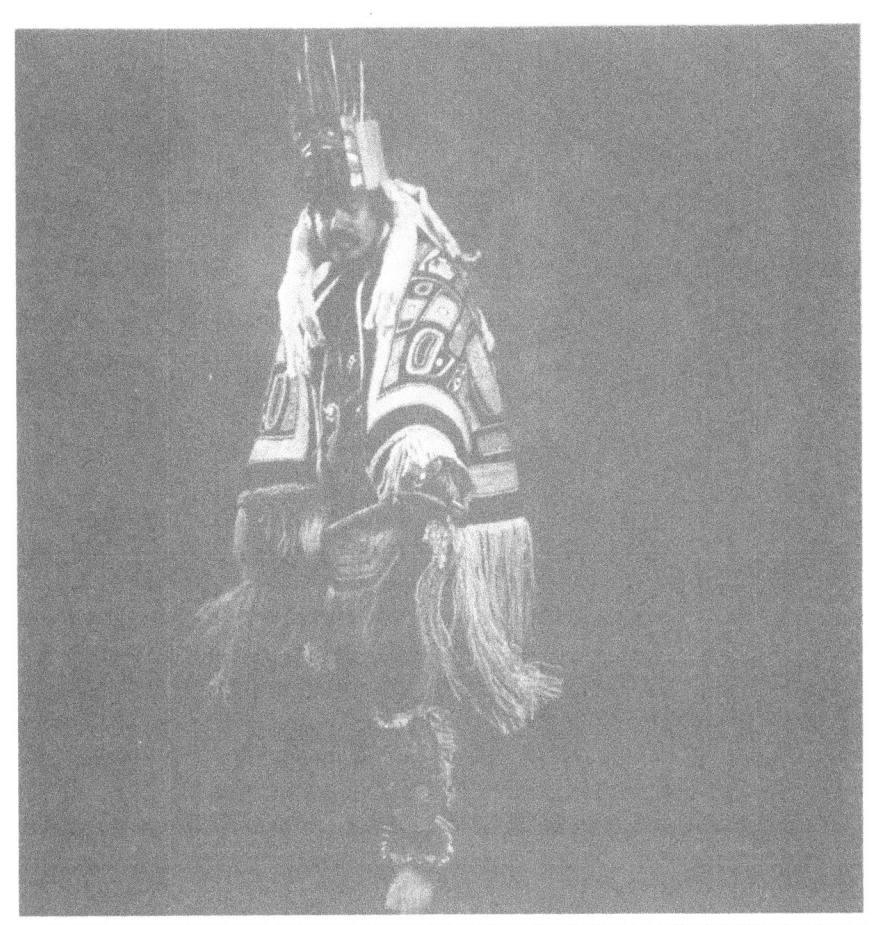

PART

ORIGIN,
CEREMONY,
AND DESIGN

I

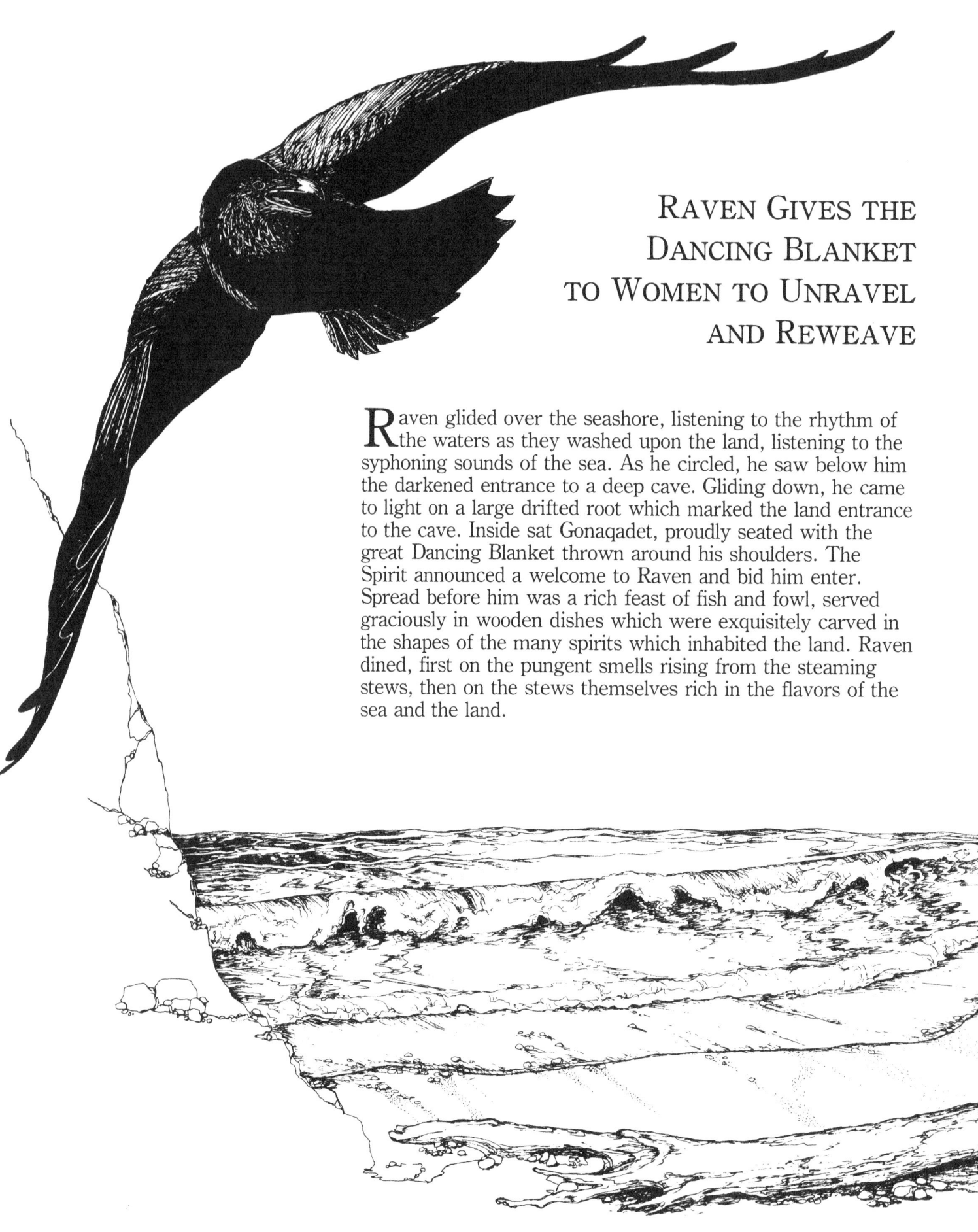

RAVEN GIVES THE DANCING BLANKET TO WOMEN TO UNRAVEL AND REWEAVE

Raven glided over the seashore, listening to the rhythm of the waters as they washed upon the land, listening to the syphoning sounds of the sea. As he circled, he saw below him the darkened entrance to a deep cave. Gliding down, he came to light on a large drifted root which marked the land entrance to the cave. Inside sat Gonaqadet, proudly seated with the great Dancing Blanket thrown around his shoulders. The Spirit announced a welcome to Raven and bid him enter. Spread before him was a rich feast of fish and fowl, served graciously in wooden dishes which were exquisitely carved in the shapes of the many spirits which inhabited the land. Raven dined, first on the pungent smells rising from the steaming stews, then on the stews themselves rich in the flavors of the sea and the land.

After Raven had finished his feast, Gonaqadet invited him to sit around the central fire and watch while many dances were performed. The beat of the drum echoed the pounding of the waves; the steady, elegant flow of the dancers' movements imprinted itself on Raven's memory so that he might take it to the villages of men. Gonaqadet himself was a dynamic dancer and more than once he donned the Dancing Blanket which his wife had woven for him in honor of their meeting and courtship. The great fringe, Nakheen, which flowed from the base of the weaving, swung about his body as he moved. White eagle down, spilling from his headdress, floated floorward to mingle with the swinging woolen strands. It was an inspiring sight, and Raven's heart pounded as the pulse of the dance grew stronger.

When the ceremony was over, the generous Gonaqadet made a long speech, offering Raven his Dancing Blanket to take with him when he journeyed to the villages of men. Raven accepted this inspired gift and in time offered it to the human race to unravel and weave again. It was in this way that women became weavers of the beautiful Dancing Blankets.

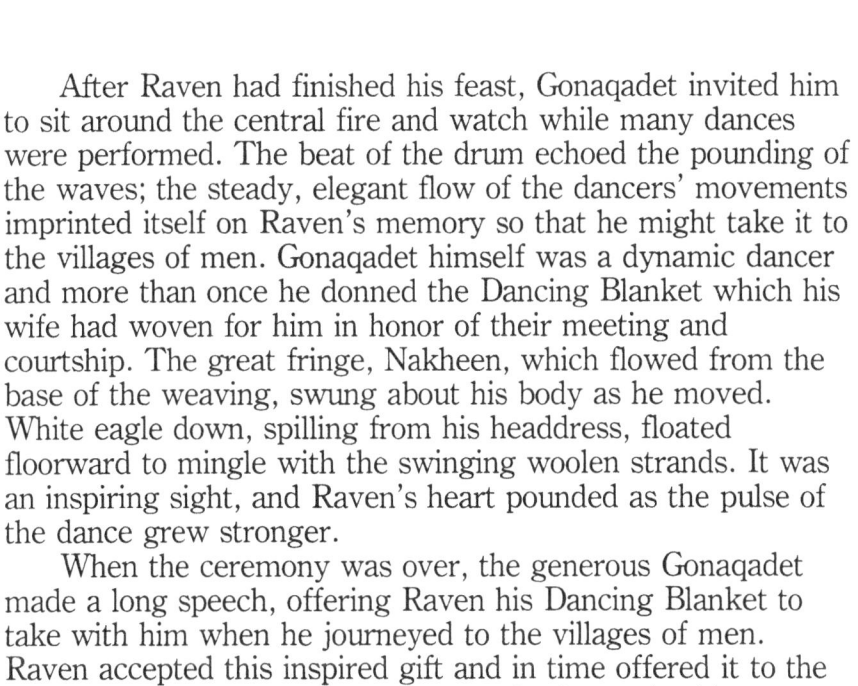
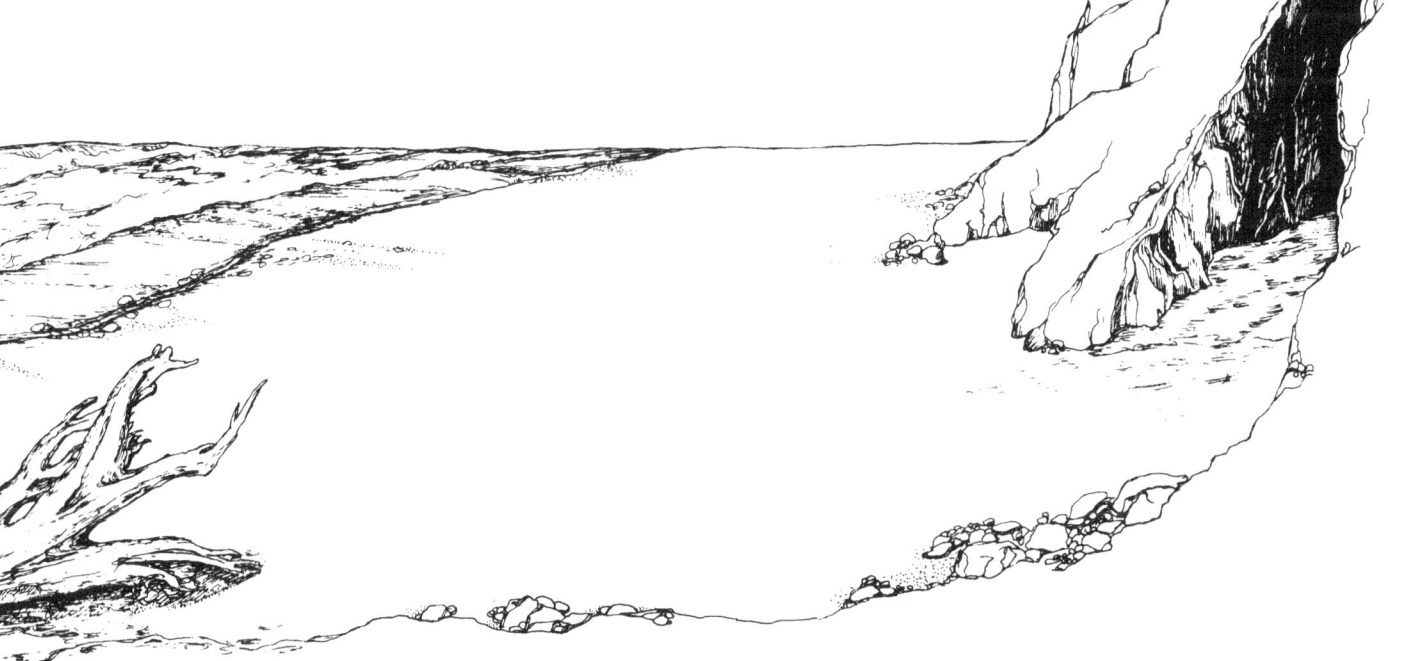

The First Dancing Apron

On the banks of the Skeena River in a Tsimshian village lived a widow with her young daughter. Although the dark days were growing lighter, deep snow still blanketed the ground and gowned the trees in ermine robes. The people and animals were hungry, for the season's stores were low and no food was to be found on the frozen land.

The fire in the center of a great chief's house burned slowly as day after day the young girl sat, facing the painted screen at the rear of the house. Beautifully carved and painted with a myriad of small figures, the screen told of the greatness of her clan and of a time of leisure and plenty. Day after day she gazed at the screen, mesmerized by the figures as they flickered in the firelight. Day after day she suffered the pain of her hunger. There came a time when the figures on the great screen took possession of her and, forgetting her hardships, she began to weave a waist robe filled with the forms of the firelight.

Slowly, the weaving grew; slowly, the snows melted. The spirit of spring spread itself across the land, swelling small buds into blossoms and broadening the bellies of women. Working the designs of her men into soft woolen strands, the

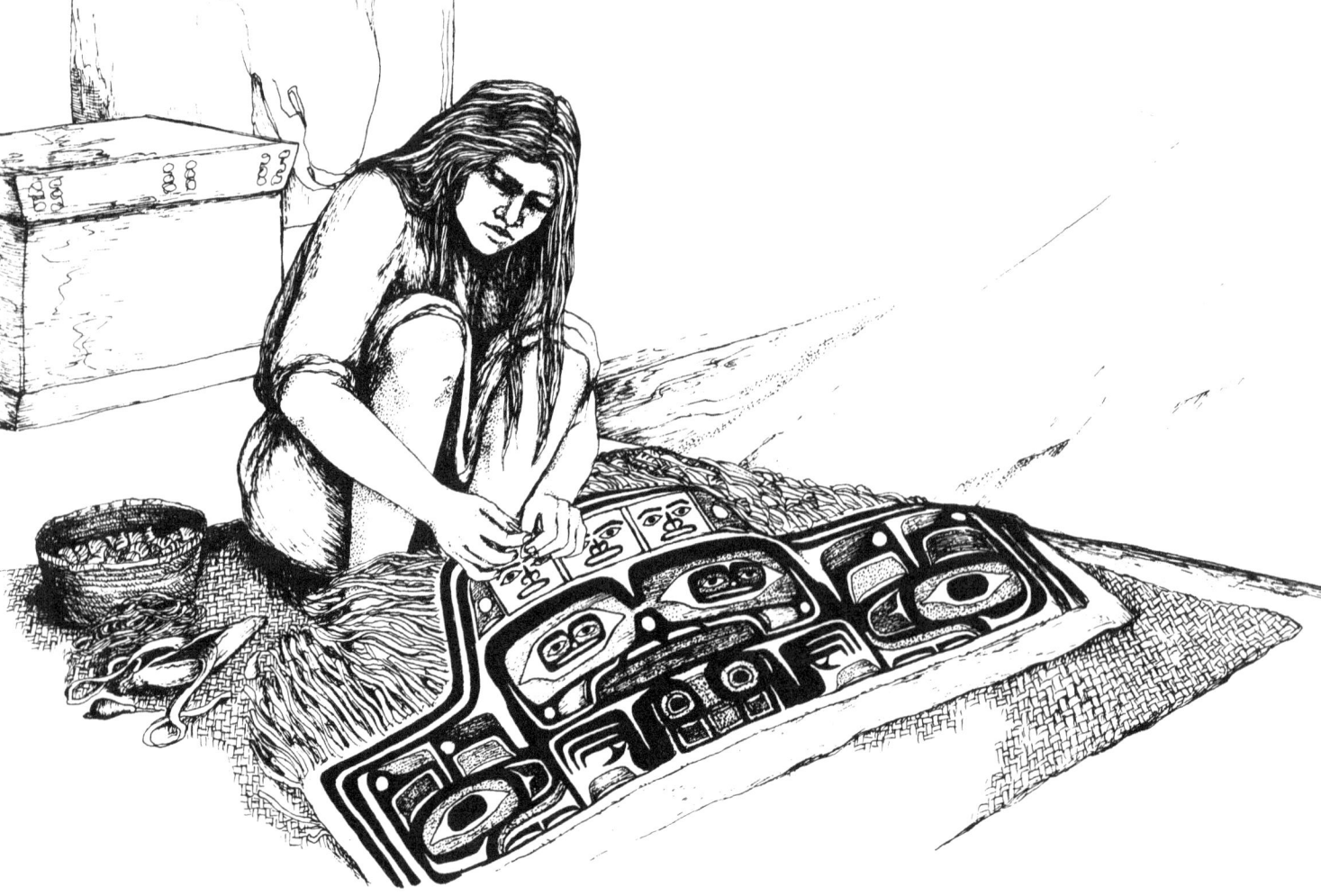

young woman wove, creating an apron of subtle beauty. When the weaving was completed, she attached it to a caribou hide and added layers of leather fringe. While listening to the trickle of melting snow, she carefully sewed puffin beaks, each with a tiny feather inside, in a flowing curve beneath the weaving. To the tails of the bottom row of fringe she sewed clattering deer hooves. The apron was finished. As she moved to wrap it carefully in intestine cloth, the rattle of the beaks spoke of the melting snows and of the summer that was soon to come.

The summer did arrive, and with it the son of the chief, seeking her hand in marriage. Greatly honored, she presented the apron to his father. To validate the privilege of owning such a beautiful garment, the chief gave a feast, sacrificing many slaves and dancing in the apron. People marveled that such a masterpiece could be created in wool; its fame spread throughout the land and commissions for similar garments came to the woman. She and her mother shared the secrets of the weaving with the women around them, and in this way the Tsimshian became renowned for their creation of the exquisite Dancing Aprons.

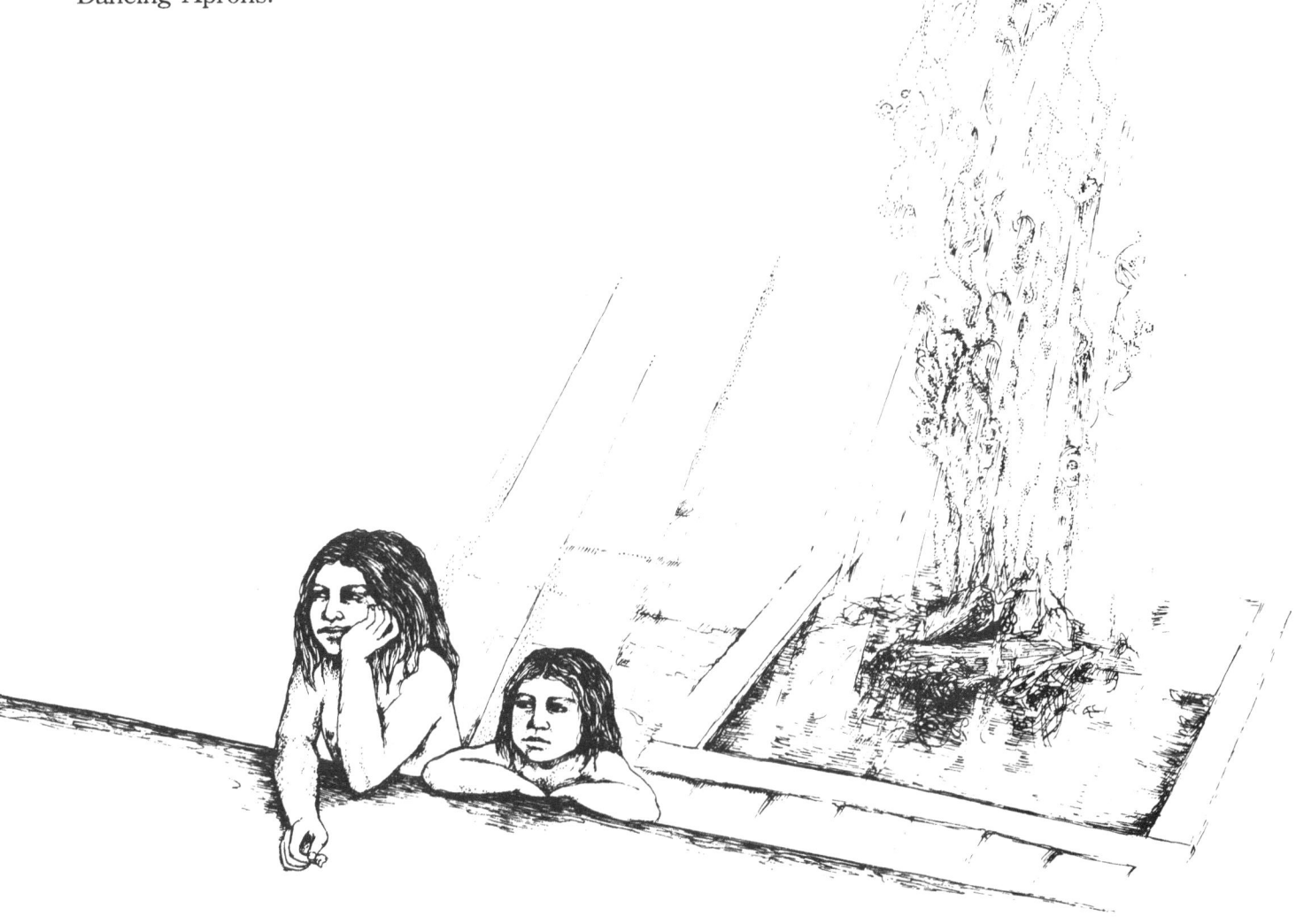

Tsimshian to Tlingit

Legend has told us that long ago women of the Tsimshian tribe were the first to produce the twined ceremonial garments. The word in the Tsimshian dialect for these weavings is "gus-halai't" and is translated by Lieutenant Emmons in his 1907 monograph, *The Chilkat Blanket*, as "dancing-blanket." Later, knowledge of this type of weaving traveled through intermarriage to the families of the Tlingit: the Tongass, the Stikine, and the Chilkat. The Tlingit name for the garment is "Nakheen" and is interpreted by Emmons as "the fringe about the body." This refers to the flowing warp fringe which sways about the body when the robe is worn in the dance.

The name "Chilkat Blanket" by which it is known today was coined by European traders in the late 1800s as a commercial tag for an important trade item. Most likely they were so called because the greatest producers of the Dancing Blanket at that time were the Chilkat women whose villages lay at the head of what is now called Lynn Canal. The term "blanket" is misleading, as it is actually a robe worn only on ceremonial occasions. However, as the name is well established, the original qualification of "dancing" will be used here in order to indicate its very special nature.

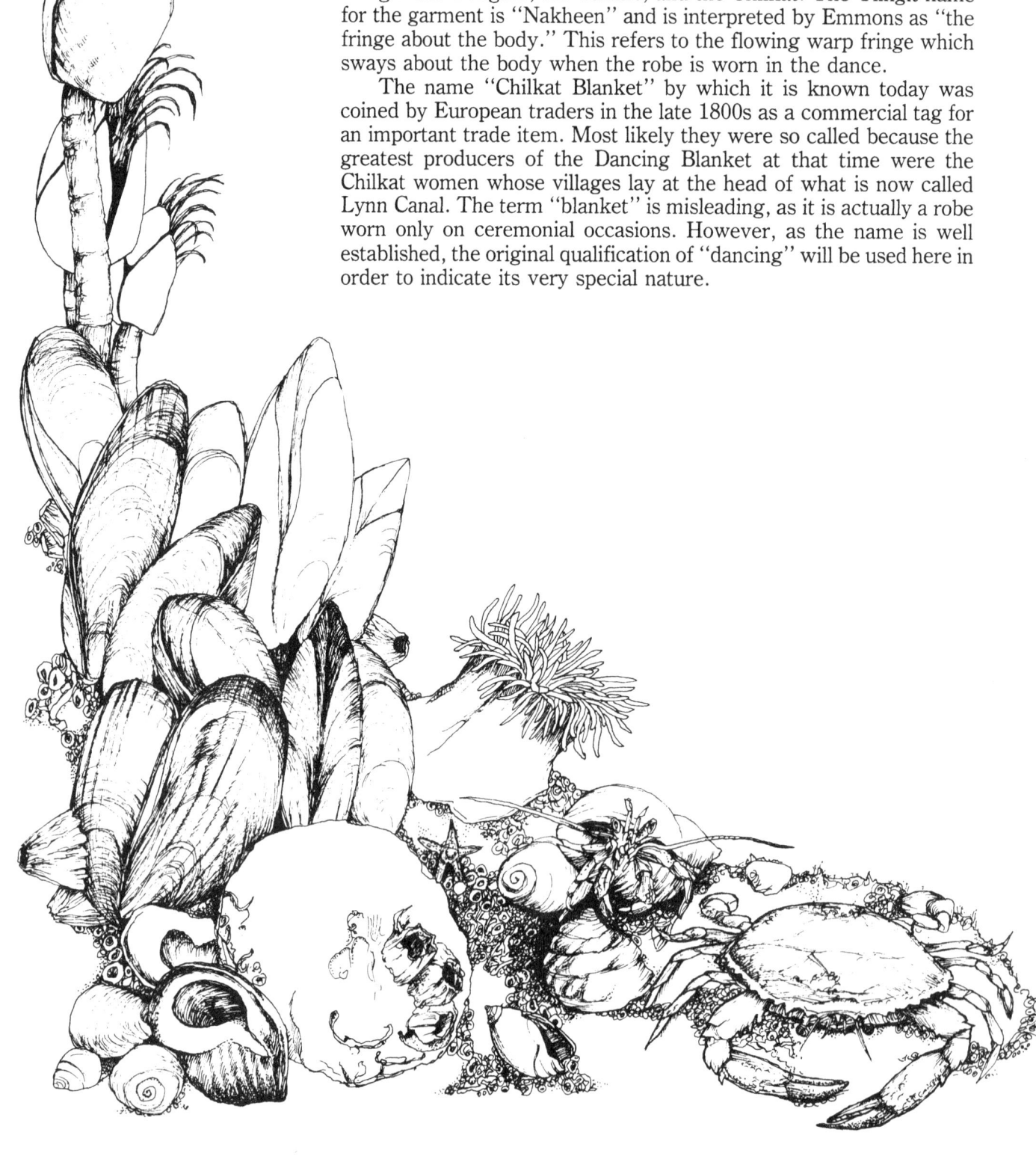

THE ELEMENT OF TIME

"The People of the Northwest Coast were rich. Their sea even richer. They were enormously energetic, and they centered their society around what was to them the essence of life: what we now call 'Art.'"

- Bill Reid, famed Haida artist

The northwest coast of North America, from Vancouver Island in British Columbia to Yakutat, Alaska, is a land which abounds in natural food resources. Two hundred years ago, the Indians who inhabited this land could gather enough food during the spring and summer months to last them for the entire winter. While the harvest months were spent in campsites near the fishing and hunting grounds, winter found the people at home in permanent villages built of sturdy plank houses. These houses, and the fires within them, provided extended families with protection against the cold of the winter and with a gathering place for the telling of tales and the presentation of dramas. With their food stores in, the people of the coast had time to create objects of pride both for everyday use and for the great winter ceremonials.

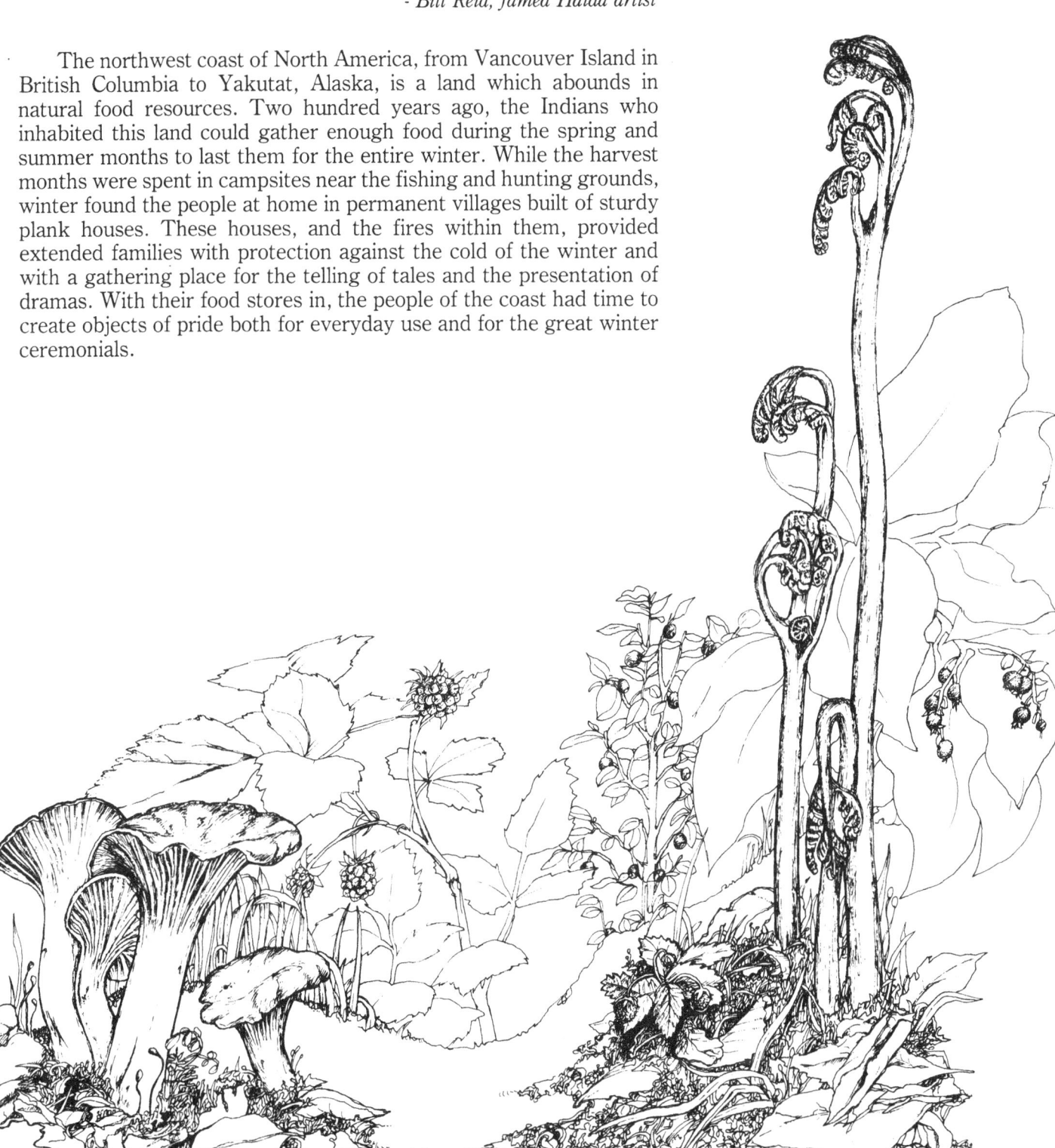

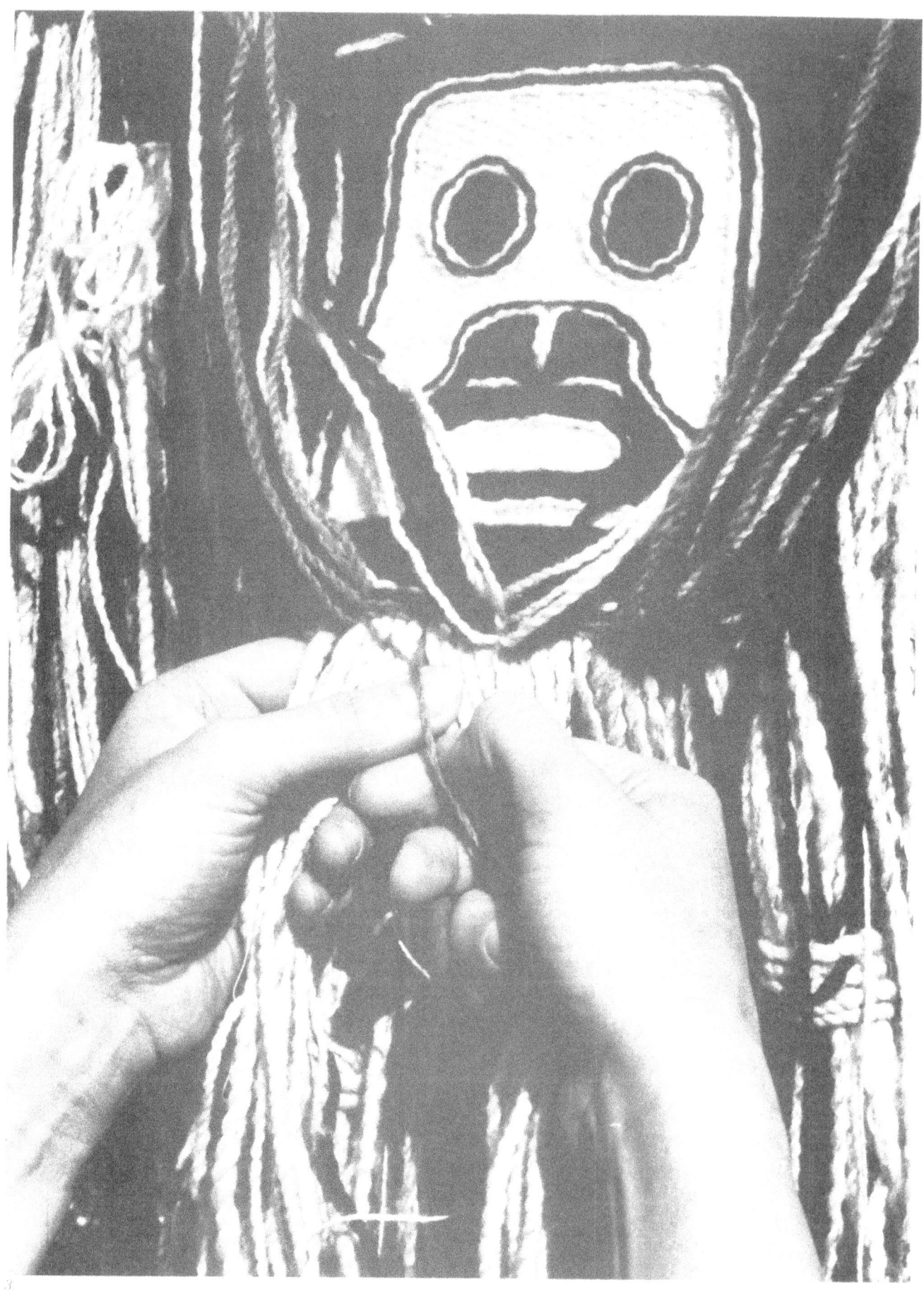

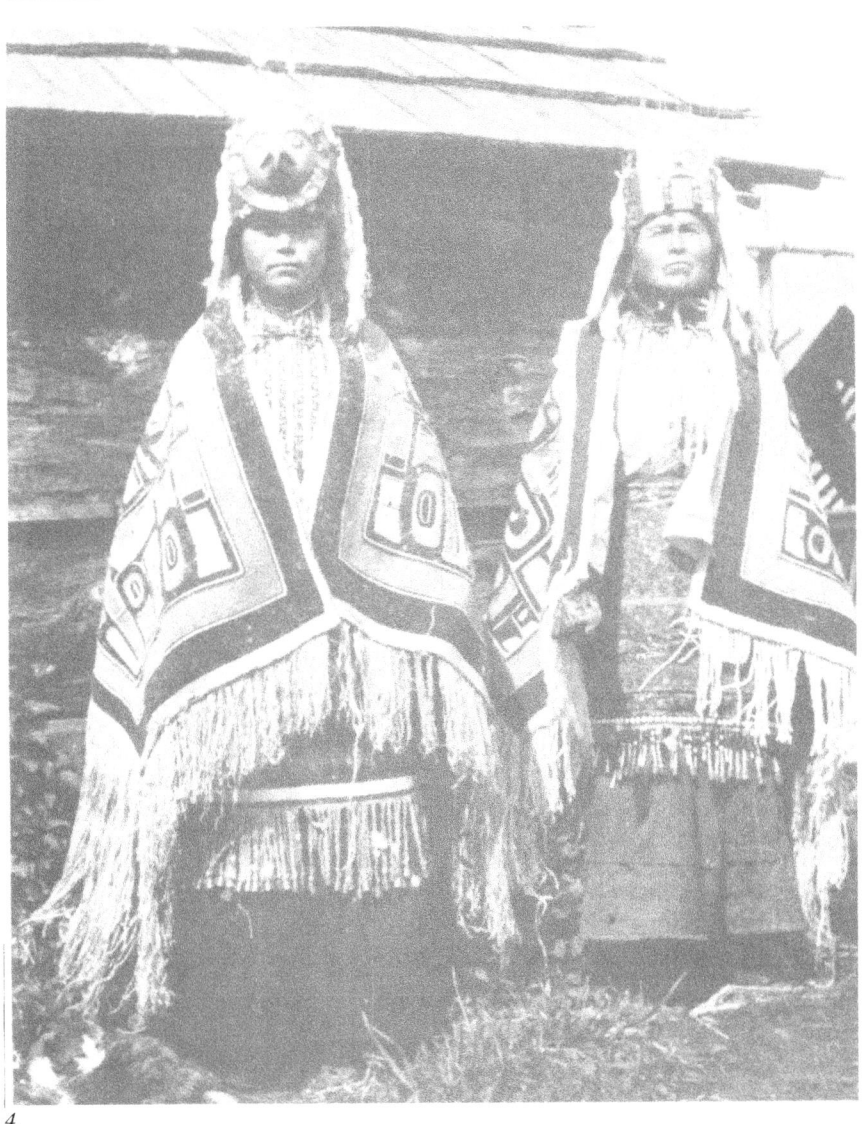

4.

3. Weaver: Cheryl Samuel

4. Two Tsimshian women from Kitwanga wearing Dancing Blankets, 1910 (G.T. Emmons photograph: Courtesy of the British Columbia Provincial Museum)

Time, indeed, was needed to weave a ceremonial garment. The weaver was a professional craftsman who most likely inherited the privilege of weaving from her mother or grandmother. The twining of a Dancing Blanket took many hours to complete. Daily progress was comparatively slow: a good weaver could complete a small face in about ten hours. Combined with the work of gathering and preserving the summer's harvest, and of daily responsibilities to the family, it would take a woman at least six months to finish weaving a Dancing Blanket.

An equally long time would have been spent in spinning all of the warp and weft yarns. Because the weaving and the spinning each took so long to do, it is probable that the spinner, with her own specialized skill, was a different person from the weaver. She, too, in time would pass her knowledge on to a younger woman, most likely a daughter or granddaughter.

Women not only wove the Dancing Blankets, but also wore them. These auspicious garments were held in very high esteem; the right to wear one was usually an inherited privilege. Furthermore, the crest figure which adorned the design field also had to belong to the owner. Initially, Dancing Blankets were designed and produced as commissioned works of art.

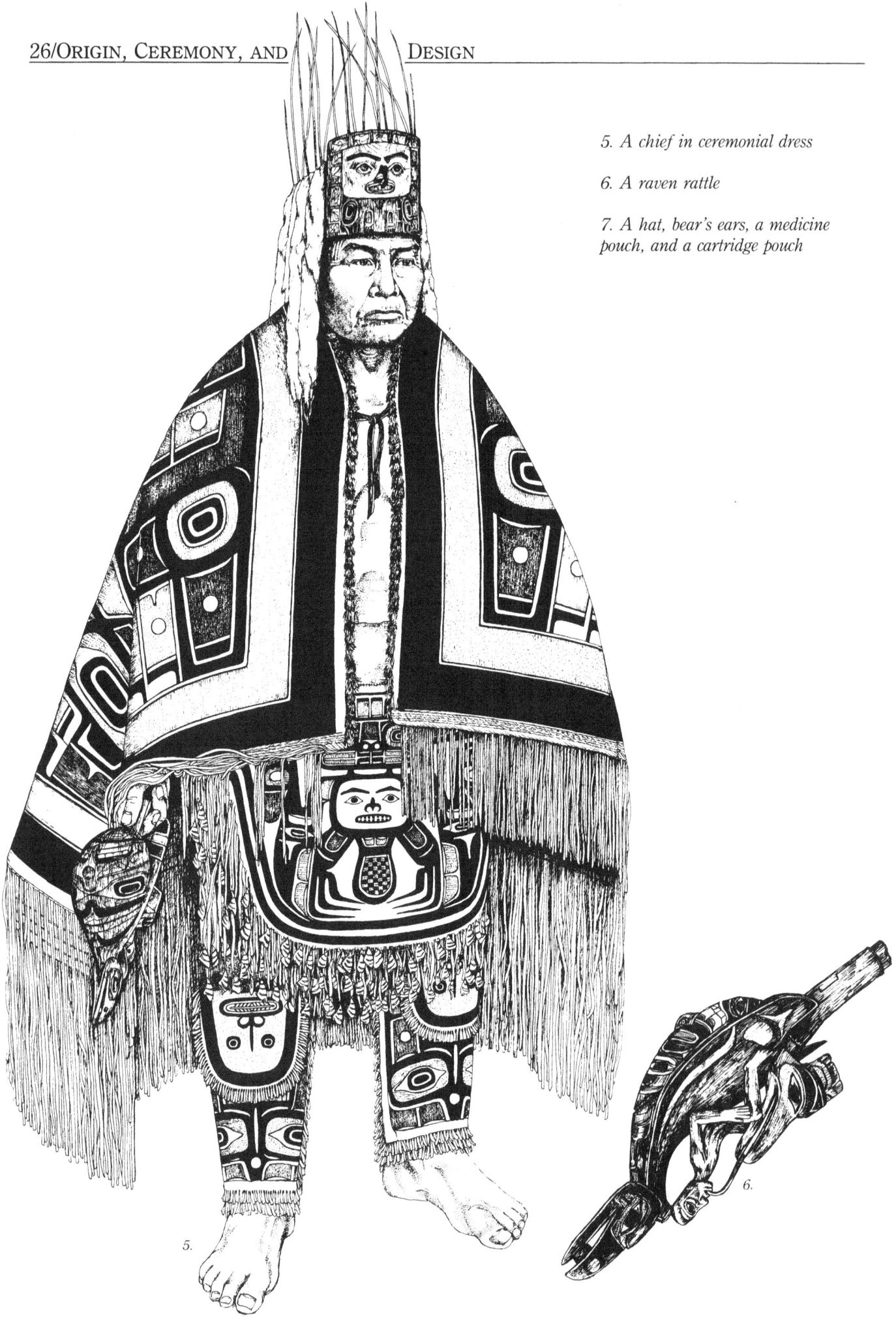

5. A chief in ceremonial dress

6. A raven rattle

7. A hat, bear's ears, a medicine pouch, and a cartridge pouch

5.

6.

A CEREMONIAL COSTUME

The ultimate in regal apparel on the northwest coast was a costume made up almost entirely of Chilkat weavings. Bill Reid, in *Indian Art of the Northwest Coast*, describes a chief in full regalia as "the most gorgeously panoplied human ever to strut the face of the earth. These costumes weren't as colorful or elaborate as, say, a Chinese emperor's brocade robes or a Renaissance churchman's gold and velvet, but the power of these designs more than makes up for that. The combination of a garment like this with the right headdress and the rest of the outfit would be overwhelming."

The Dancing Blanket itself was the focal point of the costume. Spread out flat, it is a five-sided garment with a long, curved fringe. Most often it was worn high on the shoulders, the sides tied together at the front with leather ties. Sometimes it was draped over one shoulder and under the opposite arm in the fashion of a cedar bark cape.

The expertise and versatility of a weaver was put to test in the creation of very special, small ceremonial items. Leggings, woven in pairs, were about thirty centimeters wide at the top, narrowing slightly toward the ankle, and between thirty and thirty-five centimeters long. Some styles had a fishtail extension which covered the top of the bare foot. They were trimmed with leather fringes which often had puffin bills or deer toes sewn on the ends. A hat would be made as a rectangle and finished with a shock of fur protruding from the top seam. Specially commissioned ears were woven to shape, the exterior curve accomplished by cutting warp ends as the pattern demanded. A shaman's medicine pouch was intricately twined in the shape of a ghost face. It was trimmed with blue trade cloth and outlined with a tiny pattern of beads. A wide cartridge pouch, with thongs to tie it around the waist, was made as a three-dimensional piece with a crest figure adorning the covering flap. These small, special weavings were probably individual expressions of the combined imaginations of artist and weaver, to be duplicated in spirit but not in kind.

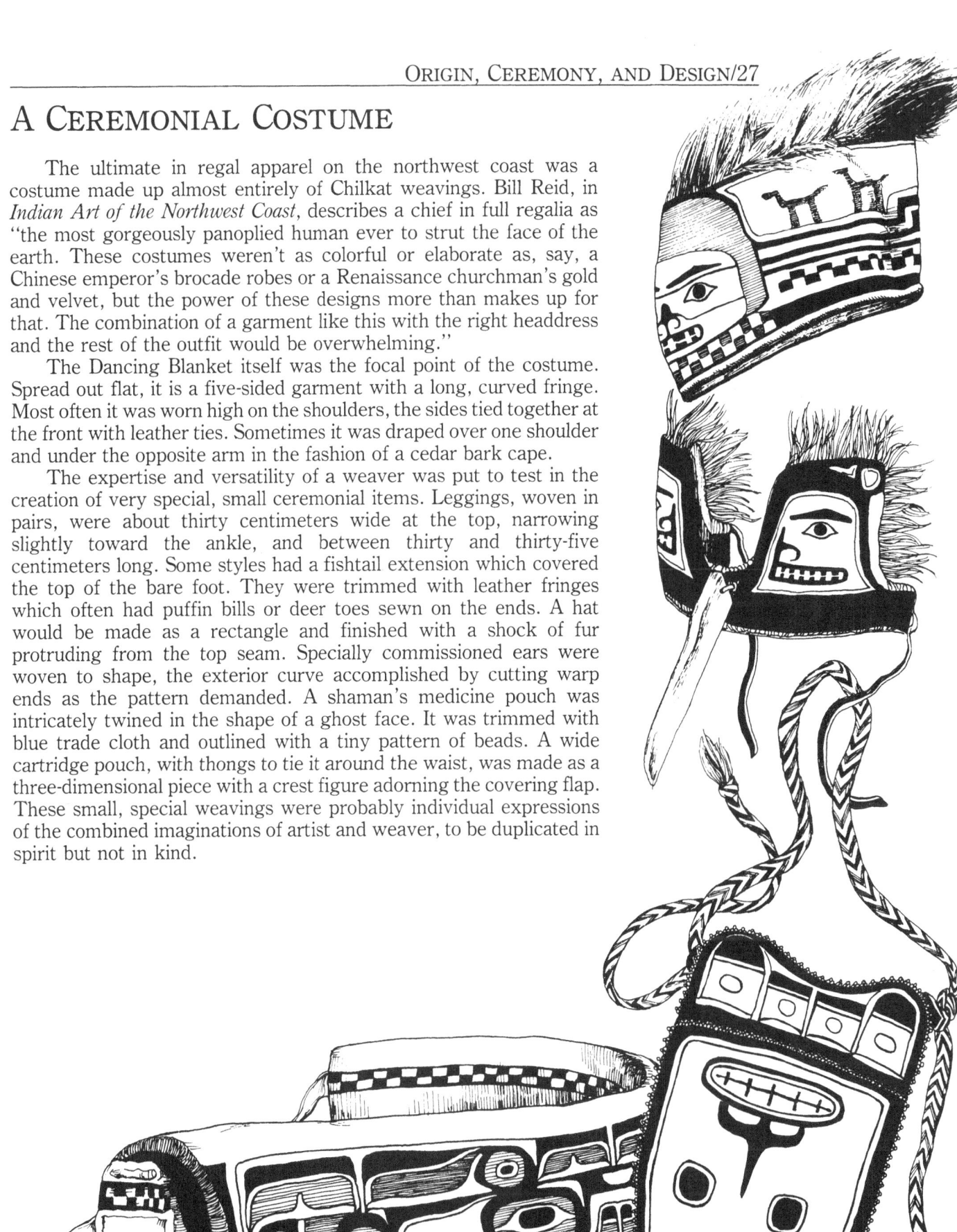

7.

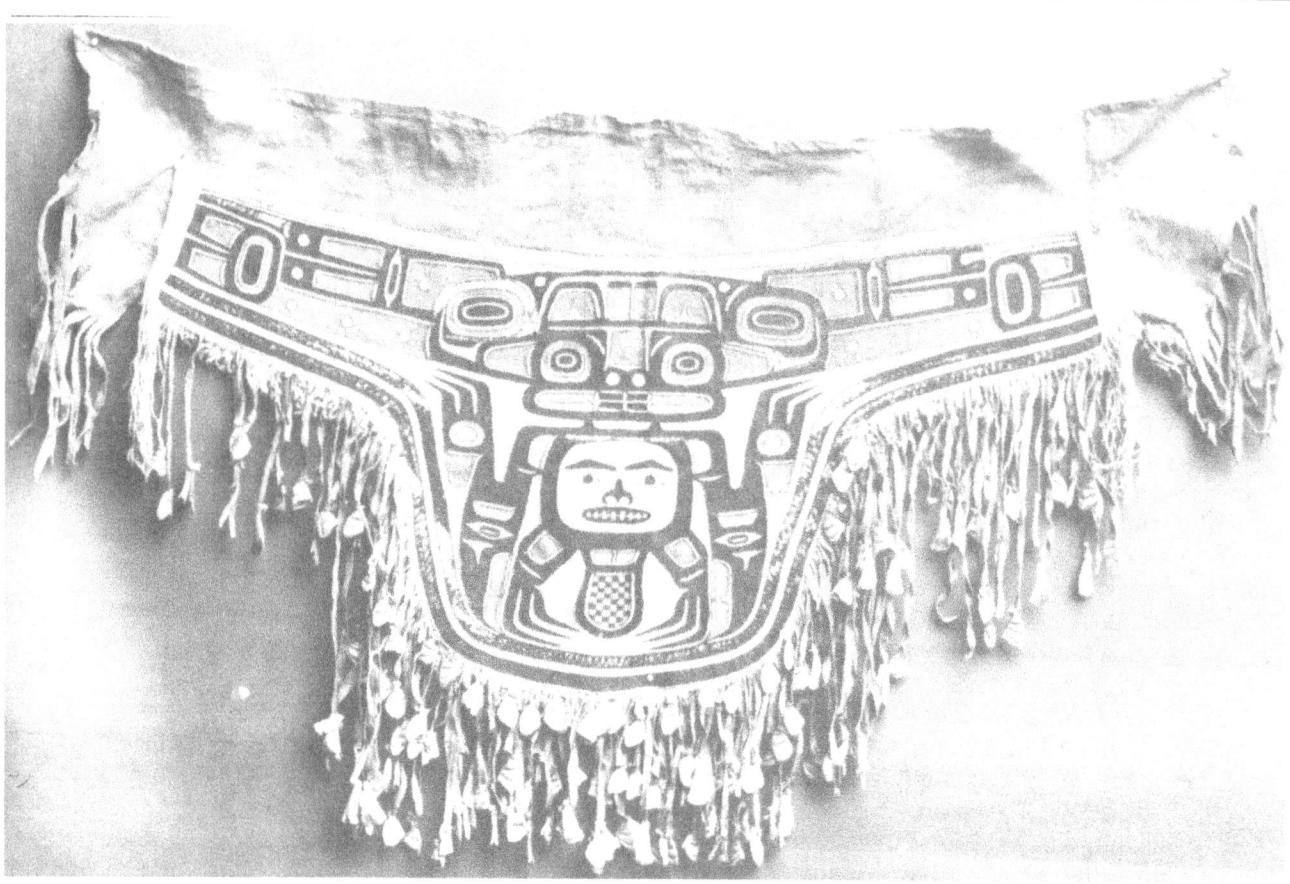

8. *This exquisite Beaver Apron, now in the Smithsonian, is woven in black, green, yellow, and white yarns. Small side braids are attached at the outer edges of the weaving and puffin beaks hang from the fringe. See also figure H in Color Plate Section. (Courtesy of the British Columbia Provincial Museum)*

The apron was a reproduction in wool of the shaman's painted leather waist robe. There are relatively few aprons in collections today and Emmons notes that their manufacture had virtually ceased by the 1800s. Emmons believes that the apron was one of the earliest products of the loom. It is not likely that many were made, however, as the greatest prestige rested in ownership of a Dancing Blanket. The aprons were fairly small and were designed so that the main figure would be seen on the front of the person wearing it. The apron shown in figure 8 measures 88.5 centimeters across the top of the weaving itself and 41.3 centimeters in depth. With the addition of the leather band and fringes, it is 114 centimeters across the top and 70 centimeters deep. More than one apron was made from the same pattern. The man in figure 9 is wearing the beaver apron that can be seen on the lowest platform in the chief's house at Klukwan in figure 10. This apron, although very similar, is not the same one as is shown in figure 8. This can be determined by a comparison of the treatment of the mouth in the human face which adorns the beaver's belly.

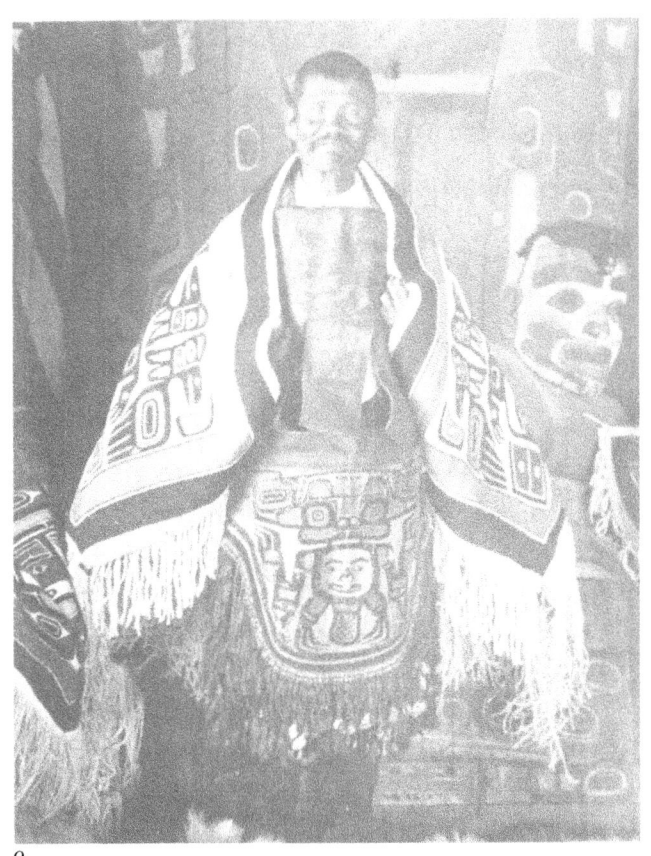

9.

10.

9. (Courtesy of the Burke Museum, University of Washington)

10. A Chilkat chief's house at Klukwan (Winter & Pond photograph, 1900: Courtesy of the British Columbia Provincial Museum)

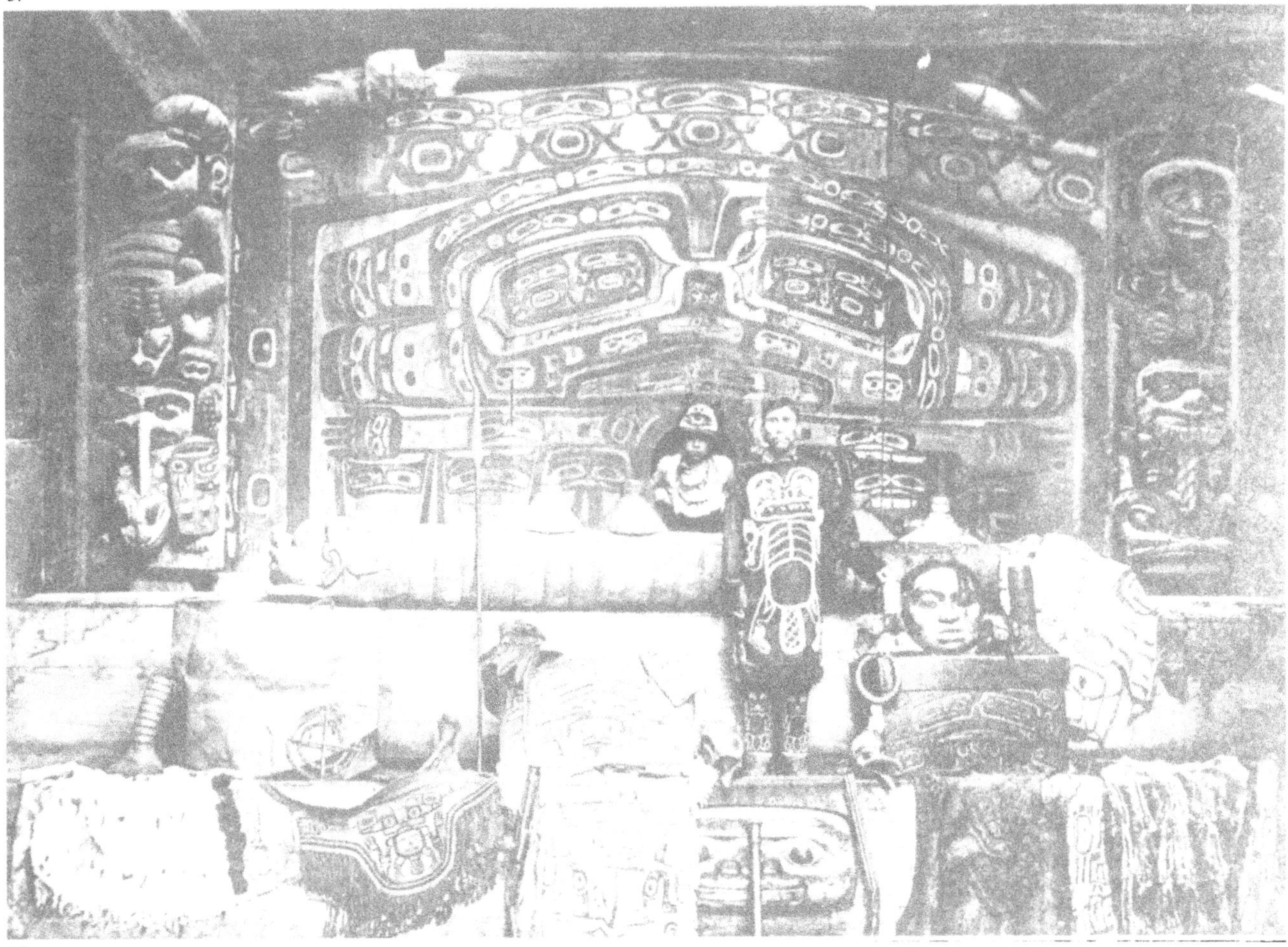

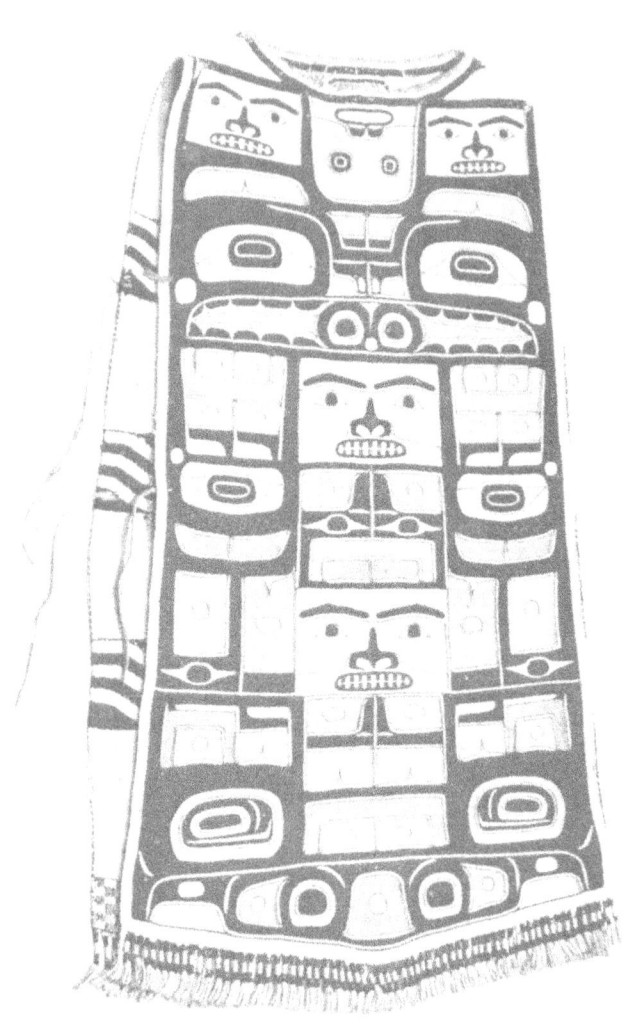

11. A sleeveless tunic (Courtesy of the National Museums of Canada, 72-2977)

Tunics, made with or without sleeves, were sometimes worn in place of an apron. These were garments, approximately 50 centimeters in width and 120 centimeters in length, which hung over the shoulders to below the knees. They were comprised of a front panel intricately designed with a totemic pattern and a back panel which sported a small ghost face at the neckline, followed by broad geometric bands on a white ground (see fig. E, Color Plate Section). The sides of these garments were usually fastened with ties, although occasionally they were woven together on one side with a drawstring join.

To complete the ceremonial costume, a chief would wear a headdress and carry a raven rattle. The headdress was composed of a small mask, painted and carved in hardwood and often inlaid with abalone. The mask was worn above the forehead and was attached to a ring. From this ring a trailing cloth adorned with ermine skins flowed down the back and sea lion whiskers extended upward. Handfuls of eagle down were placed inside the ring of whiskers.

If the chief carried only one rattle, it would be held in the right hand. The rattle represented a raven with a man lying on its back, the man's tongue being grasped by the mouth of a bird or little frog. Another bird with a curved beak rounded the breast of the raven. Rattles were carried belly up to assure the user that they would not fly away.

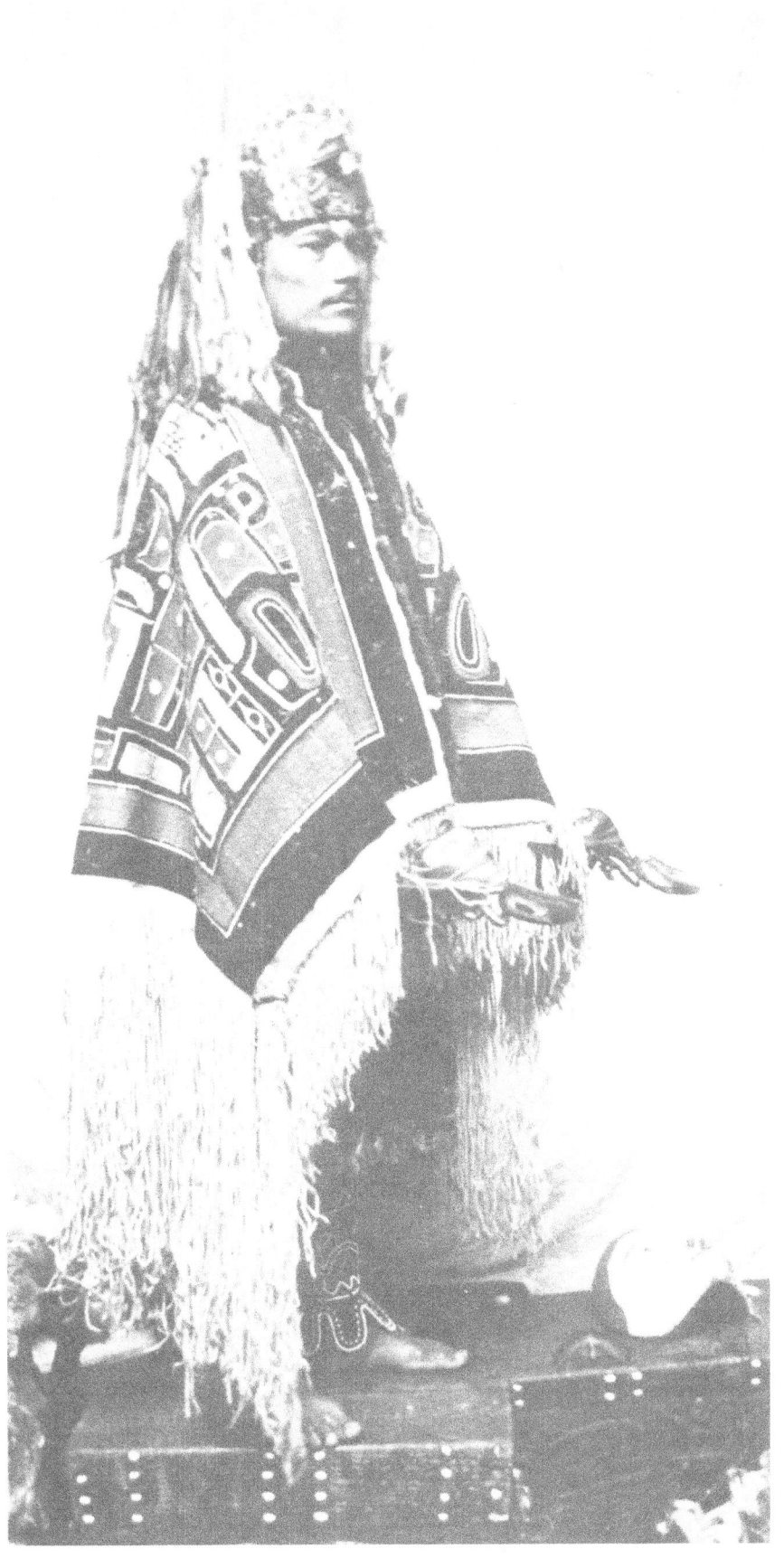

12. *A chief posing in his ceremonial costume, 1903 (Courtesy of the British Columbia Provincial Museum)*

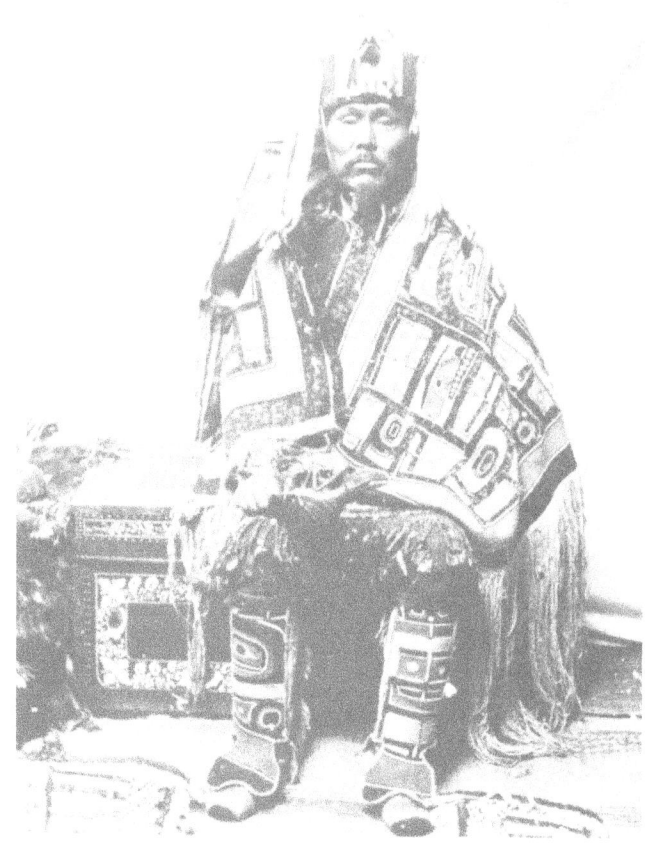

13. A chief of Kitwanga, dressed in a Dancing Blanket and wearing fish-tail leggings made from pieces of another Dancing Blanket. White eagle down clings to the wool of his garments. (Courtesy of the British Columbia Provincial Museum)

A Ceremonial Dance

While participating in a winter ceremonial, a wealthy chief would wear his Dancing Blanket and carry his raven rattle. If he owned any of the other parts of the costume, he would wear these also; otherwise, substitutions would be made. A host wearing a Chilkat Dancing Blanket would make long speeches honoring his guests and the occasion. During these speeches, he would carry an elaborately carved speaker's staff. The speeches would be followed by a great feast and the performance of dances.

The dancers wore exquisitely painted and carved masks which depicted creatures of the natural and mythological worlds. The dances which were performed mimicked the animal movements of the creatures they represented. Slow, syncopated drumbeats, accompanied by chanted song, led the performers through their dances. Costumed magnificently and seen in the light of the fire, the presence of the human dancer often dissolved into the creature being portrayed. Suddenly the house was filled with the essence of Wolf or Bear, of Raven or of Eagle. Masked dancers paused and listened, twisted and then turned with the motions of the creatures. These were people of the land and the sea; their movements in dance portrayed a keen observation of the natural world around them.

14. Tony Hunt, a well-known Kwagulth artist, wears his Dancing Blanket while performing a Head-dress Dance. He has inherited the right to wear a blanket from his Tlingit great-great-grandmother, Mary Ebbets Hunt.

One particular dance, called the Headdress Dance, was performed in the Dancing Blanket itself with headdress and rattle. The photographs of Tony Hunt which appear in this volume were taken during a performance of this dance.

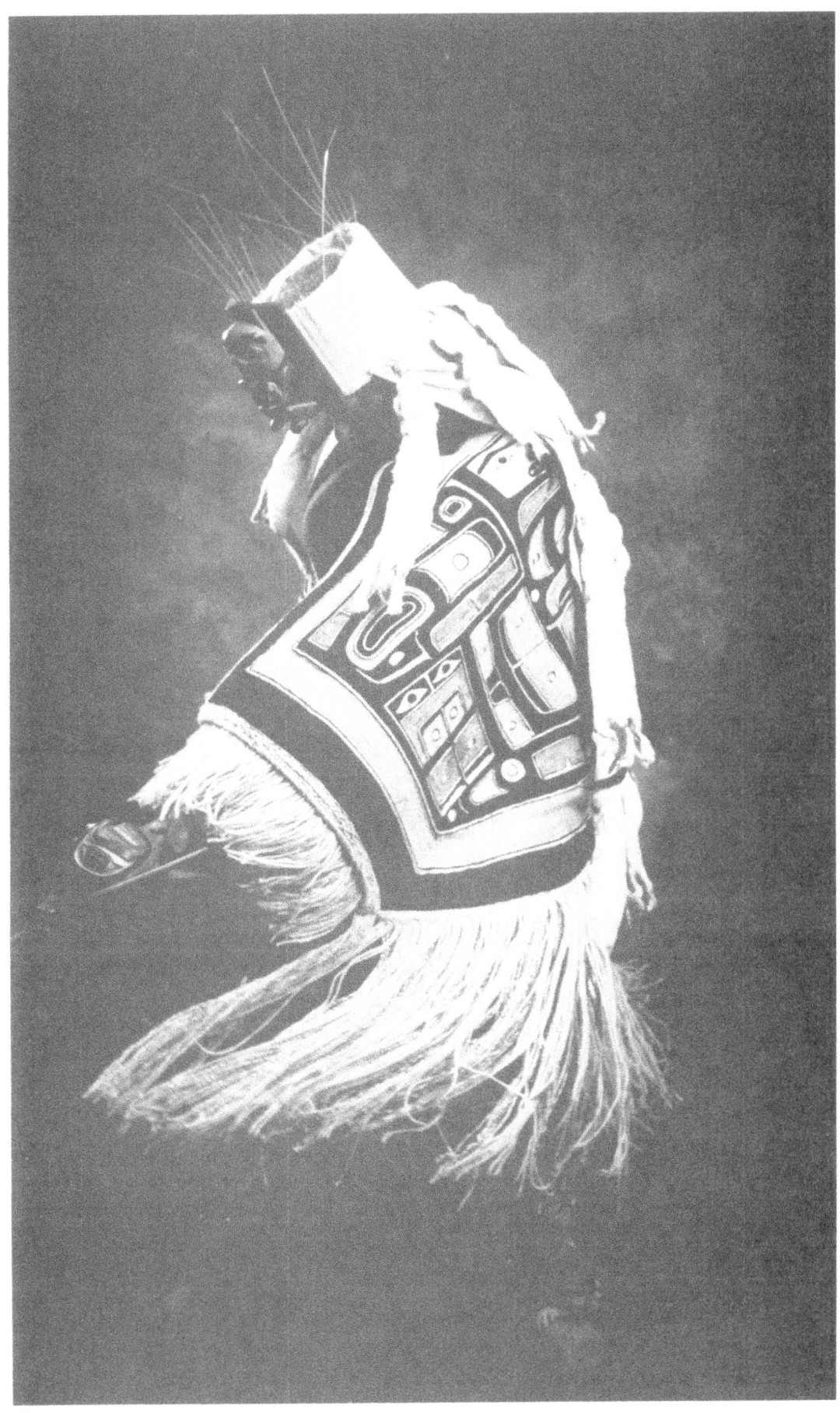

14.

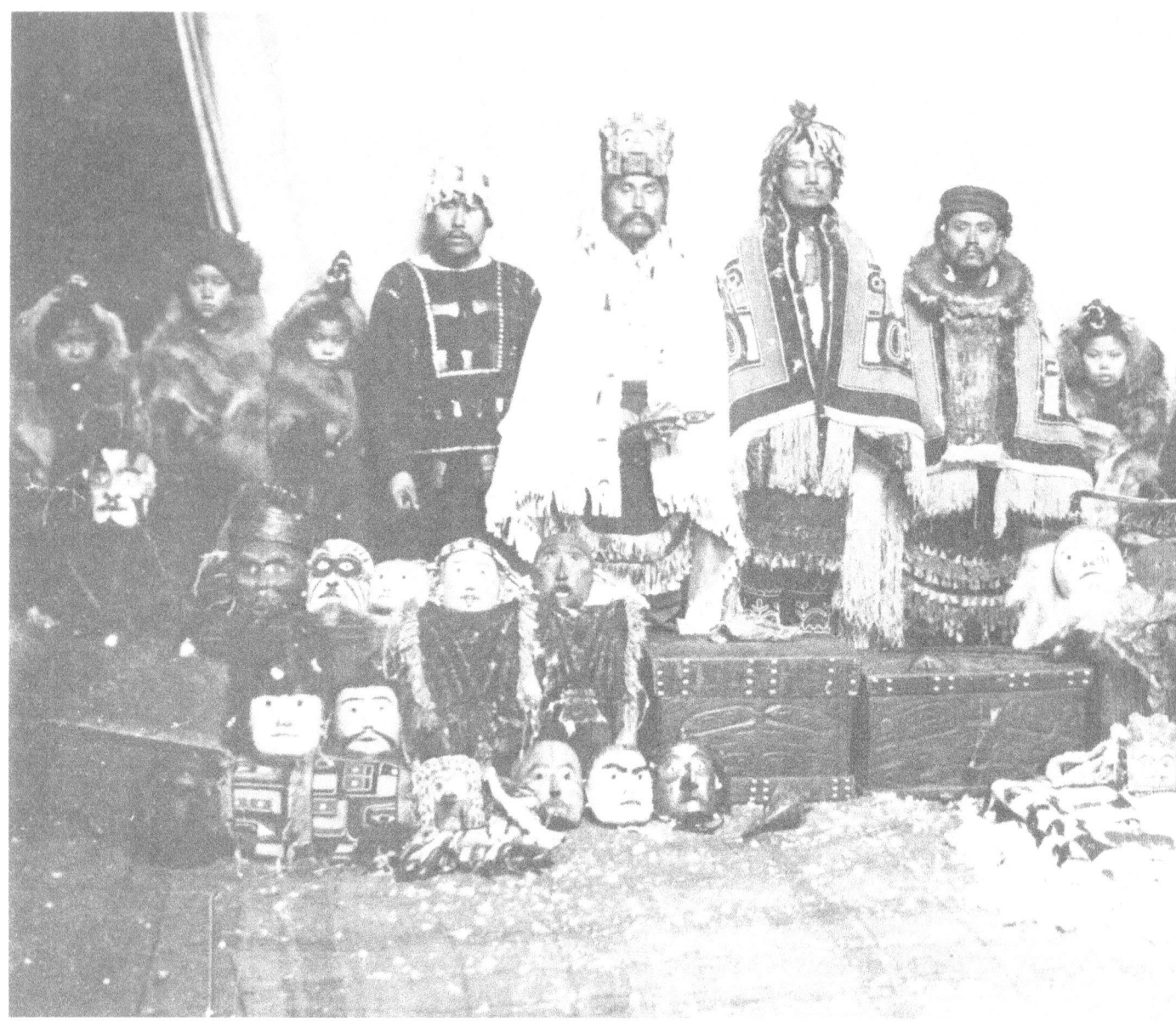

15. Men, women, and children in attendance at a ceremony. Eagle down covers the cedar bark mat on the floor, indicating a dance has taken place. (Courtesy of the British Columbia Provincial Museum)

SYMBOLS OF WEALTH

One of the ceremonial occasions which took place in the winter was called the "potlatch." This was an extensive social affair involving speechmaking, feasting, singing, and dancing. Its conclusion was marked by the host's presentation of the rights or privileges he claimed—such as the right to display a certain crest, to own a name, or to raise a totem pole. His ownership of these privileges required validation by the invited guests, who witnessed his presentation and who received payment from him in the form of gifts.

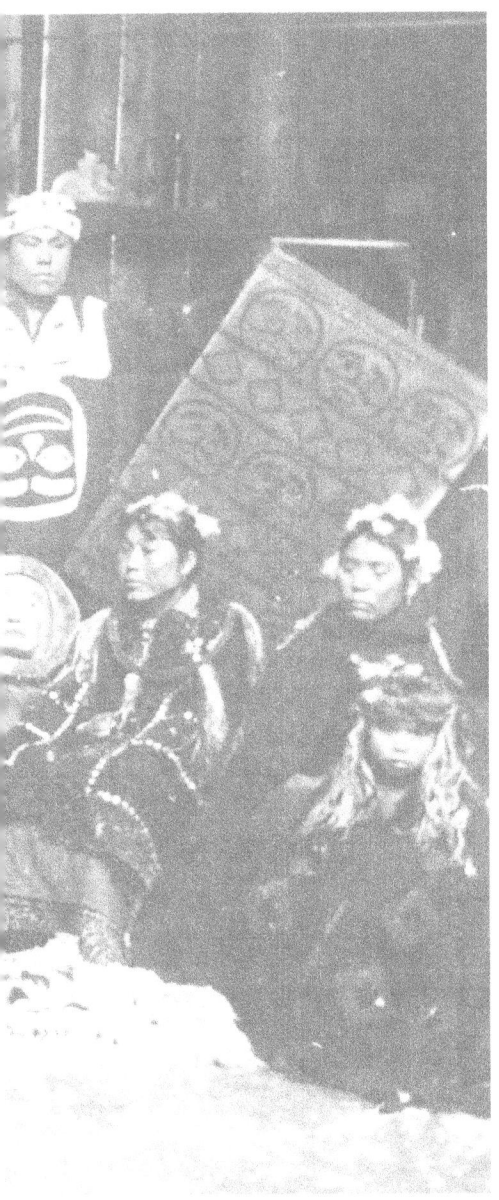

The Chilkat weavings were symbols of wealth. To own them endowed a chief with great prestige; to give them away gave even greater glory, for only the wealthiest of chiefs could afford to dispense with such valuable items. If a Dancing Blanket was to be given in potlatch and if there was no chief of high enough rank to receive it, the blanket might be cut into strips and distributed to a number of persons of prestige. These greatly coveted strips were taken home and made into ceremonial garments such as aprons, leggings, hats, or bags. Occasionally, the strips of one blanket would be reassembled to form a shirt. The man in the photograph in figure 16 is wearing such a shirt, reconstructed from a fine, old blanket. The neckline is bound with leather to which a fringe of mountain goat yarn has been attached. Sleeves cut from the same blanket were added to complete the garment. Generally speaking, there was little attempt to match the designs in "potlatch" garments.

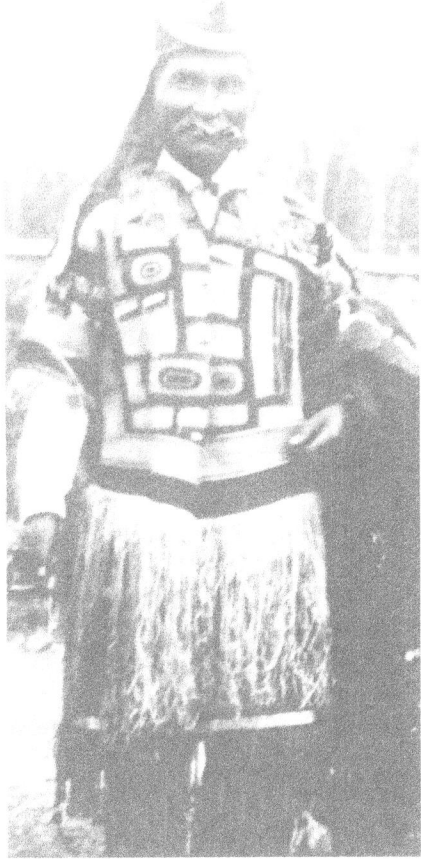

16. A Tsimshian chief wearing a potlatch dance-shirt which is now in the Glenbow Museum in Calgary (Courtesy of the British Columbia Provincial Museum)

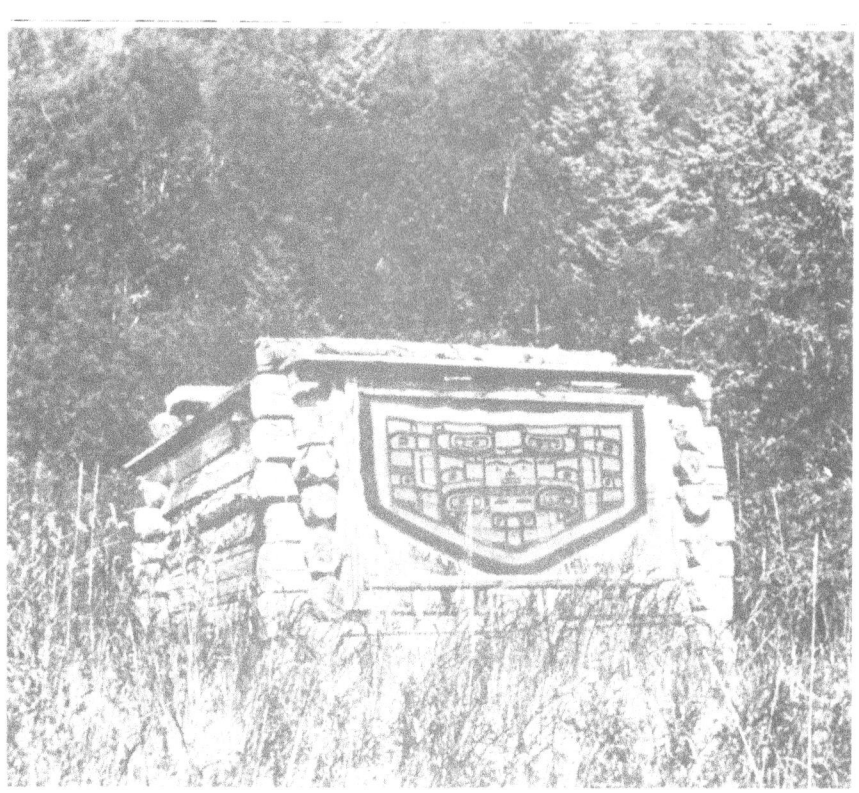

17. A grave house (Courtesy of the British Columbia Provincial Museum)

As a final show of prestige, when a chief died he was dressed in his ceremonial garments and laid in state amidst a display of his wealth. A mourning ceremony took place which lasted for four days. On the final day, a funeral pyre of yellow cedar logs was built and people gathered to feast and sing in honor of the dead. Special dishes filled with steaming fish, clams, and goat meat were burned so that the spirit of the deceased would not go hungry. Ordinary blankets were thrown on the fire so that the chief would not be cold. The prized Dancing Blanket was set aside to be hung on the grave house, where the remains of the chief would reside in a special box. As the body was burned, the fires of cremation warmed the living and a great smoke blanket enfolded the dead man's soul. The Dancing Blanket, subject to its own death through the decaying forces of wind and weather, continued to hail the glory of the chief and the wealth which allowed him to sacrifice such beauty.

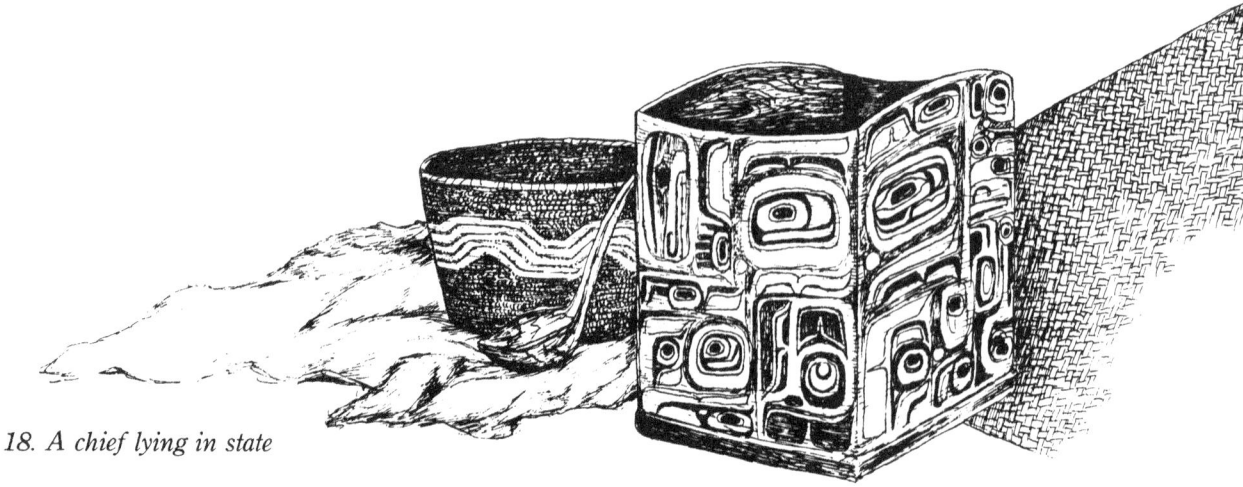

18. A chief lying in state

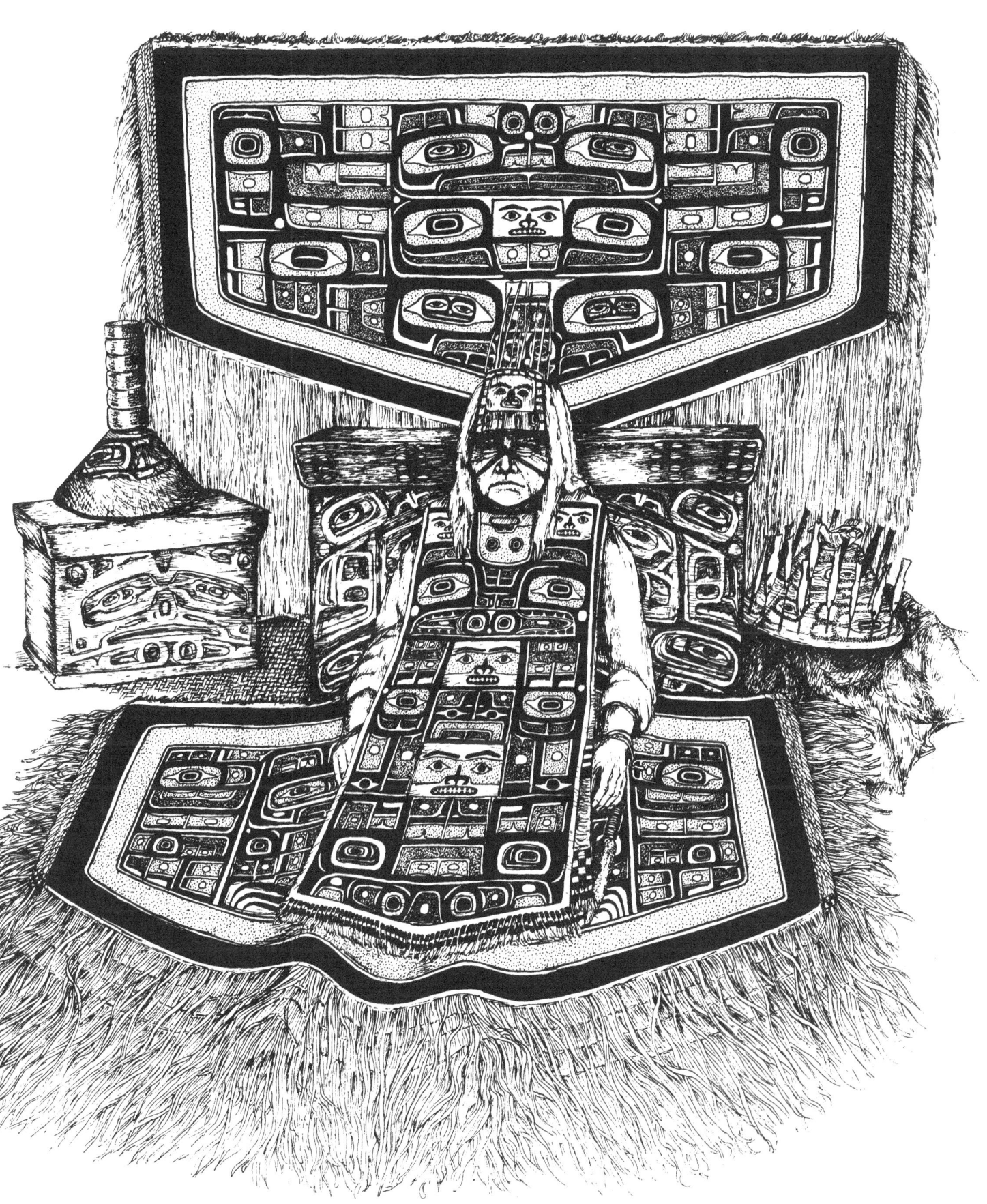

THE DESIGNS ON A DANCING BLANKET

Emmons states that the Dancing Blanket "is a family robe, elaborate in ornamentation, pleasing in color-effect, but above all a vehicle for the exhibition of the emblem of the clan." The emblems, or crests, of the northern tribes were stylized animal figures of mythological beings which were passed on from generation to generation through legend and tradition. The crest figures seen on the weavings were not confined to garments alone. The peoples of the northern coast applied these designs to virtually everything from towering totem poles to the tiniest tools. Inside their houses, painted and carved boards, such as the one in figure 19, were tied to the posts which supported the roof beams. These boards were made in sets of four and each depicted some aspect of the social history of the clan. There is a striking similarity between these painted boards and the shape of and designs on the front panels of the woven tunics. This can be seen in a comparison of the pattern board for a tunic (fig. 20) and a tunic itself (fig. 21) with the house post board in figure 19. The house post boards seem to have sloping shoulder lines, necklines, and some even have hatch marks which are identical in their placement to shoulder gussets of the tunics.

19. A painted and carved house post board (Courtesy of the British Columbia Provincial Museum)

20. A pattern board used in weaving a tunic (Courtesy of the Portland Art Museum)

21. This Tlingit chief is dressed in a tunic twined from a pattern board similar to the one in figure 20. (Courtesy of the British Columbia Provincial Museum)

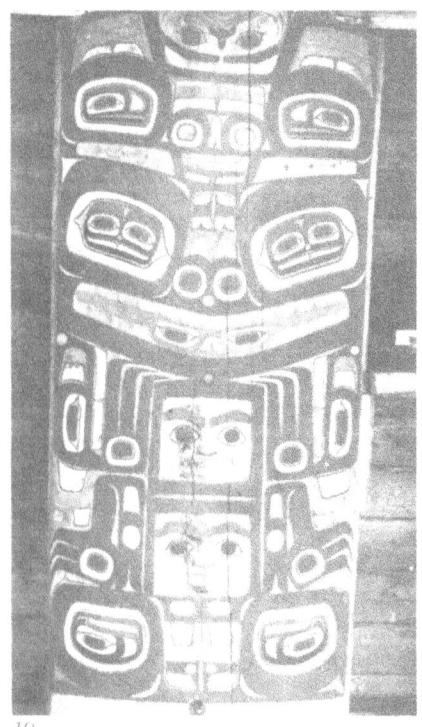

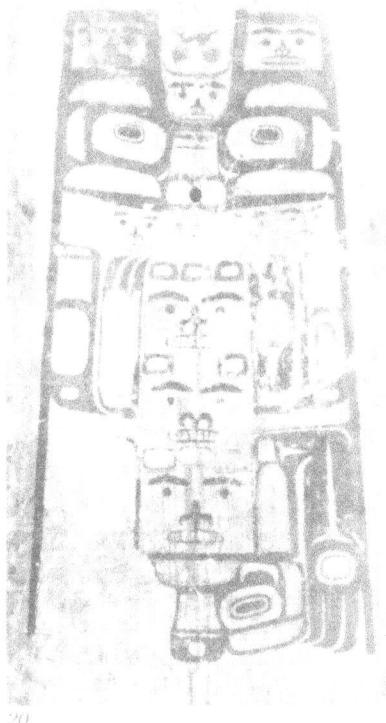

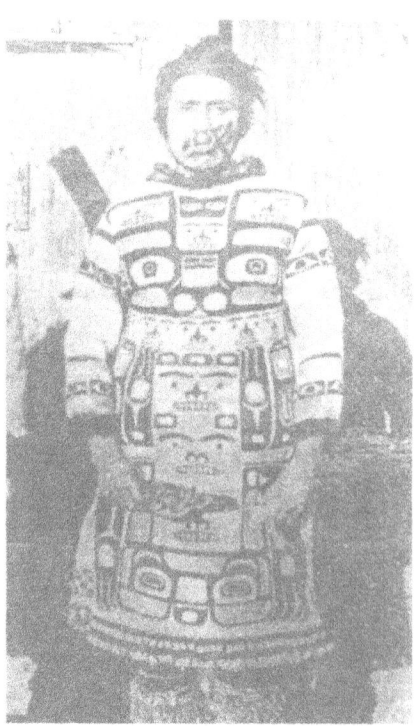

19.

20.

21.

The design field of the Dancing Blanket is covered with one or more crest figures. Some of the designs are easily recognized, but the great majority, although eyes and feet may be recognizable in themselves, are very difficult to combine into a total form. This is not only true for contemporary viewers; early anthropologists often received varying interpretations of a single crest figure from the Indians themselves. Franz Boas, when he wrote his discussion of the interpretations of design in the Dancing Blankets, states that he gave photographs to Dr. John R. Swanton and asked him to procure interpretations from the Indians at Sitka. The results are often at great variance with interpretations of the same designs collected by Emmons. One blanket might contain a figure deemed a "diving whale" by one person and a "wolf with young" by another. Certain symbolic features, such as the checkerboard tail of the beaver, give clues to the identity of the figure, but the interpretation of these clues can differ greatly. Suffice it to say that with a knowledge of the design principles used, the main figures on the blankets can be located, although their original identity may never be known.

In its overall plan, the Dancing Blanket is bounded by three bands of solid color. A narrow white band, which includes the side braids, is at the extreme periphery, followed by a broad black and then a broad yellow band. Within the yellow band lies the design field. The crest animal was organized on this field by the designer depending on his preference for handling the space. Bill Holm, in his definitive work, *Northwest Coast Indian Art, An Analysis of Form*, defines categories which serve to describe the handling of the design elements. Two of these categories—*configurative* and *distributive*—can be applied to the Dancing Blankets.

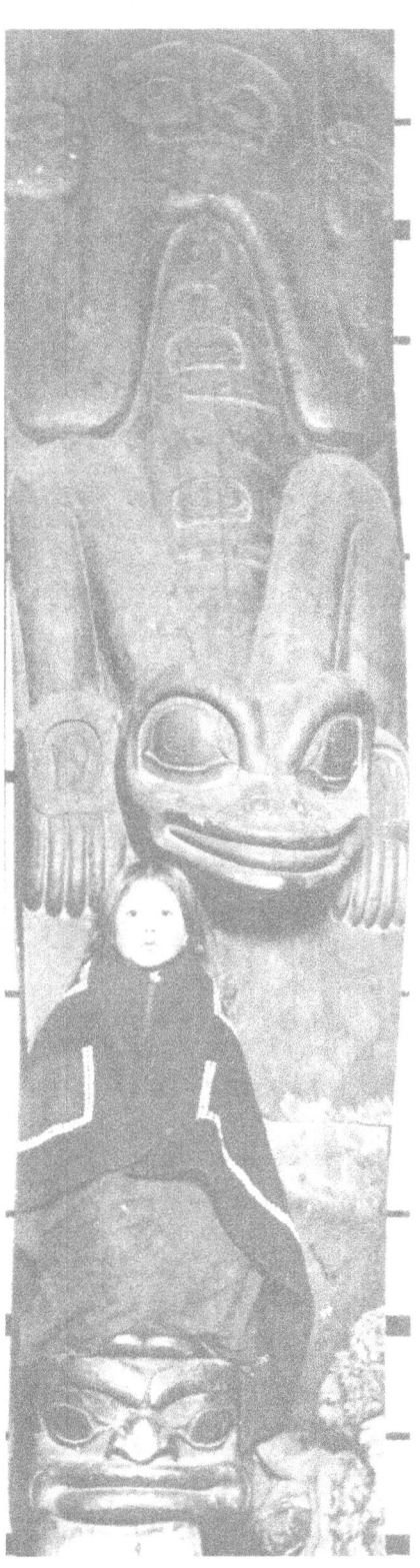

22. Carving of a frog (Courtesy of the British Columbia Provincial Museum)

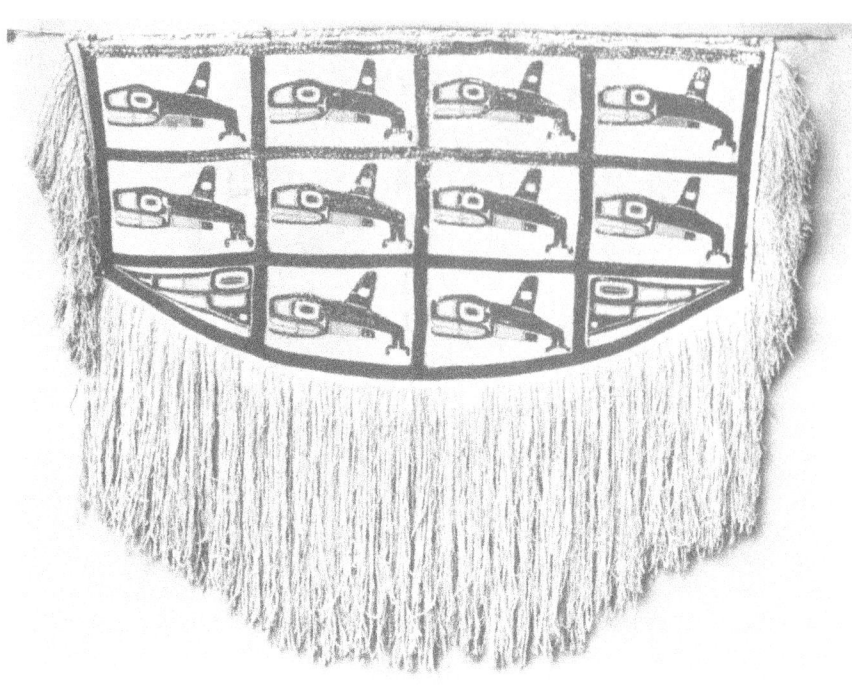

23. A configurative design (Courtesy of the Field Museum, Chicago)

Configurative: The crest animal in the configurative style of design is shown in its natural anatomical form while still being constructed with the conventionalized elements of the art. It is quite possible to identify the creature. The beautiful "Killer Whale" Blanket is an excellent illustration of this type of design. There are not very many blankets which were woven in this style.

Distributive: The major emphasis of the distributive style of design is on filling the entire available space. The parts of the animal are arranged to fill the design field regardless of their anatomical relationships. This destroys any recognizable silhouette, making the creature very difficult to identify.

Paneled Distributive: Due to the arrangement of the designs on a majority of the blankets, it is necessary to divide the distributive category into a subcategory which shall be called paneled distributive. The design field itself in this category is divided into three distinct panels: one large central panel flanked by two smaller side panels. White lines emphasize the divisions. Within these panels the designs are distributive.

The designs of the distributive blankets are ambiguous. Their meanings are hidden in the minds of their creators, to be interpreted by study, intuition, or native memory. It is, however, possible to learn to look at these designs and to distinguish the shape of the creatures within them with some confidence. This can be done by recognizing the lines which define the form. Bill Holm has described these lines, calling them *formlines*; they are black in color and flow over the entire surface of the design field.

The black formlines in the central design panel delineate the main figure on the Dancing Blanket. The blanket is woven on a white warp; the white areas which appear on the surface are, in fact, the background. The blue and yellow shapes are neither background nor main figures. They are the body of the forms, colored according to specific conventions.

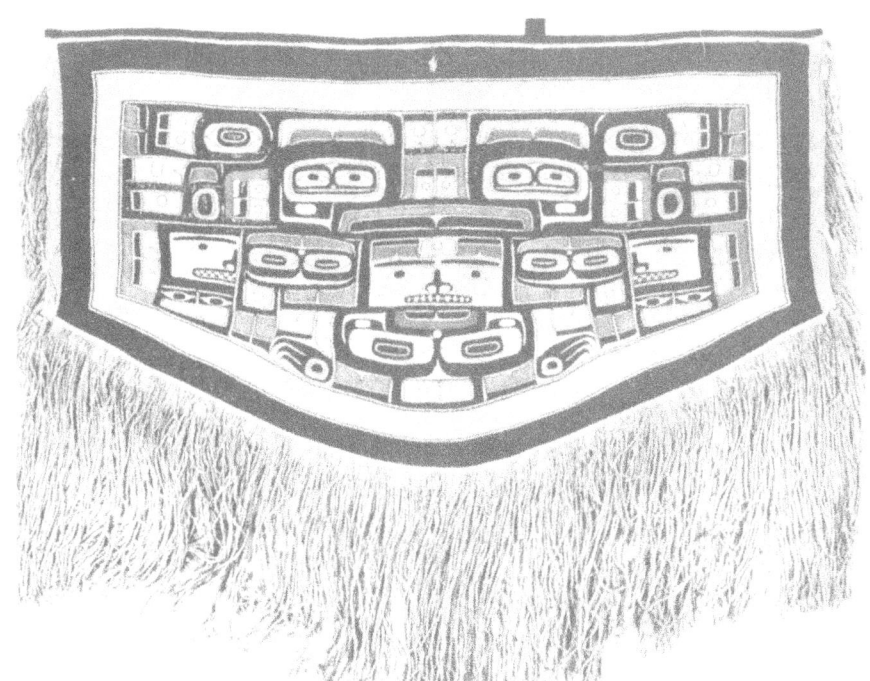

24. A distributive design (Courtesy of the American Museum of Natural History)

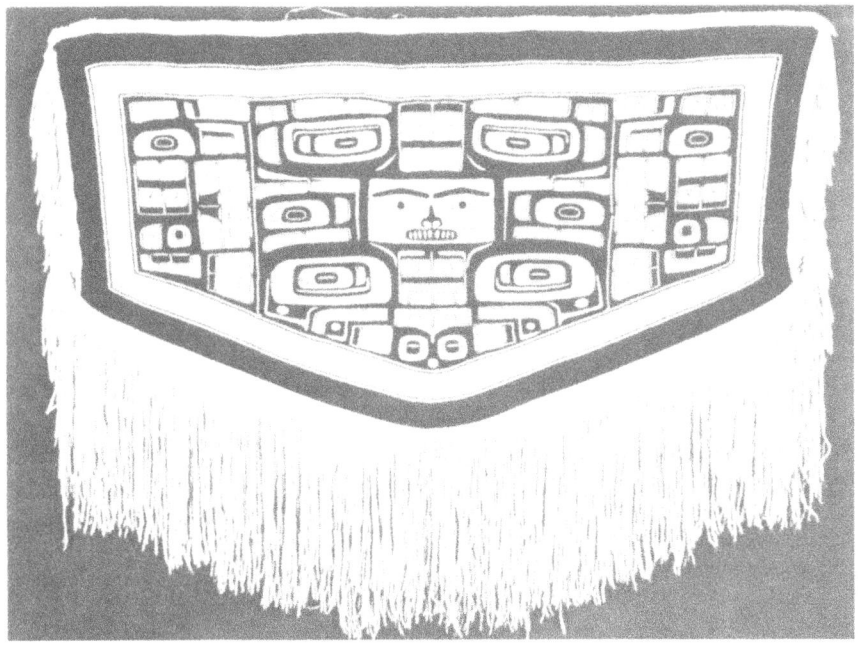

25. A paneled distributive design (Courtesy of Dr. Allan W. Lobb)

By eliminating all patterning except the formlines, the figure of the main animal should become clear. In the following pages, three blankets are presented along with painted interpretations of the main animal figure in the design field.

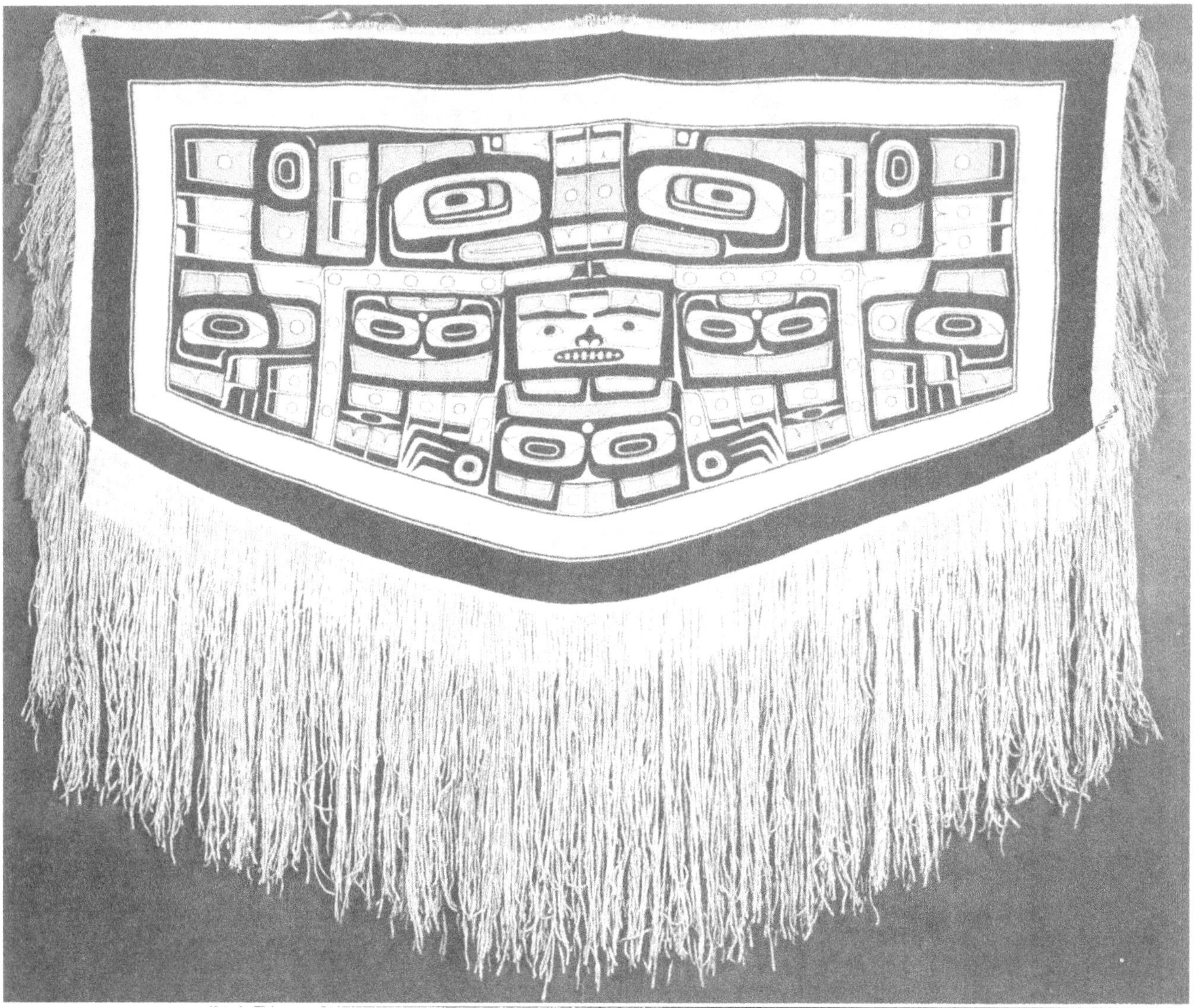

26.

26. and 27. According to Emmons, the figure in this Dancing Blanket represents a sea-bear; Boas calls it a standing eagle. Whatever the identity, the painting depicts the basic formline structure of the creature. (Photograph courtesy of the American Museum of Natural History)

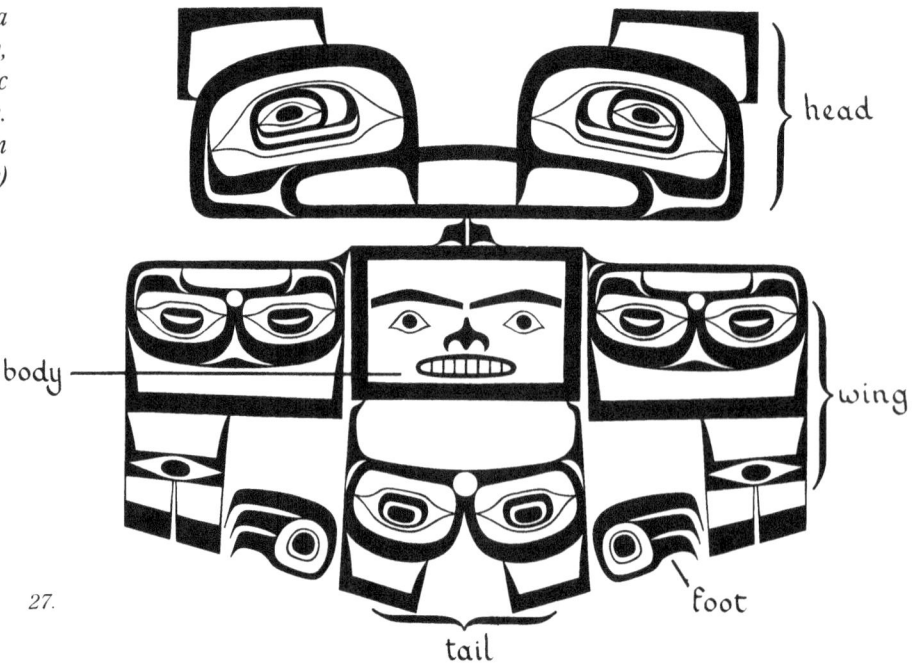

27.

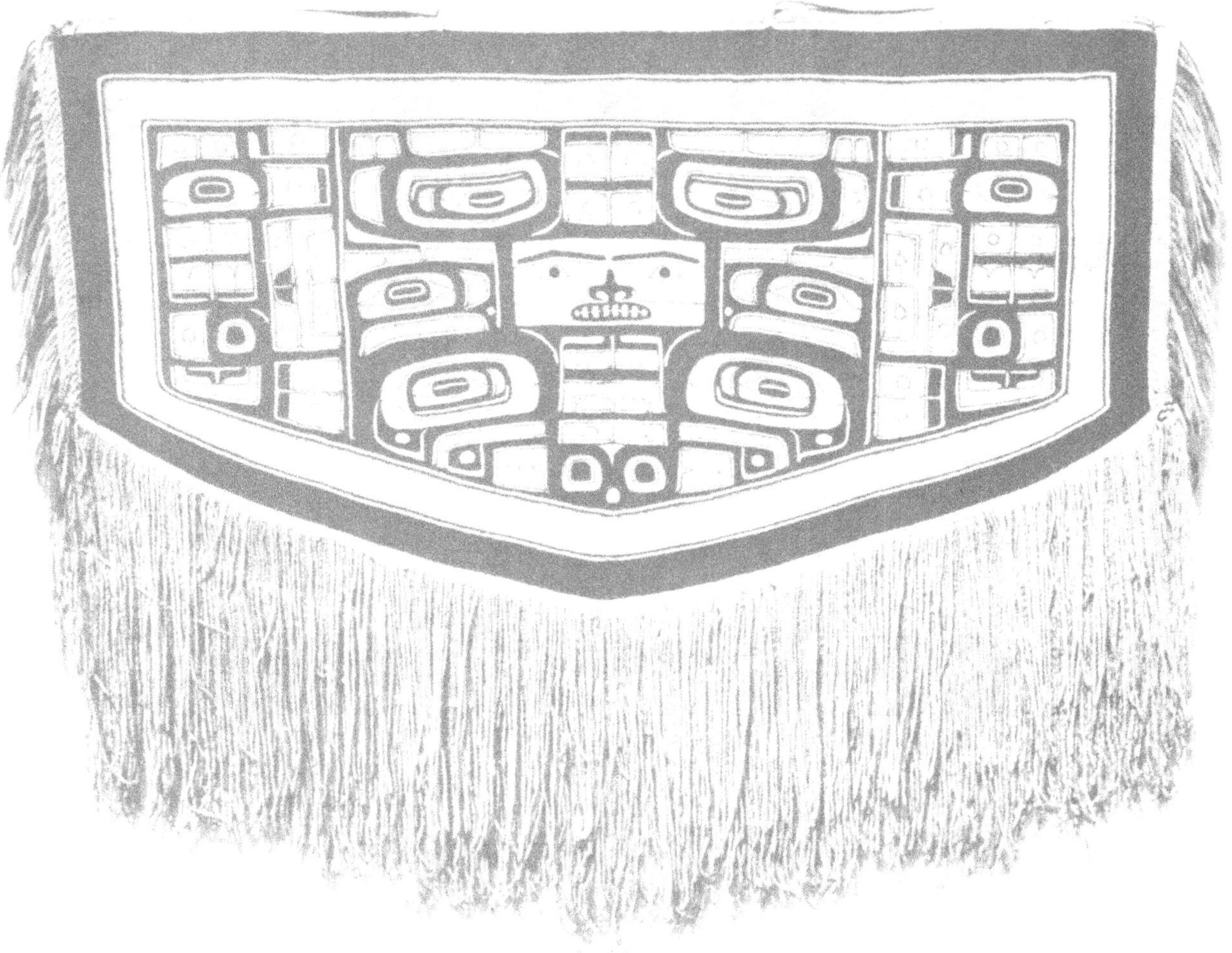

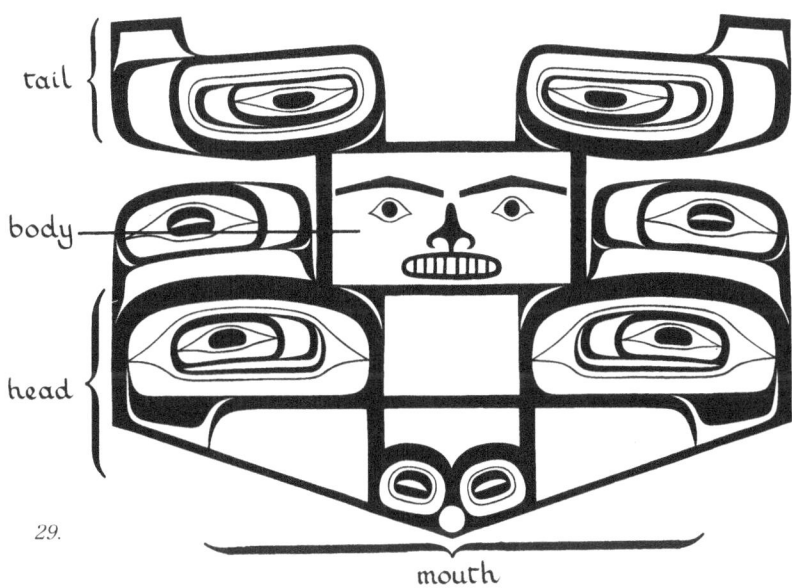

28.

29.

28. and 29. Emmons calls the design in the central panel a diving whale. The head, with its nostrils and mouth, is shown at the bottom of the design. The central face represents the body. (Private Collection: CS)

tail

body

head

mouth

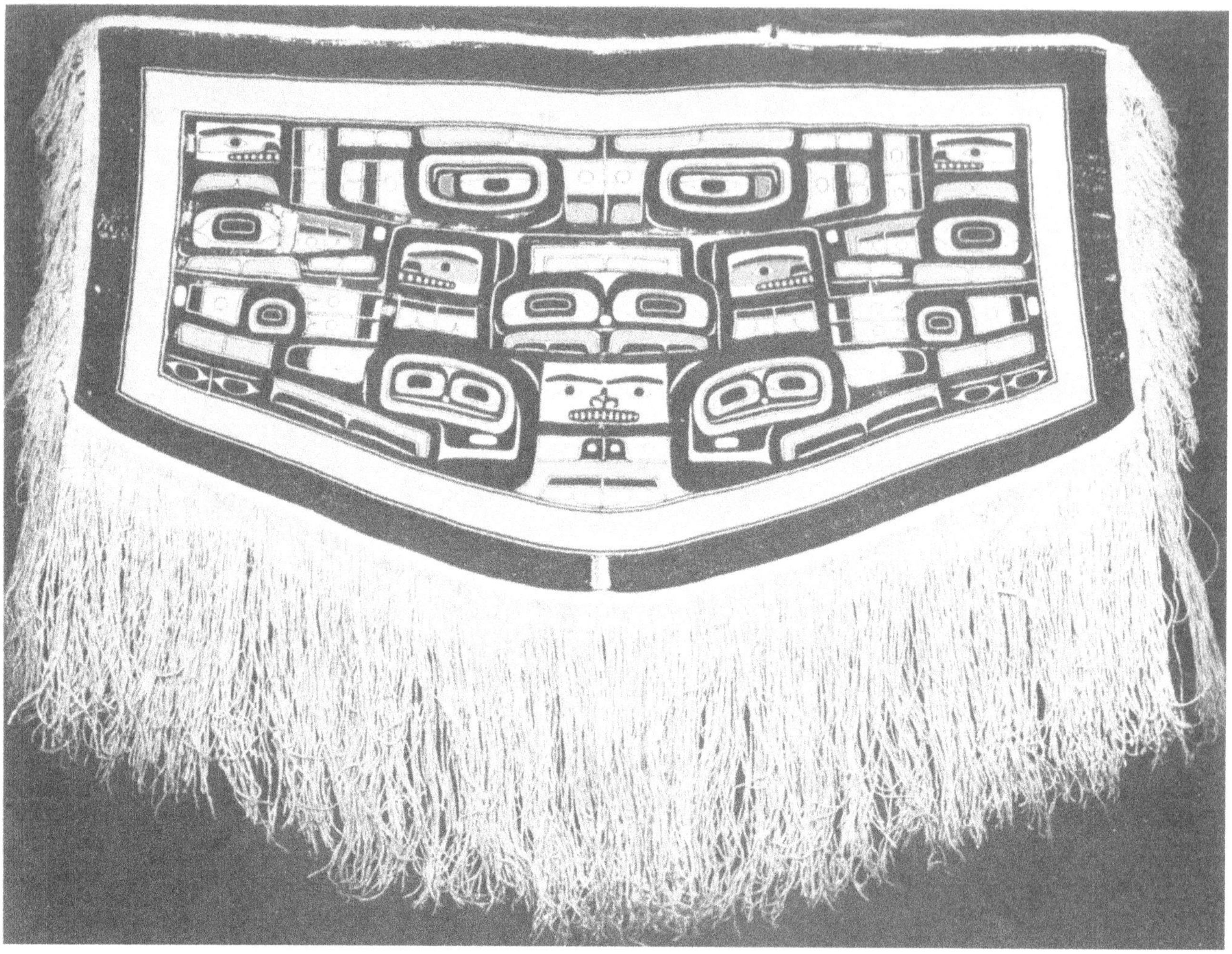

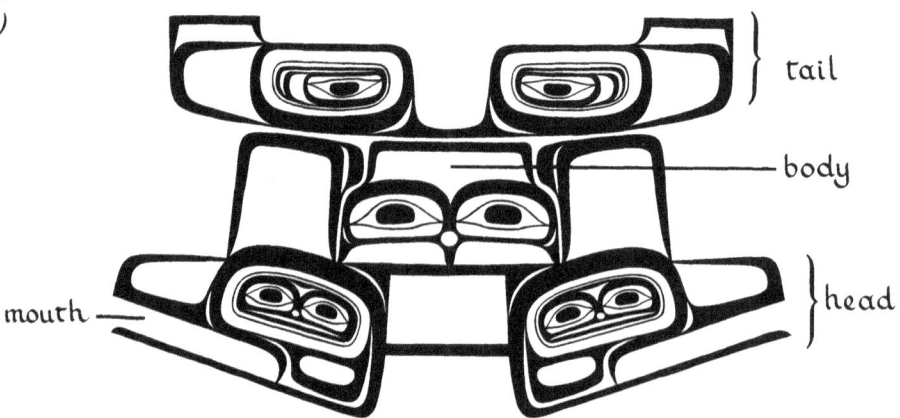

30.

30. and 31. Possibly another whale,
this one is split down the belly and
splayed so that in profile the nose is
pointing outward. (Photograph
courtesy of the British Columbia
Provincial Museum)

tail

body

head

mouth

31.

How the Design is Affected by the Weaving

The technique which the Tlingit women developed in order to weave the men's designs allowed them to create almost any curve imaginable. However, even the cleverest weaver had her limits; to weave across the entire width of a blanket was an unmanageable task and a special technique, called a "drawstring join," was introduced to break the line of weaving. The drawstring needed to be introduced on a vertical line; the weavers and designers must have worked together to determine what overall design arrangement was practical and where it could be straightened out to allow for a drawstring join. Likewise, although curves were possible, square shapes were easier to execute and the curvilinear shapes of the painter's art were often squared. As the weavers and painters worked together, a style of design developed which became a recognized carving and painting style and was used in the majority of Dancing Blankets.

The Pattern Board

A pattern board, from which the design of the Dancing Blanket was taken, was fashioned and painted by a male artist. These boards, upon which full-sized renderings of the designs we painted, were made of cedar planks finely adzed to a smooth surface. The designs on the blankets were symmetrical, and because of this only one-half need be painted; the weaver could mirror the images on the other side. Generally, pattern boards were paintings of the right side of the weaving, including the middle of the central design panel. The left side of the central panel might be outlined, but most of the details were left out. The boards were painted only in black; the weaver understood the conventions of the art and could color the shapes accurately. They also only included the design field, as most blankets had black and yellow borders so that indication of these was not necessary.

Pattern boards were highly valued and were used more than once by the same weaver. The designs on the boards were faithfully translated into wool, each portion being measured by means of a small piece of inner cedar bark which could be marked with the thumbnail. The cedar bark templates which the men used to paint the designs were also helpful in establishing the correct curves. Painters were known to copy a pattern board or even a blanket, changing only the smallest of details and leaving the main design elements intact. The slightest variation in pattern between two seemingly identical blankets indicates that each was woven from its own pattern board. Occasionally a pattern board would carry two designs: one on one side of the board and a different one on the other.

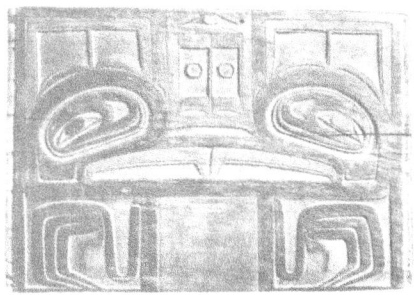

32. One side of a carved chest, showing a similarity in style between the carving and weaving designs (Courtesy of the Burke Museum, University of Washington: CS)

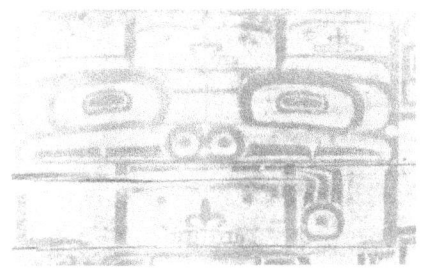

33. A pattern board with a central design similar to the carved chest in figure 32 (Courtesy of the British Columbia Provincial Museum)

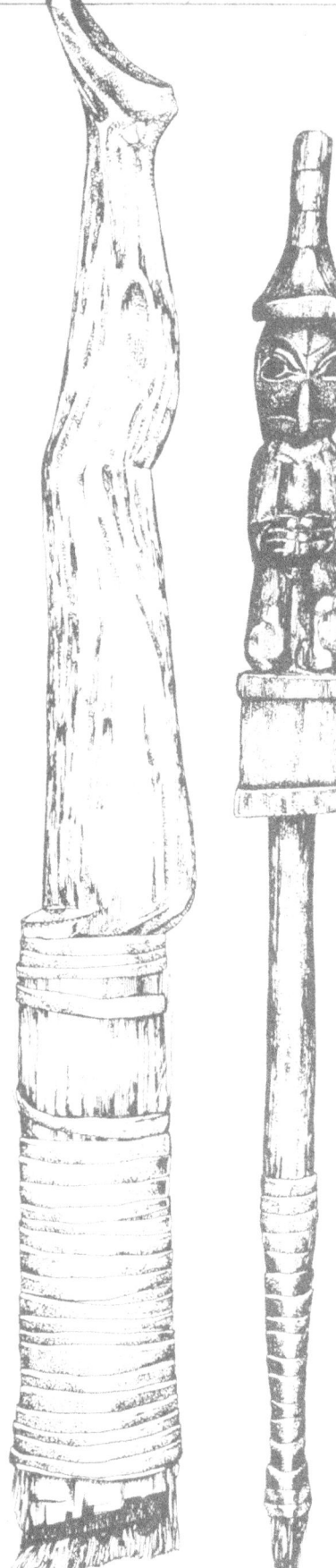

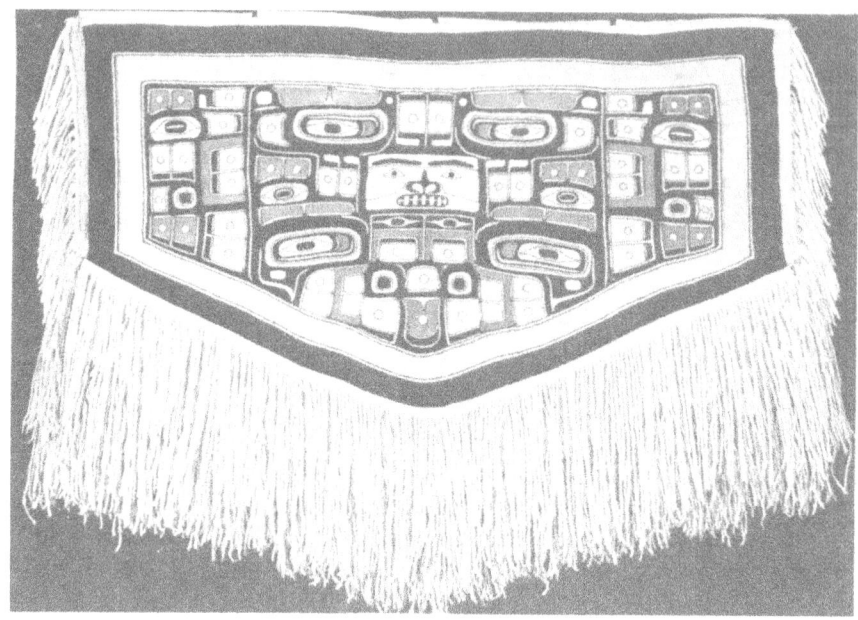

35. A Dancing Blanket almost identical to the pattern board below. The greatest number of blankets with the same design were woven from this pattern. (Courtesy of the British Columbia Provincial Museum)

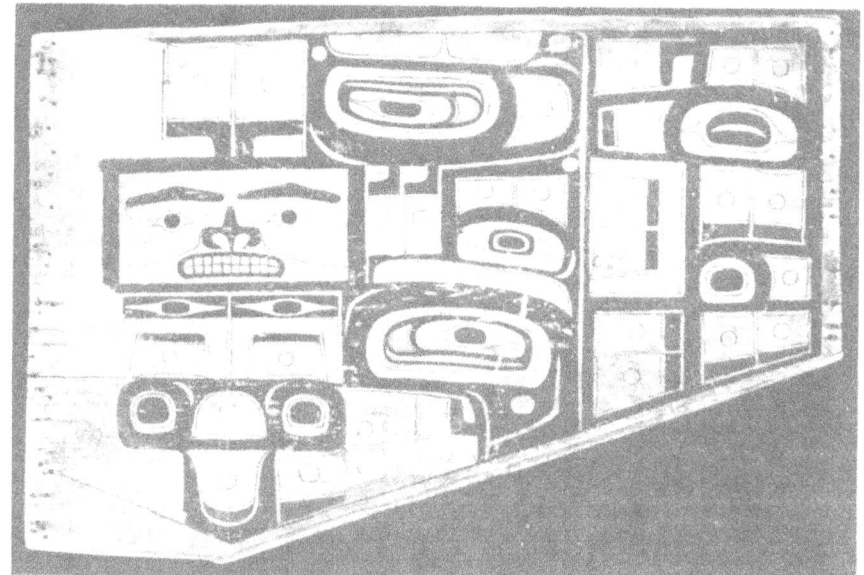

36. A pattern board from Klukwan (Courtesy of the British Columbia Provincial Museum)

34. Carved paintbrushes

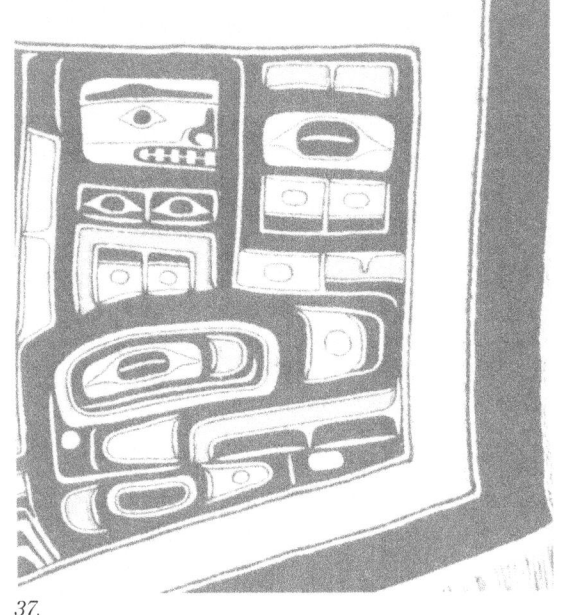

37.

37. A side panel of a blanket showing the primary formlines in (a) below. (Courtesy of the British Columbia Provincial Museum)

The Forms of the Design

In order to weave the designs accurately, a woman needed to understand the principles of the art. Various terms, defined by Bill Holm in *Analysis of Form*, are used today to identify the different design elements:

Primary Formlines (a) are the major element of the design. They constantly vary in width as they delineate the body of the main figure.

Ovoids (b) are bean-shaped forms, some elongated and some more circular. All are convex on the top and sides and straight or slightly concave on the bottom. They are found right side up, upside down, or sideways in the design field.

Primary Formline Ovoids (c) are the black ovoids used in delineating the main figure.

Sockets (d) are found directly within the primary formline ovoids.

Eyelid Lines (e) are the black lines, in the shape of an eye, which are found within a socket.

Inner Ovoids (f) are found within the sockets or within an eyelid line.

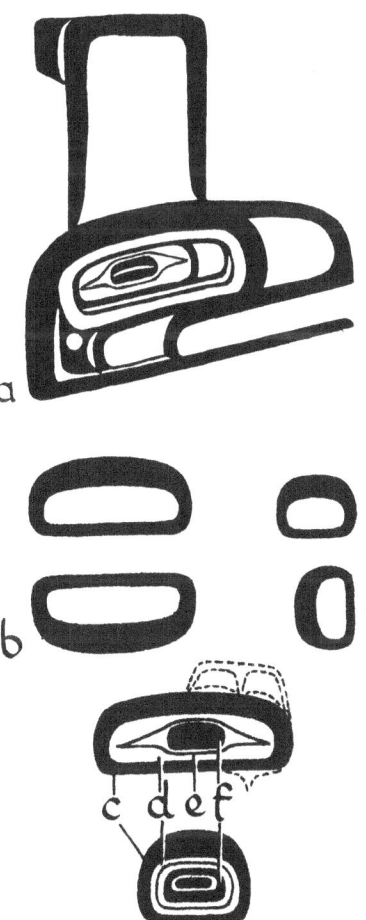

38. Design forms

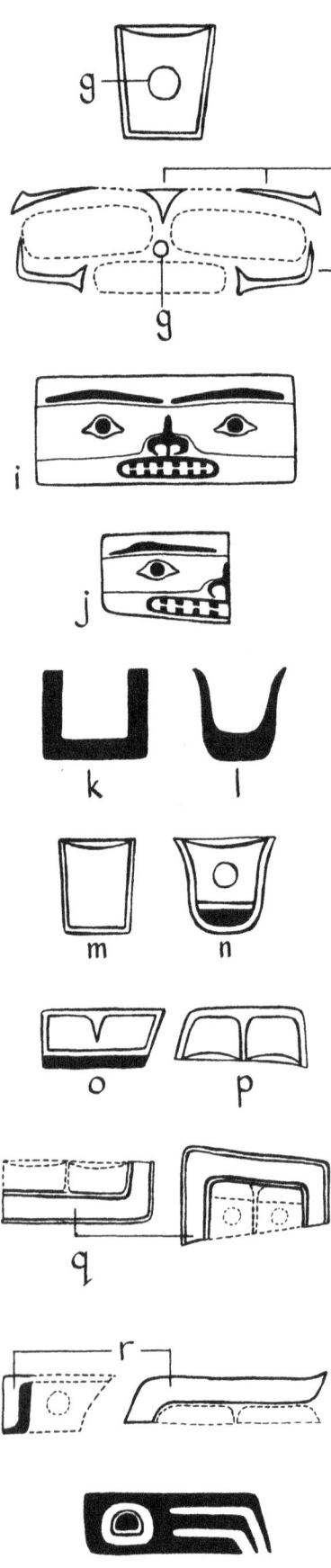

Circles (g) are small, perfectly round, and are placed within the U shapes or between two merging primary formlines.

Resultant Forms (h) are the white shapes which result when two primary formlines meet against the background.

Faces (i & j) are usually found within the body of the main figure; they also appear in between the tail fins or in and between the ears. They are human in character, containing recognizable eyes, nose, and mouth shapes. Sometimes they are placed in profile in the side panels *(j)*. Faces are never the face of the main creature depicted in the design.

Primary Formline ∪ Shapes (k & l) take the shape of the letter U. They are elements of the painted art, *(l)*, which, in the woven form, have become considerably squared *(k)*. They surround the inner U shapes and combine with other primary formlines to depict the main figure.

Inner ∪ Shapes (m & n) comprise the majority of figures in the design field. They are most commonly seen as a rectangle with a crescent at one end. Some inner U shapes are rounded at the bottom *(n)*. They can be found right side up, upside down, or sideways, the top being indicated by the placement of the crescent.

A Split ∪ (o) is a U shape with a crescent which comes to a point.

Paired Us (p) are inner U shapes which lie side by side.

Squared L and ∪ Shapes (q) are found either vertically or horizontally within the design field. Occasionally, an L shape will have circles in it.

S *Shapes (r)* are gracefully curved figures resembling the letter S.

Feet (s) are easily recognizable as such and are always the feet of the creature being depicted.

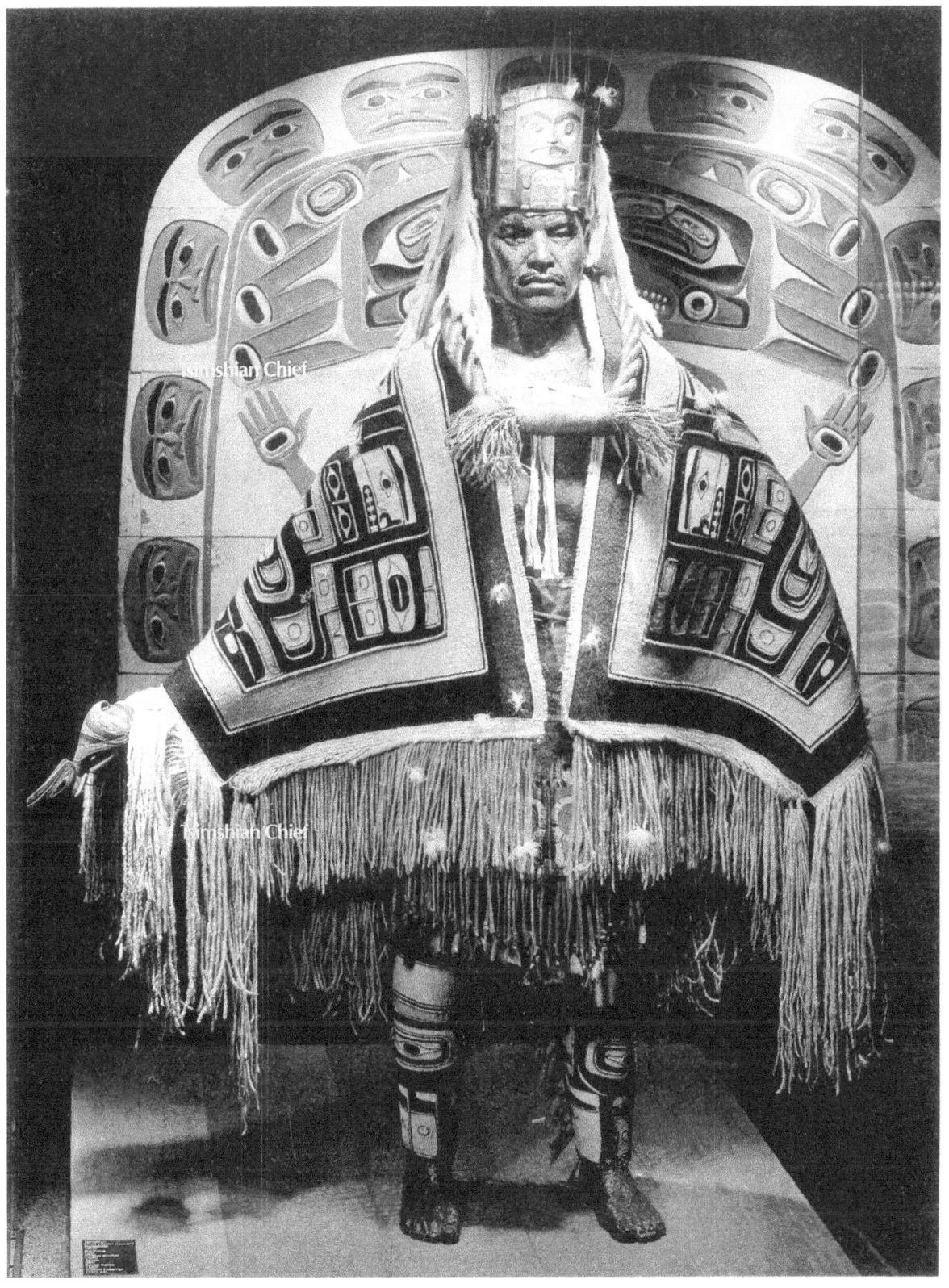

*A. On display in the British Columbia Provincial Museum is a fine model of
a Tsimshian chief dressed in ceremonial garments. (Courtesy of the British
Columbia Provincial Museum)*

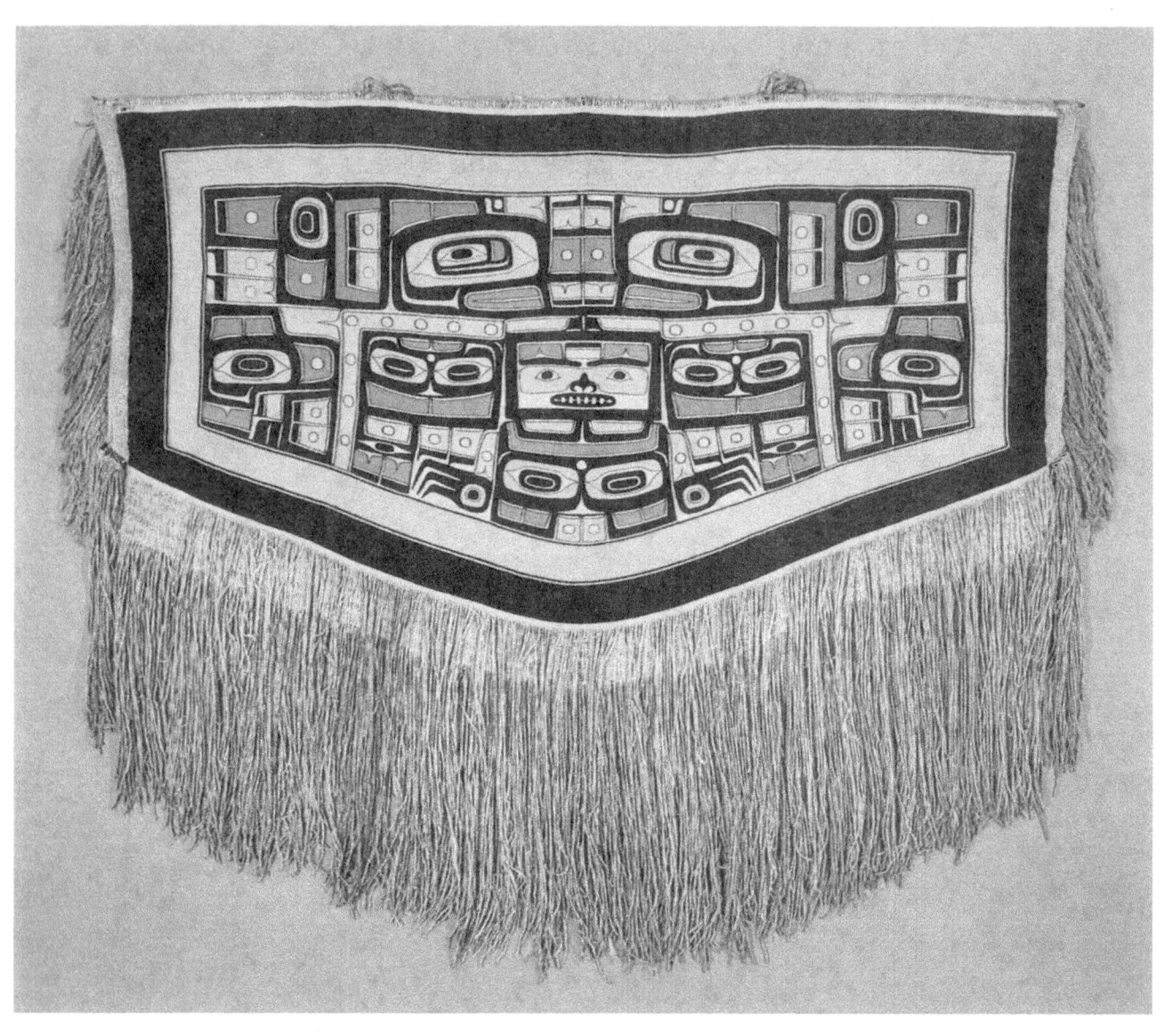

B. The yellow-green dye in this Dancing Blanket indicates it is probably one of the older blankets. (Courtesy of the American Museum of Natural History)

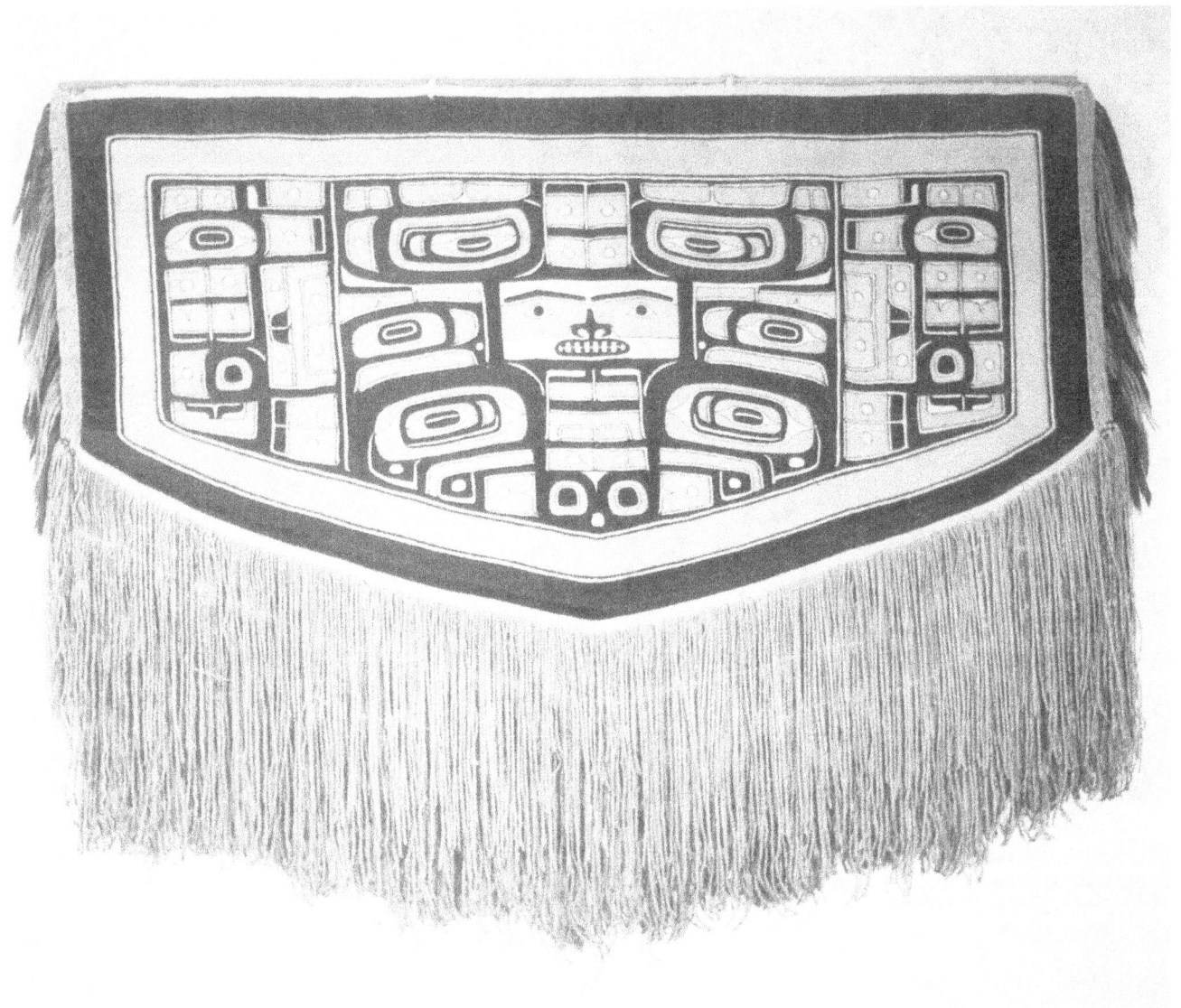

C. The use of the blue-green dye was well-established by the time this finely woven Dancing Blanket was made. (Private Collection)

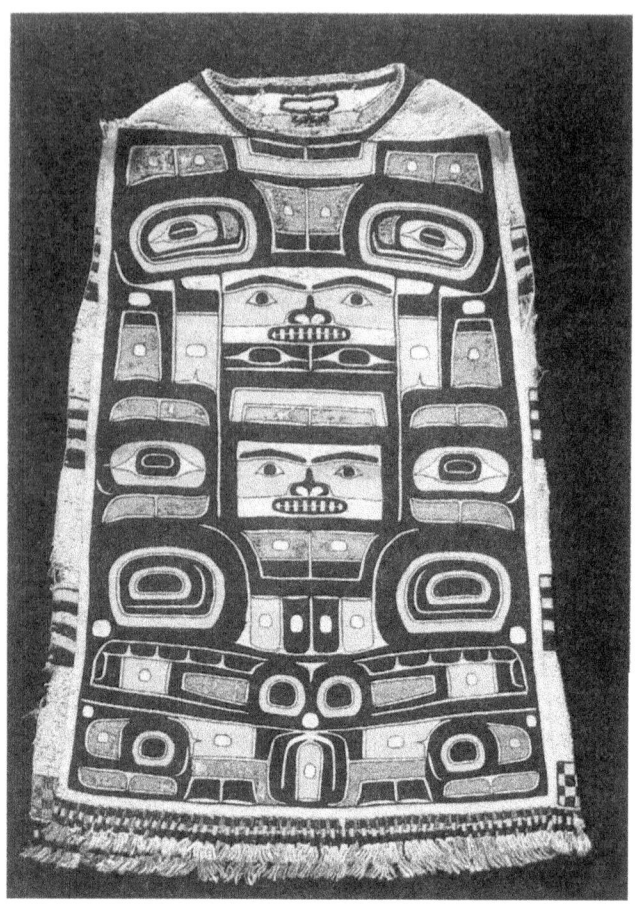

D. The front panel of this sleeveless tunic is completely covered in a totemic design. (Courtesy of the National Museum of Natural History, Smithsonian Institution)

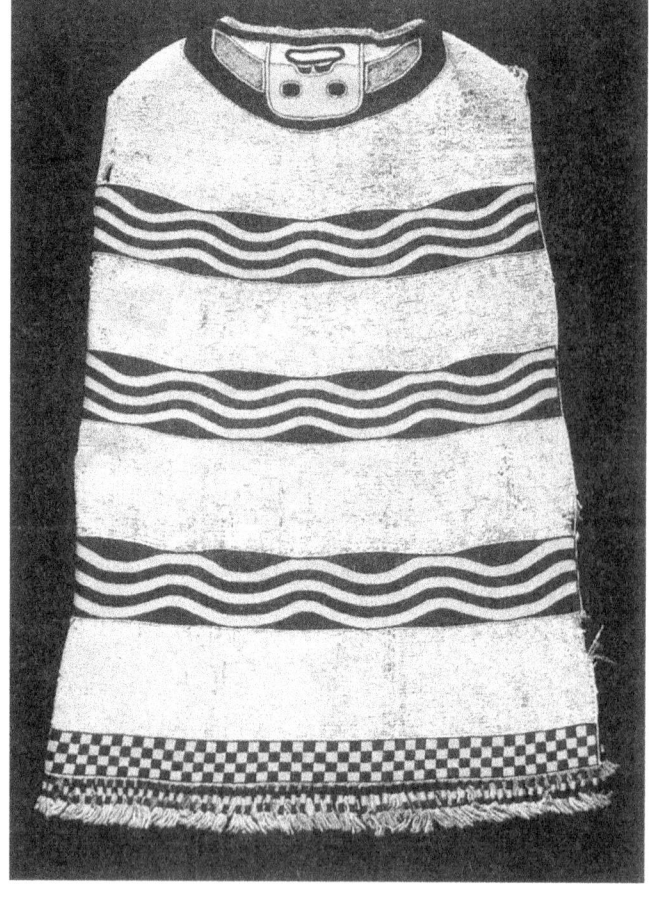

E. The back panel of the tunic in the above photograph. (Courtesy of the National Museum of Natural History, Smithsonian Institution)

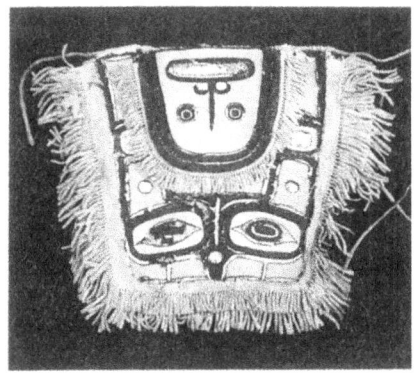

F. This legging is one of the only leggings in museum collections today which was actually woven as a legging. (Courtesy of the National Museum of Natural History, Smithsonian Institution: CS)

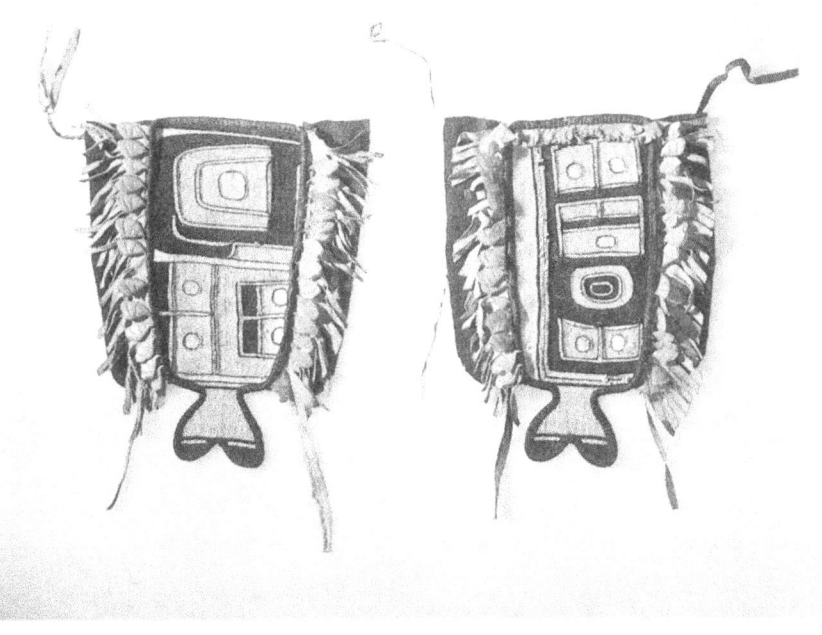

G. Leggings made from pieces of a Dancing Blanket. The designs on pairs of leggings made from potlatch pieces usually did not match. (Courtesy of the National Museum of Natural History, Smithsonian Institution: CS)

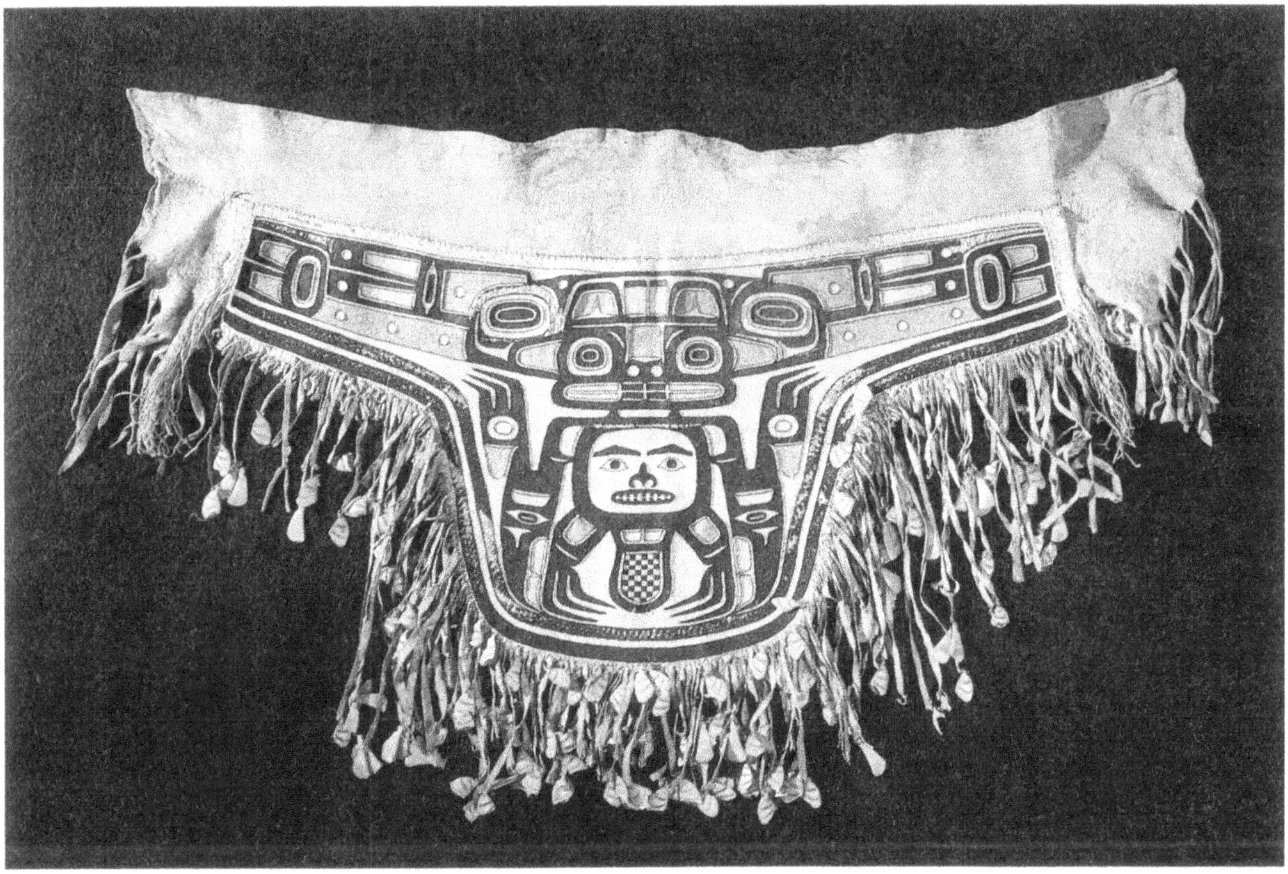

H. A Beaver Dancing Apron (Courtesy of the National Museum of Natural History, Smithsonian Institution)

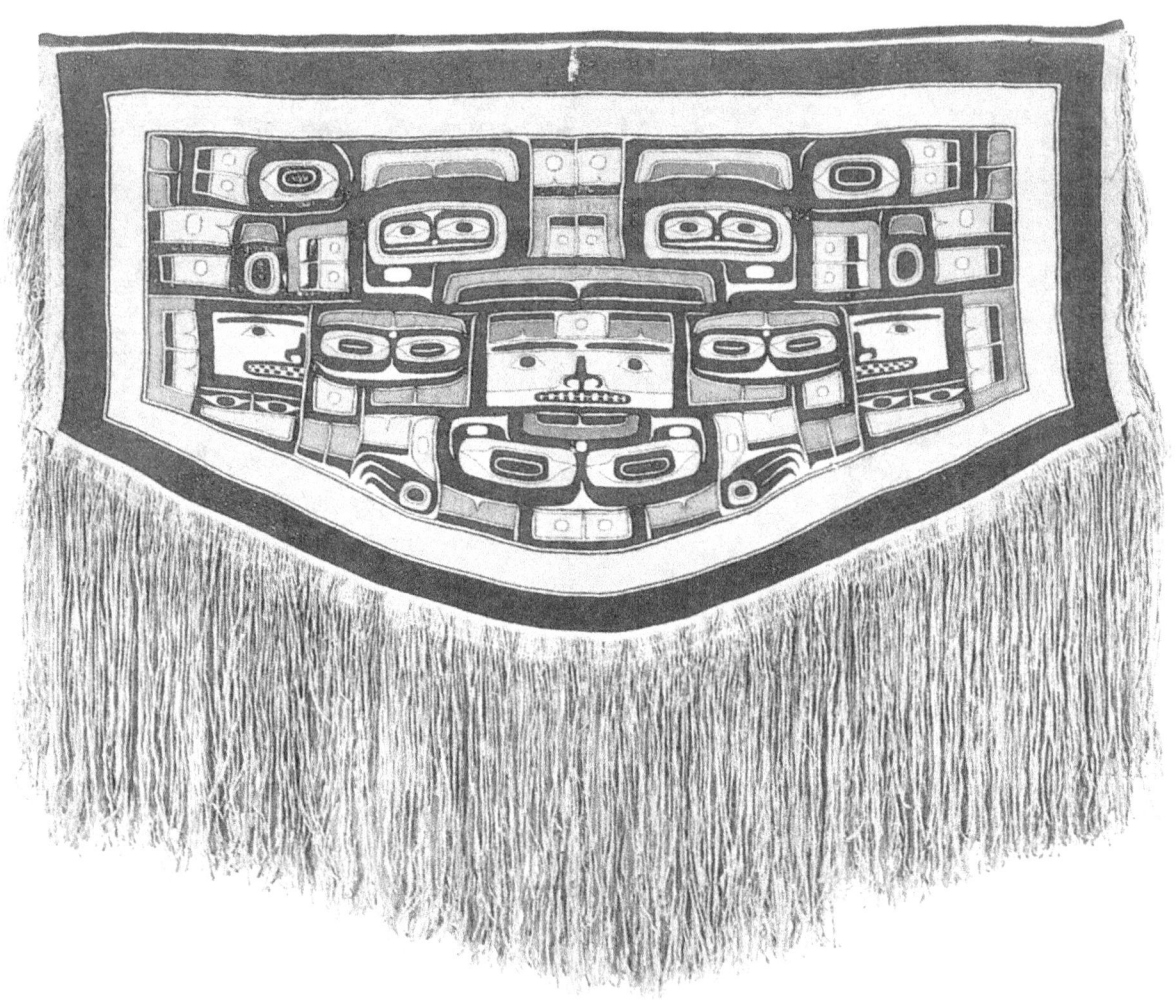

I. In this Dancing Blanket, blue-green dye has been painted over the yellow-green dye in some areas. (This was done only on the front surface; the back shows no blue-green whatsoever.) (Courtesy of the American Museum of Natural History)

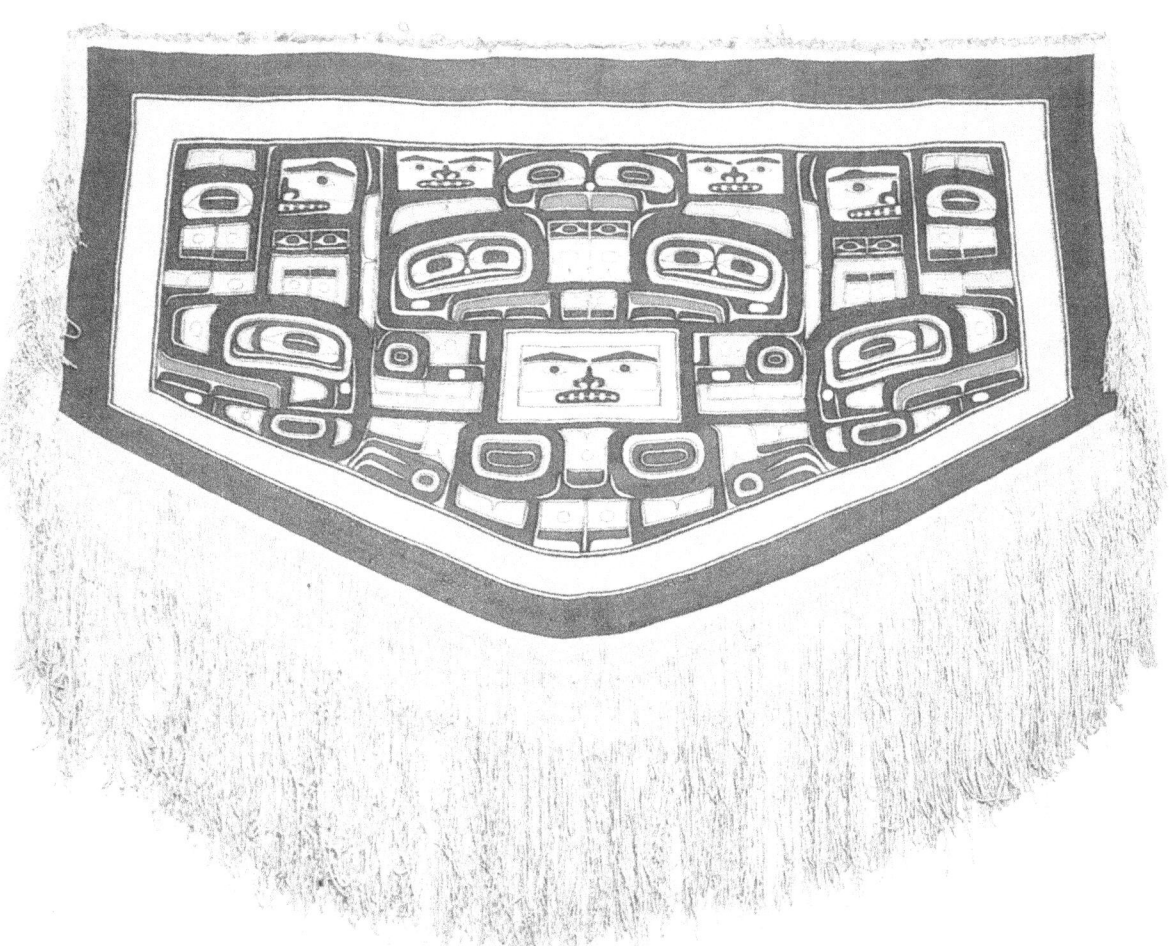

J. The Dancing Blanket in this photograph is one of a very few weavings in which red can be found. (Courtesy of the Santa Barbara Museum of Natural History. Photograph by Paul Olsen, Brooks Institute of Photography)

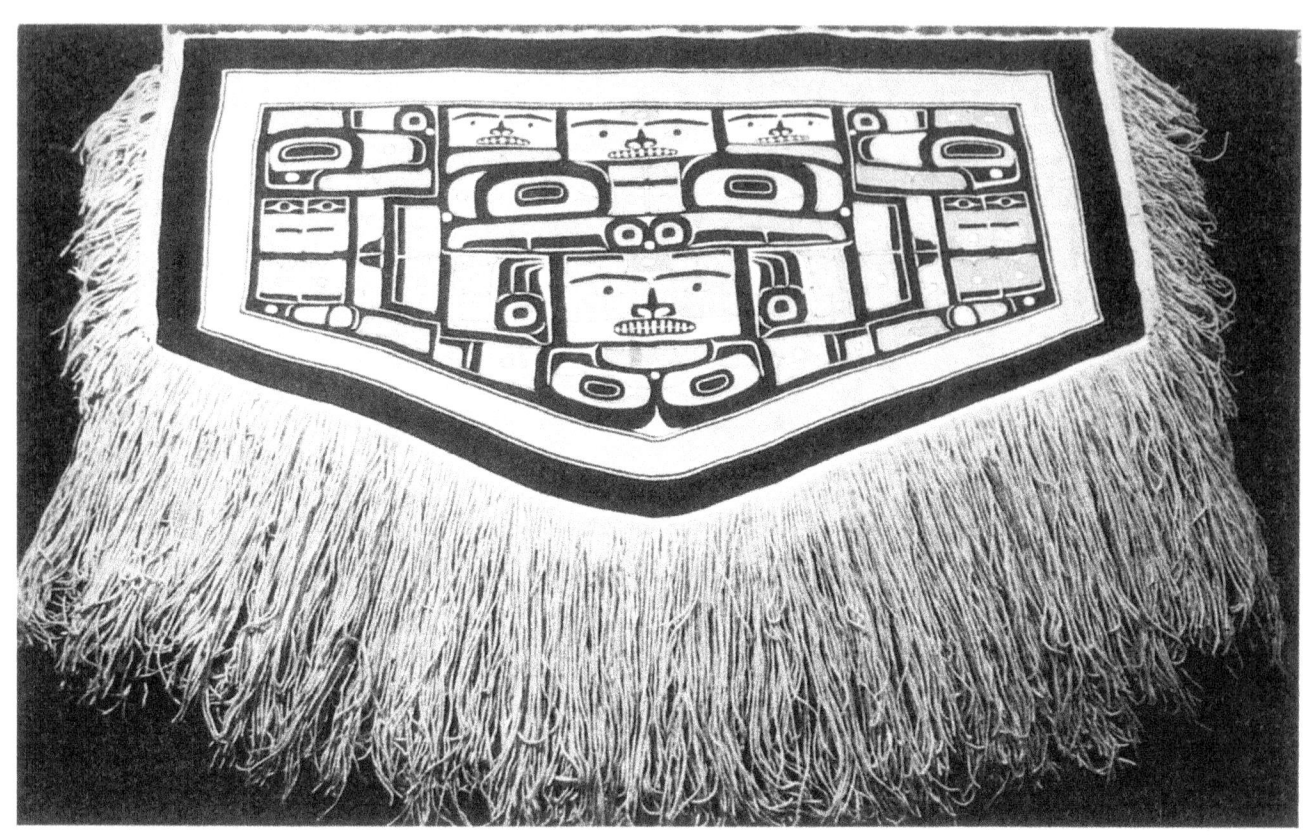

K. A superb example of a Dancing Blanket (Courtesy of the American Museum of Natural History: CS)

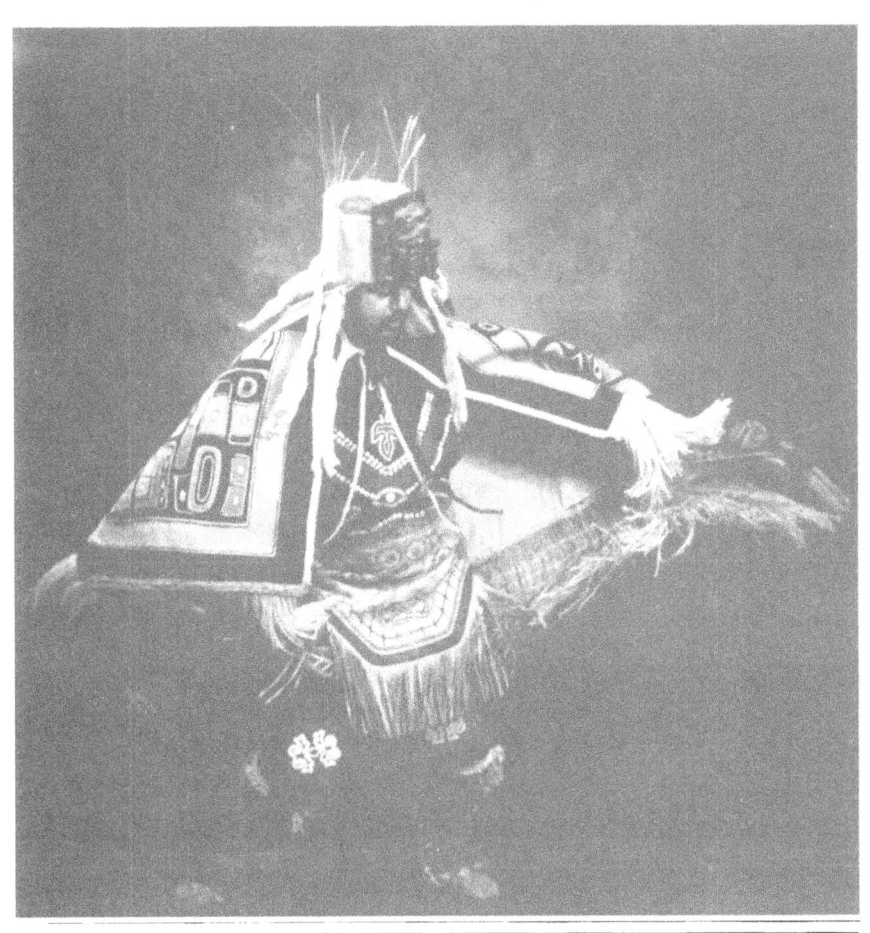

PART

MATERIALS, SPINNING, AND DYEING

II

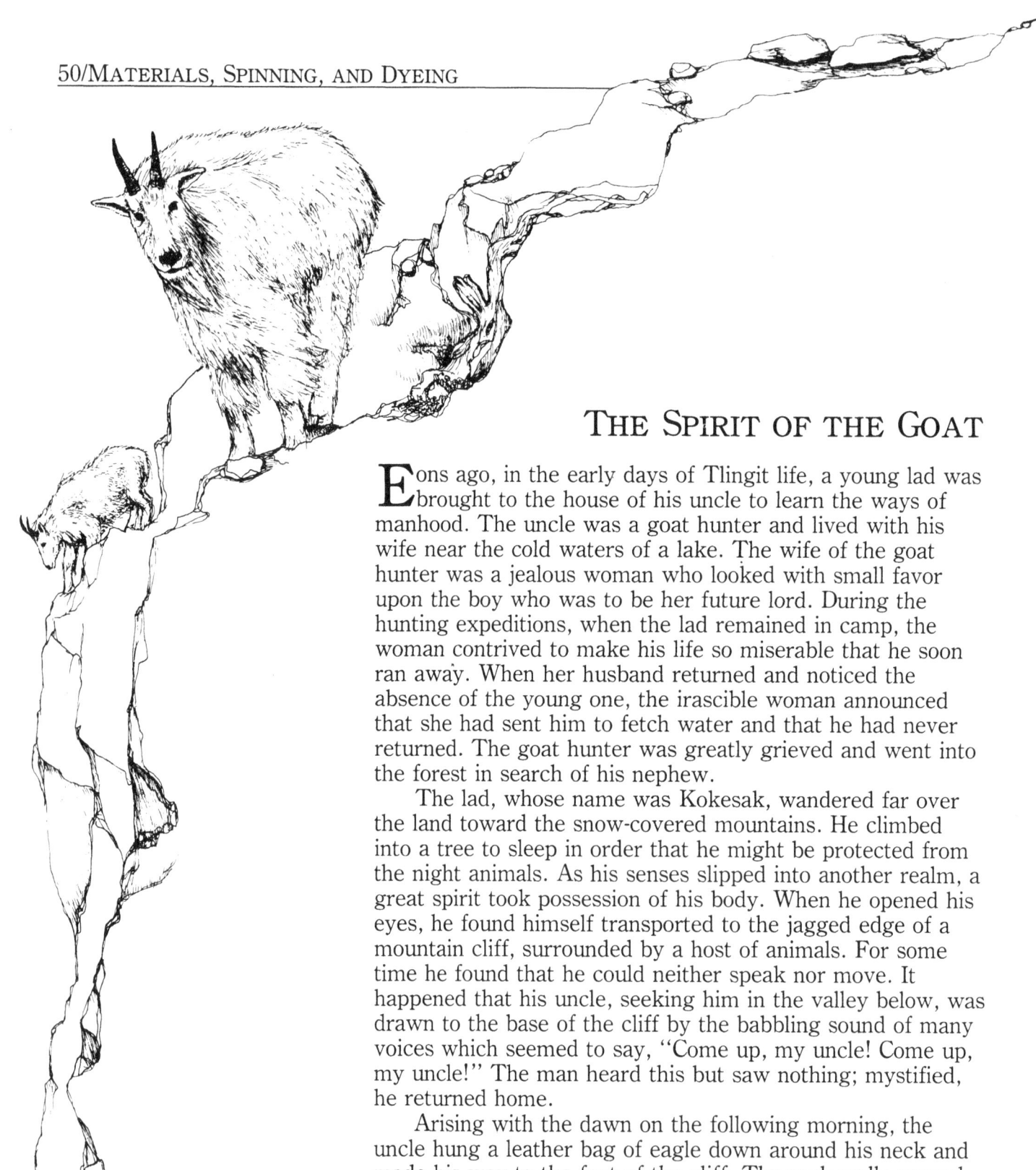

The Spirit of the Goat

Eons ago, in the early days of Tlingit life, a young lad was brought to the house of his uncle to learn the ways of manhood. The uncle was a goat hunter and lived with his wife near the cold waters of a lake. The wife of the goat hunter was a jealous woman who looked with small favor upon the boy who was to be her future lord. During the hunting expeditions, when the lad remained in camp, the woman contrived to make his life so miserable that he soon ran away. When her husband returned and noticed the absence of the young one, the irascible woman announced that she had sent him to fetch water and that he had never returned. The goat hunter was greatly grieved and went into the forest in search of his nephew.

The lad, whose name was Kokesak, wandered far over the land toward the snow-covered mountains. He climbed into a tree to sleep in order that he might be protected from the night animals. As his senses slipped into another realm, a great spirit took possession of his body. When he opened his eyes, he found himself transported to the jagged edge of a mountain cliff, surrounded by a host of animals. For some time he found that he could neither speak nor move. It happened that his uncle, seeking him in the valley below, was drawn to the base of the cliff by the babbling sound of many voices which seemed to say, "Come up, my uncle! Come up, my uncle!" The man heard this but saw nothing; mystified, he returned home.

Arising with the dawn on the following morning, the uncle hung a leather bag of eagle down around his neck and made his way to the foot of the cliff. The rock walls proved inaccessible, so he loosened his pouch and tossed a handful of the light white feathers into the air. They floated higher and higher until they were lost from sight. Suddenly, a large feather sailed earthward, driven by an invisible force, until it blew directly into the opened leather pouch. Late that night, as the hunter made camp in the woods, he was startled by rustling, gnawing sounds coming from the pouch. He hastened to open it, and in doing so was astonished to see his nephew step out.

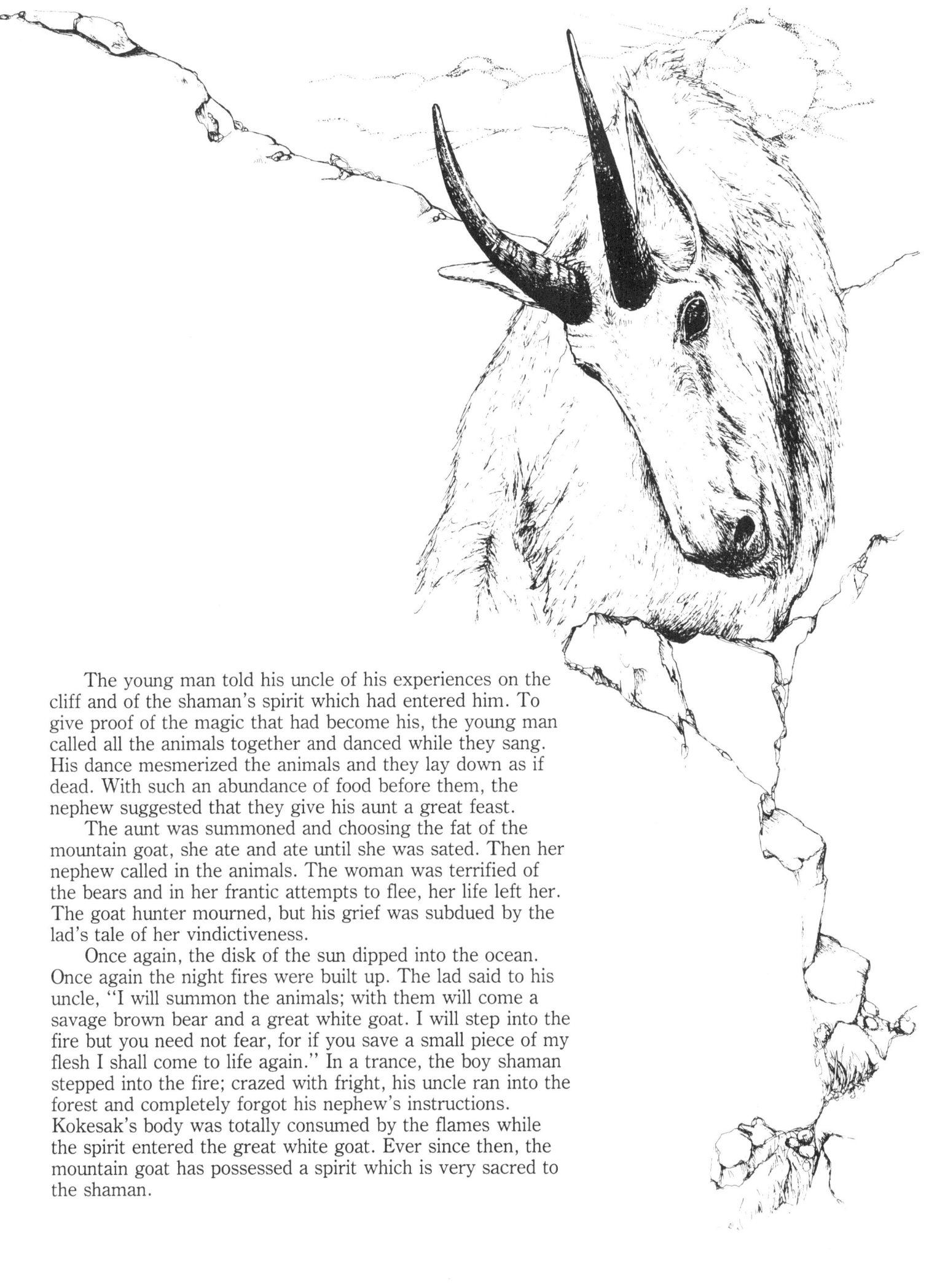

The young man told his uncle of his experiences on the cliff and of the shaman's spirit which had entered him. To give proof of the magic that had become his, the young man called all the animals together and danced while they sang. His dance mesmerized the animals and they lay down as if dead. With such an abundance of food before them, the nephew suggested that they give his aunt a great feast.

The aunt was summoned and choosing the fat of the mountain goat, she ate and ate until she was sated. Then her nephew called in the animals. The woman was terrified of the bears and in her frantic attempts to flee, her life left her. The goat hunter mourned, but his grief was subdued by the lad's tale of her vindictiveness.

Once again, the disk of the sun dipped into the ocean. Once again the night fires were built up. The lad said to his uncle, "I will summon the animals; with them will come a savage brown bear and a great white goat. I will step into the fire but you need not fear, for if you save a small piece of my flesh I shall come to life again." In a trance, the boy shaman stepped into the fire; crazed with fright, his uncle ran into the forest and completely forgot his nephew's instructions. Kokesak's body was totally consumed by the flames while the spirit entered the great white goat. Ever since then, the mountain goat has possessed a spirit which is very sacred to the shaman.

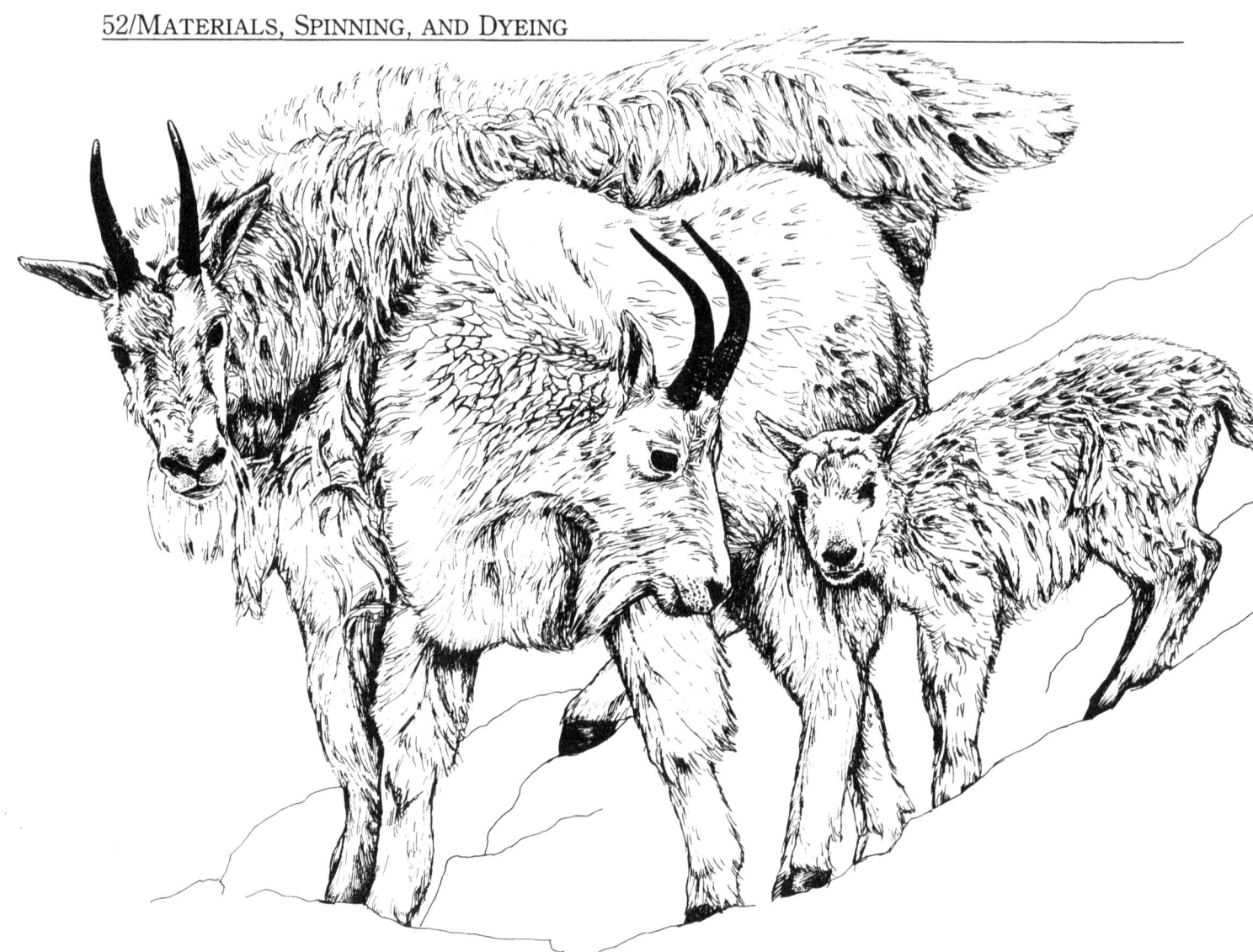

Mountain Goats

The wool of the mountain goat was the major material used in spinning the warp and the weft for the Dancing Blanket. The Tlingits, living inland near the trails which crossed the high mountains, were able to hunt these animals and bring them back for use in many ways. The hides were tanned, the fleece removed and used for spinning fine yarns, the horns carved into beautiful spoons, the intestines dried and fashioned into pouches and protective sheets, and the meat and fat eaten.

Mountain goats dwell high on the cliffs of the great mountain ranges, living on grasses in the summer and fall seasons and in winter, foraging beneath deep snow drifts for tiny lichens, mosses, and ferns. Life on the high cliffs has endowed the mountain goats with acrobatic ability. They are very deft at maneuvering on the precipitous rocky ledges. If caught on an ever-narrowing ledge, a goat has been seen to turn around by walking its hind legs over its head, against the vertical cliff, until it has described a half-circle on the rock and is facing the opposite direction. The cliffs provide safety and a home free from

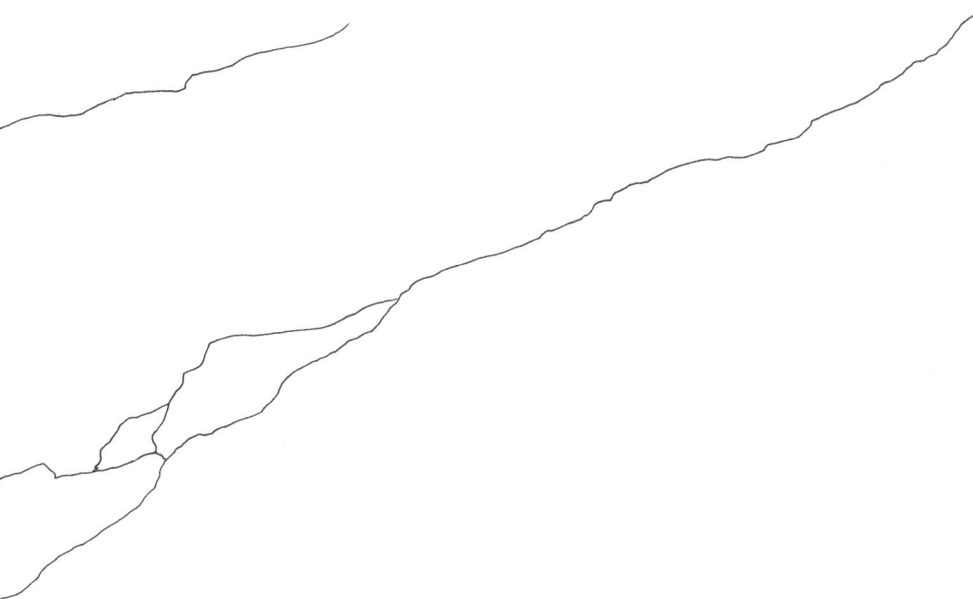

most predators. This is, however, a mixed blessing, for they are also the animals' greatest enemy. A misplaced step may plunge an unlucky beast to a premature death. A goat's entire life-span is only about twelve years.

In the early nineteenth century when European traders, trappers, and explorers first encountered the white mountain goats, they sent back tales of a great mythical beast which appeared and disappeared on the cliff faces. Mounds of white snow were seen to heave, rise, and transform themselves into this snow-white creature. The gravity-defying dexterity of the goats made them appear as marionettes controlled by a magical god.

The Europeans were not alone in their wonder over these magnificent creatures. The native Tlingits hunted them and knew their ways, and knowing them led to a belief that they housed a very sacred spirit. The magical powers of the shaman linked themselves with the seeming magic of the goat, inspiring mystery and awe in the people.

MOUNTAIN GOAT WOOL

Winters are cold and icy on the high mountain cliffs; animals need warm coats to protect them from the winter blizzards. The mountain goat wears a robe of two layers: hollow guard hairs, sometimes twenty centimeters in length, lie like a coarse rug over an inner down of extremely soft fine wool. It is this downy wool that the natives recognized as an ideal fiber for spinning fine weft yarns.

It was the work of the men to provide the goat skins from which the women would remove the wool. The skins were taken from the animal and, if not used immediately, were hung to dry in the open air. When it came time to remove the fleece, the woman would first spread the goat skin before her and sprinkle it with a soft, white powdered clay. This clay was obtained from deposits in the ground, molded into rounded balls twelve to sixteen centimeters in diameter, and baked in a fire until dry. The balls were then powdered and beaten into the fleece with a long flat stick until much of the dirt and oils had been removed and the wool looked snowy white. To remove

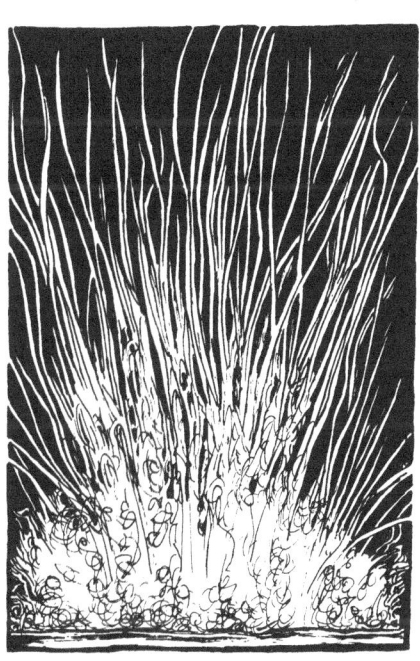

39. A section of the hide of a mountain goat showing the wool and guard hairs

40. A wool beater, used for cleaning fleece

the wool and hair from the hide, the skin side was wetted and the hide then rolled and left to sit for several days. The roots of the fibers would loosen during this time so that the fleece would readily release from the hide. Sitting on the ground, the woman would take the skin across her knees and push the fleece from her, rolling it off the hide in large patches. These she would set aside in low, flat baskets, repeating the process until the entire fleece was free.

The long, stiff guard hairs, if spun, would produce a very coarse yarn. This was not desirable and therefore these hairs had to be eliminated. Having removed the fleece in large patches, the arrangement of fibers had not been disturbed and the woman could easily pull the hairs out of the wool. Some of the finer hairs might remain, but these would not affect the final product.

Mountain goat wool is extremely soft, softer and more lustrous in fact than the finest Spanish merino fleece with which the early Russian traders and explorers compared it. Once removed from the hide, it did not need to be combed or carded in order to be spun, but simply was drawn out and rolled into roving and wound gently into balls. For safety and cleanliness, these roving balls were stored in round gut bags until the spinning began. The fleece from three mountain goats was needed to produce an average Dancing Blanket.

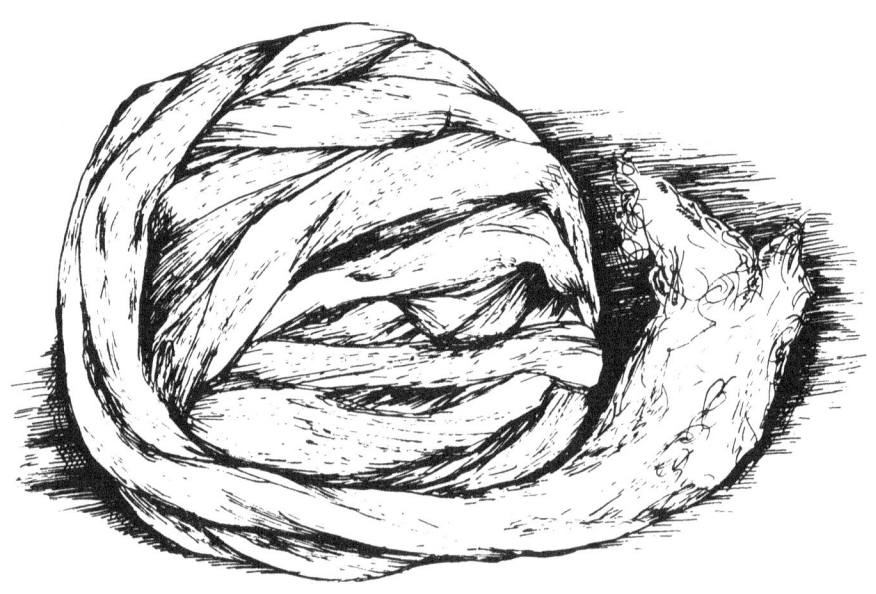

41. A ball of mountain goat roving

S AND Z TWIST IN SPINNING

The yarns in both the warp and the weft are made of two single S-twist strands plied together in a Z twist. To spin an S-twist yarn, the wool is drawn out and turned in a clockwise direction. When looking at a strand of S-twist yarn, the fibers can be seen to echo the diagonal of the S and therefore it is called S twist (fig. 43).

In a two-ply, Z-twist yarn, two S-twist strands are twisted together in a counterclockwise direction. The diagonal of these twisted strands mimics that of the backbone of the letter Z; hence its name, Z twist (fig. 43). In both cases, the yarns can be viewed right side up or upside down and they will still maintain the original S or Z appearance.

THE WARP

Within a Dancing Blanket, the warp was a stronger, larger yarn than the weft. It was made of mountain goat wool and the inner bark of the yellow cedar tree spun together into a two-ply, Z-twist yarn. Fine warp yarns could be as small as two millimeters in diameter, large ones as big as half a centimeter. All of the spinning was done between the spinner's hand and her knee, without the aid of a spindle.

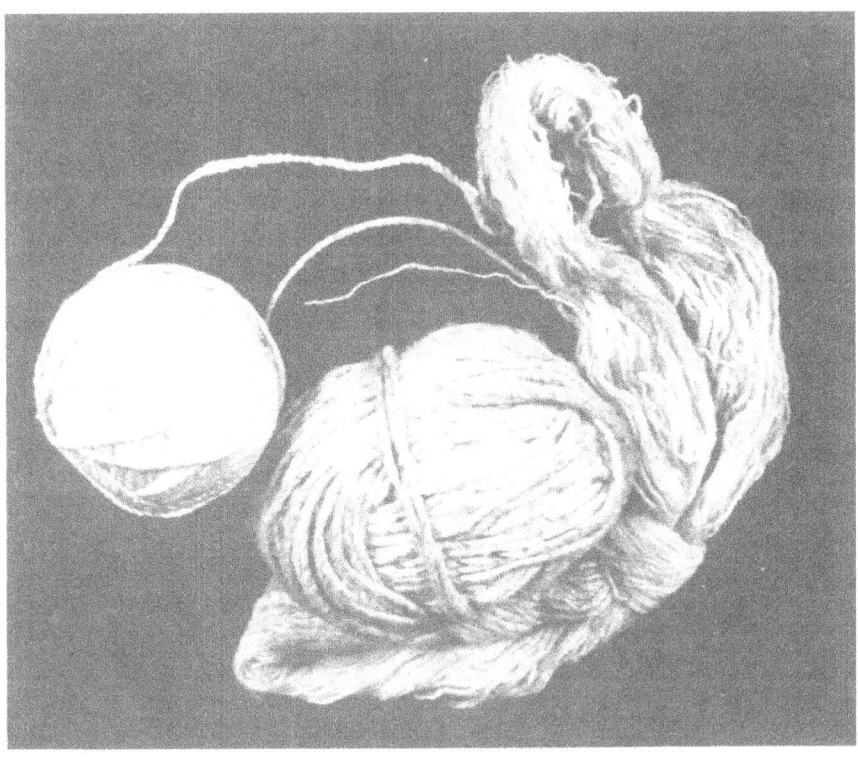

42. *The ball of warp yarn in the center is surrounded by smaller weft yarns. (Courtesy of the Burke Museum, University of Washington: CS)*

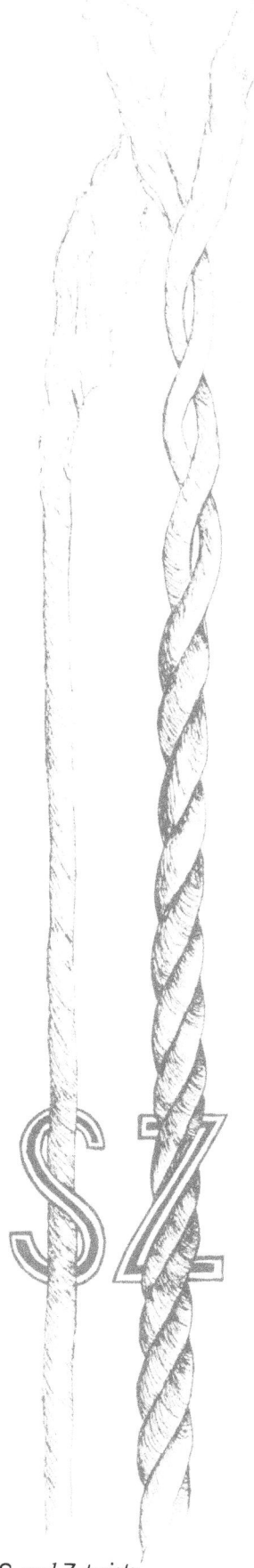

43. S *and* Z *twists*

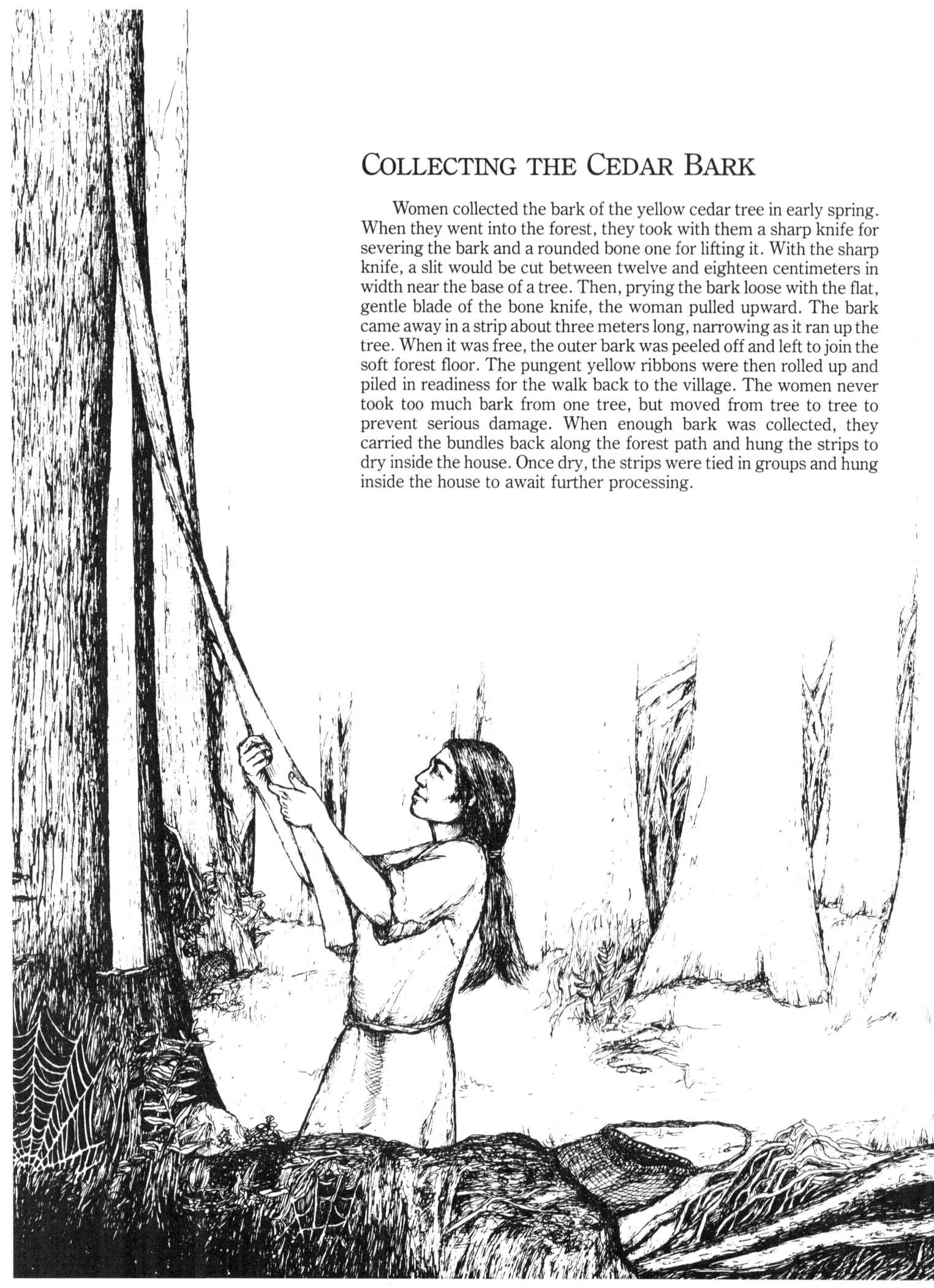

COLLECTING THE CEDAR BARK

Women collected the bark of the yellow cedar tree in early spring. When they went into the forest, they took with them a sharp knife for severing the bark and a rounded bone one for lifting it. With the sharp knife, a slit would be cut between twelve and eighteen centimeters in width near the base of a tree. Then, prying the bark loose with the flat, gentle blade of the bone knife, the woman pulled upward. The bark came away in a strip about three meters long, narrowing as it ran up the tree. When it was free, the outer bark was peeled off and left to join the soft forest floor. The pungent yellow ribbons were then rolled up and piled in readiness for the walk back to the village. The women never took too much bark from one tree, but moved from tree to tree to prevent serious damage. When enough bark was collected, they carried the bundles back along the forest path and hung the strips to dry inside the house. Once dry, the strips were tied in groups and hung inside the house to await further processing.

The dried strips of cedar bark kept indefinitely if they did not get damp. They were stiff and hard, the inner side being a yellow gold color, the outer side a rich red brown. To work with them, a woman had to boil the strips for two or three days to remove the resins. Boiled long enough, they split easily by bending the pliable ribbons of bark back and forth to loosen the layers. Remnants of the reddish outer bark were removed by rubbing a thumbnail or bone scraper down the bark strip while it was still quite wet. The bark could be separated into layers as thin as a leaf or as thick as a clamshell. The warp yarns of a Dancing Blanket needed strips as thin as blades of grass. When the women had separated the strips of yellow cedar bark, they were dried and tied again in loose bundles. As the time drew near to begin spinning, a woman would gather together the soft round balls of mountain goat roving and these bundles of cedar strips.

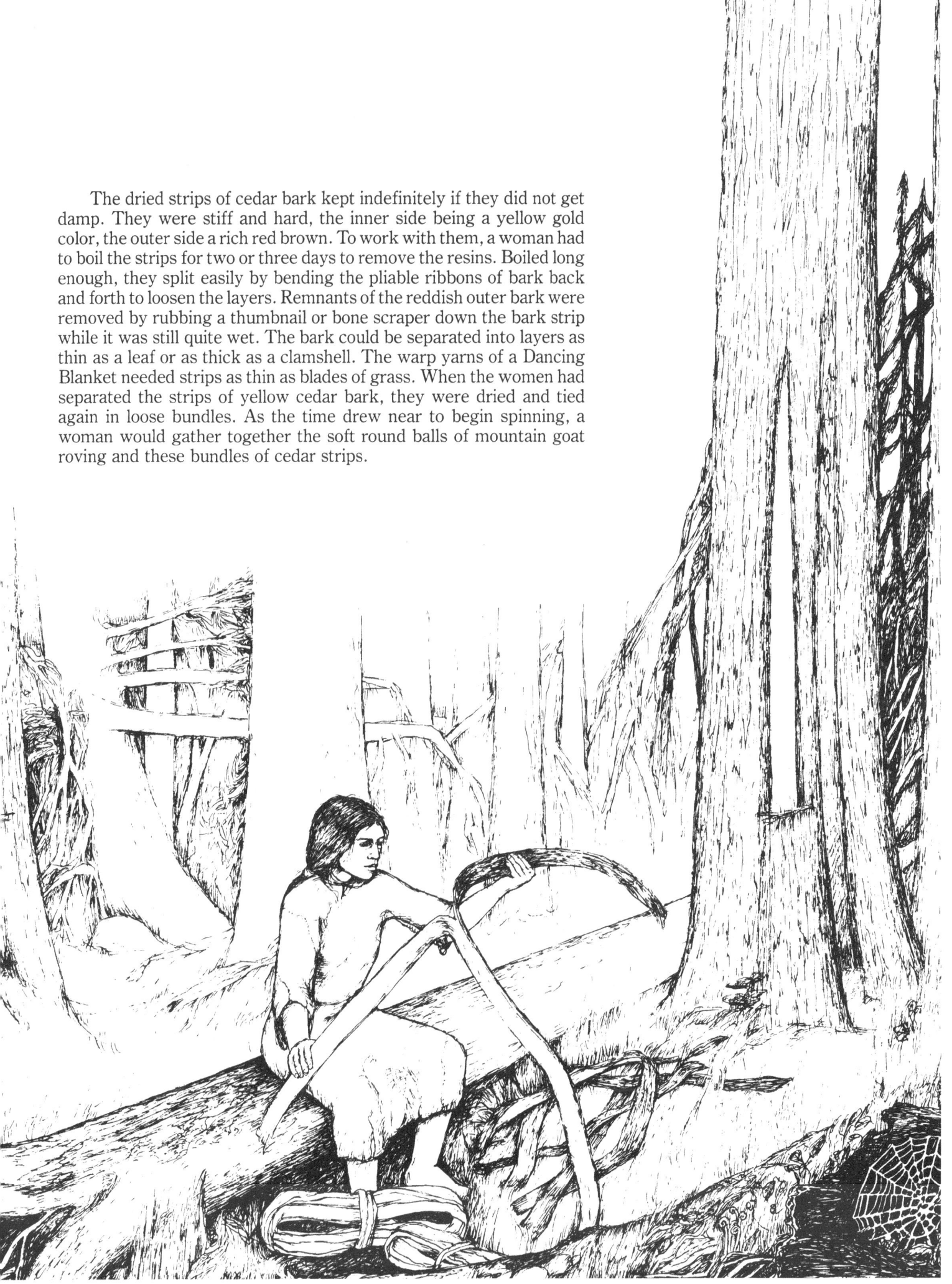

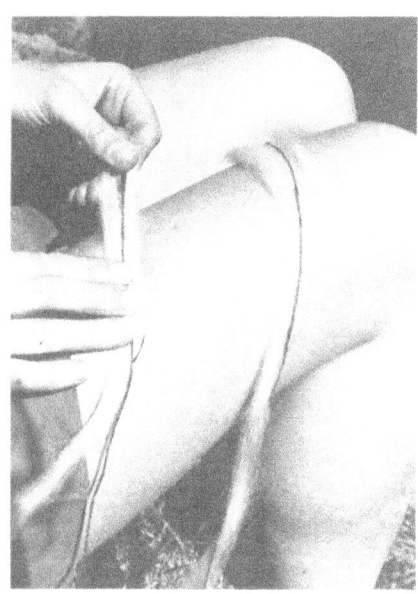 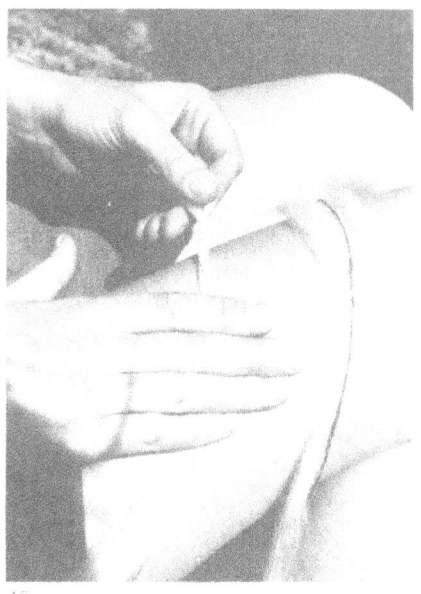 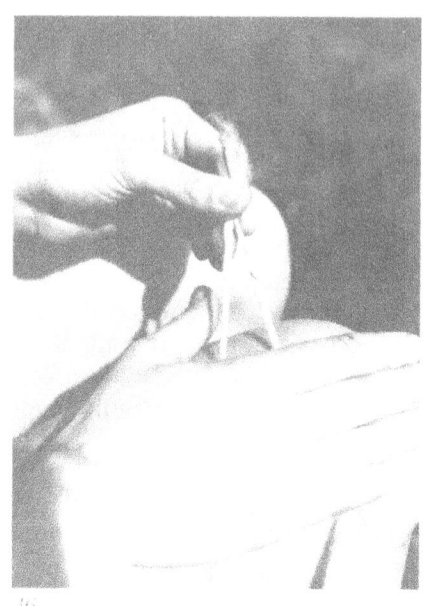

SPINNING THE WARP

STEP 1: Very little mountain goat wool is needed to put a thin covering of wool over the cedar bark. A short length of mountain goat roving is pulled out until it is very thin and filmy and approximately one centimeter wide and sixty to one hundred centimeters long. A strand of split cedar bark is wetted and then laid in the center of this roving. The mountain goat wool adheres more readily to a wet strand of cedar bark than to a dry one and the dampness of the bark helps to set the spin (fig. 44).

STEP 2: In the spinning process, two single strands are spun, simultaneously, down the leg and plied together up the leg. In preparation for this, the top four centimeters of each single strand of wool and bark are rolled loosely together down the leg to start the twist (fig. 45).

STEP 3: Holding both of these strands in the left hand, the spinner rolls them down her thigh with the fingers and palm of her right hand. The fibers of wool surround the wet cedar bark, sticking to it and covering it in one motion. It is important in beginning a ball of warp yarn to pinch the strands with the left hand at all times, or they will untwist as the yarns are being rolled. Only three to four centimeters are spun between the left and right hands, and a very tight twist is put into them. They are, in fact, overspun in order that twist remain in the single strands when they are plied. This movement may be done more than once in order to insure a tight twist. If it is repeated, the right hand must also hold the spin in the single strands while they are moved once again to the top of the leg. The motion down the leg turns the fibers in a clockwise direction and produces an S-twist yarn. The unspun tails of the strands will countertwist in the opposite direction during this action and will be untwisted at a later stage (fig. 46).

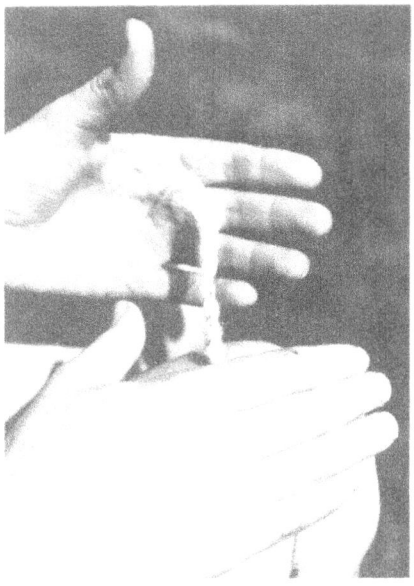
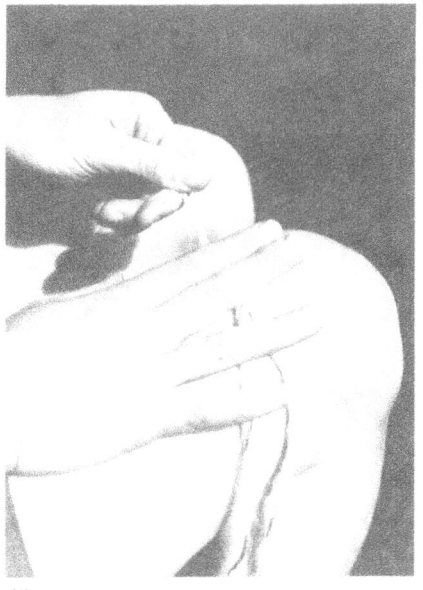
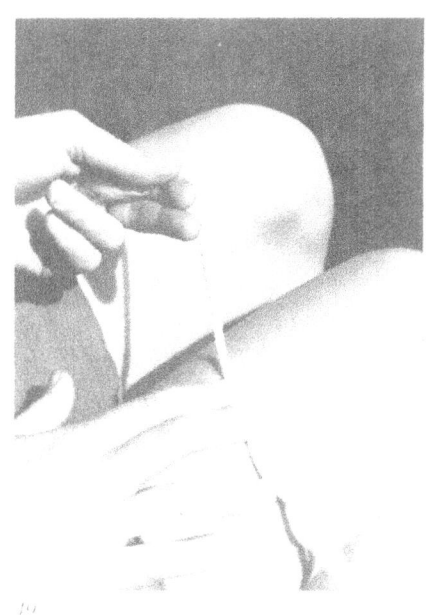

STEP 4: When the spinner reaches her knee, she continues to press the yarns to her leg with her right hand while she releases them with her left hand. Instantly the two yarns ply together in a Z twist (fig. 47).

STEP 5: The end of the plied strand is then held once again between the thumb and forefinger of the left hand. The fingers of the right hand are placed over the plied portion of the yarn (fig. 48).

STEP 6: The ply is tightened by rolling the yarn up the leg, from the knee toward the hip with the right hand. This motion tightens the twist of the fibers in a counterclockwise direction, reinforcing the Z twist. The counter twist of the unspun ends of the yarn, which occurs while spinning down the leg, is partially untwisted by the tightening of the Z twist. The remaining twist must be unloosened with the right hand while the left hand keeps the plied yarn from unspinning. An average of three twists per centimeter produces a beautifully plied warp yarn (fig. 49).

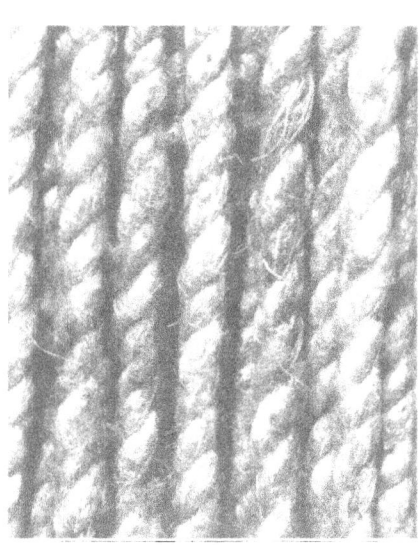

50. Beautifully spun warp yarns

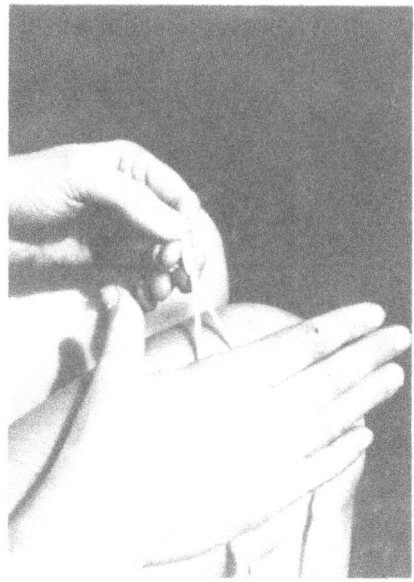
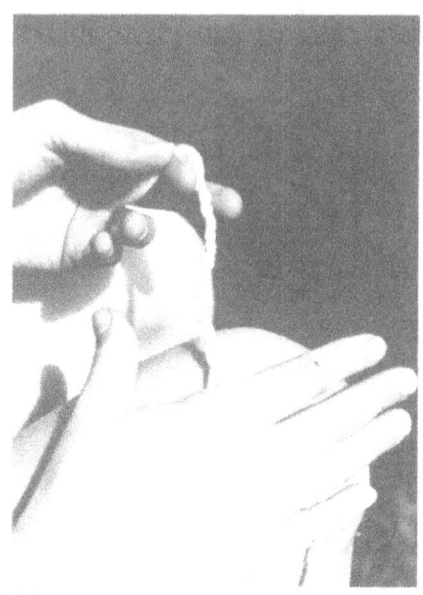

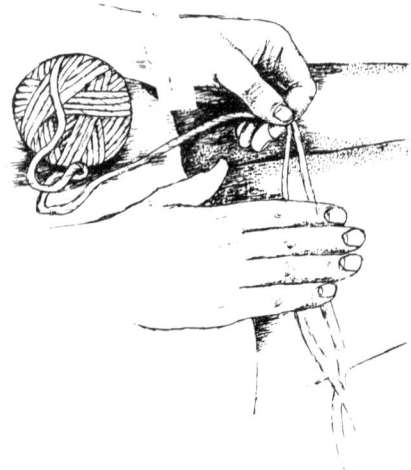

53. *The position of the spinner*

STEP 7: The spinning procedure is repeated, winding the spun warp yarn around a finger of the left hand until enough has been produced to form the beginnings of a ball. Before repeating Step 3, the two plies must be pinched between the thumb and forefinger of the left hand and spread apart under the right hand in order for them to spin separately. If this is not done, they will simply wrap around each other (fig. 51).

STEP 8: When the single plies are spun, the thumb and forefinger of the left hand release the pinched portion of the strand. The two yarns ply automatically until they reach the previously plied section. The right hand must continue to press the strands to the knees during this process so that the twist does not travel into the unspun yarn (fig. 52). Step 6 is then repeated (fig. 49).

SPLICING

Because a warp yarn is spun from short lengths of cedar bark and mountain goat wool, it is necessary to splice both of these materials (fig. 54). To splice the cedar bark, the end of a new piece of wet bark is laid next to the tail of the old piece, overlapping for about one centimeter. The spinning then continues. Mountain goat wool is spliced in the same manner, the wool being drawn out very thinly where it overlaps. In both cases, the spinning proceeds as usual once the new piece is laid in. It is not necessary to splice both strands at once; one ply can run out of either bark or wool and need splicing before the other one does.

As the yarn lengthens, it is wound into a ball. When a length of warp yarn has been spun, it must be unwound from the ball and stretched out to dry, care being taken to secure the end so that it does not untwist. Once dried, it is wound once again around the ball in preparation for the next day's spinning. A practiced spinner can spin about fifteen meters in an hour and will continue to add on to the same ball of warp yarn in many sessions of spinning.

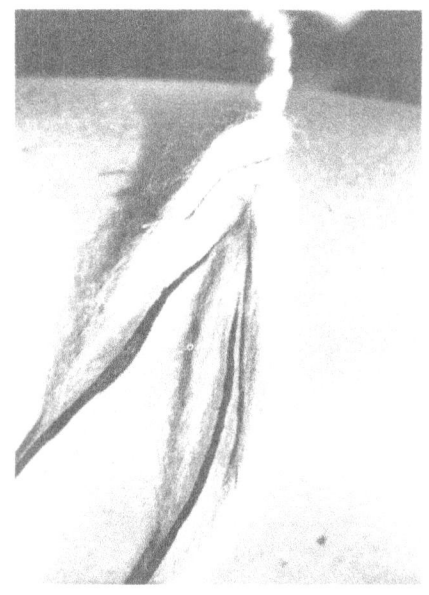

54. *A warp splice*

FORMING A BALL SO IT UNWINDS FROM THE CENTER

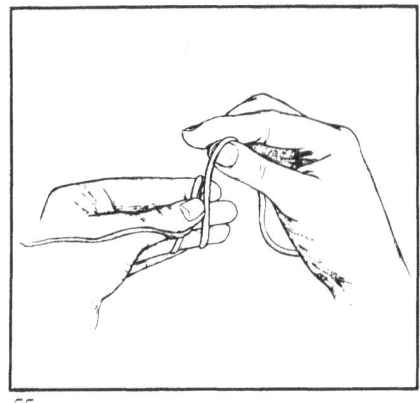

55.

STEP 1: The beginning of the yarn is held between the thumb and forefinger, about fifteen centimeters from the tail. The yarn is then wrapped around the first three fingers of the left hand (fig. 55).

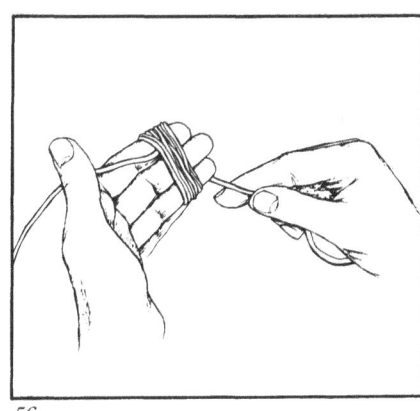

56.

STEP 2: The wrapping continues for approximately eight turns (fig. 56).

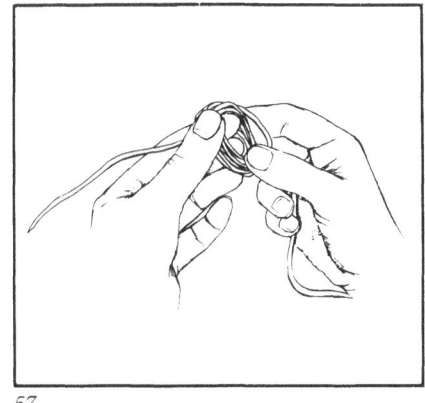

57.

STEP 3: The loops are slipped from the fingers of the left hand (fig. 57).

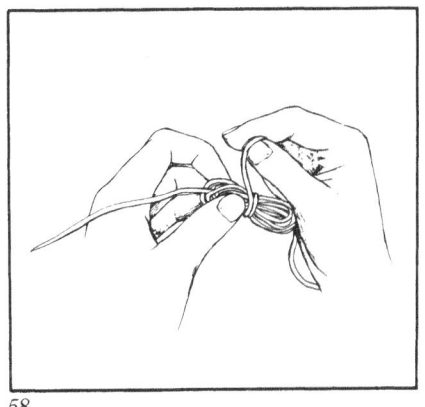

58.

STEP 4: The yarn is then wound loosely around the middle of the loops, making sure that the tail stays free (fig. 58).

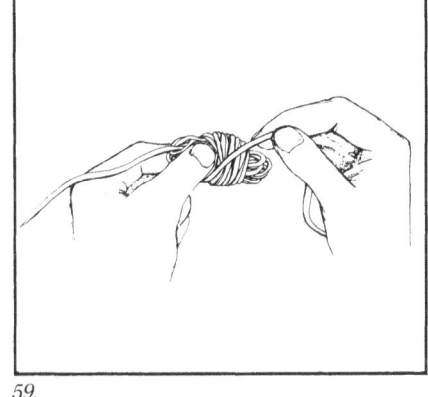

59.

STEP 5: The ball of yarn is wound very loosely so that the tail will pull out easily when it is completed (fig. 59).

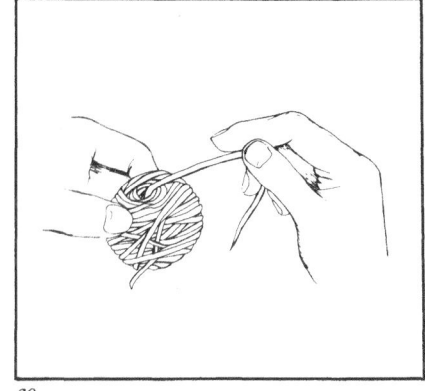

60.

STEP 6: The end of the yarn is tucked into a loop on the ball; the tail is pulled from the middle for use (fig. 60).

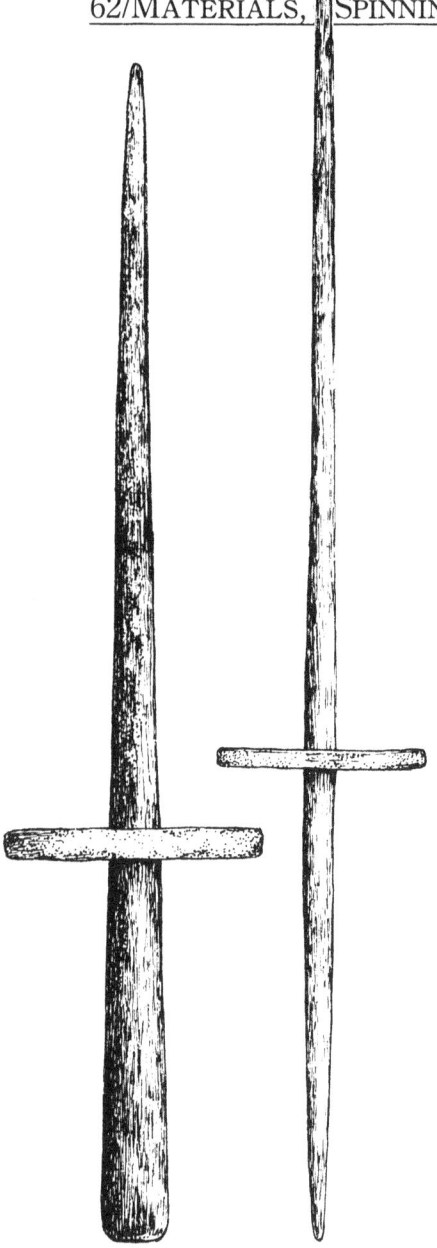

THE WEFT

The weft is the yarn which travels horizontally across the warp, the yarn with which the weaver works to create the beautiful colored designs. The weft is often of differing weights: very fine yarns are used for the innermost patterns, thicker yellow and black yarns for the outer borders. The thickest yarns were, however, no more than three millimeters wide, the finest as small as one-half millimeter in diameter. Average blankets used a yarn comparable in *size* to modern-day knitting worsted for the heavier elements, fingering yarn for the smaller ones. Many of the Dancing Blankets were made after contact with Europeans and because of this, commercial four-ply yarns are found in them. These yarns, however, are S twist in their ply, giving a very different effect when woven from the native Z-twist yarns (see p. 87, figures 94 and 95). All native yarns, whatever their size, were spun in a very regular fashion, free from lumps or undue thickening.

SPINDLES AND WHORLS

It is possible that the weft yarns could have been spun between a woman's hand and right thigh, as was described by Emmons. It is difficult, however, to do this and produce a thin yarn. Attempts to spin fine yarns in this fashion send the unspun ends of the wool twisting around in the opposite direction of the desired twist, sticking, and necessitating time-consuming unwinding. This slows the spinning process down to the point of complete frustration. With fathoms of fine yarns to spin, it seems another method would have been very welcome.

Another means of spinning did exist. Spindles and whorls of a dimension suitable for the spinning of fine yarns were present in the Tlingit villages. These were not the large and sometimes ornately carved spindle whorls of the more southern Salish, but rather, plain or simply carved whorls which measured four to six centimeters in diameter and which were made of smoothed bone rubbed with tallow. These whorls were most often flat, weighing approximately forty grams; sometimes they were made with convex outer curves which made them a little heavier (fig. 61). The spindles themselves were slender and hewn of wood, thirty to forty centimeters long, thickening slightly toward the middle and pointed on either end. One spindle, gathered in a Chilkat village, has a larger whorl and is thicker at the bottom (fig. 62). Although some of these spindles were collected from

61. On the left, a spindle collected by Emmons from the Chilkat Tlingit. It tapers from a rounded bottom, 1.5 centimeters wide, to a tip which is .3 centimeters wide. The total length is 41 centimeters. The whorl is 8.5 centimeters in diameter and weighs 80.5 grams. On the right, a spindle collected by Emmons from the Tlingit. It is pointed at both ends, slightly thicker in the middle, and measures 42.5 centimeters. The whorl is 6.5 centimeters across and .5 centimeters deep.

62. Two styles of bone whorls collected among the Tlingit

62.

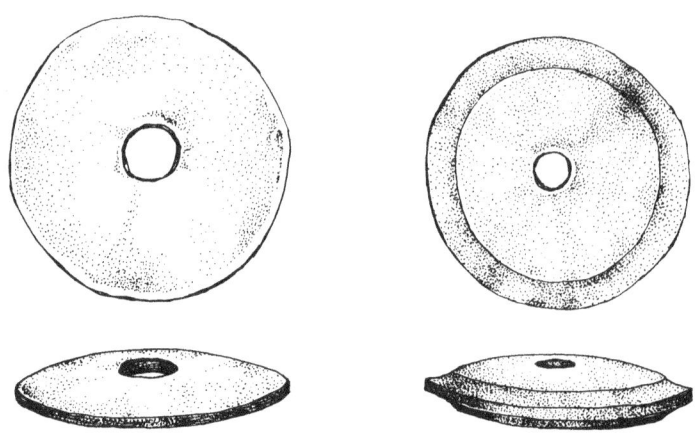

the Tlingit by Emmons himself, he does not state that they were used in the production of Chilkat yarns.

Franz Boas discusses the use of spindles similar to those of the Tlingit in his dissertation on the Kwakiutl. He states that the women spun nettle fiber or yellow cedar bark and mountain goat wool into yarns of varying degrees of fineness. It is logical that the possession of spindles and the knowledge of their use, coupled with the need to spin a great quantity of fine yarn, would cause the Tlingit women to abandon the hand and thigh method for the faster process of the spindle.

SPINNING THE WEFT

A description of spinning nettle fiber given by Boas in *The Kwakiutl* indicates one method in which the spindles were used by these southern neighbors of the Tlingit. In spinning, the woman sat on her haunches with her feet together, her knees drawn up toward her chin, and her arms around her knees. This position, called "hunkering," was a characteristic position for women while they worked. The spinner rolled the spindle down the shin of her right leg, "resting the tip of the shank between thumb and first finger of her left hand, but holding the thread as soon as it [began] to twirl around, at a distance of about 30 cm above the spindle." A motion down the leg turned the spindle in a clockwise direction and produced an S-twist yarn. In spinning mountain goat wool, lengths from the balls of roving, which were placed to the left of the spinner, were unwound as needed. Splicing would have been infrequent because of the fineness of the yarn being spun and the size of the balls of roving.

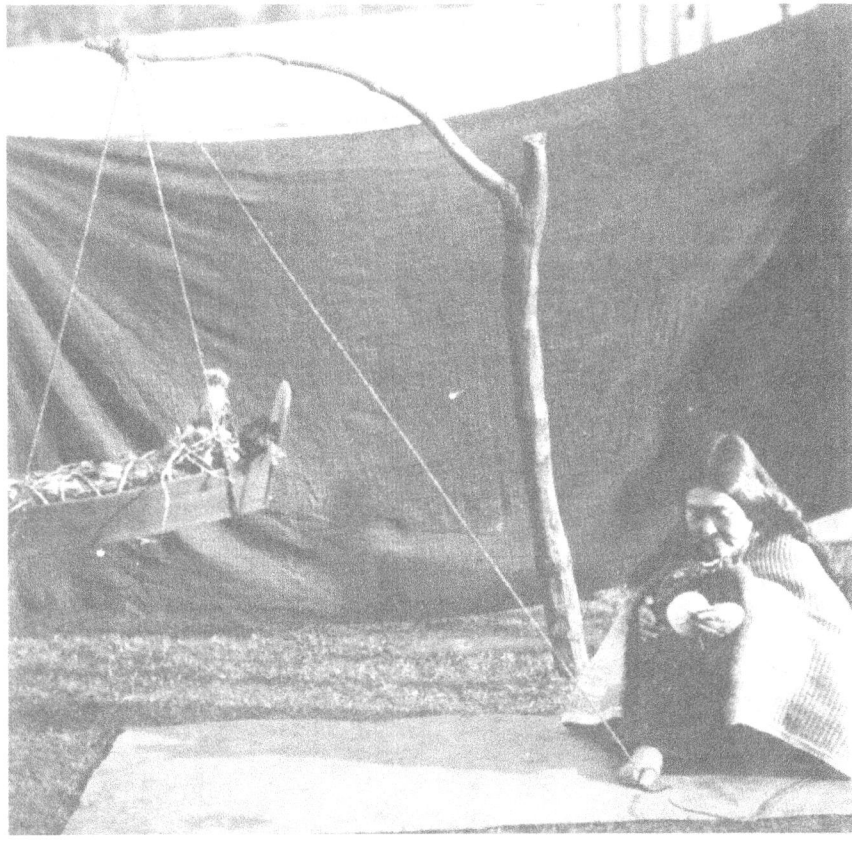

63. A Kwakiutl woman spinning with a spindle on her shin (Courtesy of the American Museum of Natural History)

When a length of yarn was spun, it was wound around the spindle above the whorl with a back and forth motion which produced a very round ball. When a ball of single-ply S-twist yarn was finished, it was pulled off the spindle and set aside to be plied. Plying was done, as described by Boas, by placing two balls in a box, holding one strand from each between separate fingers of the left hand, and rolling the spindle up the spinner's shin. This motion produced a counterclockwise spin and thus a Z-twist yarn. The yarn would have been wound on the spindle in the same fashion as the single ply.

At least three weights of weft yarn were spun: a thick one for the borders, overlay fringe, and side fringes; a medium weight for the majority of the design field; and a very fine yarn for the smallest design units. When the balls of yarn were finished, they were set aside, some to be dyed and some to be left snowy white.

SPINNING SINEW

The tough, strong sinew fibers which lie along an animal's backbone and behind its legs were the primary source of thread used by the Tlingit before contact with Europeans brought white cotton into the area. The sinew fibers were spun into a two-ply thread which was used for sewing leather garments and for the drawstrings which were used in making the Dancing Blankets. It was a woman's job to free the sinew from an animal which had been killed by the hunters and brought back to the village to be processed. Agile animals such as the mountain goat and the caribou were an excellent source for long lengths of this tough, smooth fiber.

Once the sinew was taken from the animal, it was thoroughly washed in cool fresh water and hung on a fish rack until nearly dry. It was then taken down and smoothed with the thumbnail. It was easy then to split into tiny strands by holding it between the thumb and

64. *A ball of yarn wound on the shaft of a spindle*

65. *Unspun sinew (Courtesy of the Manitoba Museum of Man and Nature: CS)*

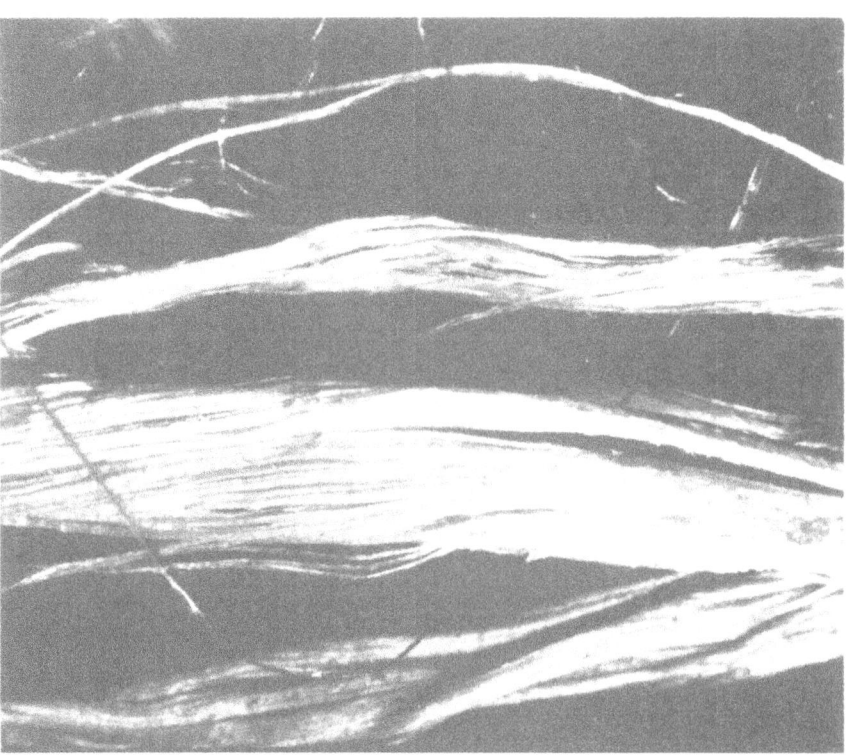

65.

first finger of each hand and pulling it apart. In preparation for spinning, the woman would draw thin pieces of split sinew through her mouth to moisten them. According to unpublished notes by Emmons, the process of spinning itself was the same as that used in spinning the warp yarns, with the exception that wool was not added.

THE SEWING POUCH

The sewing pouch of every Chilkat woman contained tools for helping her in her work. These pouches were small, oblong, and made of leather. Sometimes they were decorated around the opening with colored quillwork. A long leather thong was wrapped around the pocket to close it; into this, a wooden hook and a bone knife could be tucked.

Snuggled inside were found small tools, the most useful of which, perhaps, was the awl. Made originally of bone and later of steel with a rounded wooden or horn handle, it was used to pierce anything through which a lacing thread would be passed. It was also used in basketry to pack the wefts into position and could be useful in this way for weaving with wool. The sewing pouch contained other tools: a bear's tooth, used for flattening seams and the strands of spruce root used in making baskets; a bone scraper for cleaning skins; a nest of unspun sinew; and a woman's knife, made of mussel shell.

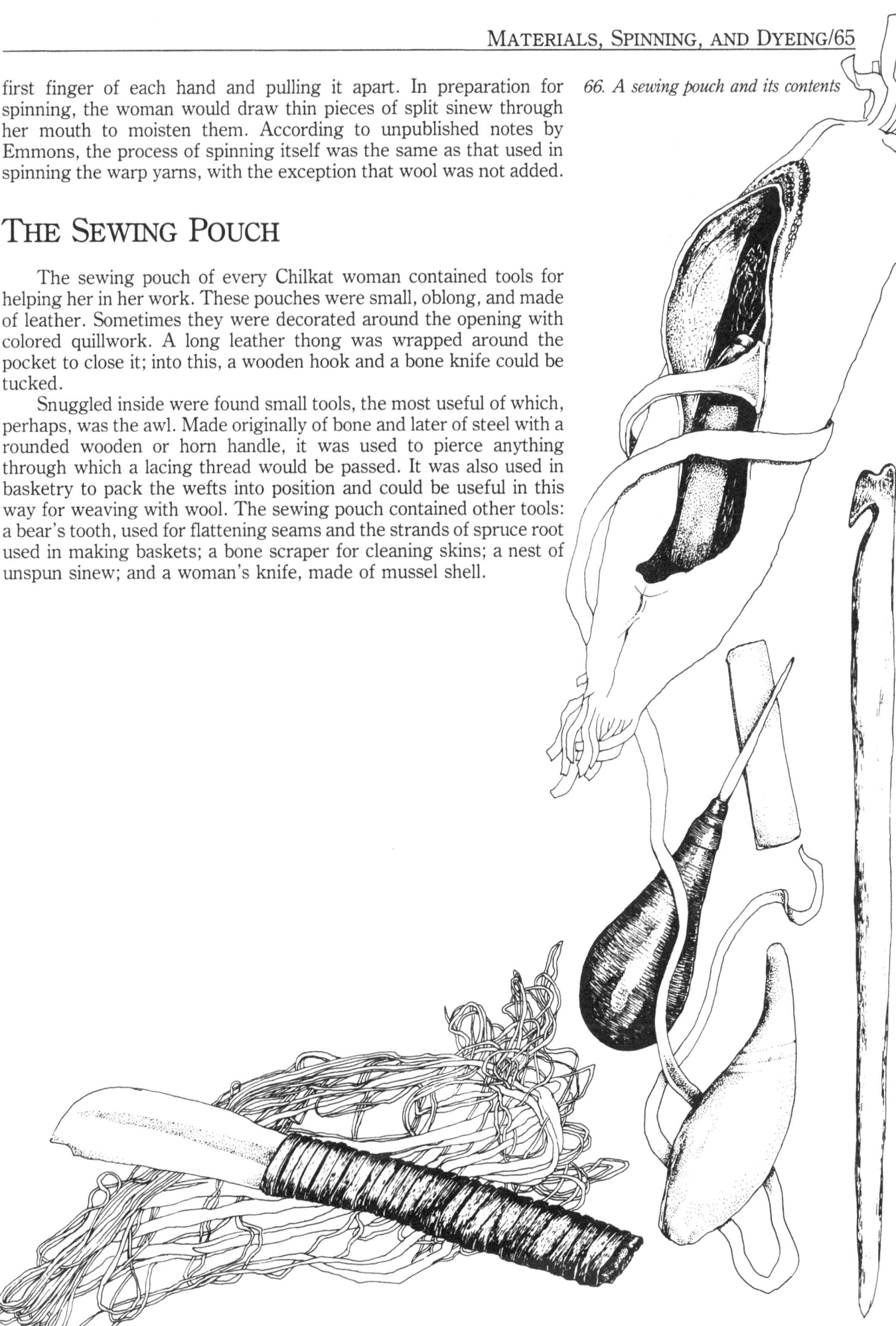

66. A sewing pouch and its contents

DYEING THE WEFT

The spun skeins of weft yarn, clean and white in their newness, had to be dyed before the weaving could begin. Originally, the blankets were woven of three colors: a very dark reddish black, a yellow, and the natural white of the wool. With the transition from geometric to formline designs, yellow-green was added to mark the differences in the design forms. When European trade goods arrived, this yellow-green was replaced by a gentle hue of blue-green. These early dyes were subject to great fading when left in contact with light. As all of the ceremonial garments were stored in wooden boxes when not being used, the process of fading was retarded somewhat. However, many Dancing Blankets show only a trace of yellow and a very pale blue on the front sides. The back sides generally retain more color than the fronts and inside the drawstring joins the original color is still present.

With the arrival of the Europeans, it became possible to use commercial yarns and dyes. The reddish-black native yarns gave way to commercially spun yarns dyed a flat black color. At first there was an attempt to duplicate the original hues of the yellow and blue-green, but the demand for these weavings on the trade markets gave birth to a change in the colors. The gentle blue-green eventually became a brilliant turquoise. A commercial yellow was introduced, very intense and not given to the slightest fading. In a very few instances, red trade yarns were employed by the weavers for use in some of the blue-green areas. These colors, along with the flat black, gave the Dancing Blankets a very different, and often garish, appearance. The mistake, however, became evident to the artistic spirits of the native people and they returned to the use of native dyes, except in the case of the blue.

It is understandable that the Indian women were receptive to experimenting with the commercial dyes and yarns which became available to them. The native dyes can still be produced, but it is disheartening to see them fade in less than ten years when exposed to constant light. For contemporary weavers who wish to reproduce these colors, Appendix II gives dye recipes which use a chemical dye that very closely matches the original dyes of the Chilkat Dancing Blankets.

BLACK DYE

The beautiful, rich black color which figured so prominently in the design came from a combination of dyes. Freshly stripped hemlock bark was used as the main source of color for the first dyebath and copper soaked in old urine produced the second, or "overdye" bath. An analysis of the black yarns by the Canadian Conservation Institute shows that some blankets have a noticeable quantity of iron in them, while others do not. The use of iron as a darkening agent was well known among many early peoples. If pieces of iron were added to the hemlock bark dyebath, they would darken the resulting color of the wool.

Iron was used for weapons and ornaments in the Tlingit country even before contact with European explorers. La Pérouse reported in 1786 that the natives of the coast "were well acquainted with methods of forging iron." This iron was obtained either through trade or from

67. Dyebaths

drifting wood. Experiments in dyeing the black yarns show that the color can be obtained with or without the use of iron, the difference being that the presence of iron produces a blacker color more quickly. Iron is very hard on wool fibers, however, making them quite brittle. Dancing Blankets which have iron in their black yarns will shed a fine black "dust" when handled due to the breakage of wool fibers.

When dyeing the black yarns, freshly stripped hemlock bark, gathered in the spring, was placed in a container. This bark had to be fresh; if gathered from a fallen log, it would not produce a black dye. Enough liquid was poured over the bark to cover it and provide a generous bath for the wool. Emmons states that this liquid was "strong urine"; experiments show that water works equally well. Skeins of yarn were placed in the bath with the bark and simmered for the best part of a day. The brew was then left to cool and steep for about a week. When the fibers reached a rich reddish-brown color, the yarn was removed from the dye and brought to a simmer in a bath of urine in which copper had been sitting for about two months. Miraculously, the brown wool turned to black. If iron was present in the bark dyebath, one minute in the copper dye would produce a rich reddish-black, fifteen minutes in it, a very deep black. If iron was not used, five minutes in the copper and urine dye would produce a brown-black, and half an hour would turn the yarns a dark, rich red-black. Once they reached the desired color, the yarns would be removed from the dyebath, cooled, and rinsed in salt water before they were dried.

Different dye lots of black faded to slightly different shades of brown. Occasionally, a twill pattern is seen in the brown areas of a blanket. This is the result of the use of two different dye lots of black for the weft; when twined together over alternating warp pairs, diagonal lines visually develop. These lines probably did not appear when the blanket was new.

YELLOW DYE

The yellow dye was obtained from a chartreuse lichen, *Evernia vulpina,* commonly called "wolf moss," which clothed the boughs of pine trees growing east of the mountain ranges. This lichen was purchased in trade from the peoples of the interior for use in the

68. Wolf moss on a pine branch

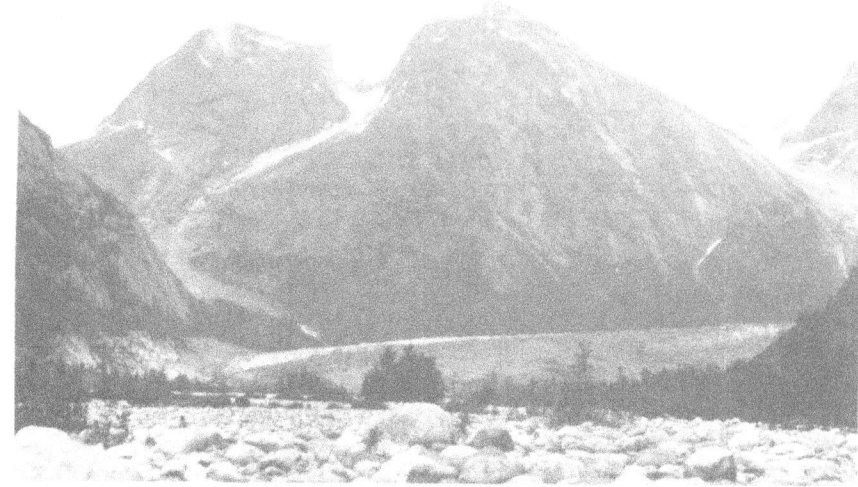

69. The moraine of a glacier behind the Chilkat River. The Chilkat Indians traveled through this pass on their trading trips to the interior. (Courtesy of the British Columbia Provincial Museum)

Tlingit communities. Yellow dye was extracted by boiling the wolf moss in fresh urine for about an hour. The musky-smelling plant would easily yield its color to the dyebath. Skeins of yarn of the proper size would then be placed into the dye and simmered briefly. Ten minutes, maximum, would produce the desired color. When a rich, strong yellow was reached, the yarns would be removed, cooled, and rinsed thoroughly in salt water before being left to dry.

FROM GREEN DYE TO BLUE

The most dramatic effect that the European trade goods had on the dyes of the Dancing Blanket was to change the yellow-green color in the blankets to a blue-green. The first weavers to use a fourth color obtained their dye from an oxide of copper and urine. The dyebath was produced by soaking copper in old urine, leaving it to settle for approximately four months. The resulting liquid was a beautiful blue-green color. Wool, when immersed in this liquid before it was heated, immediately took on this delightful hue. One can easily imagine the frustration of the weavers when they rinsed the yarns, and the color changed to a dull green. Even if left to soak for a week, the color which eventually stayed in the wool was not the blue-green of the liquid dye. Simmering yarns for half an hour produced a yarn, which, when rinsed, turned golden yellow and when dried, changed to an olive green. The weavers, wishing to brighten this color, quickly transferred the hot, wet yarns from the copper and urine dye into another bath of wolf moss and urine. The dye produced by the lichen gave a beautiful overtone of yellow to the green. This final color was acceptable to the weavers, even though they must have looked at the blue liquid of the copper dyebath and wondered what they could do to obtain a blue-green dye. The fact that the carvers and painters used a very similar blue color in their work would have made their desire to accomplish this even greater.

The answer to the blue eventually came, although not from the copper and urine dye. Research analysis of dye samples from fifteen blankets representing various shades of blue and green, done by the Canadian Conservation Institute and at the University of British

Columbia, has indicated that while there is copper present in the yellow-green yarns, *there is no copper in any of the blue-green yarns.* A ready source for the dye existed in the blue trade cloth which the natives prized so highly. The woolen trade cloth, with its wealth of color, was boiled, possibly in a bath of strong, old urine. Ten minutes in the resulting blue liquor easily dyed the weft yarns a sky blue. Following the precedent already set in obtaining the green color, the yarns would then be plunged into an overdye of wolf moss yellow which turned them instantly to blue-green. Remarkably, this color is very close in hue to the coveted blue of the urine and copper liquid.

A variety of shades of blue existed in the trade cloths. Certain of these wools were probably known to produce a desirable color, since most of the blues in the Dancing Blankets are in the same color range. Experiments with a blue wool obtained from shirts which the Tlingit made and adorned with appliquéd designs and with a similar blue wool found in the side fringes of a fine Dancing Blanket produced yarns which, when dipped in wolf moss yellow, matched the native blue-green color exactly. Another wool trade cloth found on leggings from the interior produced a blue which, when overdyed, resulted in a much greener yarn. This color, too, is found in some of the Dancing Blankets. It was not necessary to await the invention in 1856 of aniline dyes: much of the trade cloth was obtained from England where for centuries woad had been used to produce a blue cloth and where, after the 1600s, indigo had become the dominant source of blue. A determination of the original source of the blue dye has not been made at this time. However, it is likely that a variety of cloths were used to produce tones of blue which were pleasing to the weaver's eye and which satisfied her desire for a traditional color balance. The blue color that is seen today in most of the Dancing Blankets has mellowed with age considerably.

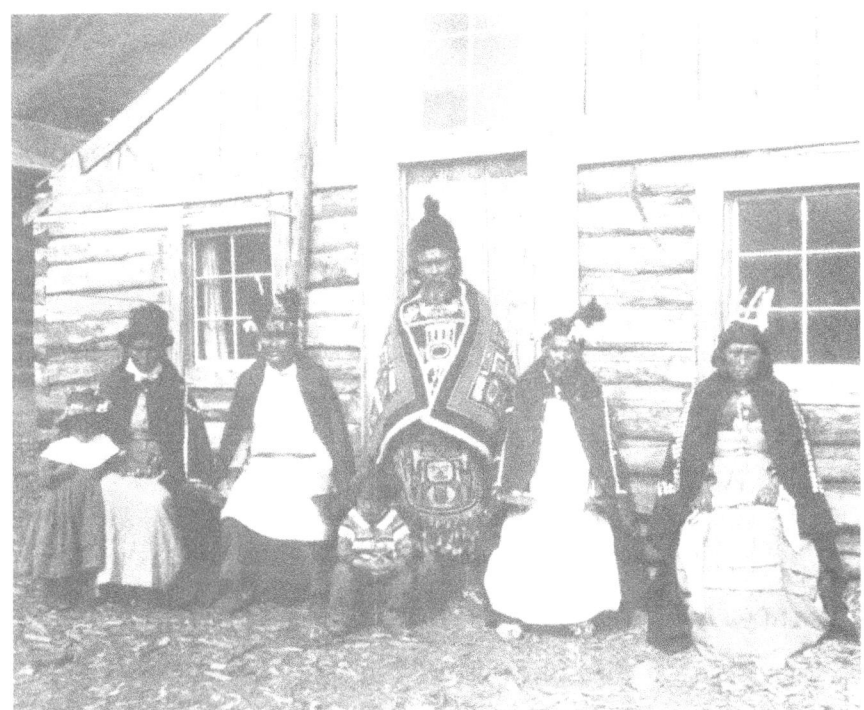

70. The influence of European trade can be seen in the dress of these Tlingit people. The man in the middle wears the Beaver Apron shown earlier in figure 8. Under his Dancing Blanket, he is wearing an appliqued shirt. (Courtesy of the Provincial Archives of British Columbia)

Coloring the Forms

Black was the main color of the Dancing Blanket and it was the only color which was painted on the pattern board. Every black shape and line on the board was woven with black weft yarn. The design was woven on a white background. With a knowledge of the art, the white areas were easily determined from the pattern board. There was no ambiguity in the coloring of the black and white areas.

There was much more yellow in the forms of the Dancing Blanket than there was blue-green. The distribution of the yellow and blue-green was not purely an aesthetic choice; specific shapes were always yellow or always blue-green. The remaining shapes were colored through knowledge of the conventions of the art. Variations in the coloring of these shapes are found, as definite rules as to what color every element of the design should be have not yet been determined. However, by observing the guidelines in Appendix III, the design field of a Dancing Blanket can be colored with the confidence that the result will fall along traditional lines.

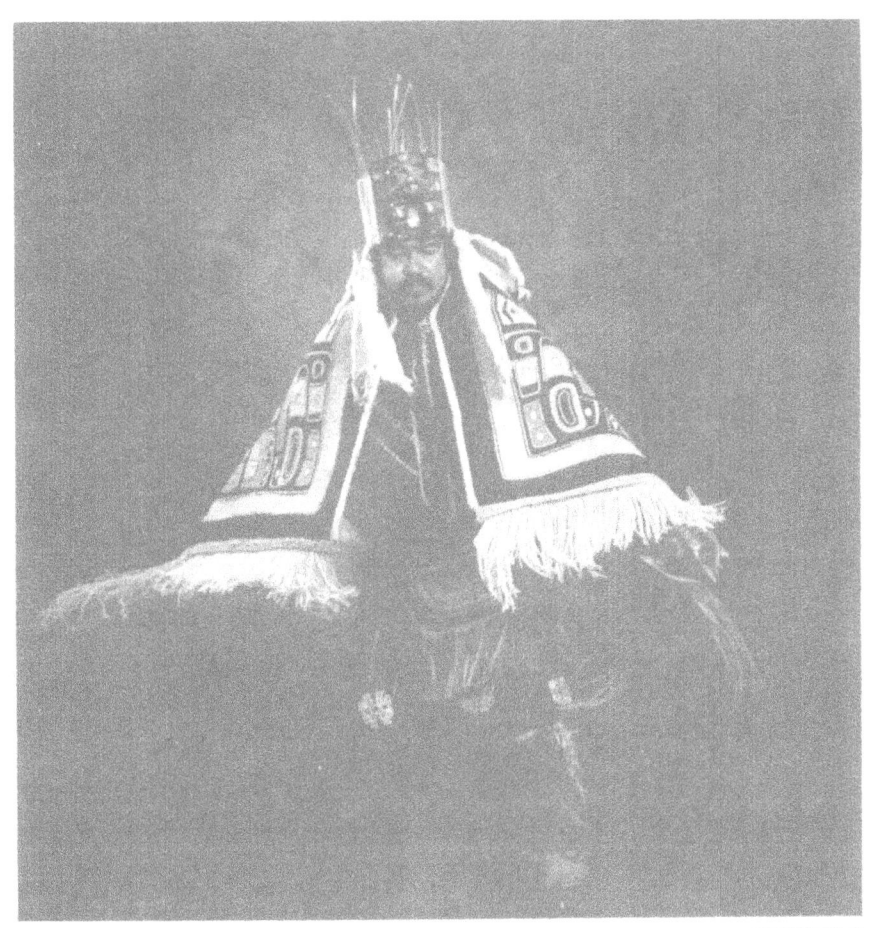

PART

EVOLUTION
AND WEAVING
TECHNIQUES

III

TWO TLINGIT WOMEN UNRAVEL THE MYSTERIES OF A TSIMSHIAN DANCING BLANKET

An old and very powerful Chilkat chief lived in a village with his two wives. These two were very clever women, expert in the weaving of spruce root baskets and accomplished as leather workers. Yearly, the men of the chief's clan traveled to the southern lands of the Tsimshian to trade for the expertly carved and painted red cedar chests and the grand war canoes for which those people were renowned. On one of these ventures, the men returned with a beautifully woven Dancing Blanket. The two wives of the chief were enthralled with the fineness of the weave and puzzled over the techniques which allowed the weaver to produce such subtle curves. They studied the blanket carefully, looking again and again at the twined yarns, trying the weaving themselves on a sample warp until they understood how it was done. The knowledge they had of basketry aided them tremendously in their efforts; they could see that the foundation of this skilled technique echoed the practices of the basket weavers. It took time to learn all the subtleties, many months of following the tiny weft strands in and out of the design. There were moments when they thought they knew how a circle was turned or how the fine outline rows were laid in, only to try it and see that some bit of knowledge was missing. More time, then, was needed to look and to think. Eventually, they felt certain that they could duplicate this fine art, but they could not weave a blanket for they had no pattern board to follow.

One night, as the elder wife slept, a magnificent Dancing Blanket sprinkled all over with white raindrops came into her dreams. She told her husband of the dream and he advised her to journey to a village of the Tsimshian and relate her story to a famous designer. The Tsimshian were well known for their artistic abilities; surely a painter there would be able

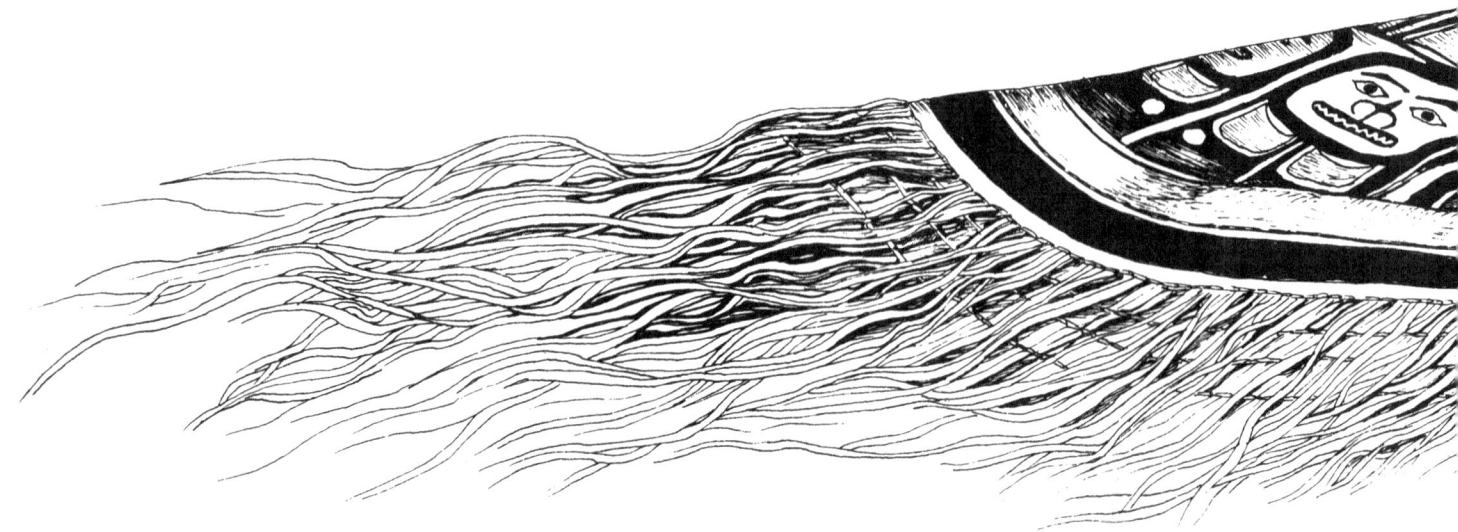

to interpret it for her. The chief's two wives went south and found a man who could feel the flow of the dream and paint its spirit on a wooden board. The two women then returned to their home and started to weave the ceremonial robe. They worked together, each weaving one side of the pattern, ecstatic when they completed one of the perfect circles. With a surge of pride, they presented the finished robe to their husband, the robe that was the first Dancing Blanket made in the land of the Tlingit.

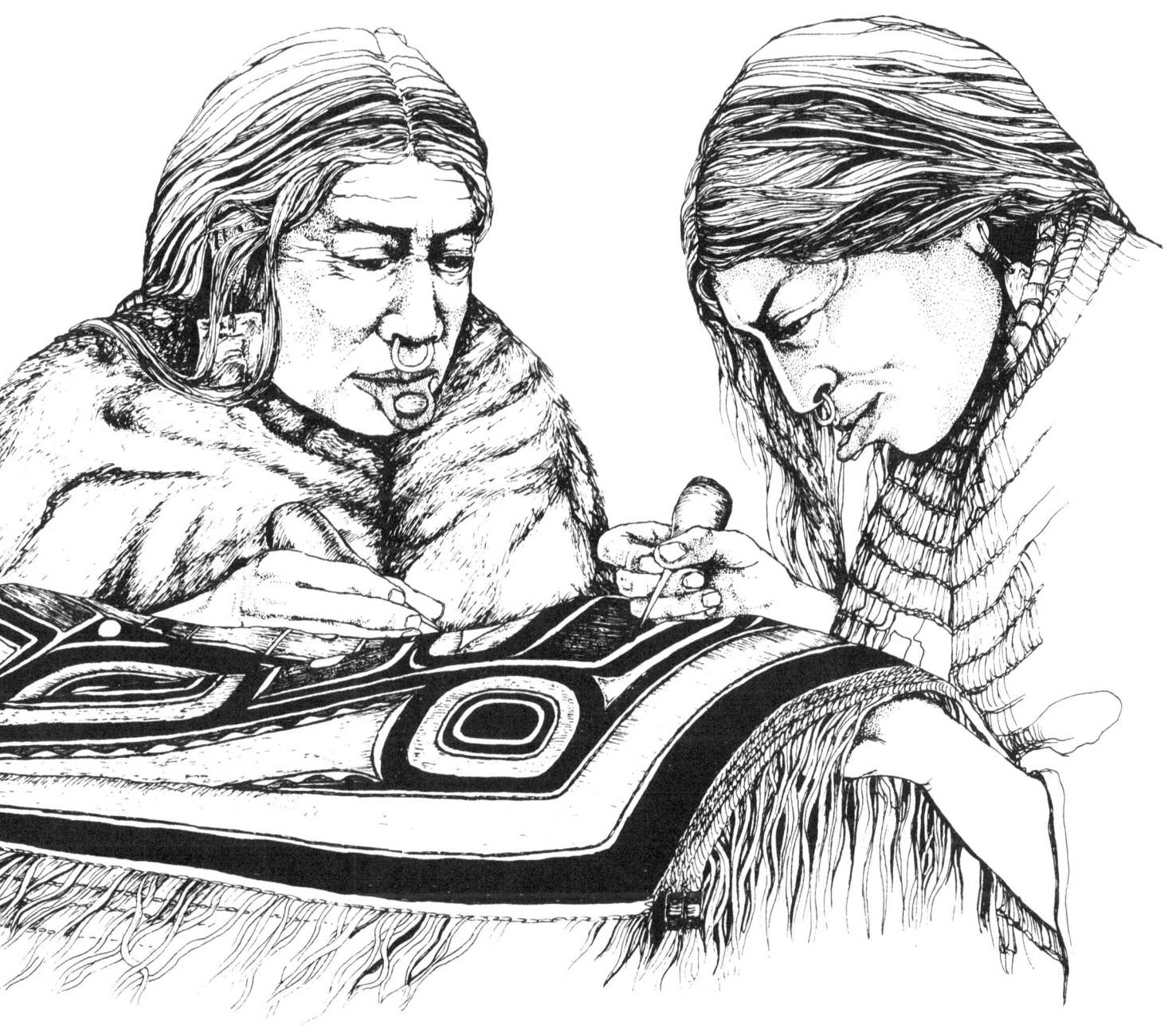

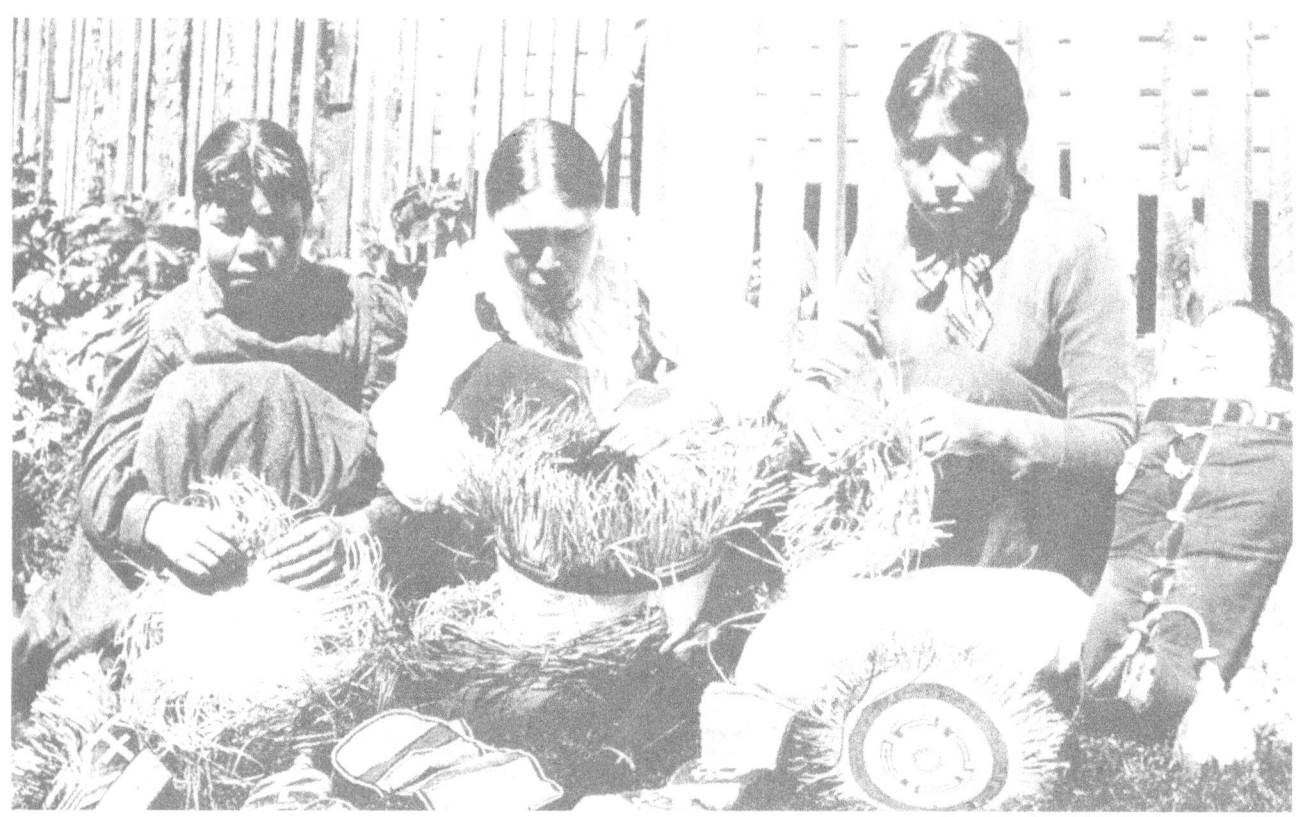

71. Spruce root basket weavers from Sitka, Alaska (Courtesy of the British Columbia Provincial Museum)

TWINED BASKETS AND TWINED GARMENTS

The skill of the Tlingit basket makers was well known up and down the coast. Fine baskets were made for every purpose: cooking, storage, feast dishes, hats, and even drinking cups. Many of these baskets were made of split spruce roots; the degree of ornamentation on them depended on their use.

The main technique used in creating spruce root baskets is two-strand twining. The weft is twined over warp splints which are crossed at the bottom of the basket. Two wefts twine together around these radial ribs in continually widening circles. As the weaving gets larger, additional splints are added to maintain an evenness in the length of the weft segments.

Ornamentation is woven into the baskets with a variety of twining techniques or with an overlay of dyed grasses. The overlay grasses are wrapped around the outer strands of the weft as the twining progresses, producing a pattern which only shows on the outside of the basket. One special technique called self-patterned twining is used within an area to create geometric patterns. This involves the lengthening of certain weft segments in a geometric progression and is done with only the natural colored root. Self-patterned twining was a common feature of the ceremonial crest hats which were highly valued by the wealthy chiefs and which displayed the finest and most elaborate work that was done in spruce root.

The primary method used by the Tlingit for the weaving of woolen fabric was also weft twining. There is a very close relationship between the techniques of twined basketry and the twining of the

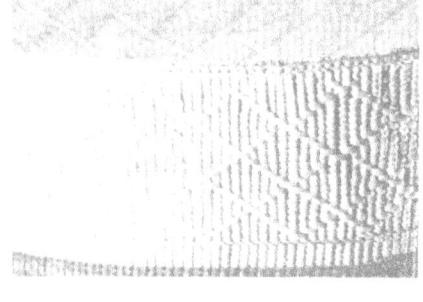

72. An example of self-patterned twining used in spruce root basketry (Courtesy of the British Columbia Provincial Museum)

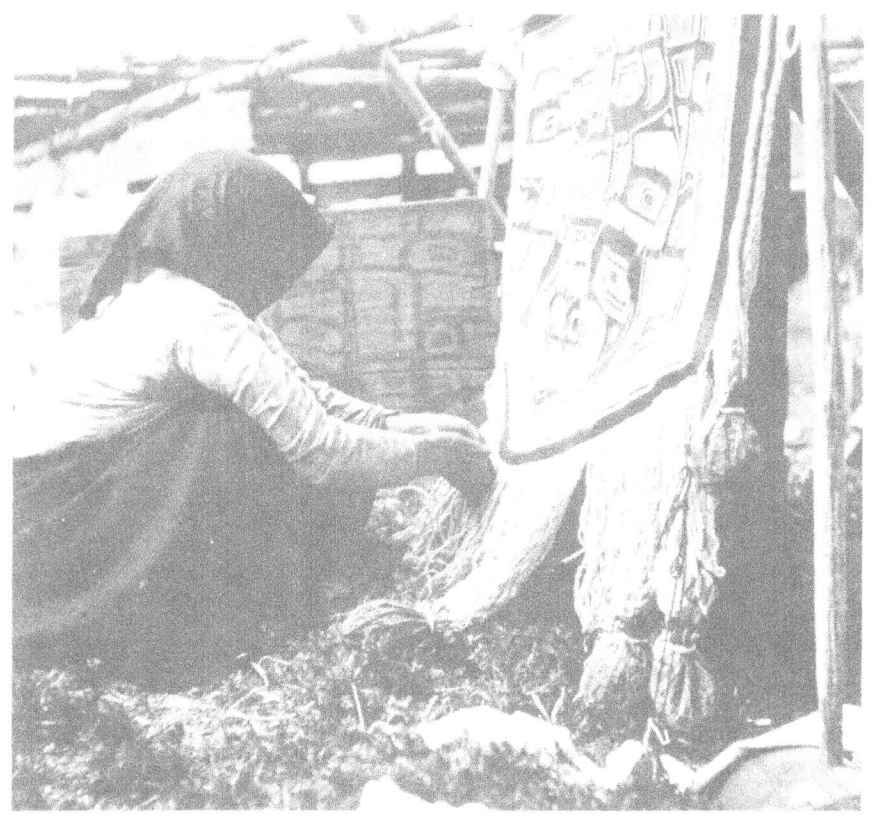

73. A weaver in Sitka working on the bottom black border of a blanket. In this photograph, taken by Emmons, the woman is probably posing. Normally, the weaving would be wound up on the beam and the gut bags would not drag on the ground. (Courtesy of the British Columbia Provincial Museum)

Dancing Blankets. Because the weavers were not bound to a loom with a warp which was under tension and an interlaced weft, they were able to think in ways foreign to other weaving traditions. It seems most likely that their skill and knowledge of twined basketry freed them to develop the remarkable techniques which were used to create the Dancing Blankets. This is especially true of the old-style geometrically patterned chief's robes. The beautiful self-patterned twining found in some baskets and in the spruce root hats is one feature held in common with these robes. When the Dancing Blanket was fully developed, two-strand weft twining and braided twining were the main techniques retained. Although the actual technique of grass wrapping was not used in wool, an important aspect of it is shared in the twining of the curvilinear designs of the weavings. This involves the movement of weft yarns through the weft, rather than the warp, an idea which is not generally found in weaving traditions. Another unusual weaving technique used in the Dancing Blankets is the addition of warp ends while the weaving is in progress to enlarge the shape. This is identical to the addition of warp splints in basketry.

RAVENSTAIL ROBES

The designs which the women wove into the baskets were not the formline designs which characterized the men's work. Rather, they were geometric shapes which were technically compatible with the twining methods used. The legendary first Dancing Blanket woven by the wife of Gonnaqadet in the earliest days of the world may well have been similar to the geometrically styled chief's robes of the Tlingit. In these garments, black and yellow patterns similar to the designs on baskets were placed on an undyed wool ground. Robes of this type

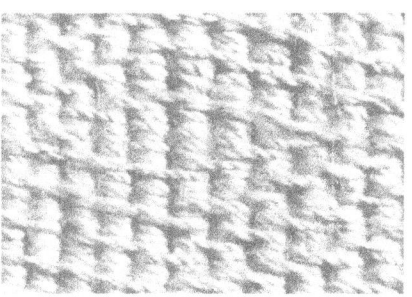

74. An example of self-patterned twining used in a woolen mantle (Courtesy of the National Museum of Denmark: CS)

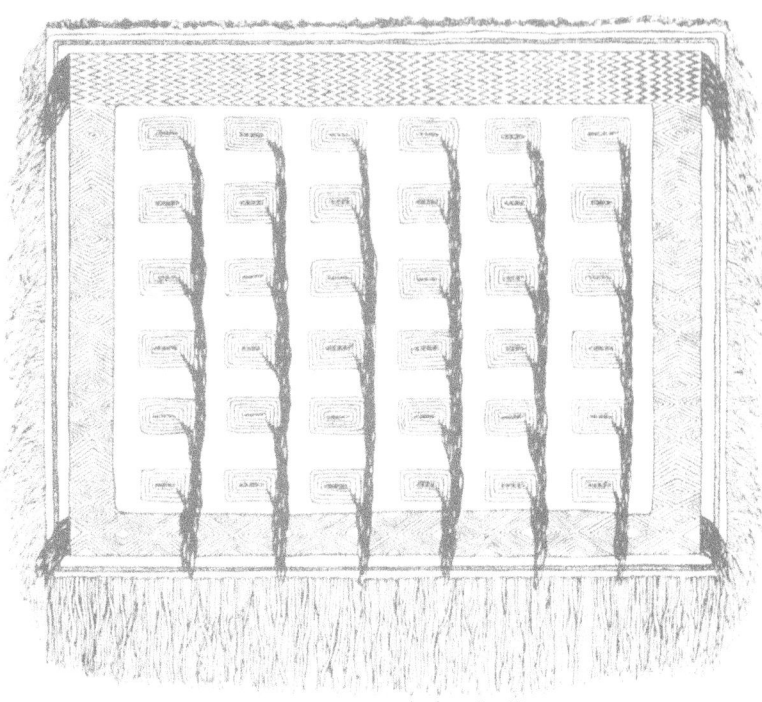

75. A pen-and-ink reconstruction of the fragments of an old-style geometric chief's robe in the American Museum of Natural History

were made entirely of mountain goat wool and hair and did not have any cedar bark in the warp. The drawing in figure 75 is a reconstruction of such a robe from fragments in the American Museum of Natural History, New York.

This very old style of weaving was observed by explorers in the late 1700s. Two very special robes in the ethnographic collection in Leningrad are similar in pattern on one side to the geometric robe just described. The other side of these garments is covered in fur with pattern showing only at the sides. In 1786, La Pérouse described such a robe, saying, "They intermingle with [the spun-wool warp] slips of otter-skin, which gives their cloaks a resemblance of the finest silk plush." These skin strips were extremely narrow and were hung on the loom with the wool warp. They were treated as warp ends, and the white skin side showed only on the patterned side of the robe.

Another style of chief's robe shows an elaboration of the geometric patterning. The "Swift Blanket," named for Captain Benjamin Swift of Charlestown, Massachusetts, is an excellent example. Robes of this style exhibit a complex, sophisticated, and well-developed weaving technique. They all follow a similar overall organization, with broad borders surrounding a central design field, fringes on three sides, and a

76. A detail of the pattern side of the Leningrad fur and wool robe (Courtesy of the Museum of Anthropology and Ethnography, Leningrad: CS)

77. The reverse side of the section of robe shown in figure 76, showing the sea otter fur (Courtesy of the Museum of Anthropology and Ethnography, Leningrad: CS)

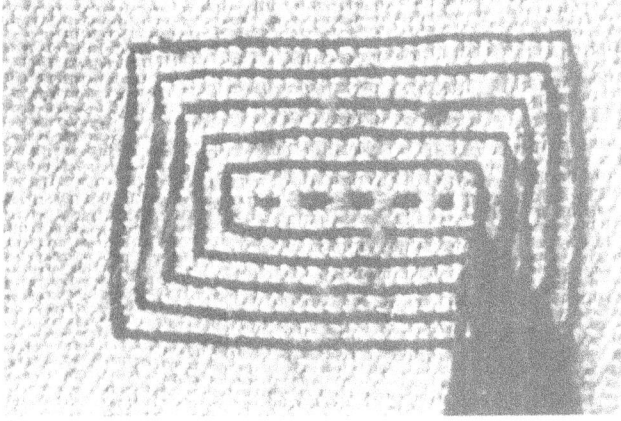

trim of fur along the neckline. The bottom fringe, which is about 26 centimeters long, is an extension of the warp ends. On one side the side fringes are extensions of the weft yarns; on the other side, they are added. The robes are all rectangular in shape, the woven portion measuring approximately 140 centimeters by 100 centimeters. They are made entirely of the wool and hair of the mountain goat. The weft is primarily wool, while the warp is wool with guard hairs added to strengthen it. The geometric patterns are in black and white, with thin yellow strips running horizontally through the bands of the central section. The inner geometric border is twined in yellow and black.

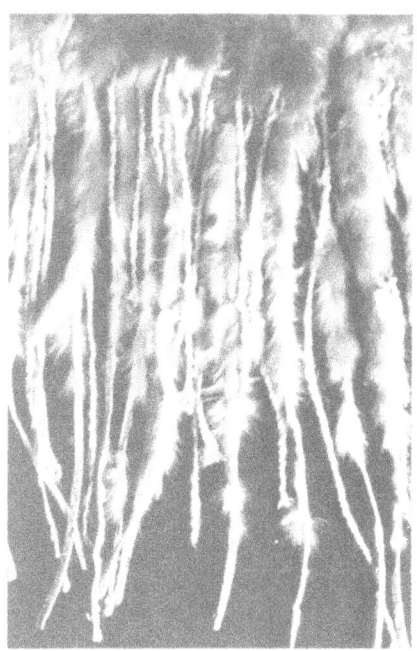

78. The fringe of the robe in figure 76 (Courtesy of the Museum of Anthropology and Ethnography, Leningrad: CS)

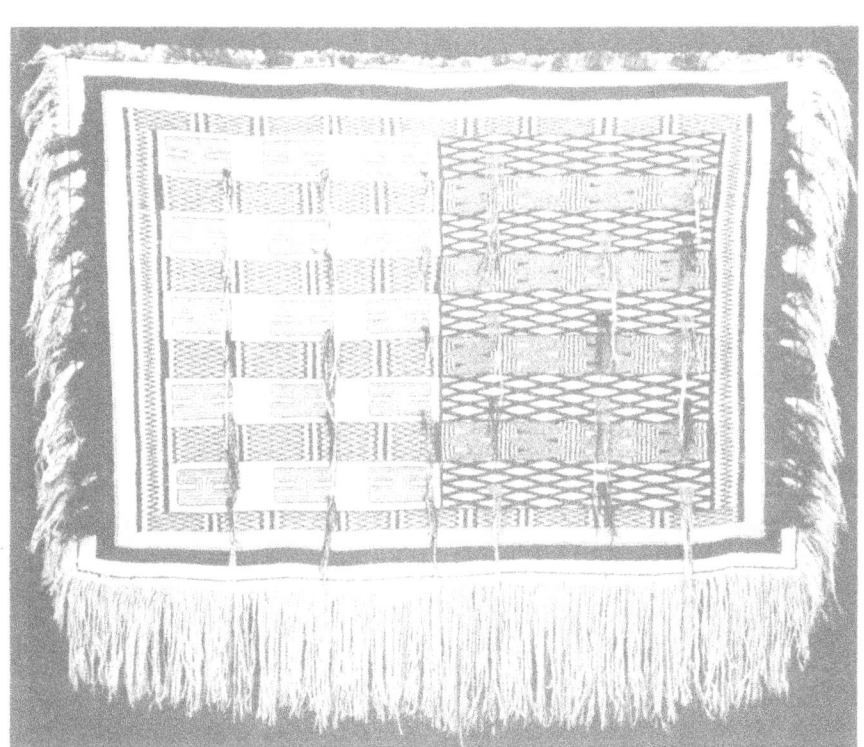

79. The "Swift Blanket" (Courtesy of the Peabody Museum, Harvard University. Photograph by Hillel Burger. Copyright President and Fellows of Harvard College 1980)

CEDAR BARK ROBES

The Ravenstail robes were garments worn only on special occasions. Everyday garments of the precontact Tlingits, as determined from the reports of the early explorers, seem to have been made primarily of skins. Farther down the coast, the southern neighbors of the Tlingit who lived near Nootka Sound made and wore twined garments of shredded cedar bark. Some of these garments took the form of a five-sided robe with a curving lower edge and a warp fringe. The neckline was wound with fur and the side fringes, when present, were not part of the weft but were added after the weaving was finished.

The cedar bark robes were twined either with a weft of cedar bark or with a weft of cedar bark which was spun with white mountain goat wool. Some of the robes were decorated with borders of geometric twining. These borders were twined with the combined

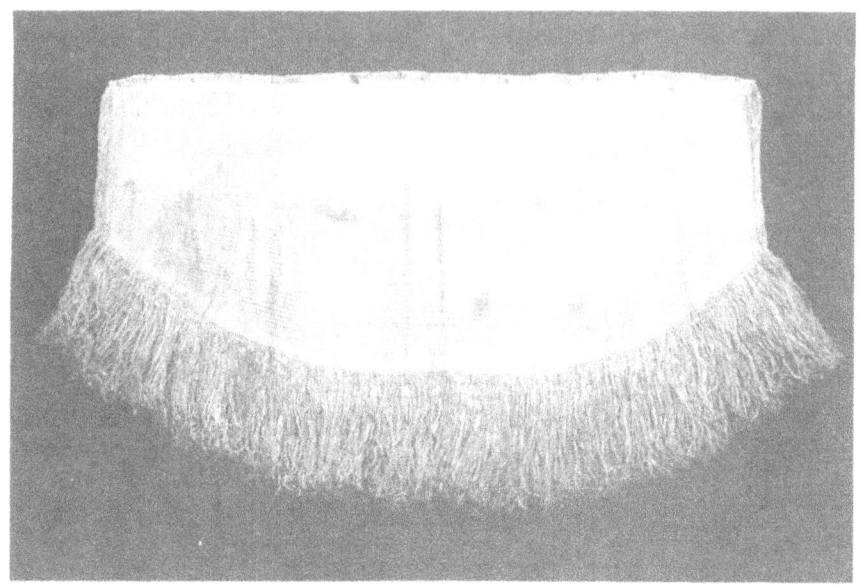

80. A cedar bark robe (Courtesy of the National Museum of Ireland: CS)

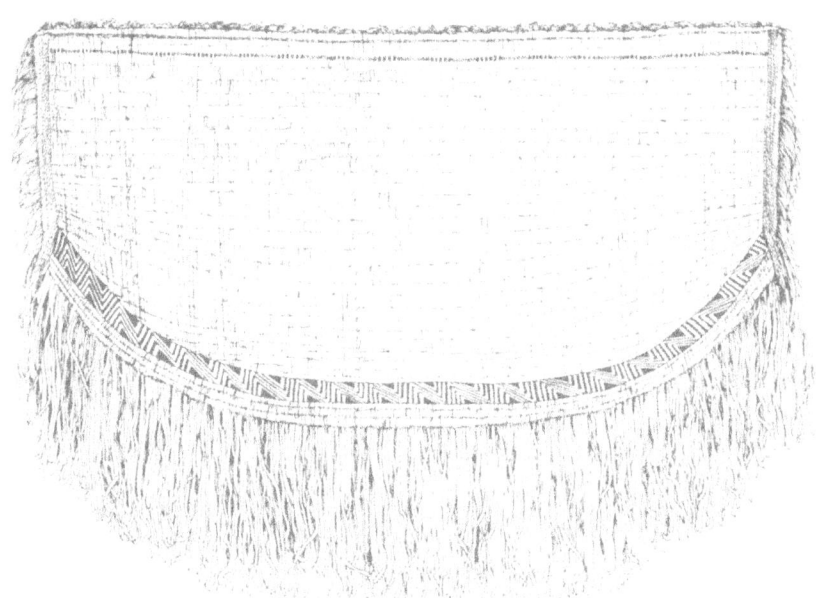

81. A cedar bark robe with a geometric border (pen-and-ink reconstruction)

cedar bark and mountain goat wool wefts, dyed yellow and a rich black. In some cases, the black weft was only cedar bark and the yellow weft was only wool. On some of these capes, stylized figures were painted in bold formline designs.

THE TRANSITION

While the women's arts of weaving and basketry produced pieces patterned primarily with geometric designs, the male artists painted and carved animal figures in a curvilinear style. These carvings and paintings visually surrounded the lives of the people. Many of the carvings were executed in very low relief. Similar, stylized paintings were also done on leather ceremonial aprons and on cedar bark robes. The weavers, living with these designs and the excitement of the artists who created them, began to discover how they could be executed in wool. Artist Duane Pasco has pointed out that the feeling of the low relief carvings is echoed on the surface of the classic Chilkat weavings. This quality was not present in the paintings on leather or bark.

It is exceptionally fortunate that on Cook's third voyage, "transitional" pieces were collected which exhibit the possible beginnings of formline weaving. One most remarkable transitional weaving is now in Vienna (fig. 82). This piece exhibits a number of twining techniques being used in an attempt to solve the design challenges. The warp, a forerunner of the warps of the Dancing Blankets, is made of split cedar bark spun with mountain goat wool and hair. This cloak is more rectangular in shape than the cedar bark robes, but it does have a curve to its bottom border. Like the cedar bark robes, it has a side fringe which is attached underneath the side braid. The warp fringe is quite long, perhaps a harbinger of Nakheen. The very beginnings of successful formline weaving can be seen in this particular piece: weft strands move out of the warp and travel over the base weft to create and outline shapes. Also, one can see attempts to create perfect circles and outline the forms. This break in traditional thinking must have been as exciting to the weaver as it is to modern researchers seeking the origins of the techniques of the Chilkat Dancing Blankets.

It seems highly probable that the classic Dancing Blanket grew out of two traditions: the cedar bark robes of the south and the geometric chief's robes of the north. Once formline weaving was established, the northern weavers began to mix it with the traditional geometric designs. The drawing in figure 83 is a reconstruction of a

82. A prime example of a transitional weaving (Courtesy of the Museum für Völkerkunde, Vienna: CS)

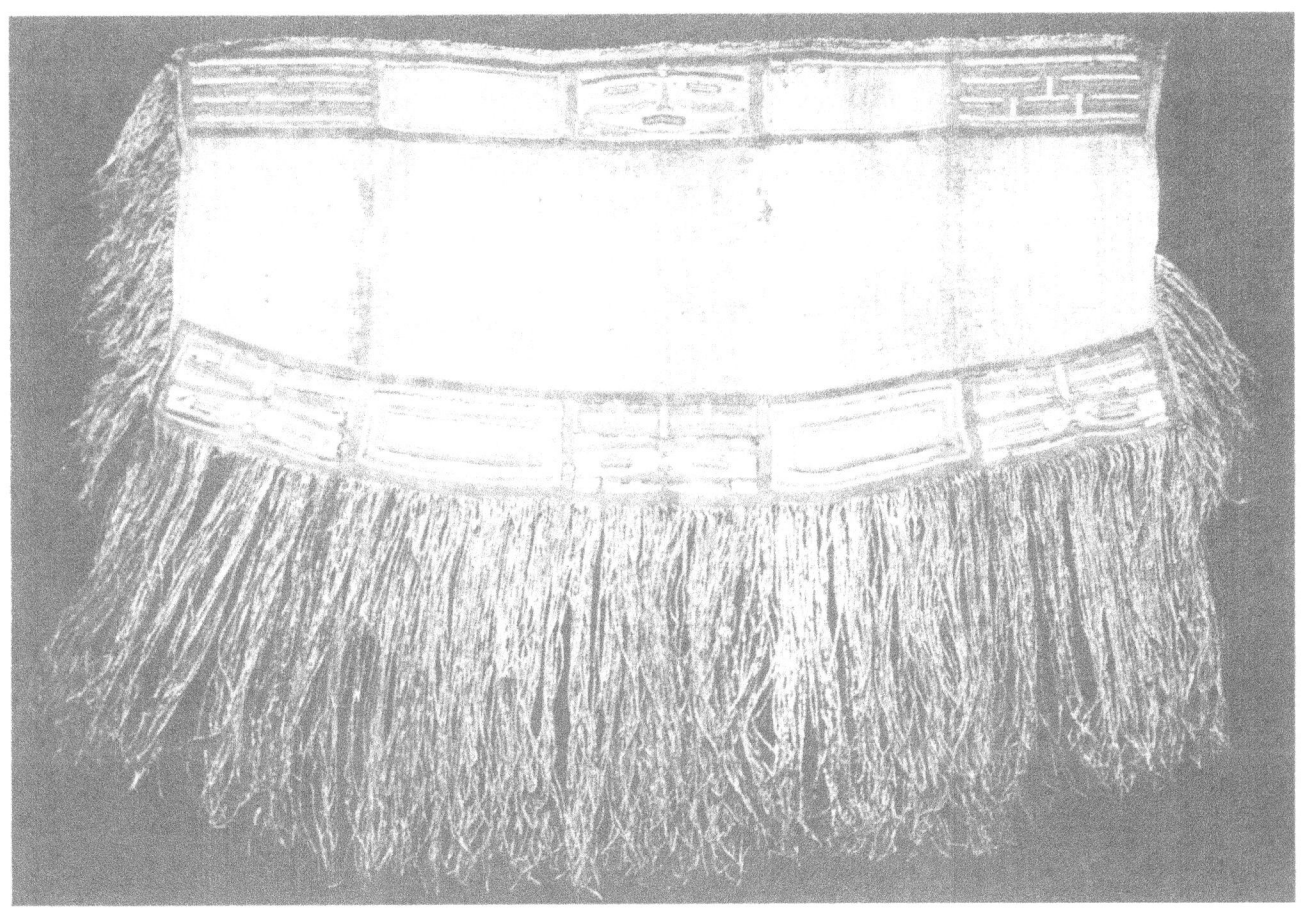

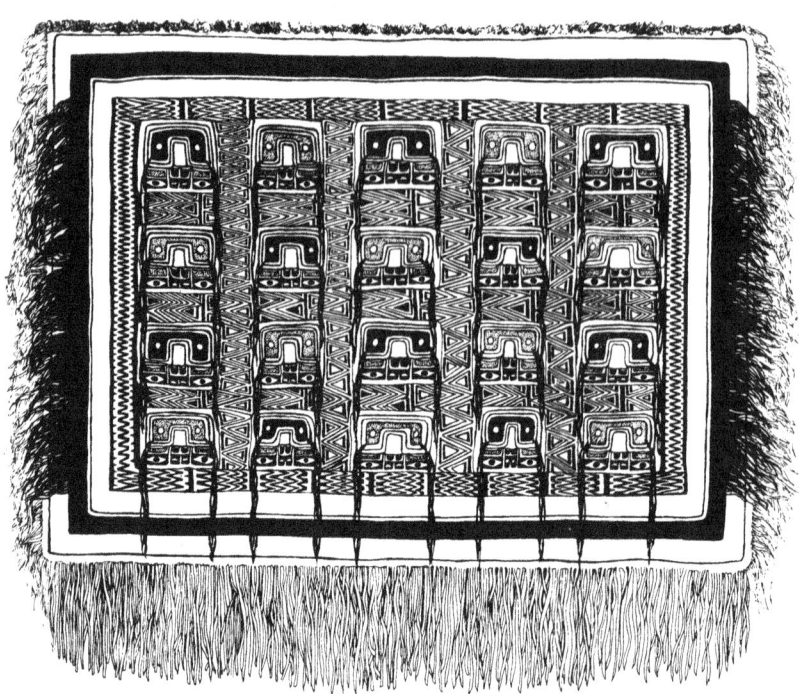

83. This drawing is a reconstruction of a robe taken from potlatch pieces. The tunic is now in the National Museums of Canada and one legging is in the Museum of the American Indian, Heye Foundation, New York.

robe which was cut up in potlatch and remade into a tunic and leggings. In it, the style of the elaborate geometric robes is easily recognized. Formline figures are fitted into the design field. The use of formline weaving made it necessary to add a fourth color, yellow-green, to the standard black, white, and yellow. With the exception of the formline figures, this robe is identical in technique and organization to the elaborate geometric robes.

Eventually, the weavers must have become so expert in forming the curvilinear shapes that men began to paint patterns which could be followed in wool. The women not only continued to develop the technique of weaving, but learned the subtleties of the conventions of the men's art in order to be able to weave the blankets accurately.

In time, the Dancing Blanket assumed its final form. Split cedar bark was added to the wool of the warps to strengthen them. The fringe became deeper and thicker with the recognition of its aesthetic addition to the dance. Added woolen side fringes complemented the warp fringe. The curve at the bottom of the weaving angled in imitation of the cedar bark robes. The black and yellow borders of the geometric chief's robes became a permanent feature of the design; within these borders, one or more figures were depicted, depending on the crest of the owner. The Dancing Blanket was a commissioned work; a wealthy chief, desiring the ultimate in noble dress, would pay handsomely for a blanket woven with his crest figure.

The beautiful Dancing Blanket in figure 84, which is now in the Portland Art Museum, exhibits remnants of the geometric tradition combined with formline weaving. A zigzag pattern is maintained in the grided bib at the top of the weaving, while a magnificent crest figure is wrapped around the main body of the blanket. This blanket, and the "Coppers Blanket" in figure 85, are both very old blankets, woven after formline weaving was thoroughly developed and before the design format was standardized.

The Coppers Blanket was donated to the Peabody Museum, Salem, Massachusetts, by Captain R.B. Forbes in 1832. It is the

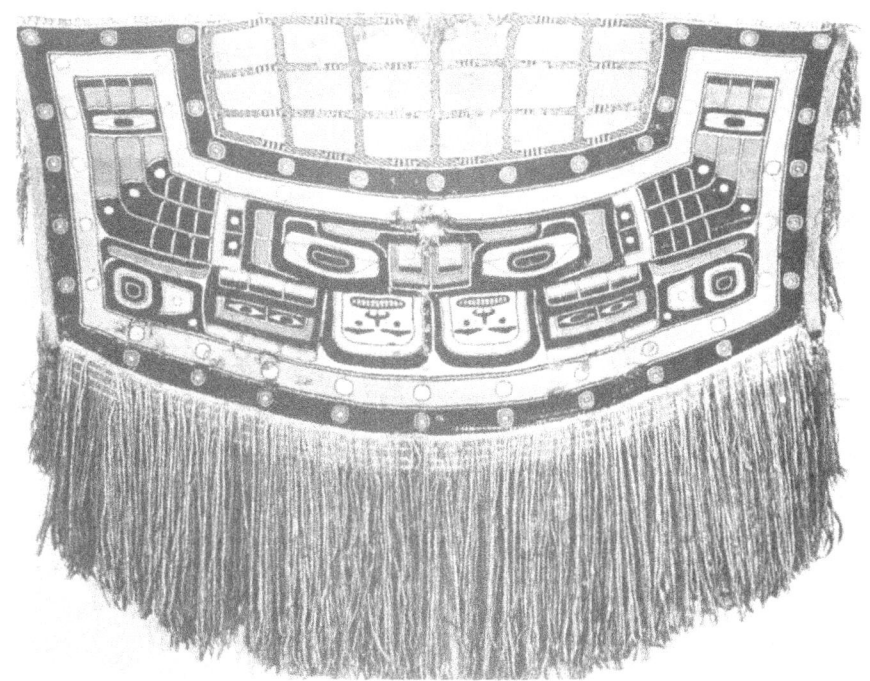

*84. A harbinger of the classic
Chilkat Dancing Blanket (Courtesy of
the Portland Art Museum)*

earliest documented weaving to exhibit formline design. In the
tradition of the older blankets, it is colored black, white, yellow, and
yellow-green and is woven of extremely fine weft with sometimes as
many as forty weft rows per centimeter. Traits which characterize the
oldest weavings are the use of yellow-green dye, very small warp and
weft yarns, the use of two-strand twining over single warp ends in the
white relief forms, the use of rigid weft twining in some of the design
areas, and the absence of commercially spun weft yarns. Many, but
not all, of the older weavings have a tie-off designed with diagonal
lines.

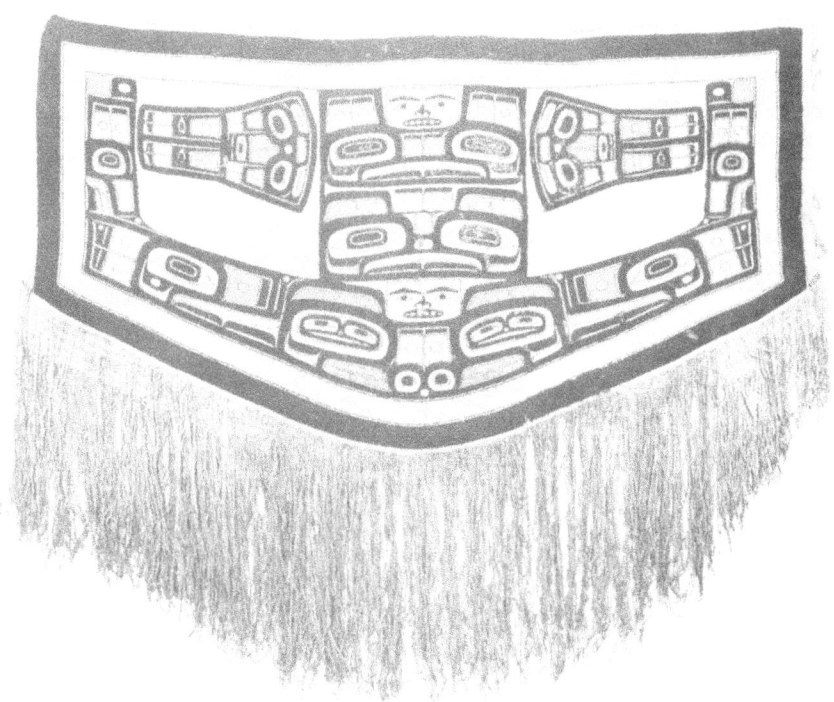

*85. The "Coppers Blanket" (Courtesy
of the Peabody Museum of Salem)*

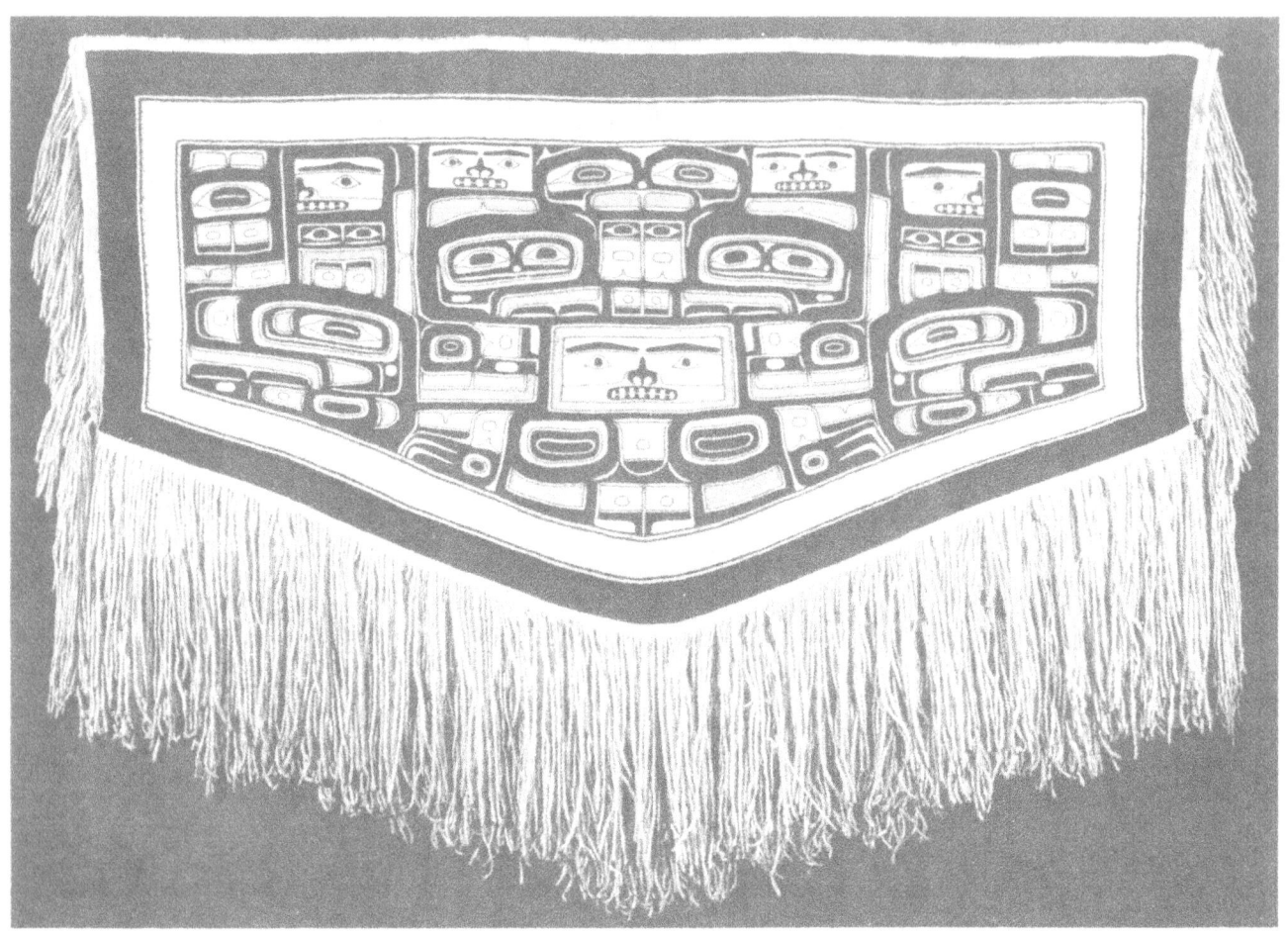

86. A classic Dancing Blanket (Courtesy of the British Columbia Provincial Museum)

Anatomy of a Dancing Blanket

The classic Dancing Blanket can be divided into several parts, most of which were constructed during the main process of weaving and others which were added once the garment was freed from the loom.

Design Field. The main body of the weaving holds the design field. In a *paneled distributive* design, this field is divided into three panels: a central panel which contains the main heraldic figure and two side panels in which minor crest figures may be depicted.

Borders. Surrounding the design field are two broad borders. The outermost one is always black and the inner one is always yellow.

Heading. The top of the blanket is called the heading and consists of a leather cord over which the warp ends are hung and rows of white twining which arrange and secure the warp before the border twining begins.

Fur. Around the heading cord is wound a strip of sea otter fur. The fur is added after the weaving is completed and provides a soft neckline finish.

Ties. Two ties, made of leather strips about forty-eight centimeters long, are attached to the heading cord and used to tie the blanket around the dancer's shoulders.

Side Braids. Along the sides of the weaving lie the side braids. These are twill braids which are attached to the black border in their middle and folded into two halves. They adorn the edge of the blanket and provide a housing for the side fringes.

Side Fringe. The side fringe is sandwiched between the halves of the side braid once the blanket is off the loom. It is made of strands of mountain goat wool. When the blanket is worn, these fringes hang vertically and complement the motion of the great fringe.

Footing. The footing lies beneath the bottom black border. Similar in size to the heading, it consists of a few rows of white twining which put a final finish on the blanket.

Warp Fringe. From the bottom of the weaving flows a great fringe which is a continuation of the wool and cedar bark warp strands.

Overlay Fringe. On top of the warp fringe lies the overlay fringe made of weft yarns of mountain goat wool which is attached to a twined row beneath the footing and which floats over the warp fringe. It is usually slightly shorter than the warp itself.

Tie-off. The tie-off is a small, twined pattern at the bottom of the side braids which binds them so they will not unravel. It is the only part of the blanket which represents the weaver's own pattern.

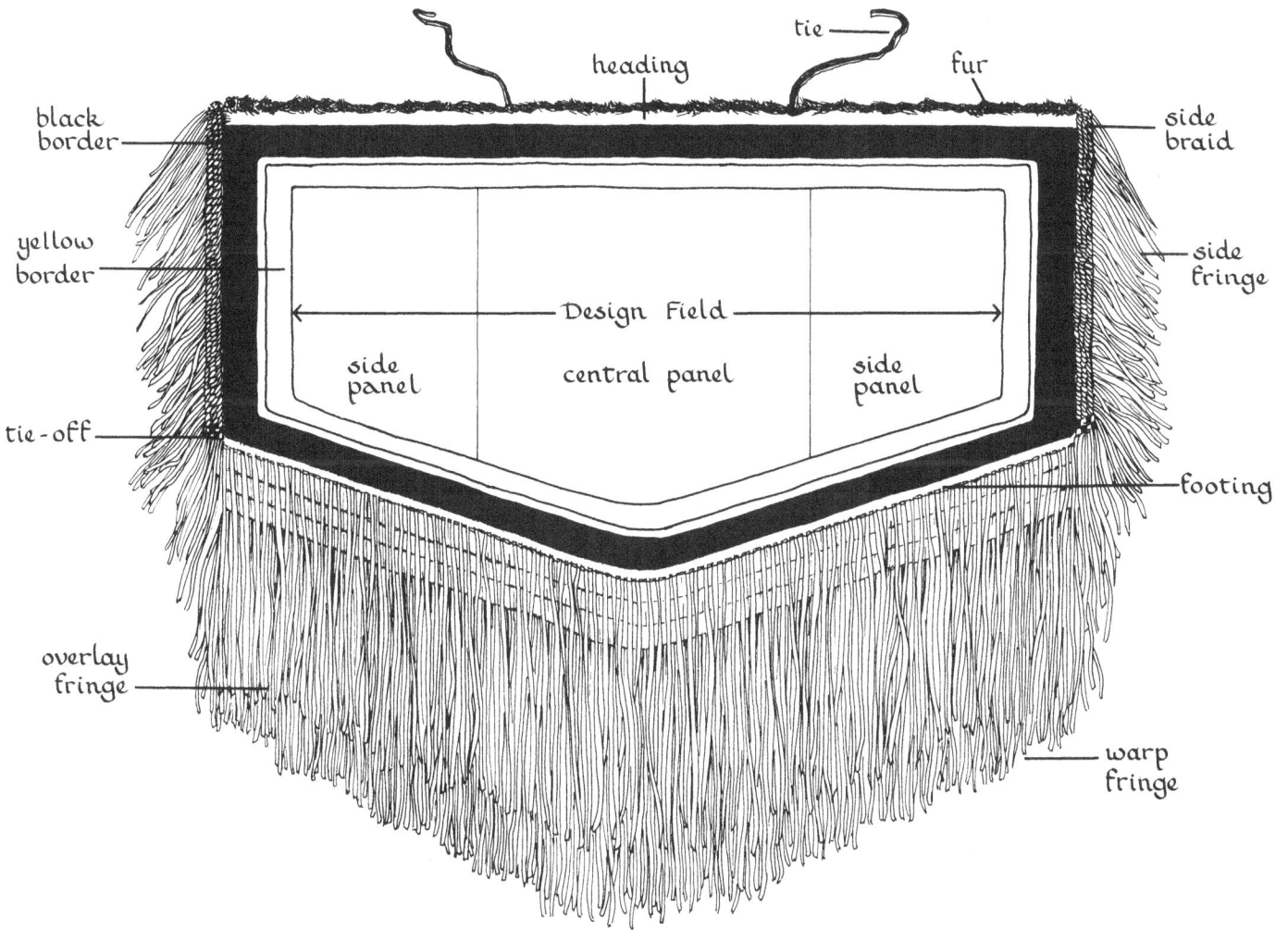

87. Parts of a Dancing Blanket

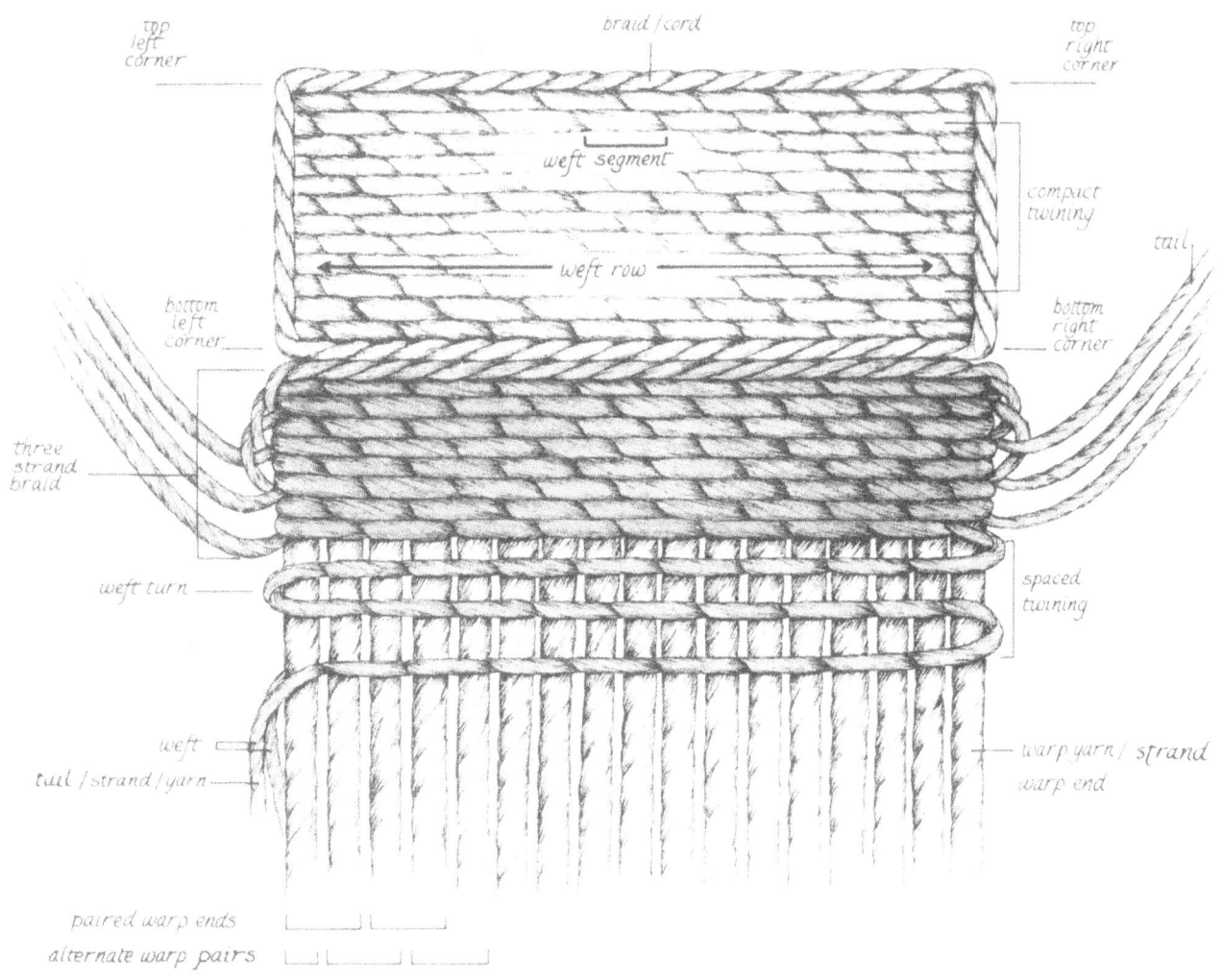

88. Chilkat weaving terms

TECHNICAL TERMS USED IN CHILKAT WEAVING

In order to speak clearly of the structure of the weave, the following terms have been given to the different parts which compose a woven area. The definitions of these terms are specific to the weaving done by the Chilkat Indians and should not be confused with a general identification.

WARP TERMS

Warp yarn. A very strong two-ply, Z-twist yarn, made of mountain goat wool and yellow cedar bark.

Strand. One piece of yarn, either warp or weft.

Warp. All of the parallel strands of warp yarn which run vertically in the weaving.

Warp end. One measured strand of warp yarn.

WEFT TERMS

Weft yarn. A two-ply, Z-twist length of spun mountain goat wool. Sheep's wool, when used as the weft, is a commercial four-ply, S-twist yarn.

Weft. Two strands which twine together around pairs of warp ends and travel more or less horizontally across the warp.

Weft row. One passage of the weft across a form.

Weft turn. As one weft row is completed, the two wefts turn around the edge warp end and begin the next row. One weft "turn" is composed of two weft rows.

Weft segment. Each enclosure of warp ends by the weft.

Alternate warp pairs. Two-strand twining which encircles paired warp ends in one row and splits these pairs in the succeeding row.

Paired warp ends. Two-strand twining which encircles the same pair of warp ends in every row.

Compact twining. Rows of twining pushed tightly together so that no warp shows.

Spaced twining. Spaces left between the rows of twining so that the warp shows.

Tail. The ends of the weft strands.

BRAIDED TWINING TERMS

Braid. A three-strand plait which outlines, or creates, a design shape and is twined into the warp or the two-strand weft.

Cord. The appearance of a braided twining row when viewed from the side.

Corners. The left or right corner at the top or bottom of a rectangular shape, with particular reference to the movement of the braided twining as it travels around these corners.

Tail. The ends of each of the three strands which make up a braided twining row.

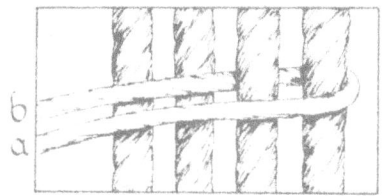

89. The beginning of two-strand twining

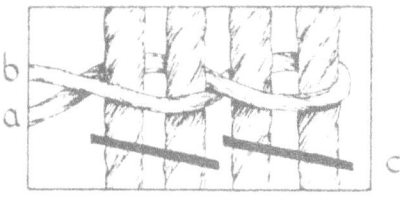

90. Two twined segments

Two-Strand Twining

To begin a row of two-strand twining (fig. 89), a strand of weft yarn is doubled around two warp ends. The two sides of this strand are now ready for use: (a), which lies in front of the warp, and (b), which lies behind the first two warp ends and then joins (a) on the front.

To twine (fig. 90), strand (a) is moved over the top of strand (b) and behind the next two warp ends. Strand (b) simultaneously travels under strand (a) and in front of the same two warp ends. This process is continued, with the strands encircling a pair of warp ends and crossing each other between the pairs. On the left side of a pair of warp ends, the strand which comes from the front always crosses over the strand which comes from the back. It is important that the cross is made in this manner, as the resulting angle of the twining must be a line which is high on the left and low on the right (c).

When a row of two-strand twining has been completed, a turn is made and the twining proceeds in the opposite direction. As the main body of the weaving is comprised of two-strand twining over alternate warp pairs, each succeeding row of weft twining splits the pairs of warp ends used in the row above it. Row 1 (fig. 91) will consequently start around two warp ends and finish around two; row 2 splits the pairs, starting and finishing around a single warp end.

To turn on the left side of a row, strand (b) moves from behind the warp, closely around the edge warp end, and to the front of it. Strand (a) moves snugly around strand (b), behind the first warp end, and then crosses over strand (b) as it comes to the front, splitting the pair of warp ends in the preceding row.

To turn on the right side of the row, strand (a), which lies in front of the edge warp end, moves closely around this warp end and behind the first pair of warp ends. Strand (b) travels around its mate and over the first pair of warp ends.

The weft strands, as they pass over two warp ends, create one segment of a row of two-strand twining (A) (fig. 92). If the letter Z is placed horizontally over a row of two-strand twining, it will be seen that the twining is done with a Z twist. As the weft yarns have been

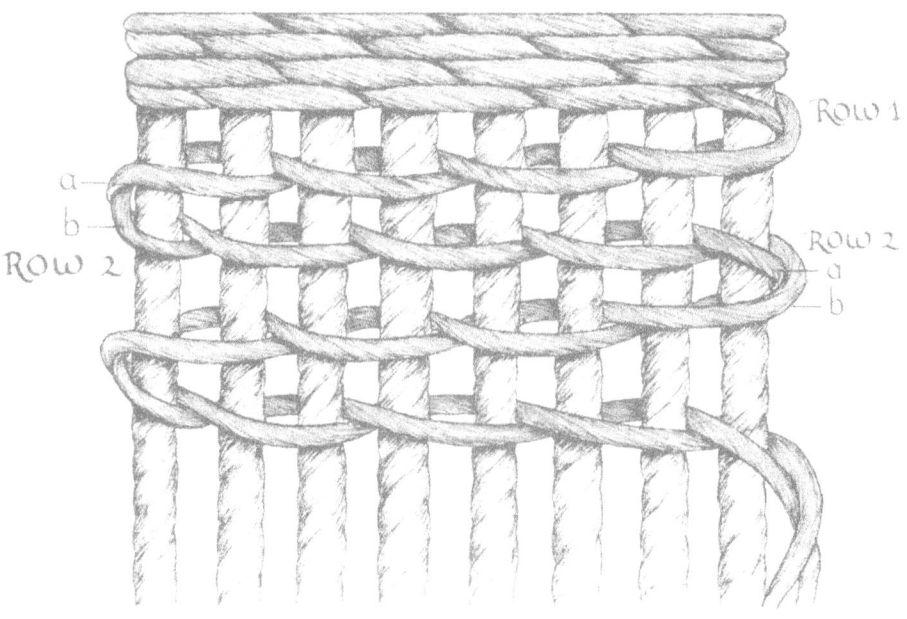

91. Rows of two-strand twining

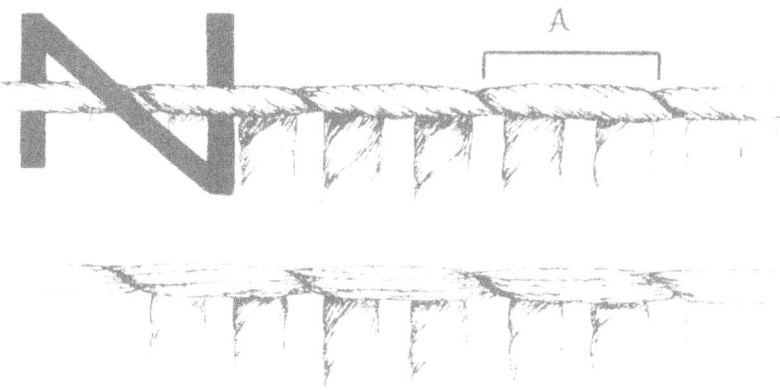

92. Twining with native yarns

93. Twining with commercial yarn

plied in a Z direction, the action of the twining turns the yarns in the direction of the ply, reinforcing the twist of the yarn and the visual angle of the twining. If the wefts were plied in an S twist, the continual turning of the yarns in a Z direction would slightly untwist them, resulting in weft segments which almost look like two parallel yarns (fig. 93). This occurred in the Dancing Blankets when commercial yarns were used.

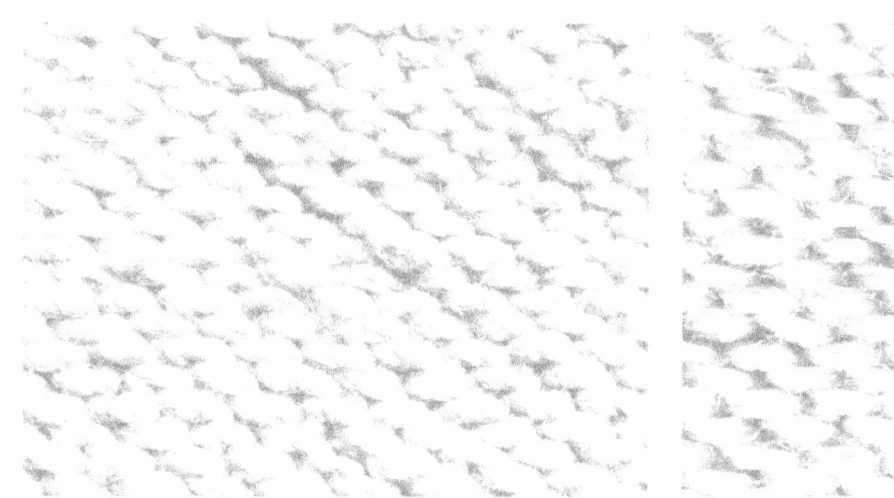

94. Native two-ply Z-twist yarn, twined in a Z direction over alternate warp pairs (CS)

95. Commercial four-ply S-twist yarn, twined in a Z direction over alternate warp pairs (CS)

TWO-STRAND TWINING: FINGER MOVEMENTS

Two-strand twining is easily executed by working the two wefts between the thumb and forefinger of the right hand, providing tension and guidance with the left hand. Chilkat weavings are worked from the top to the bottom: as two or three twined segments are made, they are pushed up with the right thumb, each row snuggling against the preceding one so that no warp shows. This form of compact two-strand twining results in what is called a "weft-faced" fabric: only the weft, and none of the warp, appears on the surface. The tension of the weft strands should be even and not tight. In two rows, a cross must occur between every warp end; therefore, space must be left between the warp ends to accommodate it. Pushing the weft up into place should be easy; if it is difficult, the weft strands are pulling too tightly in a horizontal direction.

STEP 1: When twining from right to left, the weaver grasps a small number of warp ends in each hand and inserts the weft around one pair of warp ends which are held in the right hand. The thumb and forefinger of the left hand twist the wefts (fig. 96).

STEP 2: Two warps are drawn through the weft twist with the thumb and forefinger of the right hand (fig. 97).

STEP 3: The weft is crossed again, *the strand from the front going over the strand from the back* (fig. 98).

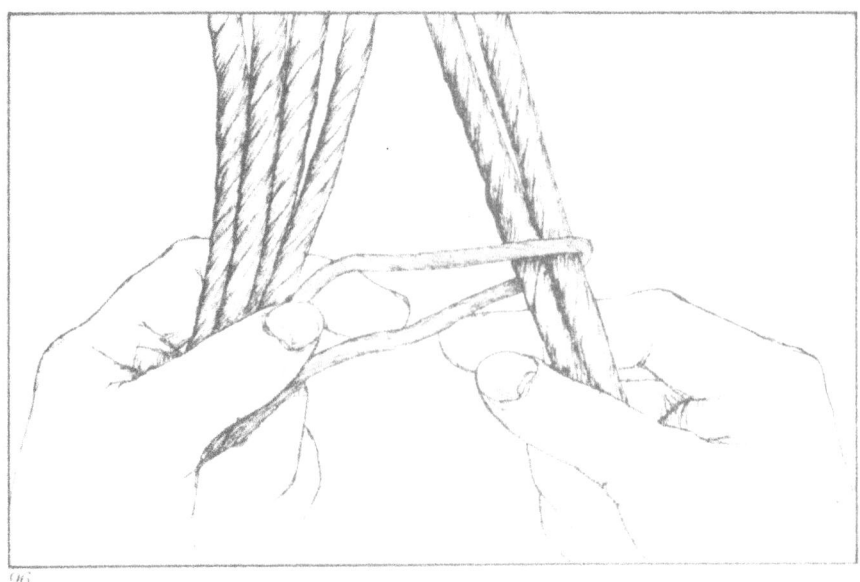
96.

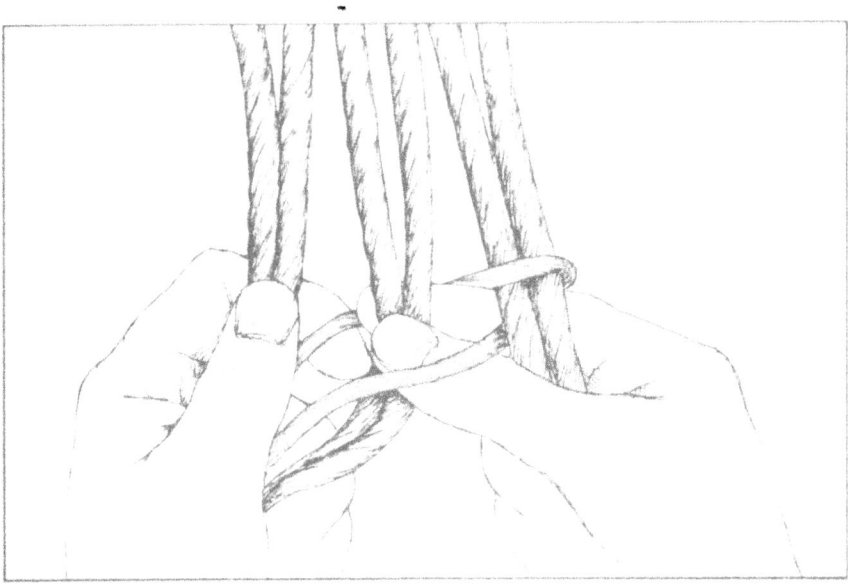
97.

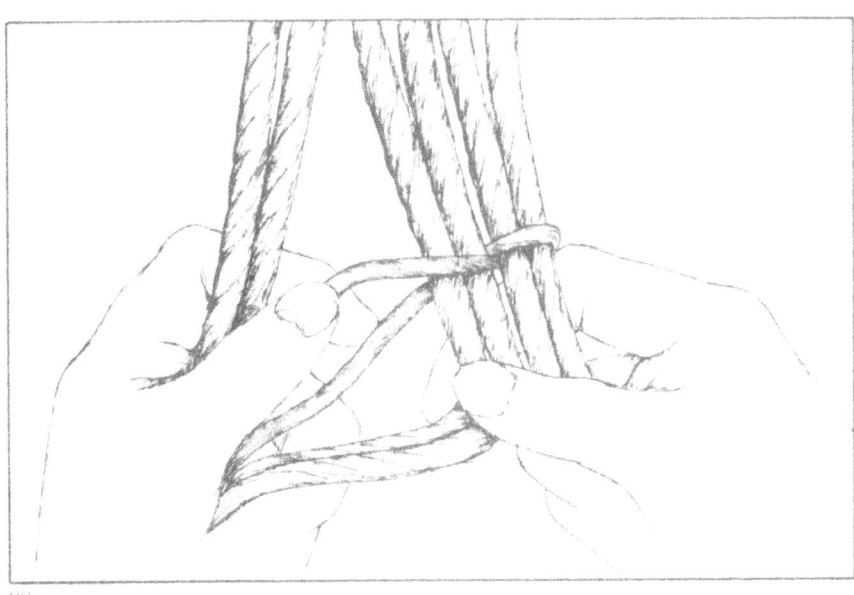
98.

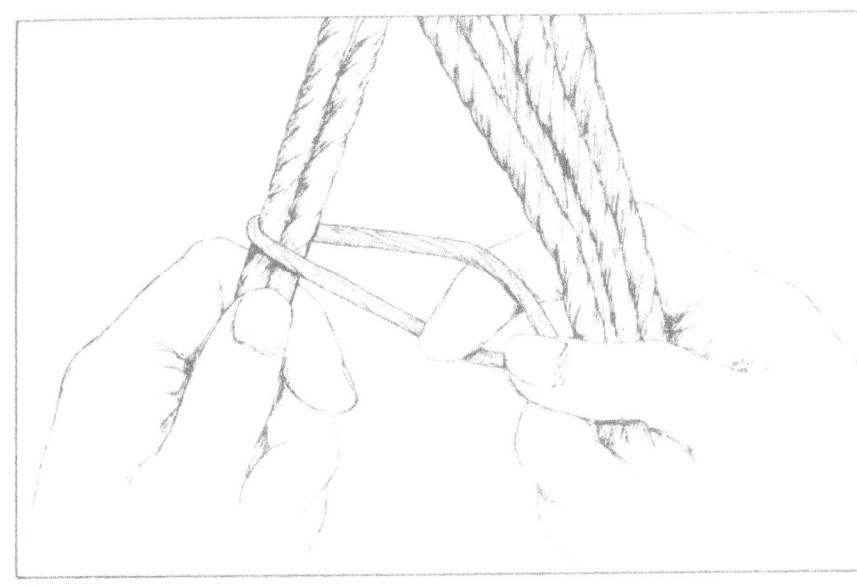

99

STEP 4: Twining from left to right entails a different motion in order to produce a Z angle of twist. The thumb and forefinger of the right hand twist the wefts (fig. 99).

STEP 5: Two warp ends are drawn through the weft twist with the thumb and forefinger of the left hand (fig. 100).

STEP 6: The weft is crossed again, *the strand from the back going over the strand from the front* (fig. 101).

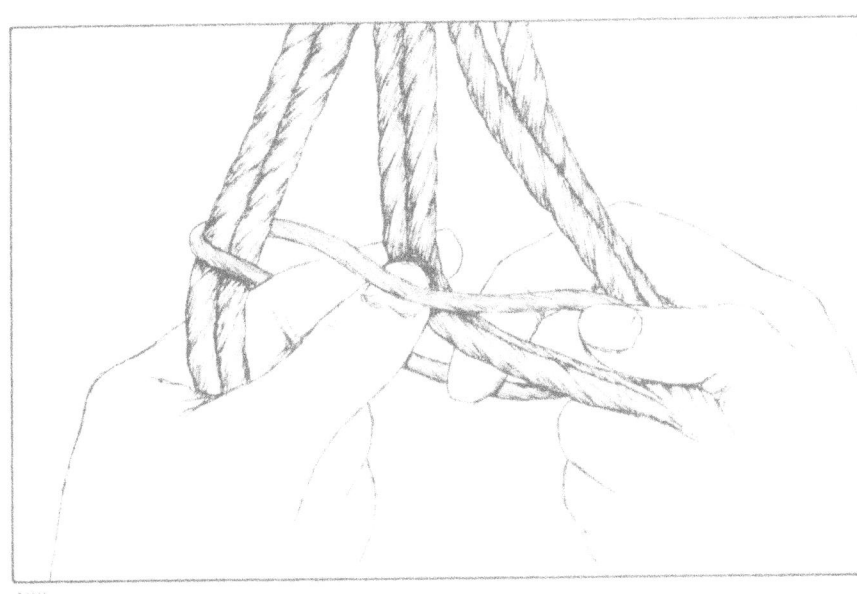

100

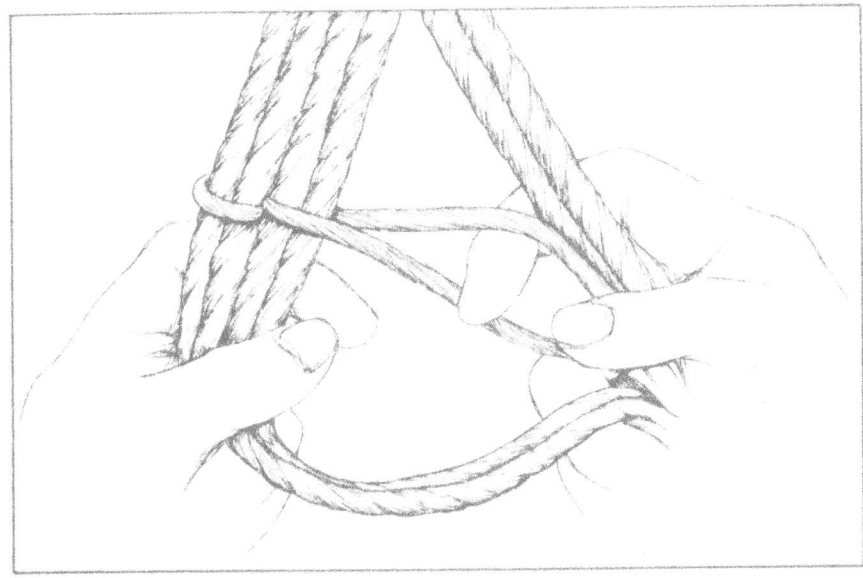

101.

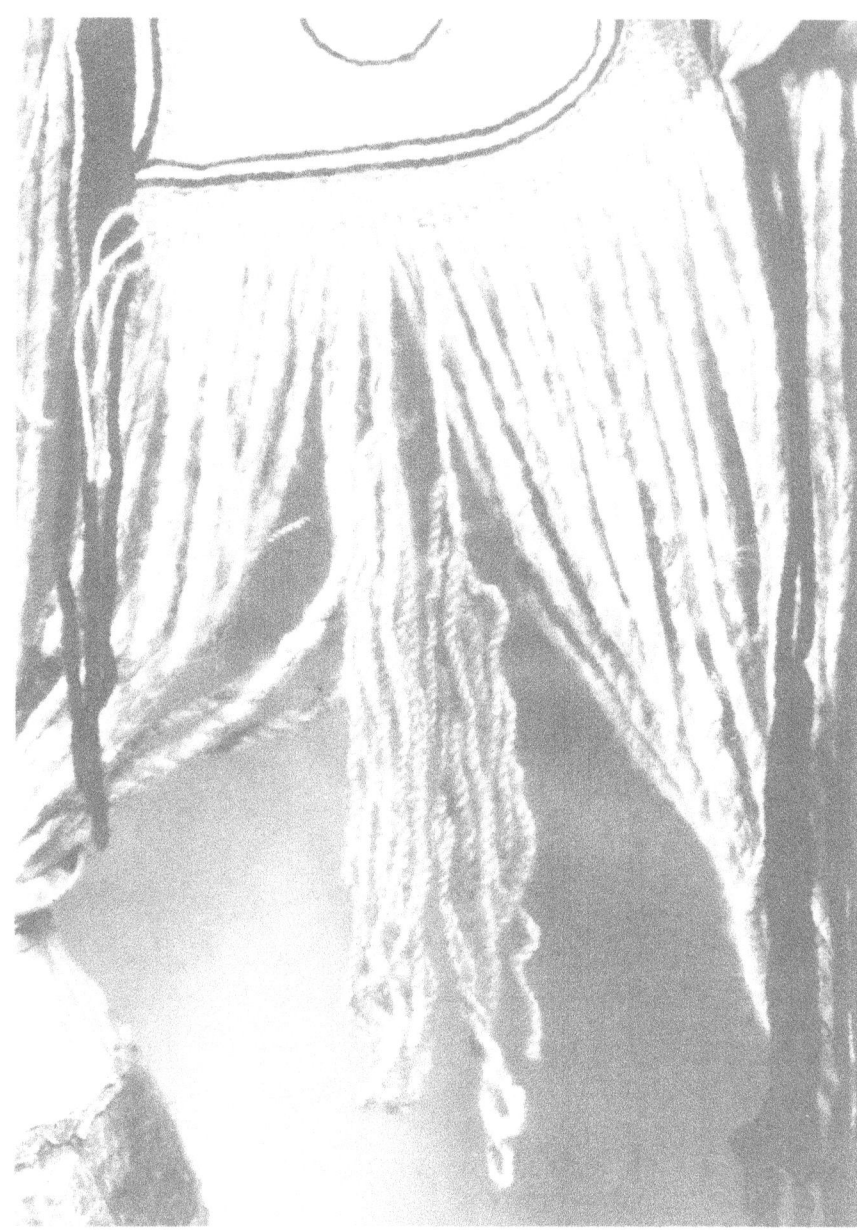

103. Slipknots in the two-strand twining yarns (Courtesy of the Field Museum, Chicago: CS)

Slipknots

In order to work with long weft yarns and avoid frequent splicing, a compact row of slipknots is inserted in the tails of each strand. These slipknots start within six to eight centimeters of the working point of the twining. They must be quite close to the work so that they will not get caught in the warp yarns. After each segment of twining is completed, the weft strands, with their slipknots, are pulled through the warp. As each weft yarn shortens, the slipknot closest to the twining is pulled out, thus lengthening the strand. Using this method, each side of the two-strand weft can be as long as the weaver desires. The row of slipknots shortens a strand to a working length of less than twenty centimeters.

102. Slipknots

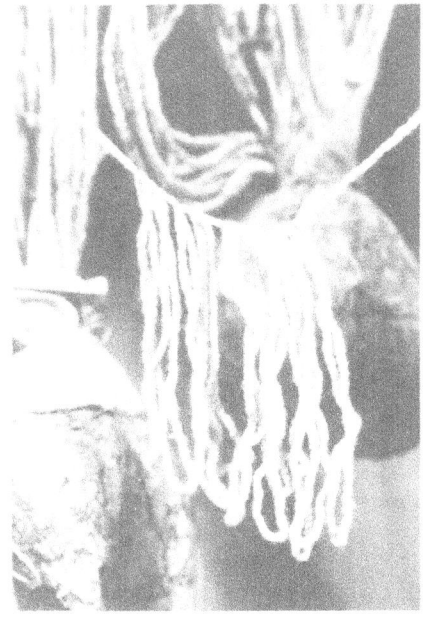

104. A row of closely packed slipknots (Courtesy of the Field Museum, Chicago: CS)

MAKING A ROW OF SLIPKNOTS

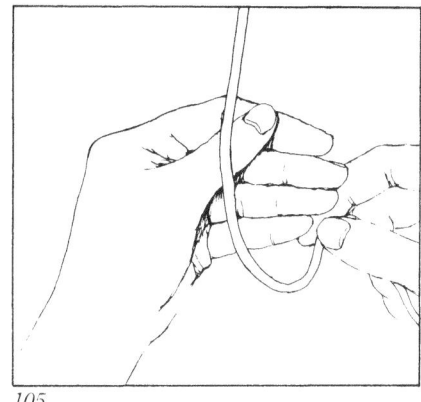

105.

STEP 1: To make a slipknot, one end of the strand is brought down and around the left hand (fig. 105).

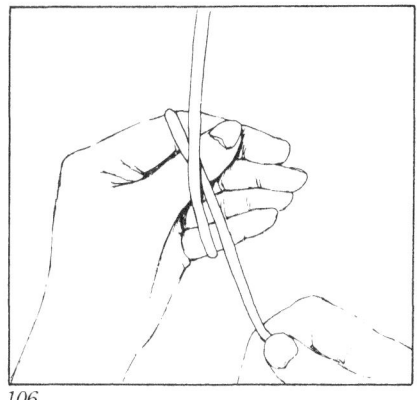

106.

STEP 2: The tail of the strand is looped around the left hand, including the thumb (fig. 106).

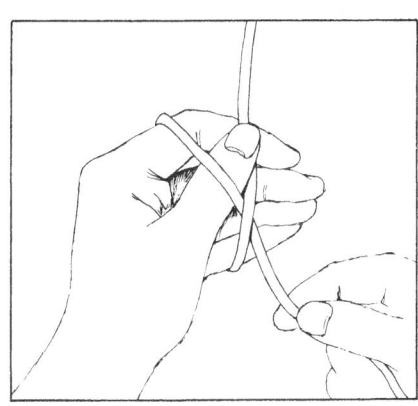

107.

STEP 3: The attached end of the strand is pinched between the left thumb and forefinger (fig. 107).

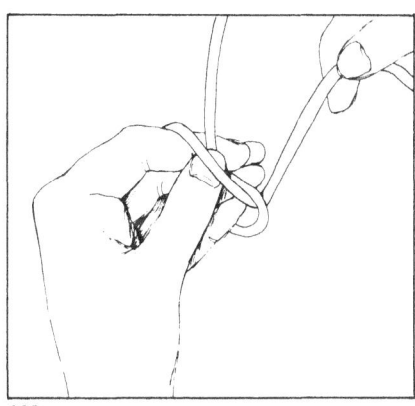

108.

STEP 4: The right hand then raises the tail of the strand, slipping the loop from the left hand. The left hand continues to pinch the strand (fig. 108).

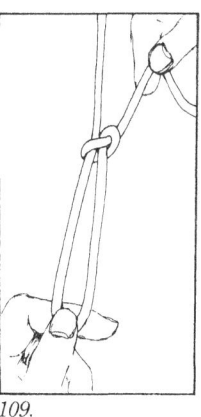

109.

STEP 5: The knot is then tightened by pulling up with the right hand. The next slipknot is worked in the same manner and pulled close to its neighbor (fig. 109).

SPLICING THE WEFT

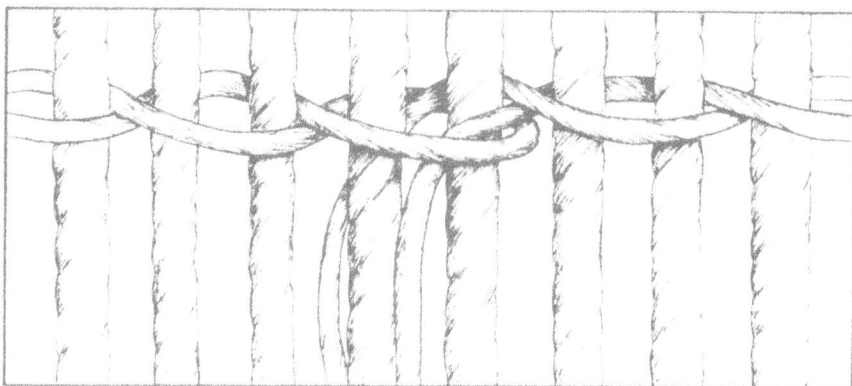

110. A splice in the weft

If the weaver runs out of weft while working in one area and wishes to continue with the same color, she must splice in new weft strands. To do this, she works with the old weft until approximately six centimeters remain on each strand. These short wefts are then dropped alongside a pair of warp ends (fig. 110). A new weft is measured, doubled, and inserted around the last pair of warp ends that the short wefts encircled. This will produce a doubled weft segment which rarely shows, because the two short strands slip down inside the new weft and lie next to the warp ends. These short ends are left to hang vertically and are twined for the next centimeter with the warp ends adjacent to them. When they are firmly secured by the weft, they can be cut off. Due to the complexity of the braiding which occurs on all sides of a form, it is preferable to splice a two-strand weft in the center of the form. If it appears that the wefts will run out near the border of a figure, it is easier to stop twining near the center and leave longer tails hanging next to the warp ends.

WEFT JOINS

The figures in the designs of a Dancing Blanket are woven in four colors and must be joined together in the weaving process. There are four methods commonly used in joining two colors of weft within a figure: a *diagonal join,* a *dovetail join,* an *interlock join,* and a *stepped interlock join.*

DIAGONAL JOIN: METHOD I

Diagonal joins create the curves at the tops of ovoids and the "lazy lines" of the vertical borders. A lazy line is made between two wefts of the same color and can be seen on the front and the back of the weaving. It is not covered by braids.

To create the diagonal join in figure 112, the left weft rounds warp end #6 in turn (A), while the right weft turns around warp end #7. In turn (B), the left weft retreats one warp end, turning around #5. The right weft will consequently advance one warp end and turn around #6. This process continues for the length of the join.

A diagonal join may occur between two colors of weft. The two wefts need not be twined simultaneously; all of the black may be completed before the yellow is worked (fig. 113). Furthermore, the diagonal may be very shallow, the black moving back two or more

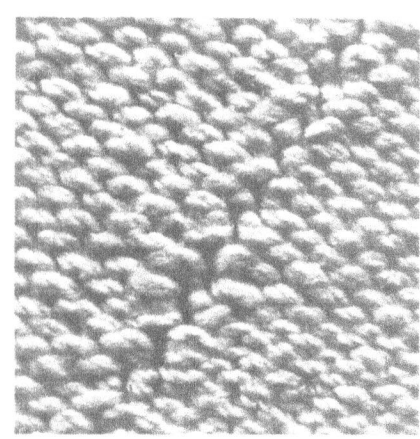

111. A lazy line (CS)

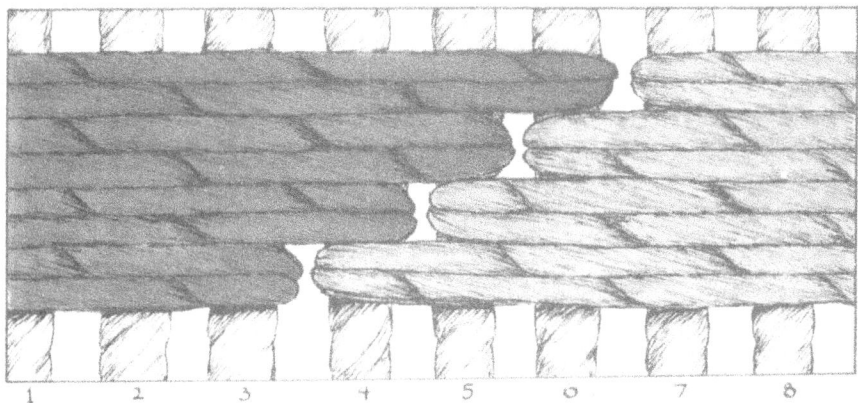

112. A diagonal join

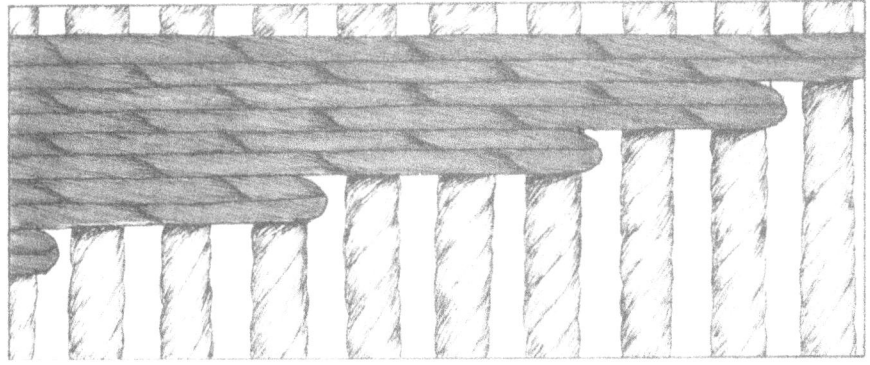

113. The top portion of a diagonal join which will form a curve

warp ends each row. When curves are created in this way, the join is covered on the front of the weaving with braids.

DIAGONAL JOIN: METHOD II

Another type of diagonal join is started, as shown in Method I, by first twining and retreating the desired number of warp ends, (a) (fig. 115). A second weft is then worked at an angle to the diagonal line of the first weft (b). This join is used in creating the formline ovoids and is not covered by braids.

A variation shows weft (a) twined to a horizontal line and weft (b) meeting it at an oblique angle (fig. 116). This method is used in the black and yellow borders where they turn to angle along the bottom of the weaving.

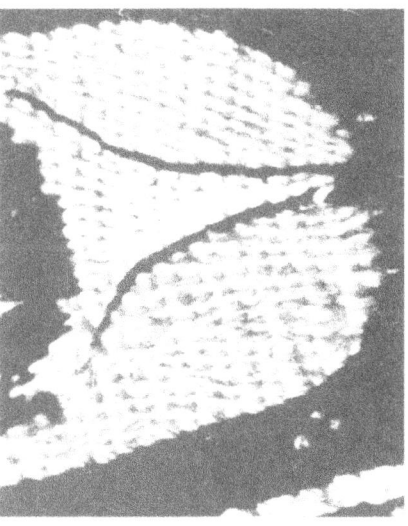

114. A curve created by a diagonal join (CS)

115. and 116. Examples of diagonal joins, Method II

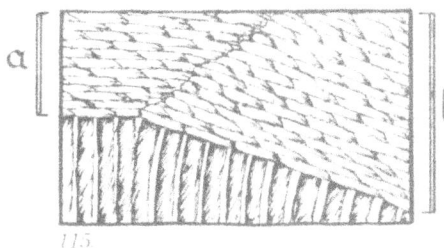

DOVETAIL JOIN

Dovetail joins are often found between the black and yellow vertical side borders and are always covered with braids on the front of the weaving. In this method, the two colors advance and retreat

117. A dovetail join

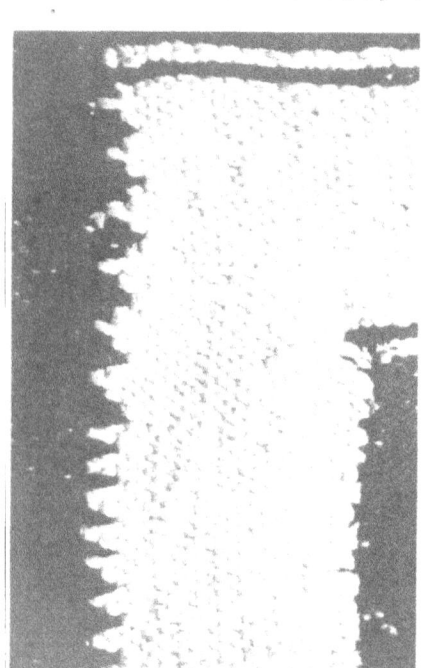

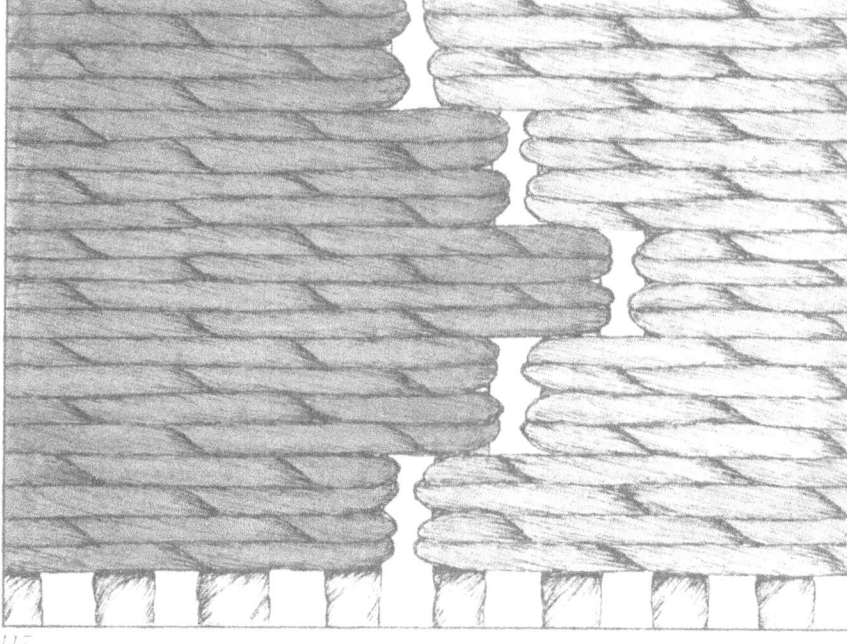

117.

118. A variety in the patterning of the dovetail join shows between the black and yellow borders on the back of the weaving. (CS)

within the space of two or three warp ends, forming a geometric pattern. One weft turn, or two at the most, may be taken around each warp end. In these joins, the two colors are worked simultaneously and the patterns of the join may vary along the length of the border.

119. An interlock join

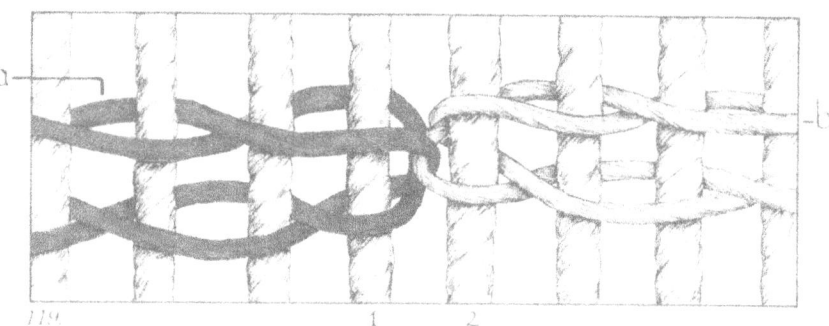

119.   1   2

INTERLOCK JOIN

Within the main design field, figures are usually joined by interlocking the two colors of wefts and covering this interlock with braids. An interlock join takes place between two warp ends. The two colors are twined toward each other until they meet at the point in the design where the weaver wishes to make a join. The front strand of the black weft (a) then encircles the back strand of the yellow weft (b) and travels behind warp end #1. The black weft is then twined to the left. The back strand of the yellow weft, having interlocked with the black weft, continues in front of warp end #2 and is twined with its partner to the right. The interlock is used to join wefts in a vertical line, and the two colors must be worked simultaneously.

120. An interlock join seen from the back side of the weaving (CS)

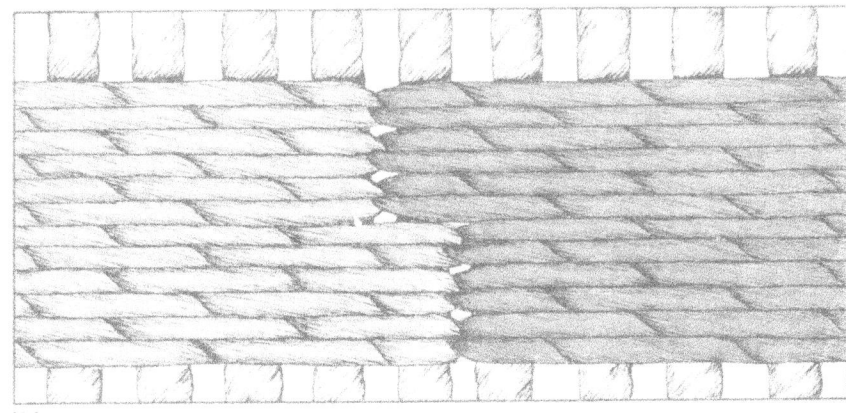

121. A stepped interlock join

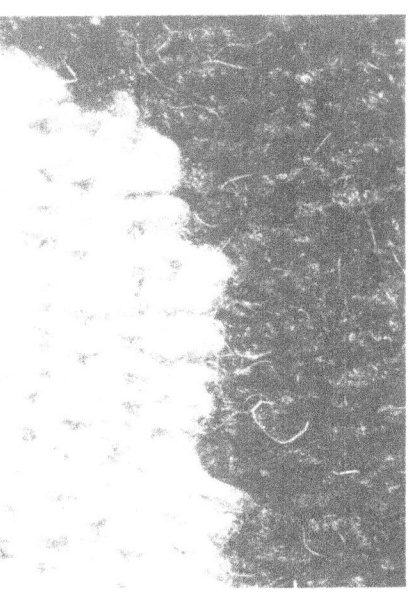

STEPPED INTERLOCK JOIN

In this method, the interlock join and the dovetail join are combined to create steep diagonal lines. Braids always cover the join on the front side of the weaving. If the weaver wishes to join two wefts for three or more rows in a vertical line, she must use an interlock. If she wishes to gradually move this vertical line to the right or the left, she may step the interlock one warp end at a time in either direction.

122. A stepped interlock join seen from the back side of the weaving (CS)

DRAWSTRING JOIN

An average Dancing Blanket is a little over a meter and a half wide; given this width and the crouching position from which she

123. The designs on this loom are being worked between drawstrings.

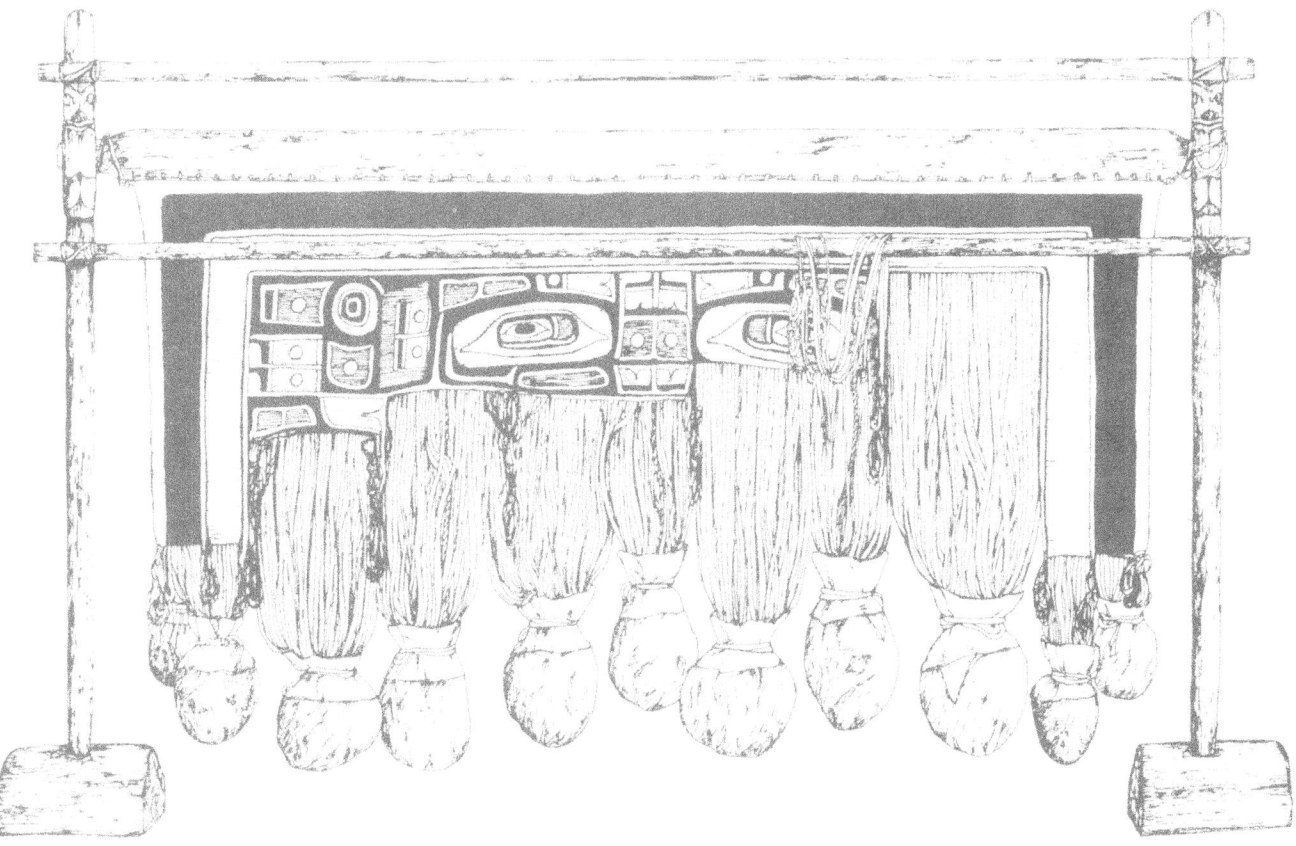

weaves, the weaver benefits greatly from a technique called a *drawstring join.* The use of drawstring joins eases the complexity of the weaver's task by allowing her to stop her twining at any vertical line which appears on the pattern board. The many intricate forms of the design field require the utmost concentration and skill in their execution; to have to cope with too many shapes at one time would tax the abilities of even the cleverest weaver. An awareness of the presence of drawstrings has led many writers to believe that the Dancing Blankets were woven in strips and sewn together. This is a misconception, for they were actually twined together in this very ingenious manner.

The drawstring, made at one time of a spun sinew strand and later of cotton seine twine, is dropped along a warp end which coincides with a vertical line in the design. The weaver can then stop her horizontal progression at this line and return across the shape she is twining. When she has finished the shape, she twines the form adjacent to it, attaching the weft to the drawstring. This join is very strong; ultimately, there will be no division in the fabric. Furthermore, the join does not appear on the front surface, as it is completely covered with braids (figs. 124 and 125).

Drawstrings can be inserted for very short distances. Due to the method of twining, the outside edge of a curved form contains a straight line (see p. 157). A drawstring could therefore be placed on this line (figs. 126 and 127).

124. A drawstring join covered by braids on the front of the weaving (CS)

125. The drawstring join shown from the back of the weaving. The yellow and black wefts are attached to the drawstring. (CS)

126. A ∪ shape with a drawstring join on the inside edge of the crescent (CS)

127. The back of the ∪ shape, showing the placement of the drawstring join (CS)

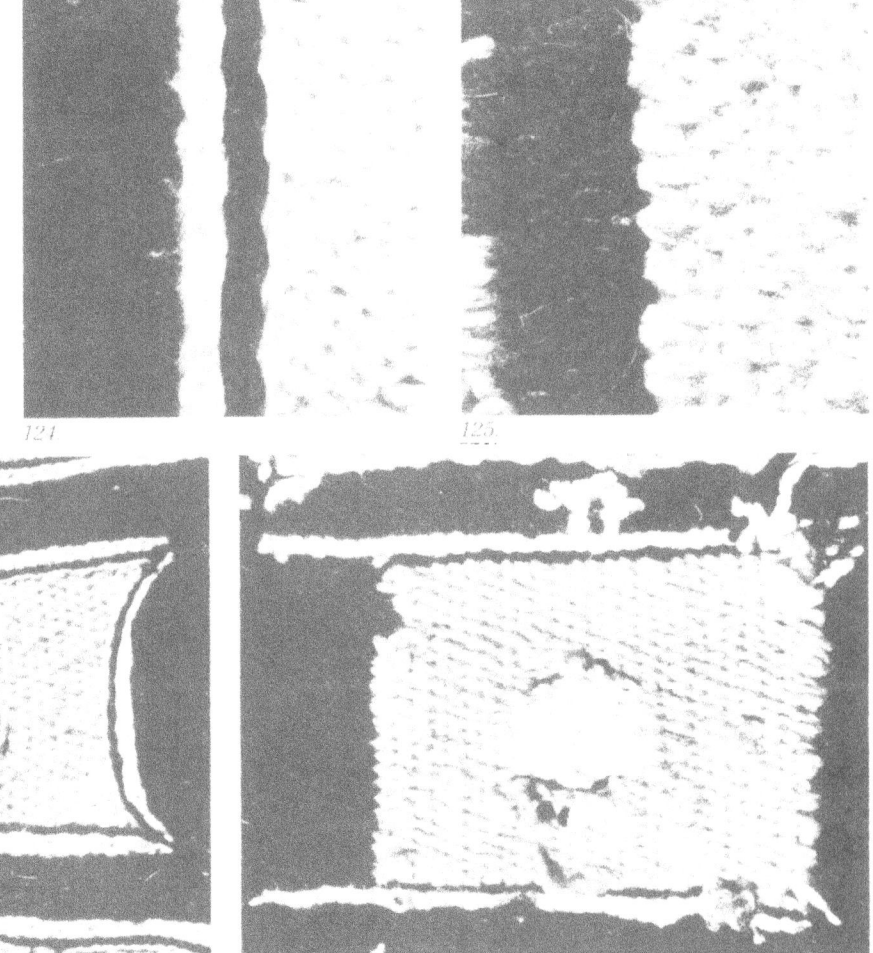

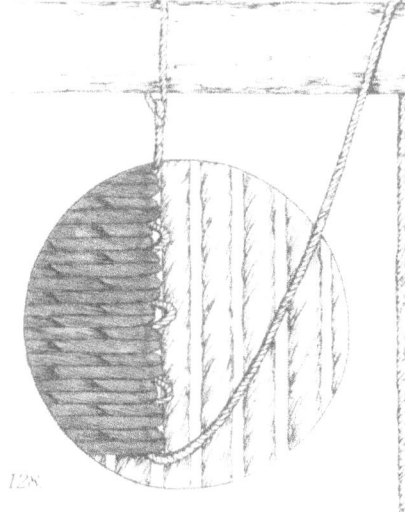

128

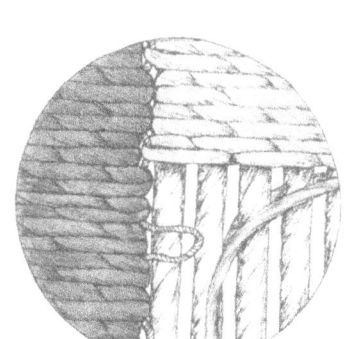

129

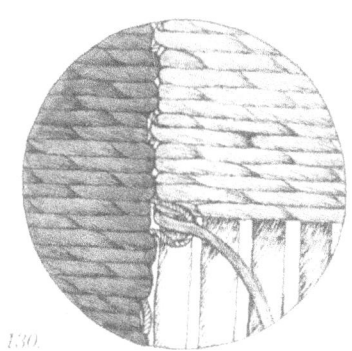

130

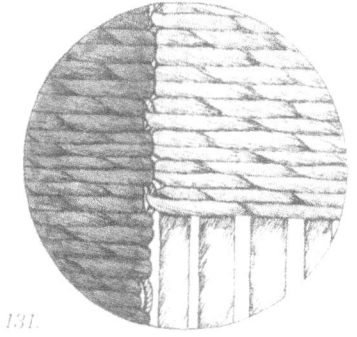

131

INSERTING A DRAWSTRING JOIN

All of the following illustrations are viewed from the back of the weaving.

STEP 1: A drawstring is tied to the cross-slat or the loom beam and dropped alongside the area to be woven. As the twining progresses, the drawstring is included with the edge warp end for two turns, and then left out for one turn (fig. 128).

STEP 2: When weaving the adjacent side, a loop of the drawstring is pulled out. Four rows are twined to advance the weaving to the point where the loop emerges (fig. 129).

STEP 3: In the next weft turn, one of the two weft strands is inserted in the drawstring loop and the twining then proceeds from left to right (fig. 130).

STEP 4: The drawstring loop is pulled tight by tugging gently on the bottom of the drawstring or by pulling out the next free loop (fig. 131).

When a drawstring join has been completed, the sinew is untied from the cross-slat or beam and knotted on the back directly above its entry. At the bottom, it is woven in with the warp for a short way and then cut off. On the front of the weaving, this join is completely obscured by the rows of braids which travel over it.

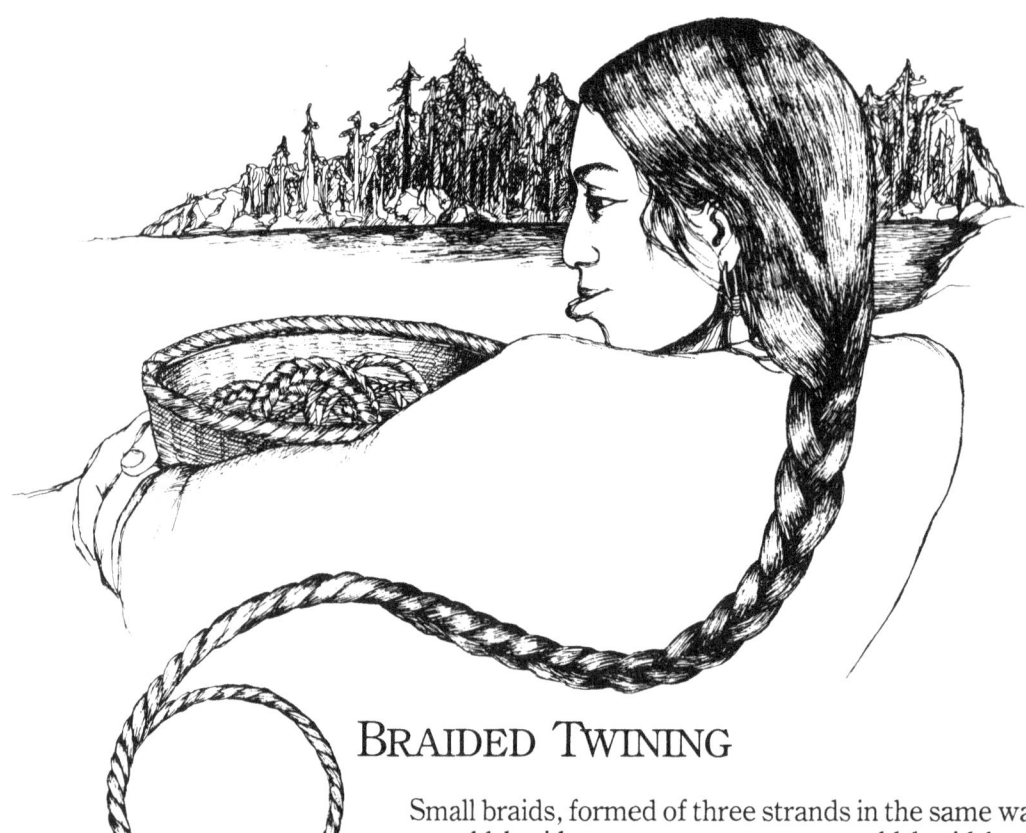

BRAIDED TWINING

Small braids, formed of three strands in the same way that a fisherman would braid a rope or a woman would braid her hair, were an important element in the construction of a Dancing Blanket. Seen only from one side, the braids formed outlines around all of the shapes in the design, giving a weaver the freedom to create clean and gentle curves.

Braided twining was used extensively in Chilkat weaving. Disregarding usual weaving conventions, the small braids were twined into either the warp or the weft. *This is the most remarkable technical accomplishment of the Indian weavers.* As the outline strands were freed from their dependence on the warp as a base, they could travel at any angle over the surface of the weaving. No longer restricted to elements which traveled only horizontally, the weavers could form the curvilinear shapes of the formline designs.

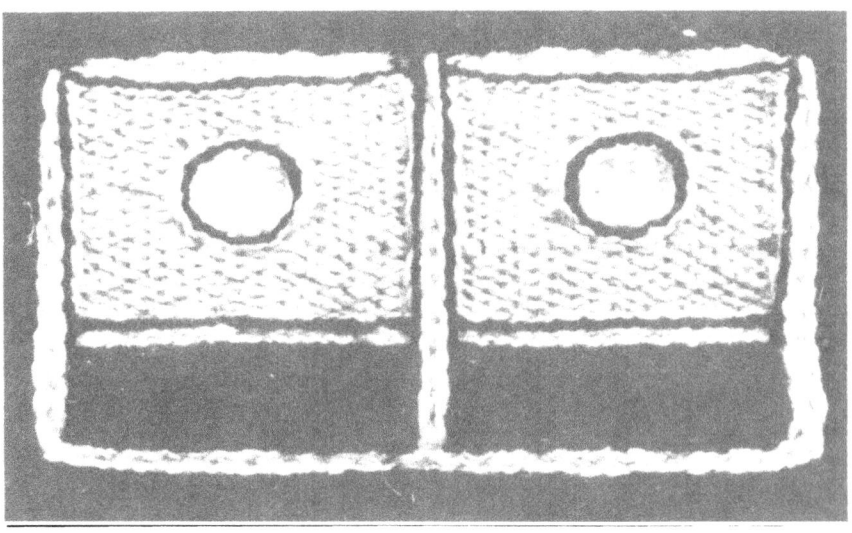

132. Little braids outline and define the figures in the Dancing Blankets. (CS)

BRAIDED TWINING OF THREE-STRAND TWINING?

Braided twining can be confused with another technique called three-strand twining. In three-strand twining, the three strands are not interlaced with each other before twining around the warp. One strand simply passes over or under the other two and then behind the next free warp end. When both the braided twining row and the three-strand twining row are seen as cords on the front of the fabric, it is impossible to tell from the front which technique is being used. A simple way of determining this is to compare the angle of the weft segment created on the back side of the fabric with that on the front. If the angle lies in opposition to the slant of the row on the front, the row is braided (fig. 133). If the angle on the back is identical to the angle on the front, the row is twined (fig. 134). Each of the three strands in both twining and braiding travels over two warp ends and under one. On the back of the fabric, the row appears to travel over single warp ends.

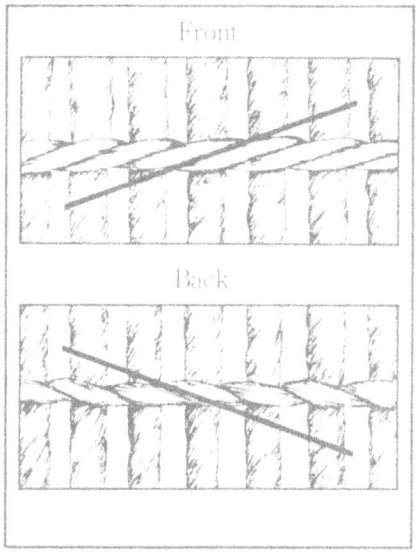 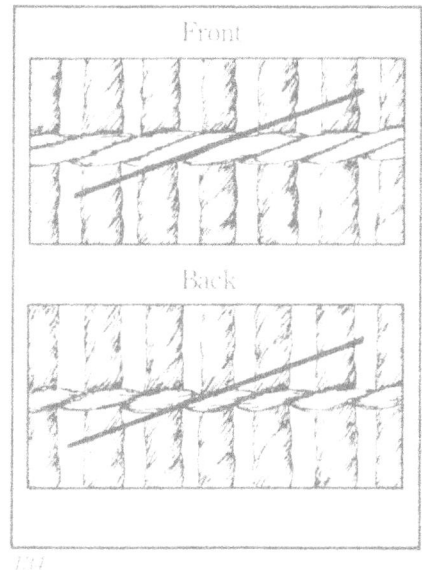

133. Braiding

134. Twining

THE CROSS-SLAT

The tails of the braided twining rows must be organized so that they can be put out of the way when they are not actually being used. To do this, the strands are first shortened with the slipknot technique. In forms where the braid is to travel only a short distance, such as a circle or the dividing line between two U shapes, slipknots are not necessary as short strands of yarn are used.

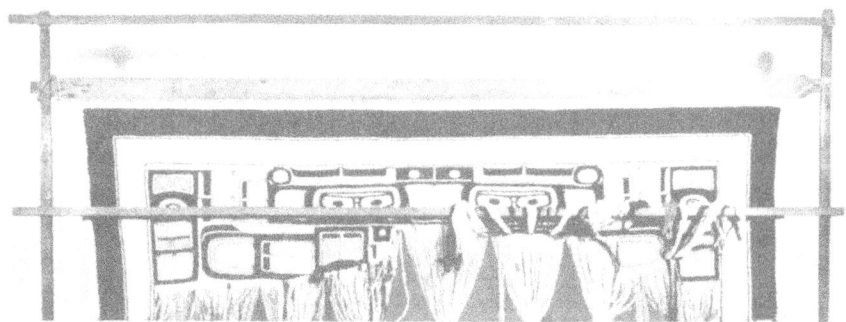

135. A cross-slat lashed to a loom (Courtesy of the Field Museum, Chicago: CS)

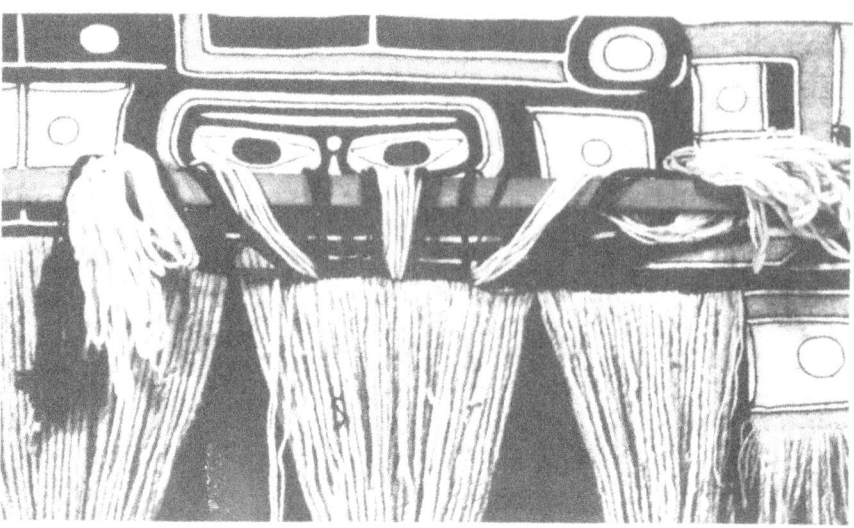

136. The tails of the braided twining rows placed over the cross-slat (Courtesy of the Field Museum, Chicago: CS)

To keep the three strands of all braids out of the way of the two-strand twining, a cross-slat is placed across the front of the weaving and lashed to the upright posts of the loom. The tails of the braids are placed over this cross-slat, thus holding them up and away from the line of weaving. The cross-slat itself is a thin piece of wood which is very flexible; the weaver can pull it away from the weaving to insert the thick bundles of slipknots. In the top rows of weaving, the cross-slat is not needed because the braid strands can be thrown over the loom beam.

THE TECHNIQUE OF BRAIDED TWINING

To form a three-strand braid which will twine around the entire perimeter of a form, three yarns must first be measured and cut. To enter the braid, the middle of one strand is placed in the center of the shape (fig. 137a). One-half of the strand is raised to the right side of the shape (fig. 137b); this is the point along the strand of yarn where it should be inserted around a warp end to begin the braid. If the strand is simply doubled and inserted, the left side of the braid strands will be considerably shorter than the right. When a braid is measured in this manner across the form, the tails will be of equal length after it has been braided (fig. 137c).

137. Measuring a strand for a braided twining row

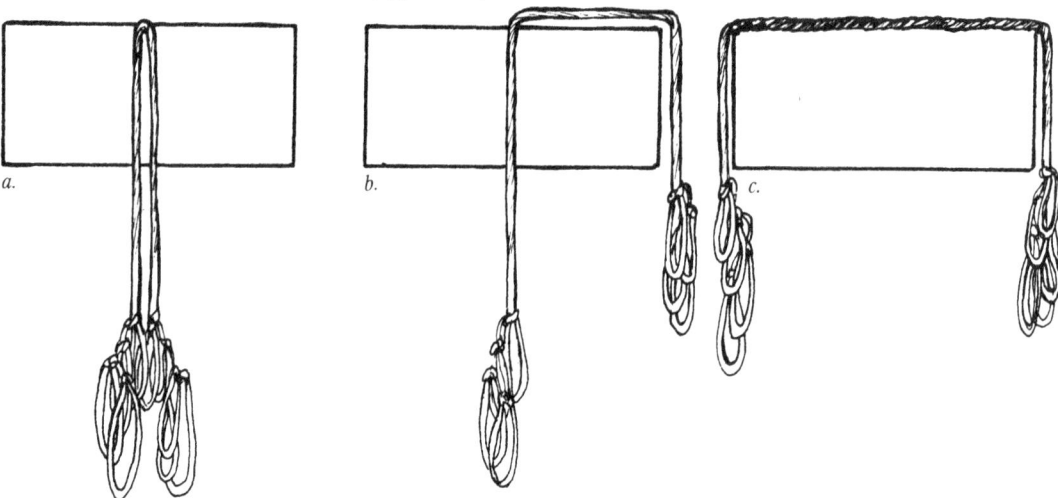

a.   b.   c.

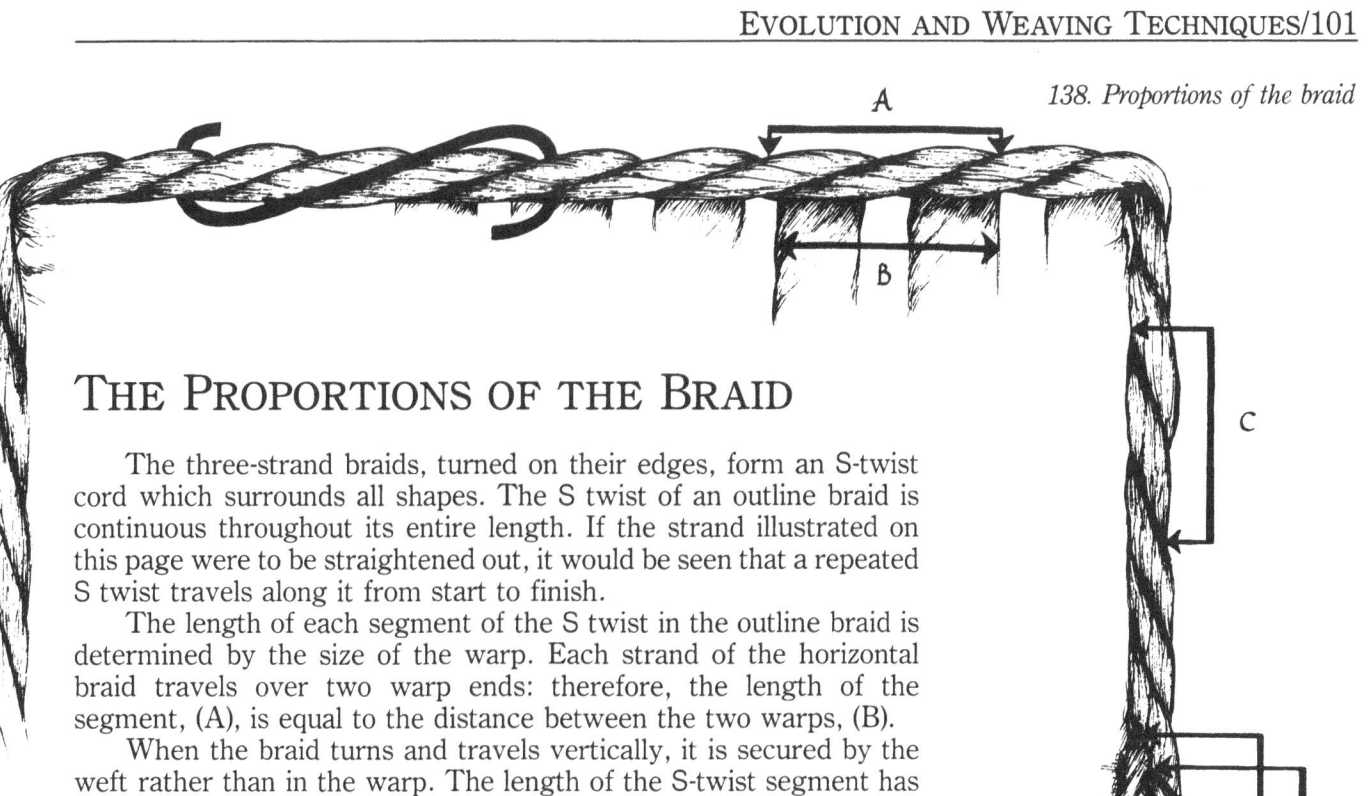

THE PROPORTIONS OF THE BRAID

The three-strand braids, turned on their edges, form an S-twist cord which surrounds all shapes. The S twist of an outline braid is continuous throughout its entire length. If the strand illustrated on this page were to be straightened out, it would be seen that a repeated S twist travels along it from start to finish.

The length of each segment of the S twist in the outline braid is determined by the size of the warp. Each strand of the horizontal braid travels over two warp ends: therefore, the length of the segment, (A), is equal to the distance between the two warps, (B).

When the braid turns and travels vertically, it is secured by the weft rather than in the warp. The length of the S-twist segment has been set by the horizontal braid. This length must be maintained vertically (C) in order to produce an evenly twisted cord. There are many more weft rows per centimeter than there are warp ends; therefore, a number of "free" rows are twined between each insertion of the braid strands. This number is determined by the number of weft rows, (D), which equal the distance between the two warps, (B). In the case illustrated, six weft rows, or three weft turns, are equal to the width of two warps, with the braid being caught in the first turn. The second and third turns are twined without inclusion of a braid strand. A single strand of the braid travels vertically three times the length of the twist (E) before it is once again inserted in the weft, but only one-third appears on the surface (F).

Entering a Braid Which Twines around the Perimeter of a Form

STEP 1: Strand (a), which has been previously cut and measured, is placed under warp end #1. The two ends of the strand, (a1) and (a2), are hung over the top of the cross-slat and spread in a V. They should hang at unequal lengths. Warp end #1 is the warp end which lies at the extreme right-hand side of the shape, wherever this shape may occur on the warp. For clarity, the following drawings will exclude warp ends which lie to the right of the figure being woven (fig. 139).

STEP 2: Strand (b) is placed under warp end #2, which lies to the left of warp end #1. The tails of the strand, (b1) and (b2), are spread in a V over the cross-slat, both lying to the left of the tails of strand (a) (fig. 140).

STEP 3: Strand (c) is placed under warp end #3, its tails, (c1) and (c2), spread in a V and hung over the cross-slat to the left of the tails of strands (b). The strands (a1), (b1), and (c1) will be used to work the top horizontal braid. The strands (a2), (b2), and (c2) will go around the corner and outline the right side of the figure (fig. 141).

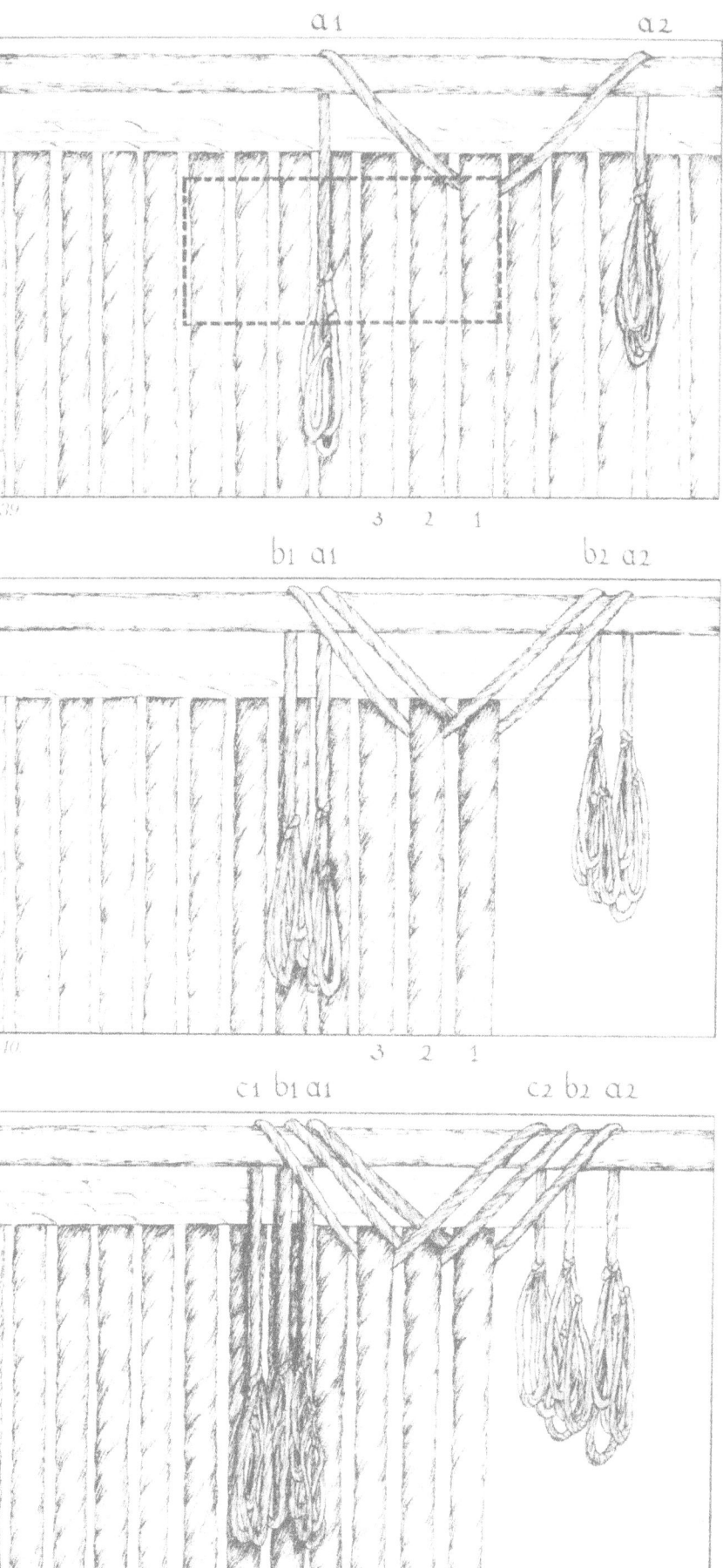

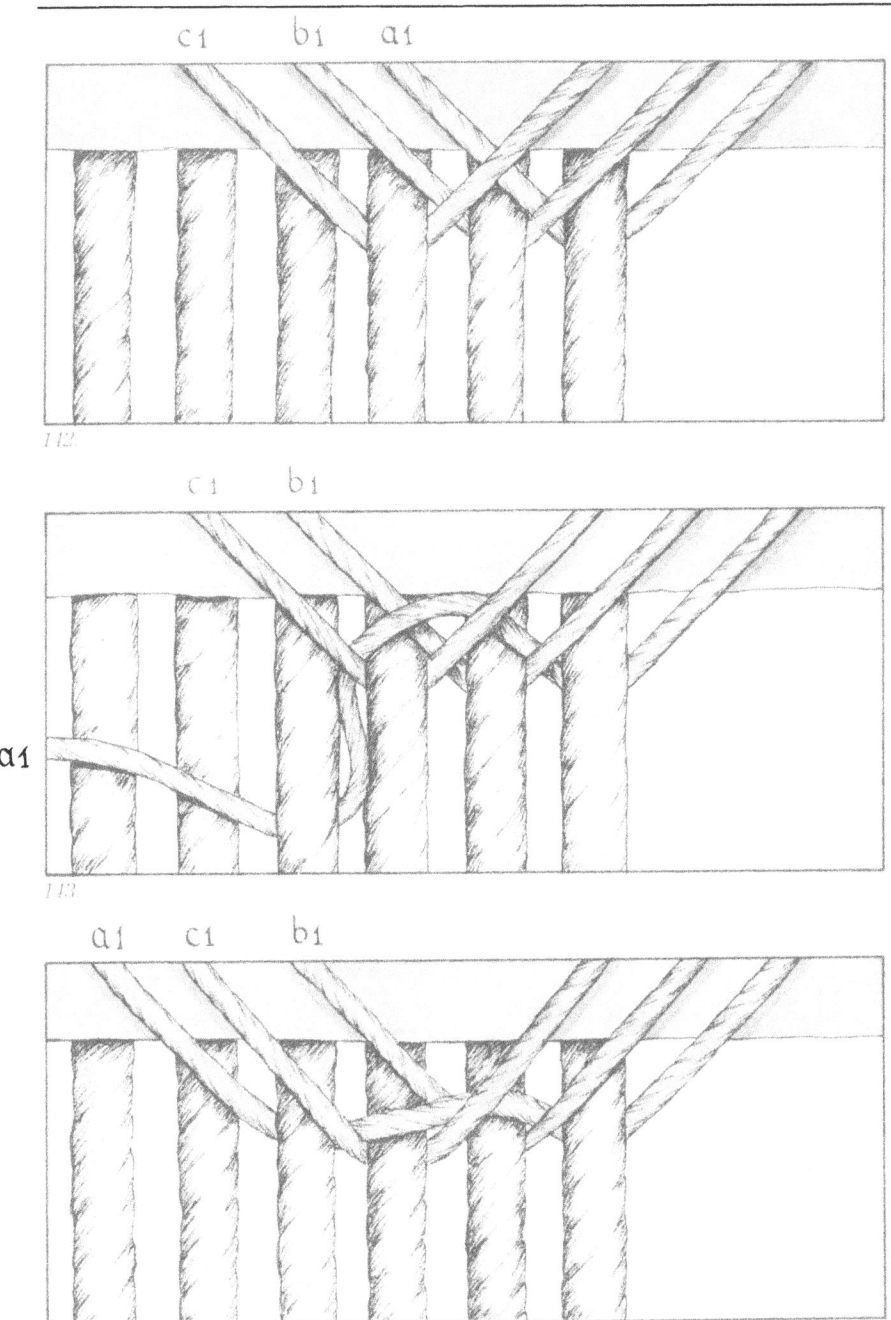

BRAIDED TWINING:
RIGHT TO LEFT

STEP 1: The yarns labeled (a1), (b1), and (c1) will be used to braid from right to left. The unlabeled strands are ready to turn the right-hand corner (fig. 142).

STEP 2: Strand (a1) is removed from the cross-slat and placed in front of (b1), behind (c1), and under the next successive warp end (fig. 143).

STEP 3: Strand (a1) is tightened into position and returned to the cross-slat. In the next step, (b1) repeats the action of (a1), traveling between (c1) and (a1) and under the next warp end. It should be noted that each strand in this braid goes over two warp ends and under one, the braid occurring as a result of splitting the second two strands (fig. 144).

Entering a Braid from the Right Which Only Travels Horizontally

Sometimes it is necessary to braid across the top or bottom of a form without traveling down the sides. A special method of entering and finishing this braid is used.

Step 1: A strand of white yarn is measured which is one and one-fourth the width of the form. The strand is doubled and is placed around warp end #1, with both of its tails going over the beam to the left. Strand (a1) lies to the left of (a2) (fig. 145).

Step 2: A single length of white yarn is measured which is one and one-fourth the width of the form. One end is placed between warp ends #2 and #3, letting a short tail protrude about two centimeters to the back of the weaving. Strand (b) is placed over the beam to the left of (a1) (fig. 146).

Step 3: These three strands are then braided and twined to the left side of the form. When the row has been twined to within three warp ends of the end, the first strand of the braid is dropped down next to a warp end. The second and third braid strands are subsequently dropped next to the final two warp ends. At this point, the braid is not very secure. It will be held in place by the next row of braided twining (fig. 147).

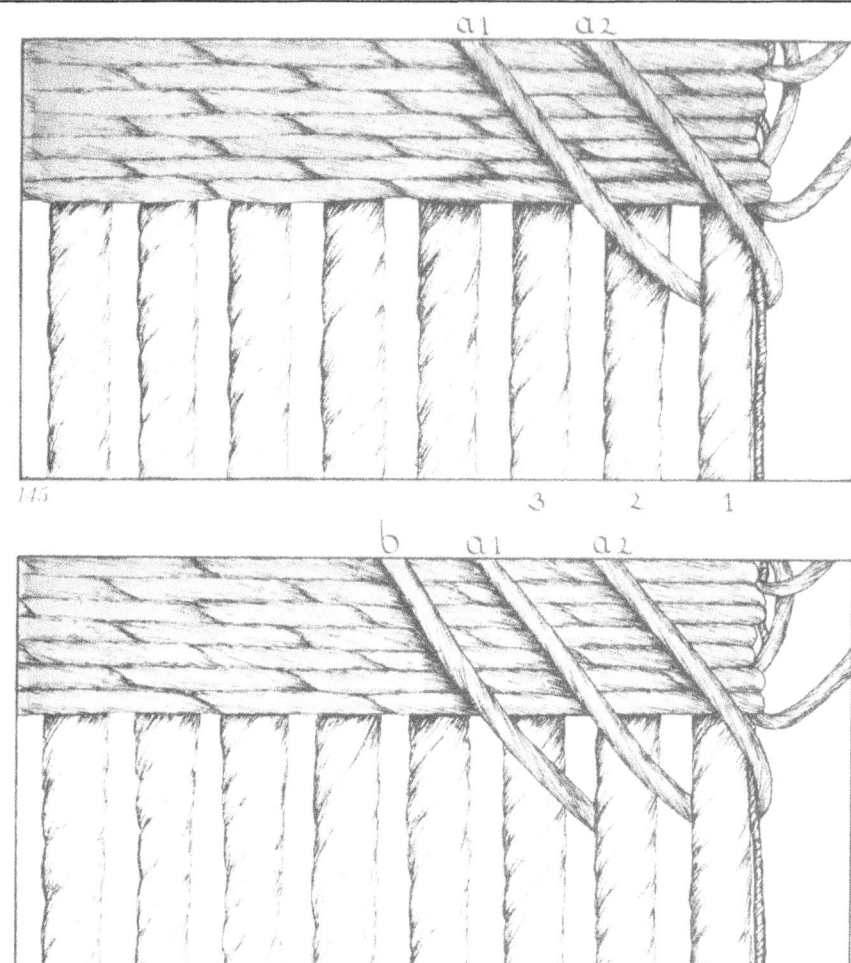

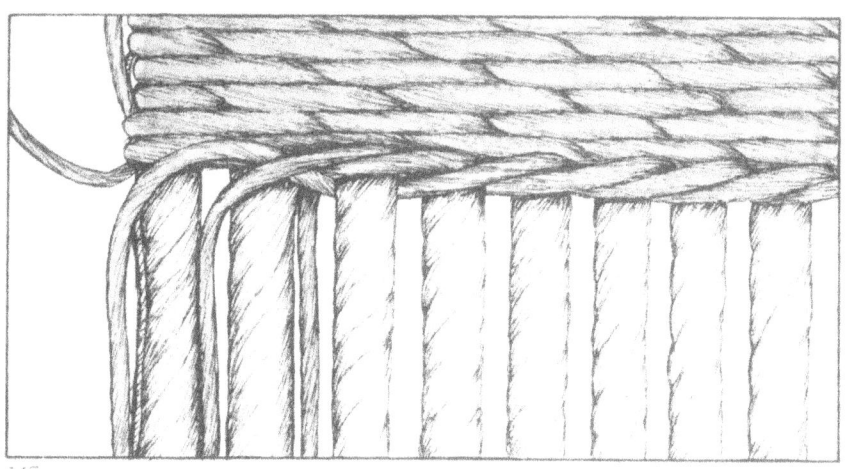

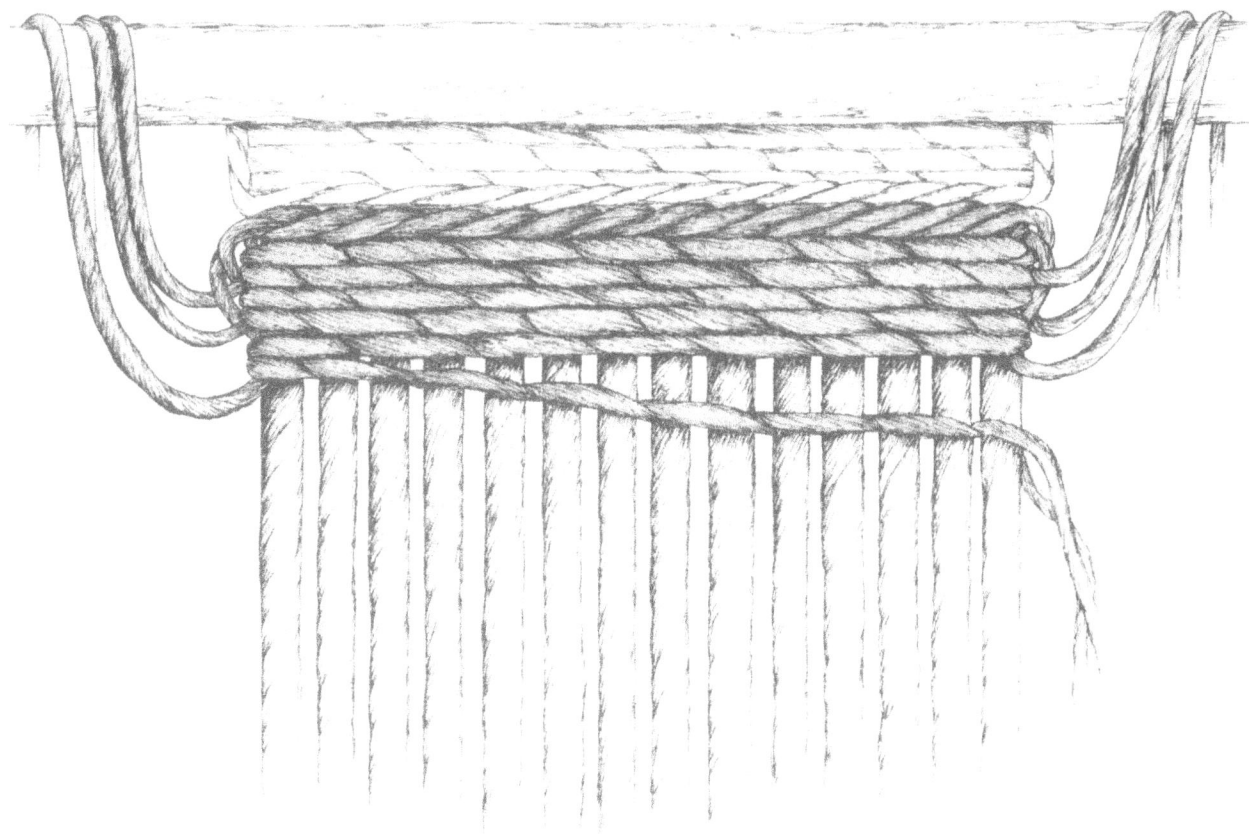

TOP CORNERS

On a square form, after the horizontal braid has been completed, the braid strands must turn at right angles and travel vertically. There is no longer any warp for them to braid into; therefore, they are inserted in the weft as it twines back and forth across a shape. Once the braids travel vertically, they appear on the front surface of the weaving, but cannot be seen on the back.

On the edge of a square shape, the braid strands are caught in the two-strand weft as it makes its turn. A braid strand is laid next to the edge warp before the weft turn is made, and is included in both rows of the turn (fig. 149).

148. In this form, the top corners have been turned.

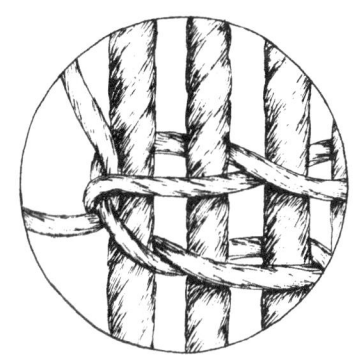

149. A braid strand caught in the turn of the weft

A Top Left Corner

STEP 1: Strands (a1), (b1), and (c1) from the horizontal braid are in position to go around a top left corner. They will be inserted successively in the first three turns of weft twining which occur under the braid (fig. 150).

STEP 2: Strand (a1) travels in front of (b1), behind (c1), and is caught in the first turn of weft twining. To keep the corner square, it is important to catch the braid strand in the row of twining which encircles one warp end at the turn (fig. 151).

STEP 3: Strand (b1) travels in front of (c1), behind (a1), and is caught in the second weft turn. Note that the second weft turn occurs in the third and fourth rows of twining (fig. 152).

STEP 4: Strand (c1) travels in front of (a1), behind (b1), and is caught in the third weft turn (fig. 153).

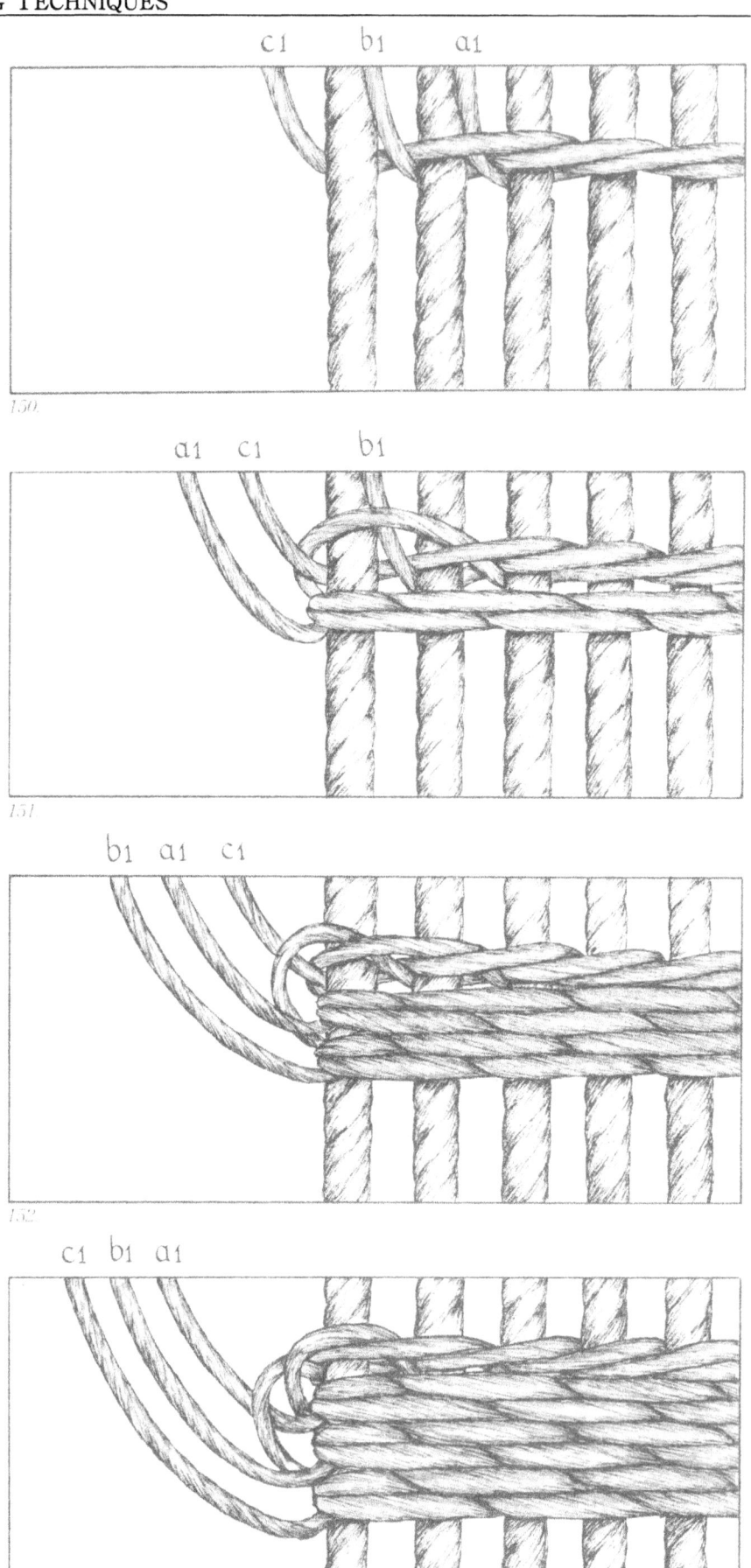

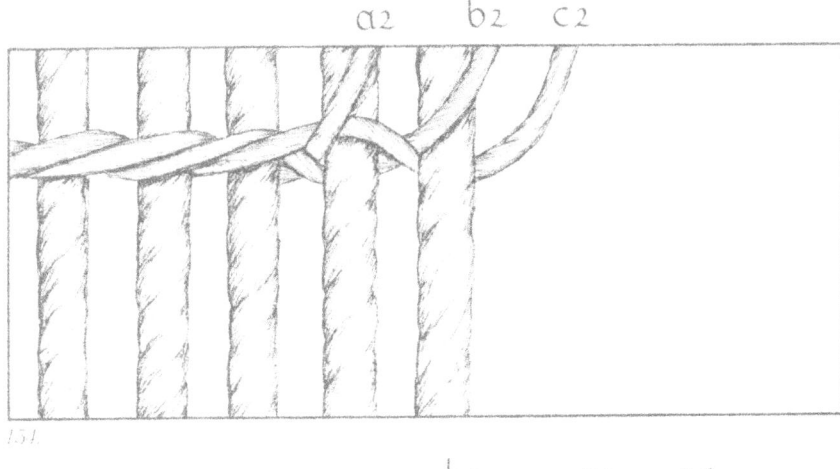

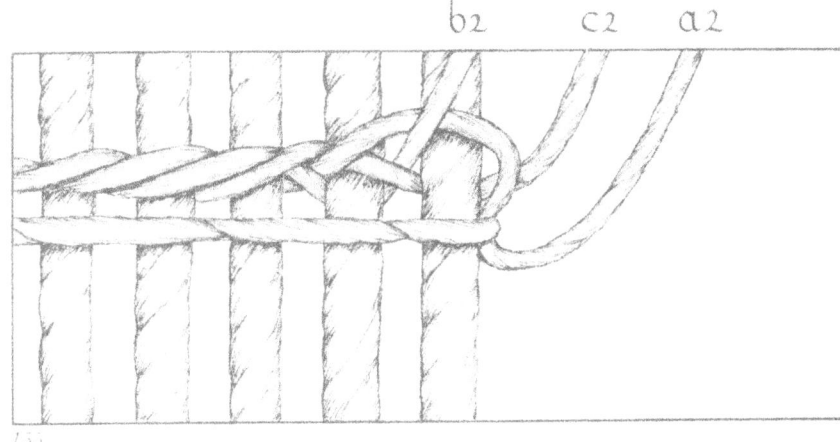

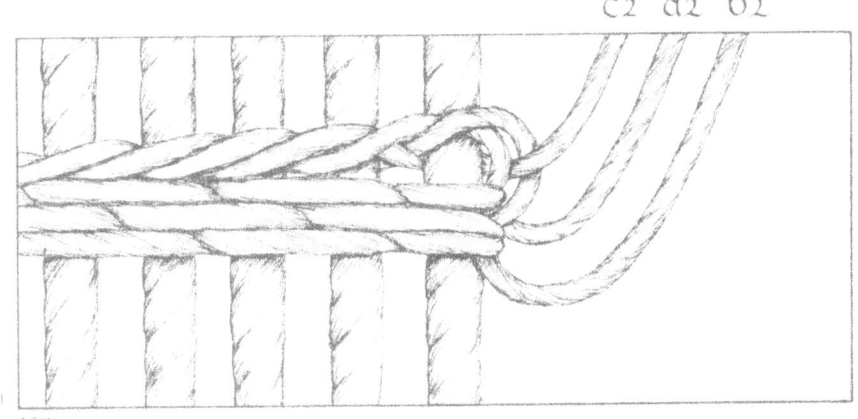

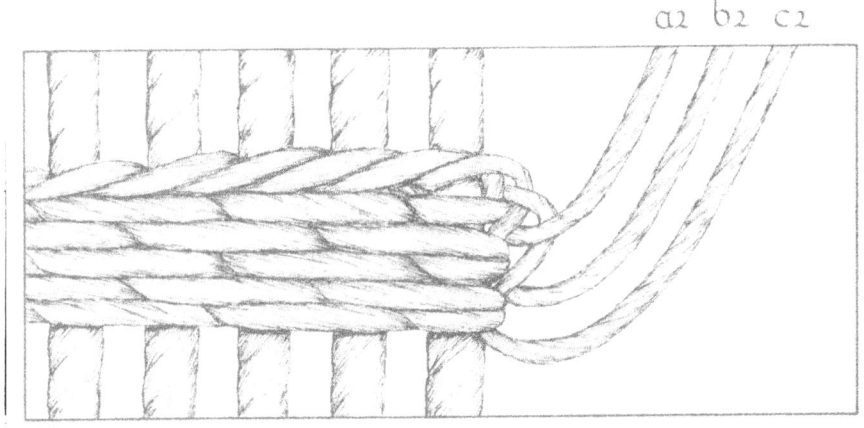

A TOP RIGHT CORNER

STEP 1: Strands (a2), (b2), and (c2) from the horizontal braid are in position to go around a top right corner. They will be held in place successively by the first row and second two turns of weft twining which occur under the braid (fig. 154).

STEP 2: Strand (a2) travels behind (b2), in front of (c2), and is caught in the beginning of the first row of two-strand twining. This weft row starts over a single warp end (fig. 155).

STEP 3: Strand (b2) travels behind (c2), in front of (a2), and is caught in the turn of the second and third rows of two-strand twining (fig. 156).

STEP 4: Strand (c2) travels behind (a2), in front of (b2), and is caught in the turn between the fourth and fifth rows of twining (fig. 157).

VERTICAL BRAIDED TWINING

STEP 1: Once a corner has been turned, the three strands on each side of the shape are in position to be braided and twined vertically (fig. 158).

STEP 2: On the left side, strand (a1) is removed from the cross-slat and dropped down in front of (b1) and behind (c1); on the right side, strand (a2) is removed from the cross-slat and dropped down behind (b2) and in front of (c2) (fig. 159).

STEP 3: Strands (a1) and (a2) are caught in the turn of a two-strand twining row and returned to the cross-slat (fig. 160).

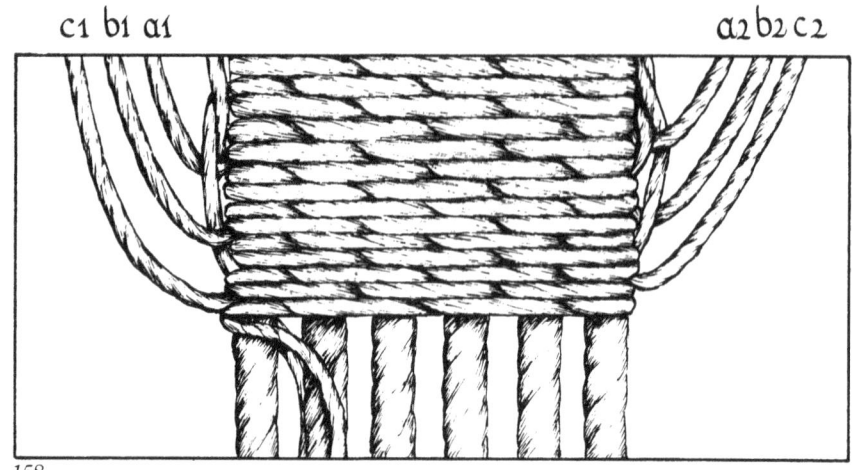

158.

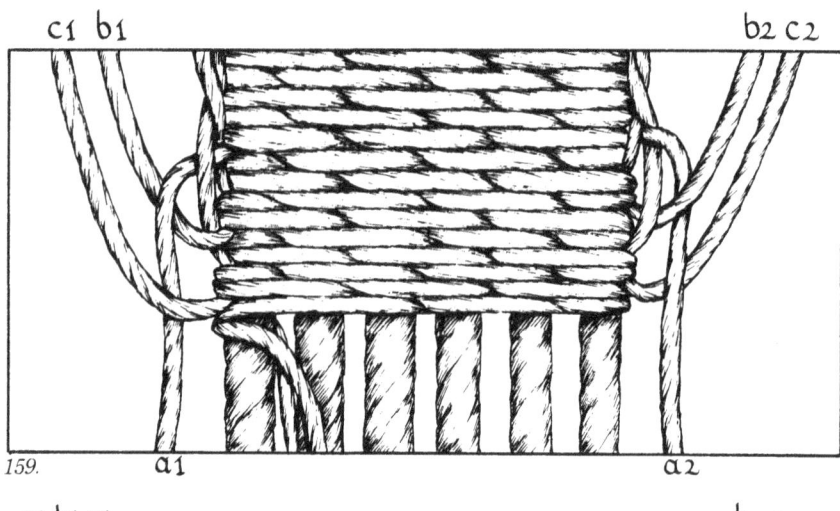

159.

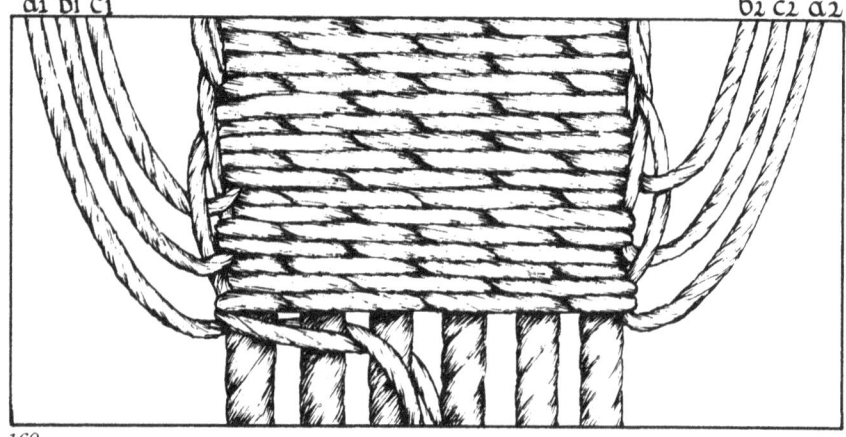

160.

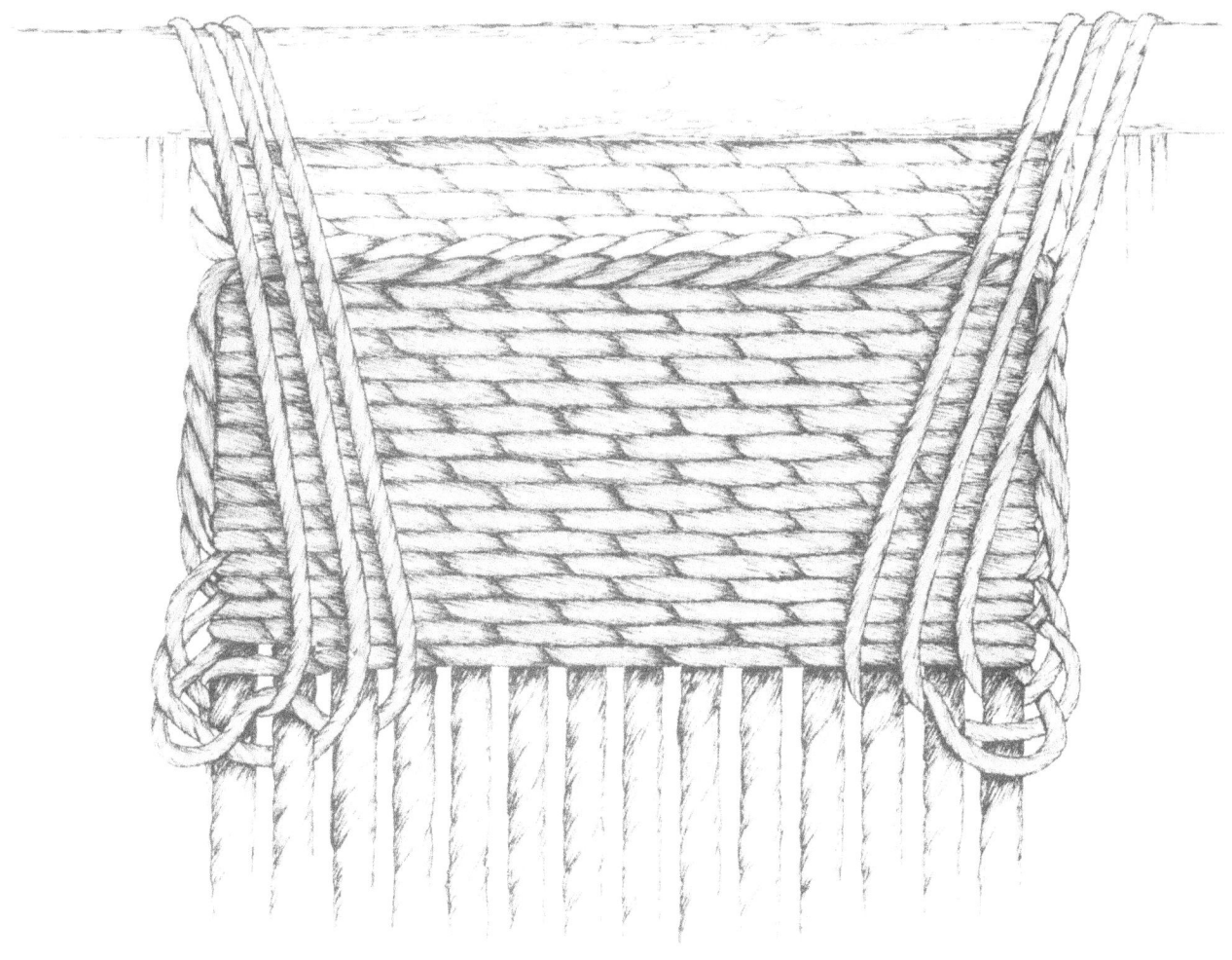

161. In this form, the bottom corners have been turned.

BOTTOM CORNERS

If a design on the pattern board has a shape which has square corners on its lower side, the vertical braids may be required to turn these corners and travel horizontally. In order to make a square corner on the lower side of a figure, the strands of the vertical braids must be caught in the three weft turns directly preceding the corner. Bringing them all close to the corner before it is braided will position them for a square corner rather than a curved one. Exceptionally tight corners are achieved by catching them in the three rows preceding the corner.

Bottom Left Corners

Step 1: Strands (a1), (b1), and (c1) from the vertical braid have been caught in the last three weft turns and are in position to braid around a left corner (fig. 162).

Step 2: Strand (a1) travels in front of (b1), behind (c1), and under the first warp end (fig. 163).

Step 3: Strand (b1) travels in front of (c1), over the first warp end, and under the second warp end (fig. 164).

Step 4: Strand (c1) travels over the first warp end and behind (a1), over the second warp end and in front of (b1), under the third warp end and up to the cross-slat. The strands are now in position to braid from left to right (fig. 165).

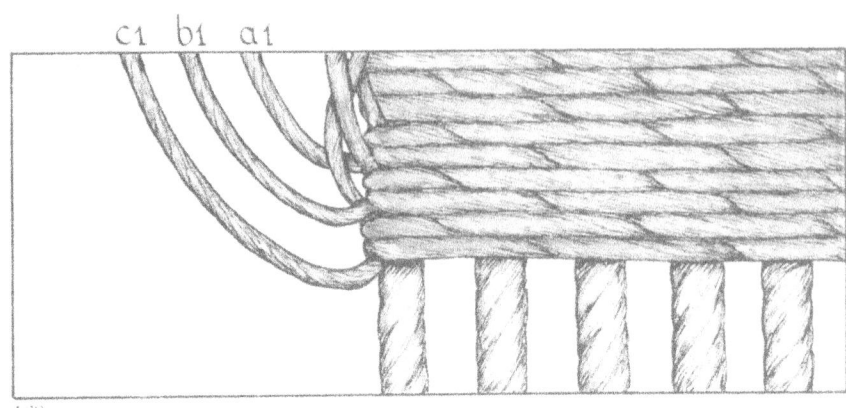

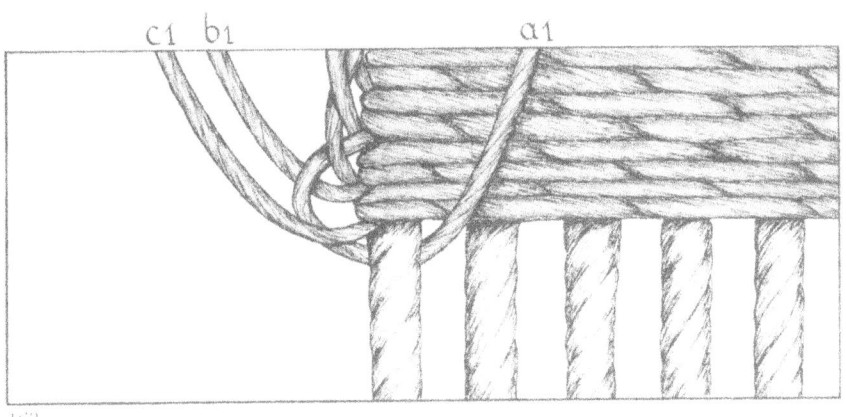

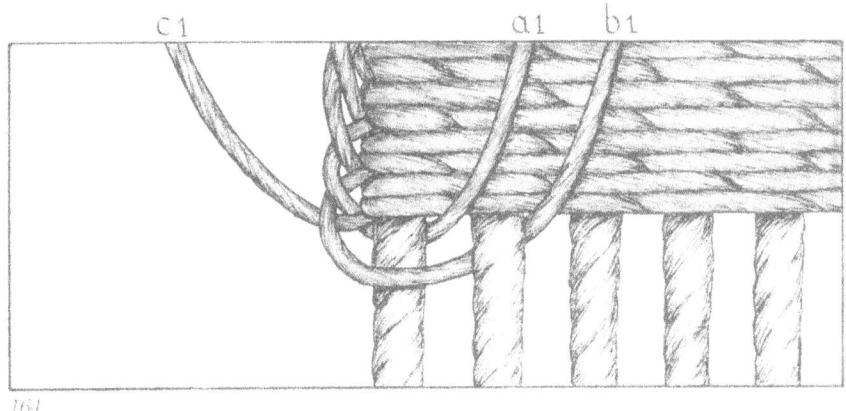

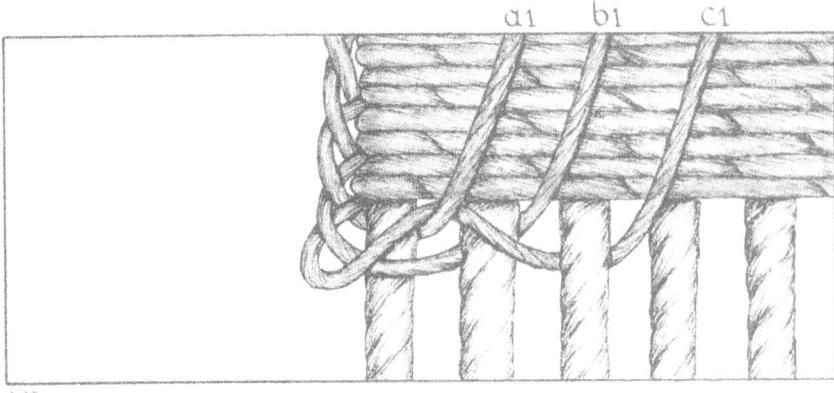

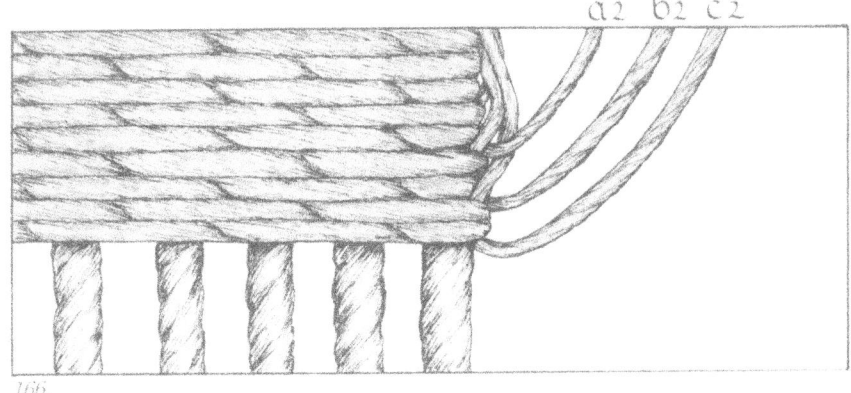

166.

BOTTOM RIGHT CORNERS

STEP 1: Strands (a2), (b2), and (c2) from the vertical braid have been caught in the last three weft turns and are in position to braid around a right corner (fig. 166).

STEP 2: Strand (a2) travels behind (b2), in front of (c2), and under the first warp end (fig. 167).

STEP 3: Strand (b2) travels behind (c2), over the first warp end, and under the second warp end (fig. 168).

STEP 4: Strand (c2) travels over the first warp end, in front of (a2), over the second warp end, behind (b2), under the third warp end and up to the cross-slat. The strands are now in position to braid from right to left (fig. 169).

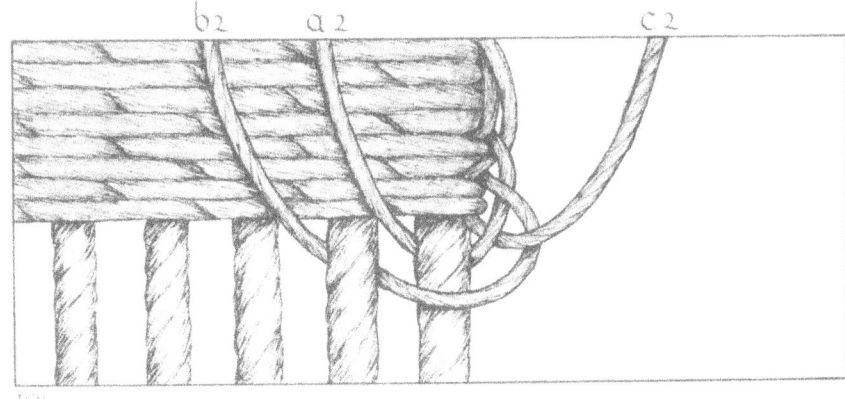

167.

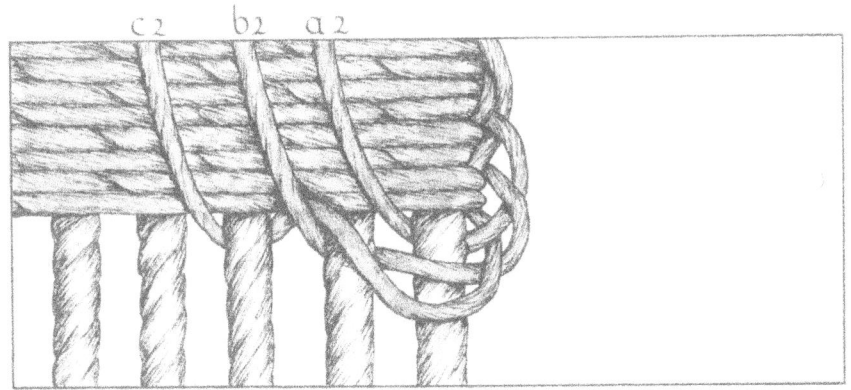

168.

169.

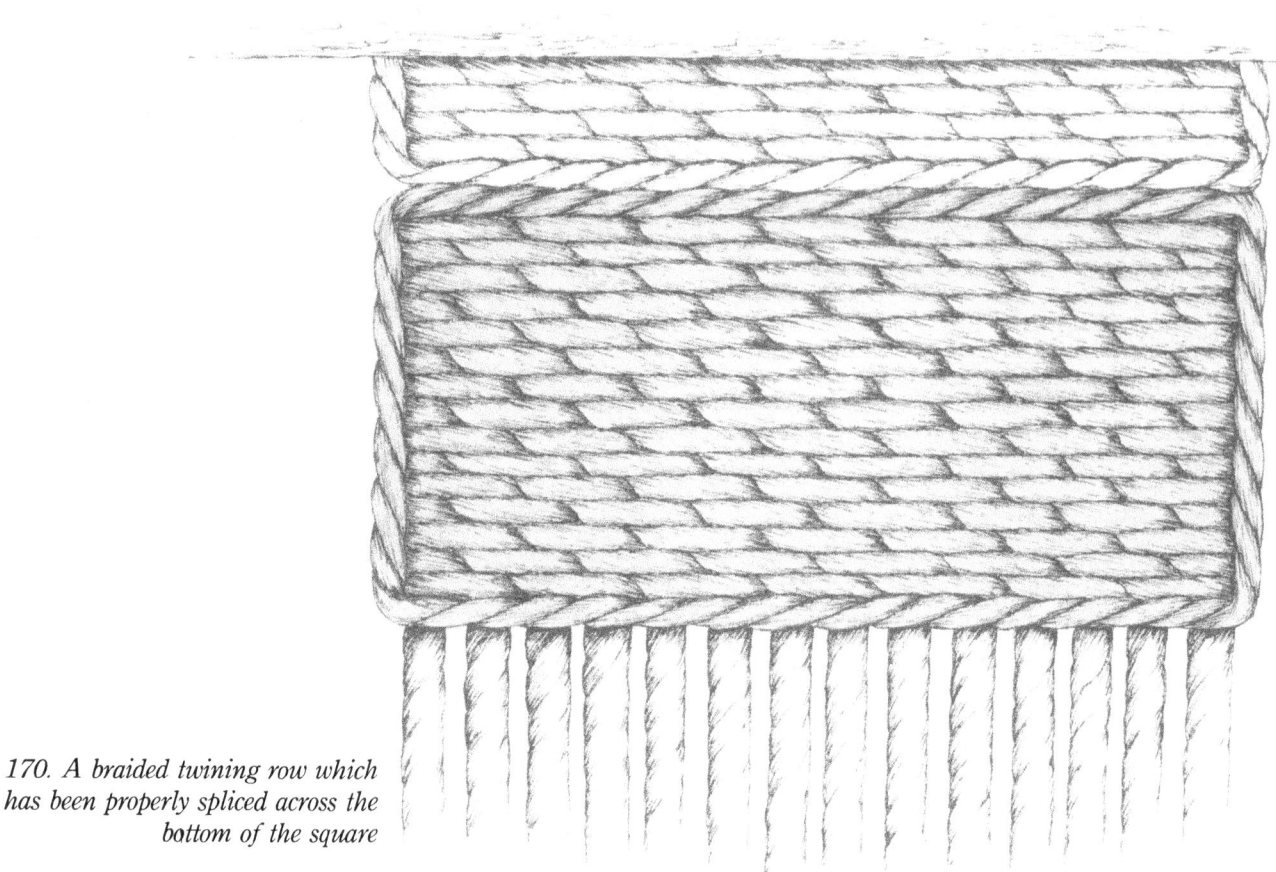

170. A braided twining row which
has been properly spliced across the
bottom of the square

Splicing a Braid

Once the bottom corners have been braided, each side of the braid can be twined toward the other along the lower edge of the shape until they meet and splice together. This splice is done so neatly that there is absolutely no evidence on the front of the weaving that two braids have been joined.

To start the bottom braid, the strands coming from the left side must first be twined toward the center of the shape. Braided twining from left to right entails a slightly different action than braided twining from right to left. This is done so that the angle of the braided line is maintained in an S twist.

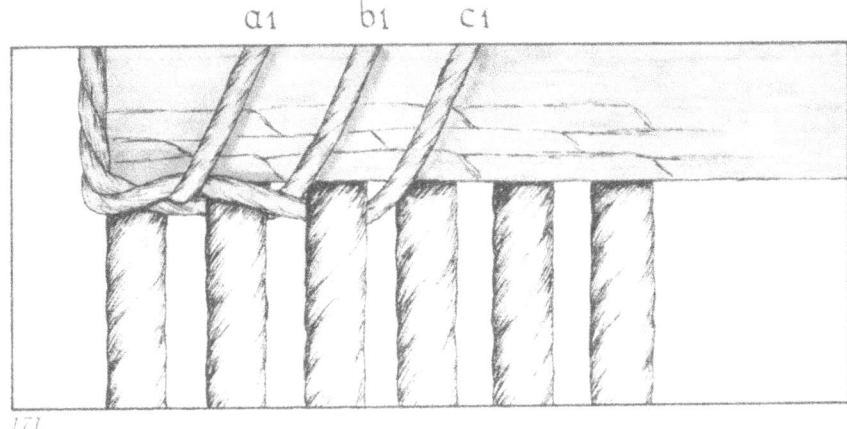

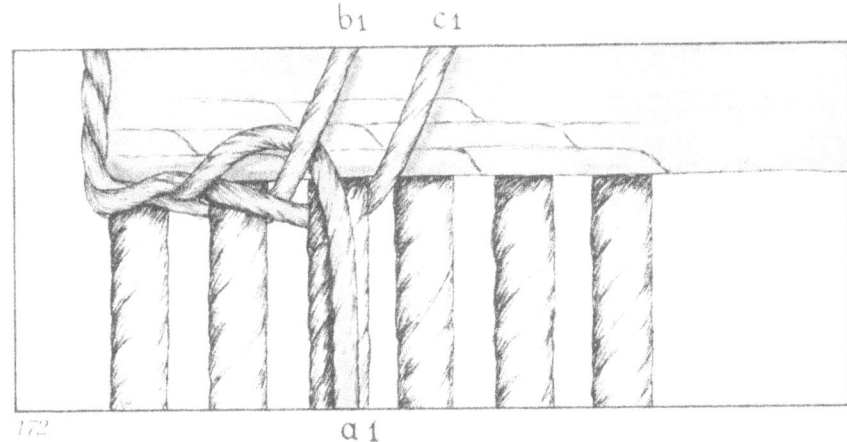

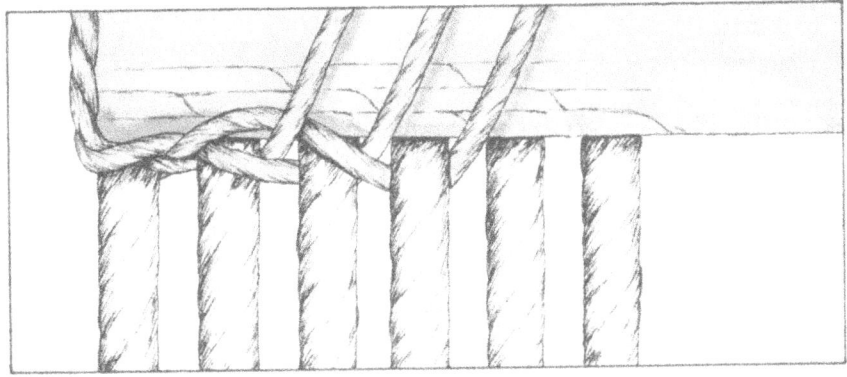

BRAIDED TWINING: LEFT TO RIGHT

STEP 1: Strands (a1), (b1), and (c1) have been braided around the bottom left corner and are ready to braid from left to right (fig. 171).

STEP 2: Strand (a1) is removed from the cross-slat and placed behind (b1), in front of (c1) (fig. 172).

STEP 3: Strand (a1) goes behind the next successive warp end and is then tightened into position and returned to the cross-slat. In the next step, (b1) repeats the action of (a1), traveling behind (c1) and in front of (a1), then under the next warp end (fig. 173).

SPLICING A BRAID
HORIZONTALLY: THE LEFT SIDE

STEP 1: After the bottom corner has been turned, the strands are worked from left to right to a point which the weaver chooses, somewhere toward the center of the shape. As there will be six tails to weave in once the braid is complete, it is better that they be kept away from the edges of the shape (fig. 174).

STEP 2: Strand (a1) travels behind (b1), in front of (c1) and drops to the back between warp ends #1 and #2 (fig. 175).

STEP 3: Strand (b1) travels behind (c1) and drops to the back between warp ends #2 and #3 (fig. 176).

STEP 4: Strand (c1) travels over warp end #3 and drops to the back between warp ends #3 and #4 (fig. 177).

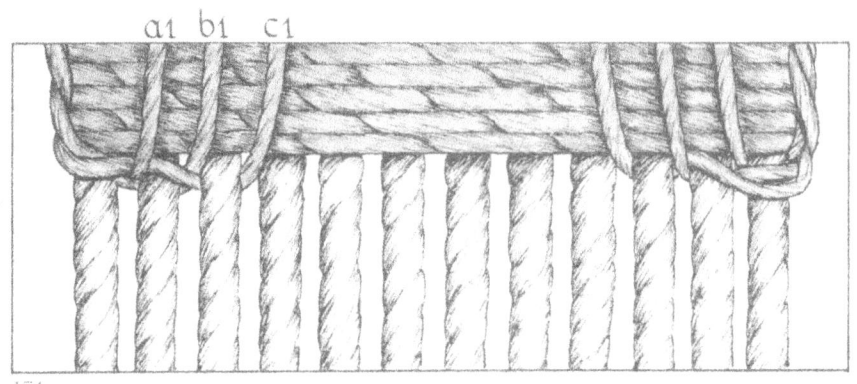

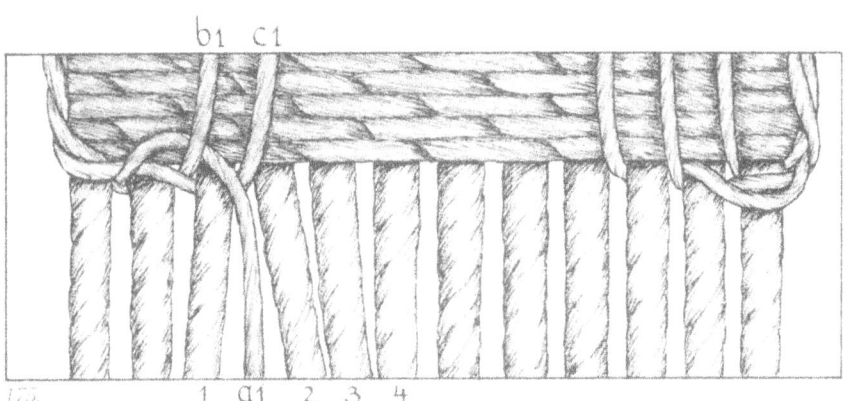

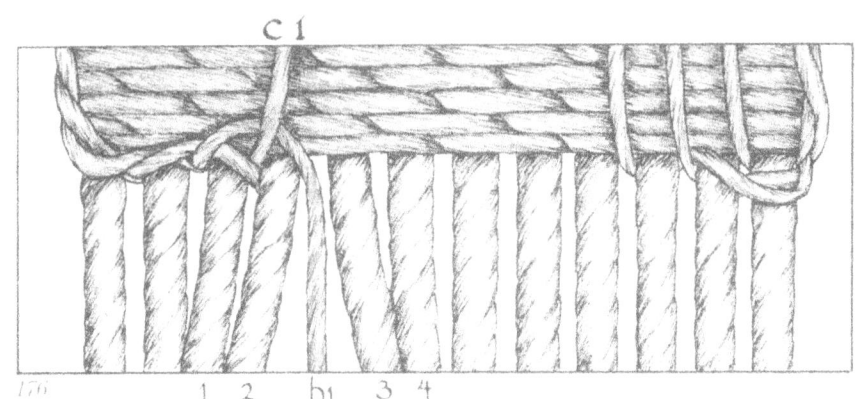

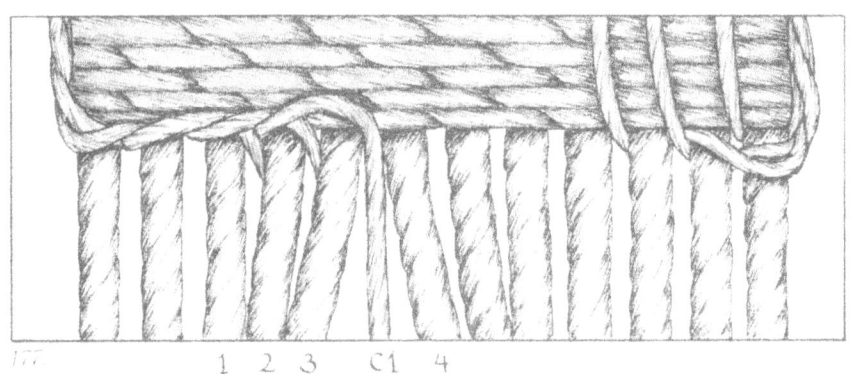

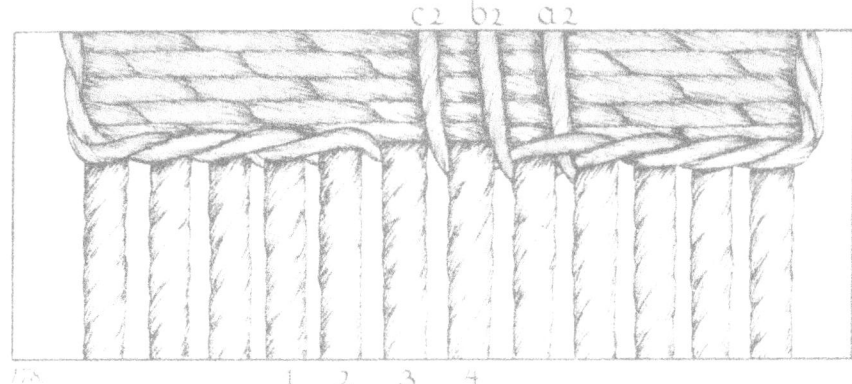

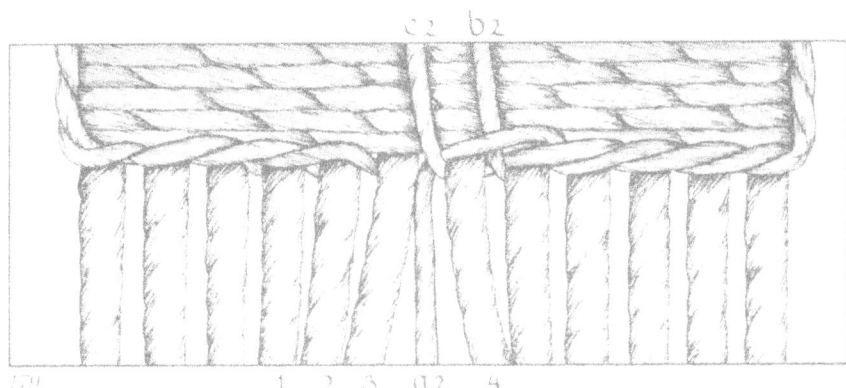

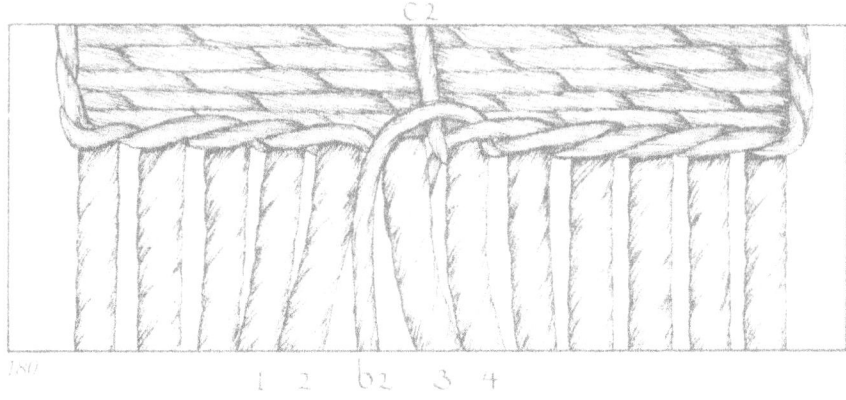

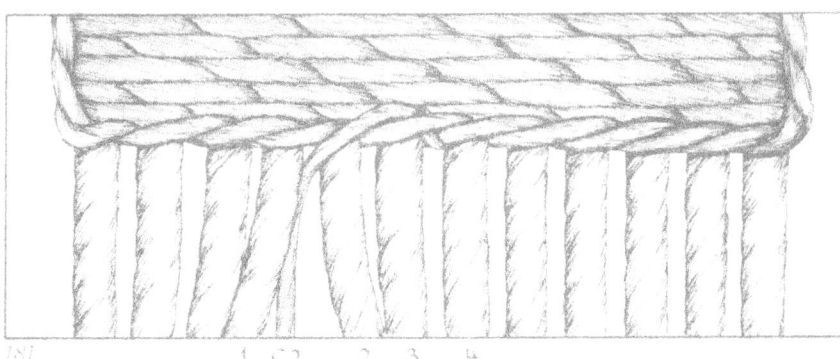

SPLICING A BRAID
HORIZONTALLY: THE RIGHT SIDE

STEP 1: After the corner has been turned at the bottom of the shape and the braid from the left has been dropped, the braid from the right is worked to the left until one warp end remains between (c2) and the final strand of the dropped braid (fig. 178).

STEP 2: Strand (a2) travels in front of (b2), behind (c2) and drops to the back between warp ends #3 and #4 (fig. 179).

STEP 3: Strand (b2) travels in front of (c2) and drops to the back between warp ends #2 and #3 (fig. 180).

STEP 4: Strand (c2) travels over warp end #2 and drops to the back between warp ends #1 and #2 (fig. 181).

All of the tails are tightened until the tension of the braid is even and the splice is perfect. The tails stay in the back if another braided row is to be finished. If not, they are dropped next to warp ends #1, #2, #3, and #4, twined for a short way with these warp ends, and then are cut off. Some weavers left them out and worked them into the weft from the back with a needle. In either case, they are not usually cut off flush with the weaving, but short tails are left sticking out on the back.

VERTICAL BRAIDS WHICH START IN THE WEFT

In some shapes, the braids which travel vertically are not ones which have rounded a corner, but are new braids which must be added to the weft.

ENTERING A BRAID VERTICALLY

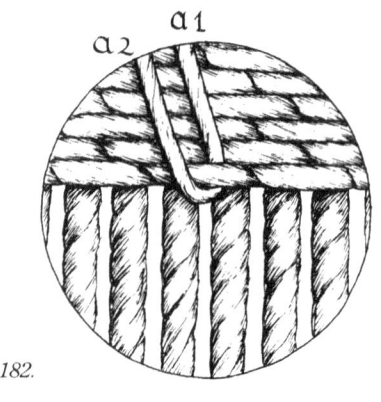

182.

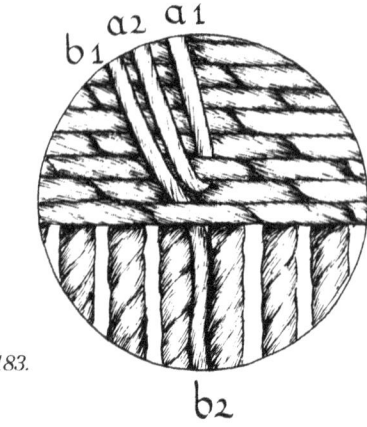

183.

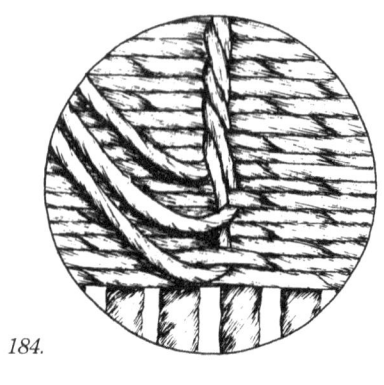

184.

STEP 1: A doubled weft strand is inserted around one weft segment, placing both tails, (a1) and (a2), over the cross-slat (fig. 182).

STEP 2: One weft row is twined underneath the inserted strand. In the next row, another strand is added, placing tail (b1) over the cross-slat and letting (b2) drop next to a warp end to be caught into the twining with the warp for one centimeter and then cut off (fig. 183).

STEP 3: The three strands are braided vertically, catching the strands in the weft and allowing the appropriate number of free weft rows between braid insertions (fig. 184).

ENTERING TWO BRAIDS VERTICALLY

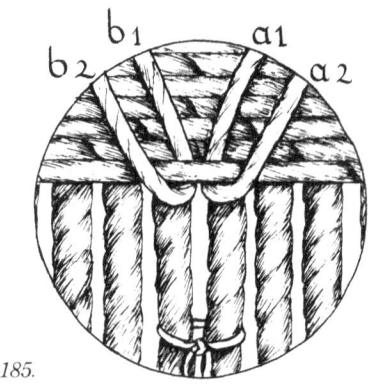
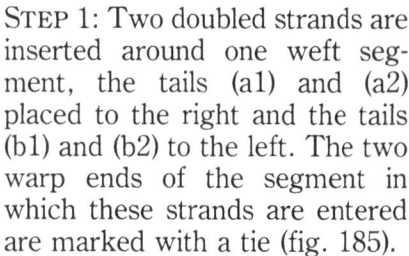

185.

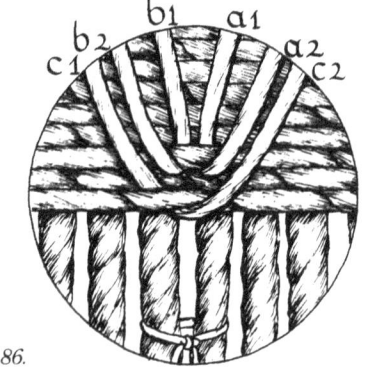

186.

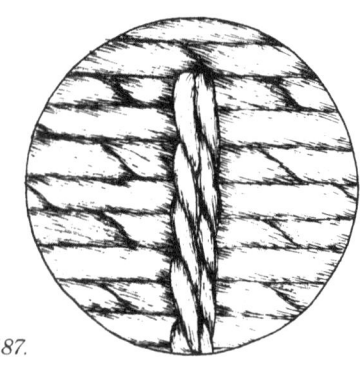

187.

STEP 1: Two doubled strands are inserted around one weft segment, the tails (a1) and (a2) placed to the right and the tails (b1) and (b2) to the left. The two warp ends of the segment in which these strands are entered are marked with a tie (fig. 185).

STEP 2: One weft row is twined underneath the inserted strands. In the next row, another strand is inserted in the segment which crosses the marked warp ends. This strand divides: (c1) goes to the left and (c2) to the right (fig. 186).

STEP 3: The strands are then braided vertically, (a1), (a2), and (c2) forming the tails of one braid and (b1), (b2), and (c1) the tails of the adjacent braid. Care must be taken to keep these two braids separate (fig. 187).

MULTIPLE BRAIDS WHICH FORM A POINT

Points, such as those in the crescents of the split Us, consist of at least six braids. These must be entered in a staggered manner in order to create a fine point.

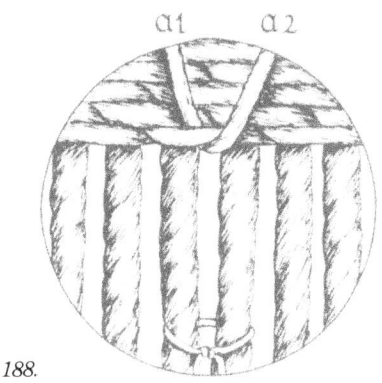

188.

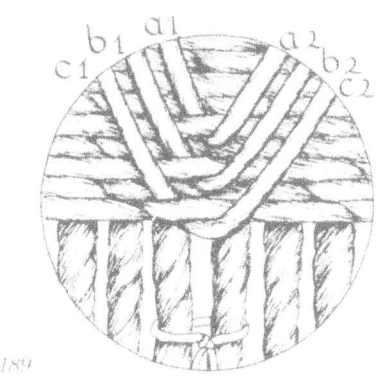

189.

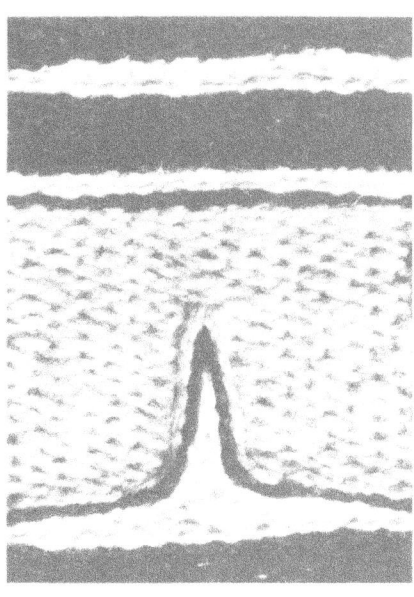

192. A fine point on a T-shaped crescent (CS)

STEP 1: A doubled strand is inserted around one weft segment, placing (a1) to the left and (a2) to the right. The two warp ends which are encircled by the weft segment in which this strand was entered are marked with a small tie (fig. 188).

STEP 2: One weft row is twined underneath the inserted strand. In the next row, another strand is inserted in the weft segment which crosses the marked warp ends. Its tails, (b1) and (b2), should be split as in Step 1. Repeat this process one more time, splitting the tails of (c) in the same manner (fig. 189).

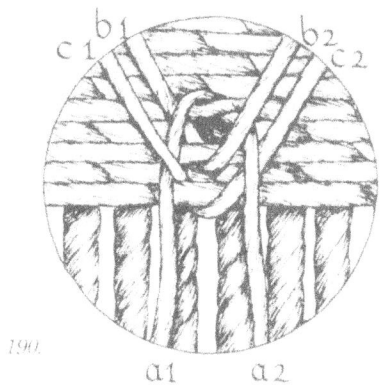

190.

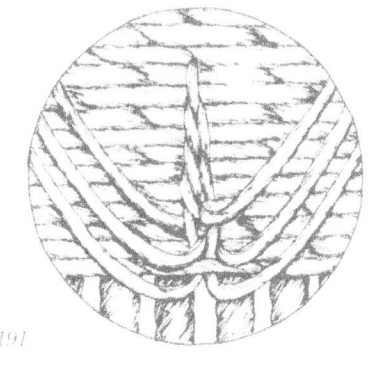

191.

STEP 3: The strands are braided, (a1), (b1), and (c1) being used for one braid and (a2), (b2), and (c2) for the other. Strand (a1) drops in front of (b1) and behind (c1), and is caught in the appropriate weft row. Strand (a2) drops in behind (b2) and in front of (c2) before it is caught in the same weft row (fig. 190).

STEP 4: This method of entering the braid strands will produce a pointed line. The line expands as more braids are entered in the same manner within it (fig. 191).

VERTICAL WEFT TWINING

There are a few occasions when two-strand twining also leaves the warp and travels vertically. This might happen in the long lines which divide the design field into three panels or when a vertical crescent needs broadening. Vertical twining is only done in white areas.

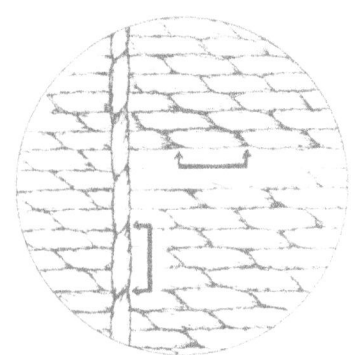

193. A number of weft rows are twined so that the vertically twined segment is equal in length to its horizontal counterpart.

194. The left side of the resultant form shown here contains vertical two-strand twining. (CS)

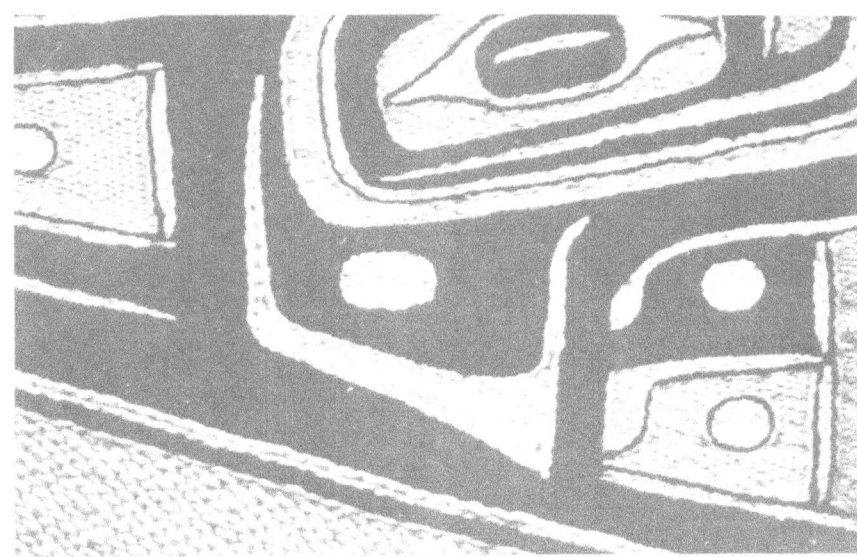

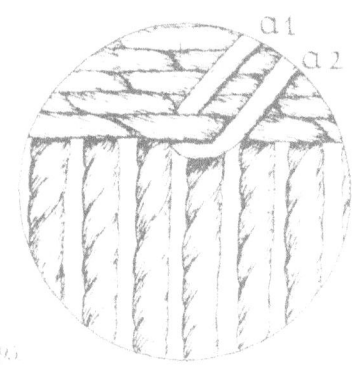

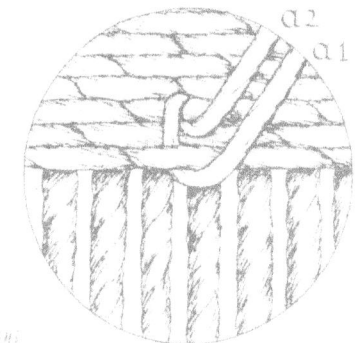

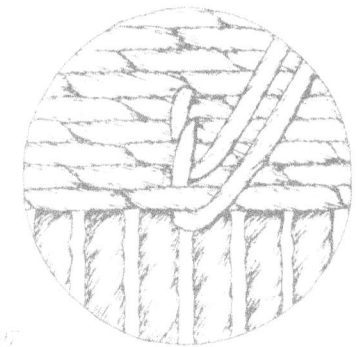

STEP 1: To begin twining vertically, a doubled white strand is inserted around one segment of the weft (fig. 195).

STEP 2: Strand (a1) is moved down to the left of (a2) and caught in one segment of the weft row (fig. 196).

STEP 3: Twining is continued in this manner, the upper strand dropping down to the left of the lower strand and catching in the appropriate weft row (fig. 197).

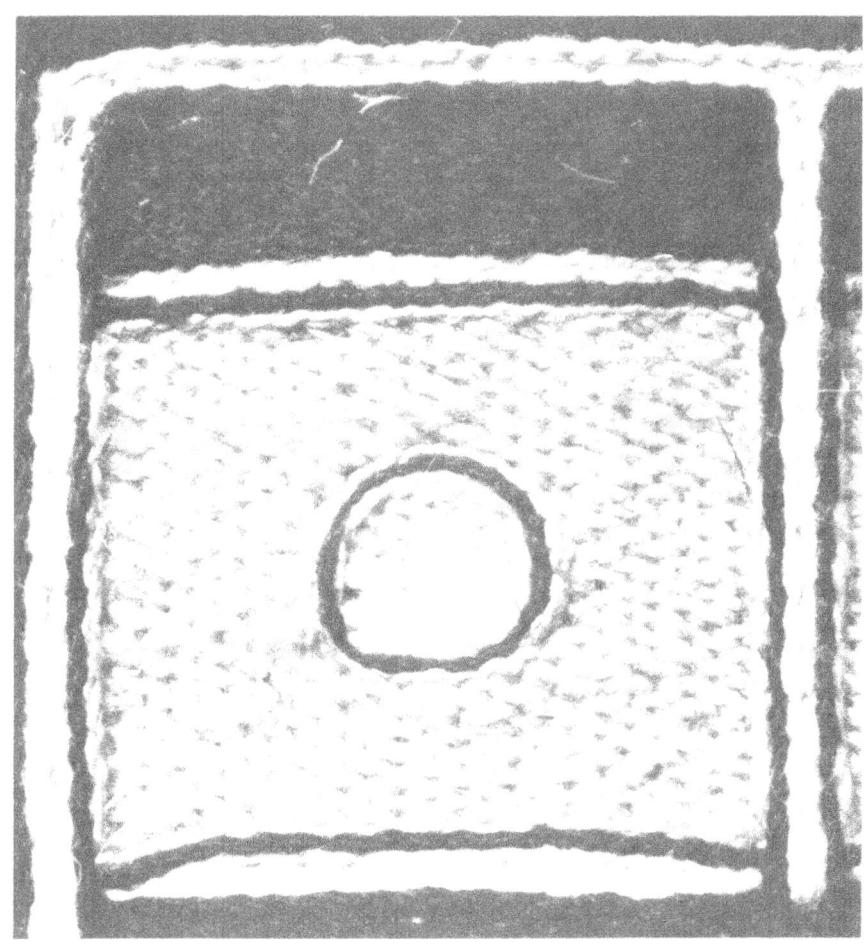

198. Small braided cords surround, outline, and even create the design forms. (Private Collection: CS)

THE USE OF BRAIDS

A braided cord in the same color as the weft surrounds every shape. Therefore, before a color area is twined, a braid of the shape's color must be inserted. This braid must travel across the top, around the sides, and underneath the shape. It need not be physically the same braid on all sides, but must give the appearance that a single braid of the weft color surrounds the form.

Outlines in black may also surround the figures. These outlines are set off by the white background. The outlines and the white ground are always made of braids. The white ground may also have rows of two-strand twining within it if the line needs widening.

The clarity of the woven figures is due in part to the twists of the braiding and twining. The braid appears as an S-twist cord on the surface of the fabric, in direct opposition to the Z twist of the weft twining. This fact emphasizes the presence of the outlines and strengthens them visually, especially in a horizontal row.

The commercial yarns which were sometimes used after the European traders had made contact with the Indians were made of a four-ply, S-twist yarn. The appearance of these yarns in braiding is quite different from the native yarns. The S twist of the ply parallels the S-twist of the braided line; the braid no longer resembles cordage but looks, instead, like a highly twisted yarn.

THE PLACEMENT OF BRAIDS OVER A JOIN

As the braids travel vertically and are worked into the weft, they completely cover the joins which are underneath them. Almost all joins have braids which travel over them; the presence of these braids cleans the uneven edges of the joins and clearly defines the figures which they help to form.

Except for the white braid at the top and bottom of the blanket, braids always travel in multiples. Two rows of braiding form the smallest group and as many as nine rows occur in some areas. The number of braids in any given area is determined by the design. The choice of the particular type of join to be used depends upon the number of braids which will travel over it and its position in the figure. Certain joins, such as the dovetail, would not be used in a pattern area which only calls for two braids.

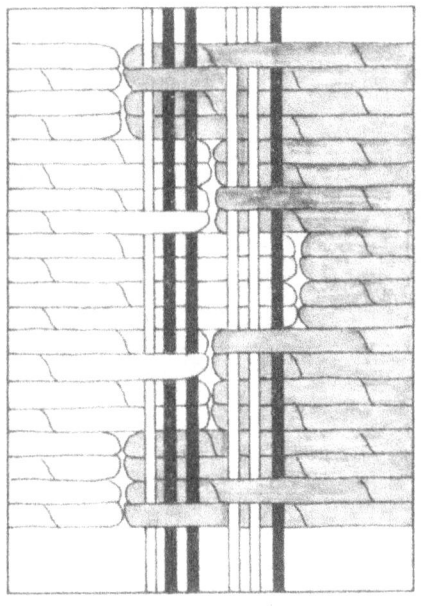

199. Braids placed over an interlock join

THE INTERLOCK JOIN AND BRAID PLACEMENT

Any number of braids can travel over an interlock join. These braids are generally divided near the middle, half on one side of the join and half on the other (fig. 199). If more than two braids fall on one side, they are caught in the segment of the weft turn which encloses two warp ends, allowing them room to lie flat next to each other. If two or four braids are placed over the join, resulting in one or two being caught on each side, they are inserted in the segment of the weft turn which encloses a single warp end. This holds them close to the join.

THE DOVETAIL JOIN AND BRAID PLACEMENT

Dovetail joins need to be covered with many braids and are generally used between the black and yellow vertical borders. Here, they are always covered with one black, two white, two black, and one yellow braid (fig. 200). As the dovetail itself travels around two warp ends, the braids are divided so that three lie over one warp end and three over the other. Large weft strands are usually used for these braids and they amply cover the spectacular patterns which some weavers incorporate in their dovetail joins.

The braid strands are always caught in the segment of the weft turn which travels over two warp ends. Because they are braiding vertically and need free rows between each insertion, their placement in the colored wefts changes with the movement of the dovetail join.

200. Braids placed over a dovetail join

THE DRAWSTRING JOIN AND BRAID PLACEMENT

With the use of a drawstring join, the braids are usually divided in the following manner: one braid runs down one side of the join and all the other braids run down the other side (fig. 201). The strands of multiple braids are caught in the segment of the weft turn which encloses two warp ends, while the strand of the single braid is caught in the segment which encloses a single warp end. This method allows enough room for the multiple strands to lie flat and secures the single braid closely to the other braids and to the join.

A general scheme for the positioning of braids over a drawstring join divides the blanket in the middle (fig. 202). The forms on the left side carry their multiple braid strands on the left side of the drawstring join. The forms on the right side of the blanket carry their

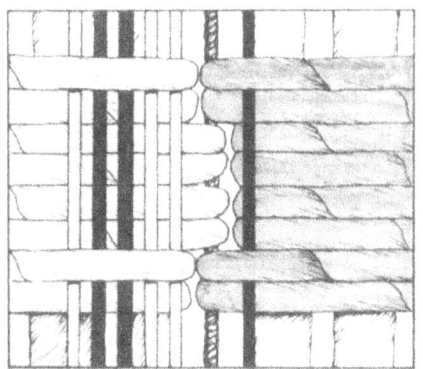

201. Braids placed over a drawstring join

multiple braid strands on the right side of the drawstring join. Figures in the very center, if surrounded by a drawstring, will most likely divide the braids evenly between the two sides of the join. Some weavers, however, did not divide the braids at all, but put them all on one side of the drawstring.

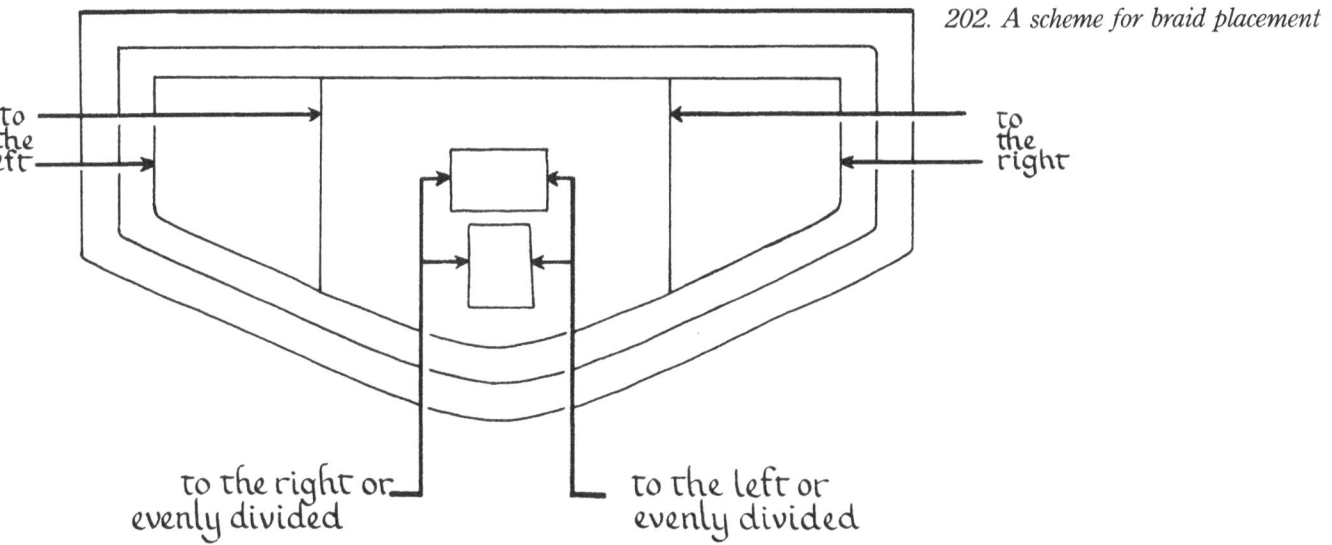

202. A scheme for braid placement

ADDED WARP ENDS

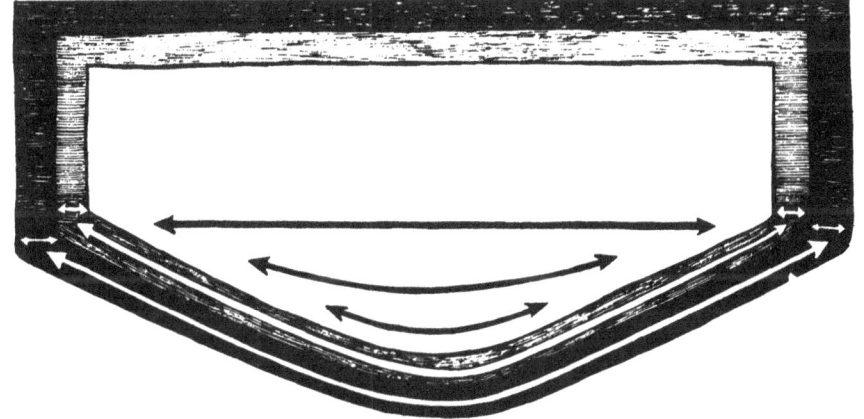

203. Direction of the weft in the woven field

The woven field of a Dancing Blanket forms a five-sided figure (fig. 203). The top of this figure is a horizontal line; the two sides do not flare out, but run absolutely perpendicular to the top line. The weft within this part of the weaving lies parallel to the top border. Changes in weft direction within the design field due to construction demands of individual forms do occur, but the overall direction of the weft in this section is horizontal. The remaining two sides form a shallow V at the bottom of the blanket. The weft within this V angles slightly. Within the black and yellow borders, the weft runs parallel to the outside edge of the bottom of the blanket.

When the weft changes its angle of weave in the bottom black and yellow borders, the warp ends automatically move to lie

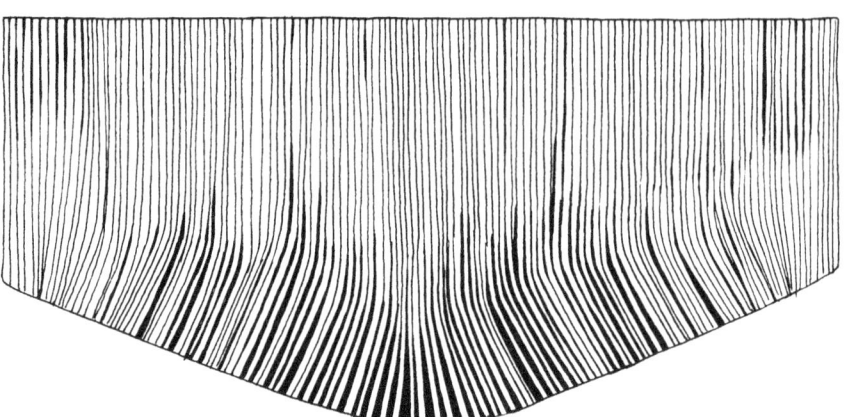

204. Direction of the warp in the woven field

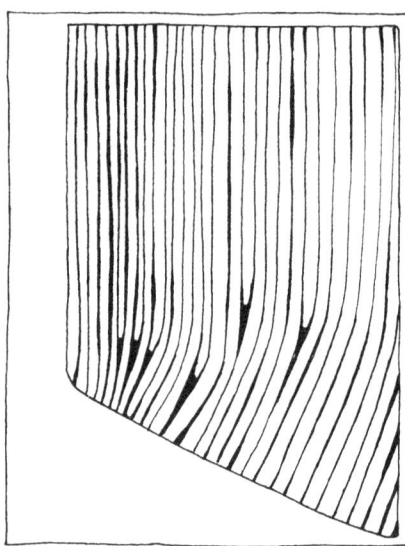

205. Cut warp ends at the outer corner of a blanket

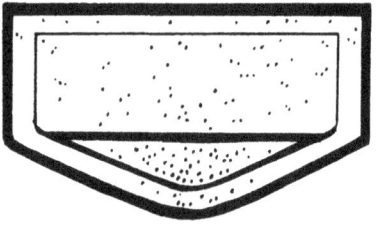

206. Approximate position of added warp ends

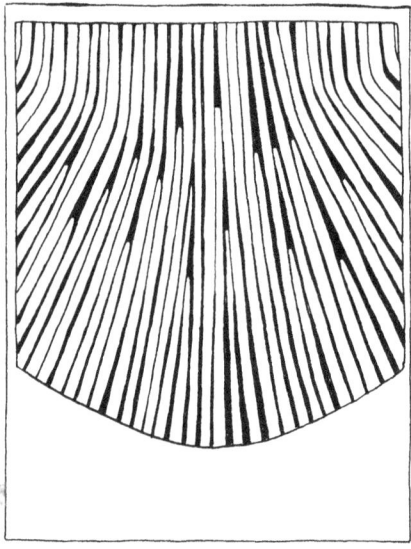

207. Warp ends added at the point of the V

perpendicular to the fell of the weft (fig. 204). This movement of the warp ends is inherent in the mechanics of twining; the weaver does not intentionally change the path of the warp ends, but the action of her fingers as she twines produces the change. In the center of the V, the warp ends will be widely spaced; at the outer edges they will bunch together.

In basketry, as the shape of the basket enlarges, more splints are added to ensure that long, weak weft segments do not occur. This is true, too, of the Dancing Blanket. Warp ends must be added in the bottom V so that the segments of the weft will be the same length as they were in the rest of the blanket. At the outer corners of the blanket, the bottom borders meet the side borders (fig. 205). The turning of the warp ends forces them to pile up. The weaver eliminates some of them so that the weaving will lie flat.

The weaver knows ahead of time that the bottom V of the blanket will be worked at an angle to the main body. To prepare for this, she adds warp ends in the entire design field, the majority of them being added in the triangular space at the bottom. As many as 50 to 80 warp ends are added across this area, the greatest concentration of them occurring near the point of the V (fig. 206). The range of the overall number of added warp ends in Dancing Blankets is from 50 to 200, the average addition being about 100. One-fourth of these may be added in the top portion of the woven field, the majority in the bottom triangular space.

METHODS OF ADDING WARP ENDS

There are two methods of adding warp ends once the weaving is in progress. Both methods may be employed in the same blanket. The effect of each method on the front of the weaving is the same; use of one or the other depends on the weaver's preference.

In the method shown in figure 209, a length of warp yarn is measured, knotted at one end, and simply inserted between two warp ends wherever it is needed. The knot pokes out to the back and can be cut off or left. Unless the knots have been worn off in the dance, it is very easy to see where warp ends were added on the back of the blanket.

In the method shown in figure 210, the new warp end is measured, cut, and then inserted alongside a warp end in the blanket. It is worked with this warp end for a short distance before the two are separated. In this way, the new warp end is secured firmly in the weft. This is a direct adaptation from basketry techniques.

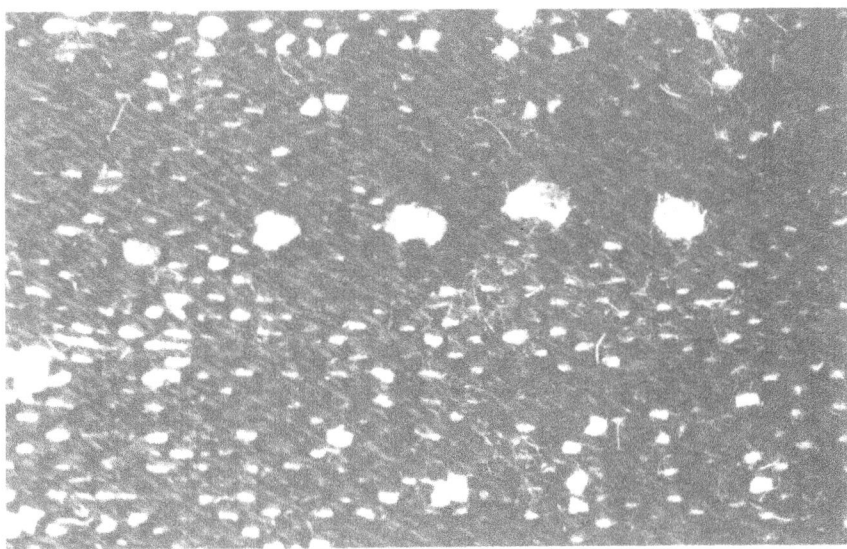

208. *Warp ends added in the middle of the bottom black border (CS)*

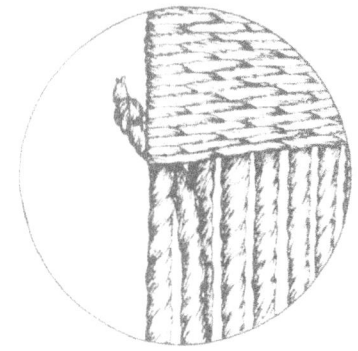

209. *An added warp end inserted between two warp ends*

In either case, the addition of the new warp ends must occur at a place within the design where it will not interrupt the rhythm of a twined row. These places occur whenever a new color is started, whether it be on the top or the side of a figure. If warp ends are to be added in the middle of a single colored area, multiples of two should be added so that the twined sequence is not disturbed.

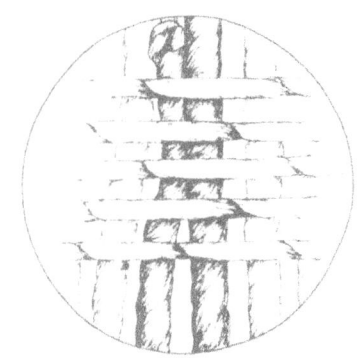

210. *An added warp end inserted alongside one warp end*

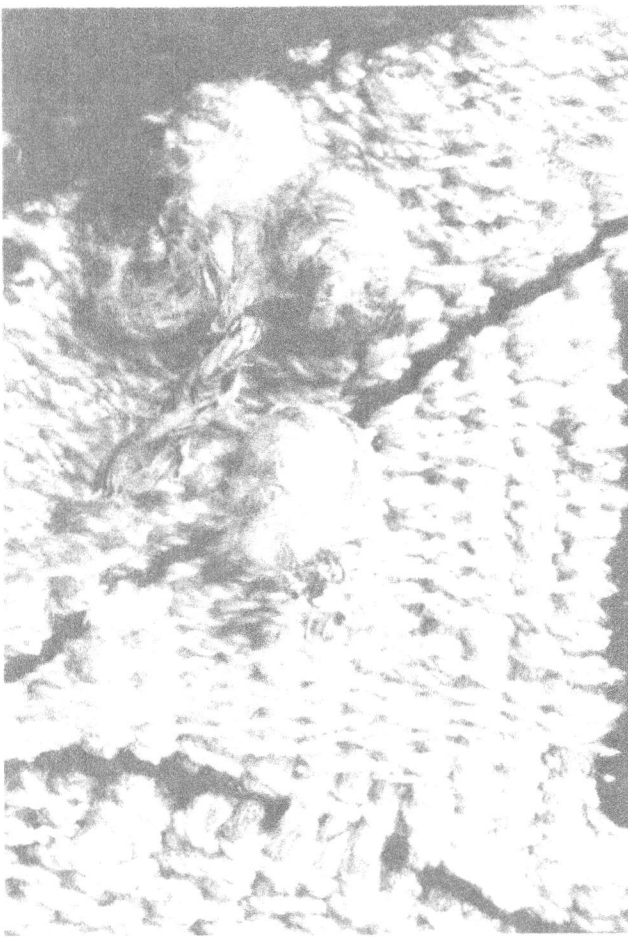

211. *Warp ends added with a knot (CS)*

Added and Deleted Warp Ends in Expanded and Contracted Shapes

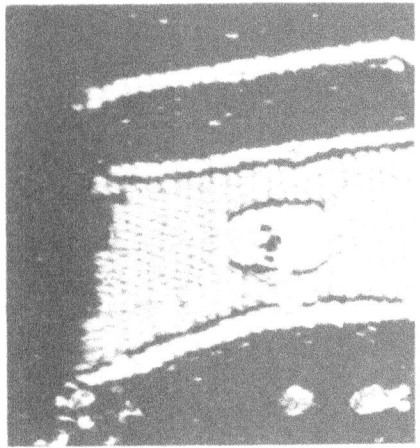

213. The side of a ∪ shape in which a stepped interlock was used to expand the form (CS)

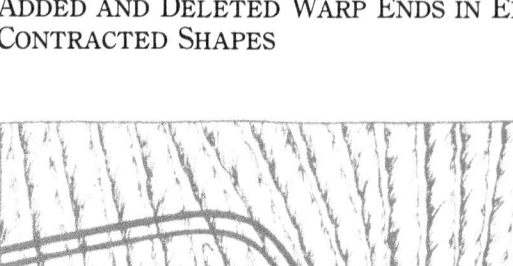

212. Added and deleted warp ends

Warp ends are added and deleted not only to shape the entire blanket, but also as a technique for expanding and contracting the figures within the design field (fig. 212). The advantage of this method of shaping is that an interlock join can run smoothly between two warp ends while the form itself changes size. Expanding or contracting forms in this manner may also force warp ends in the surrounding areas to be added or deleted in order that the weaving lie flat.

Two methods are used to shape a steep diagonal: added or deleted warp ends, or a stepped interlock. In either method, braids travel over the joins; the appearance on the front of the weaving in each case is the same.

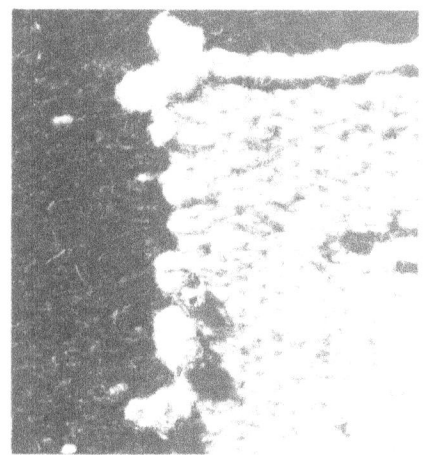

214. The side of a ∪ shape in which three warp ends were deleted to contract the form (CS)

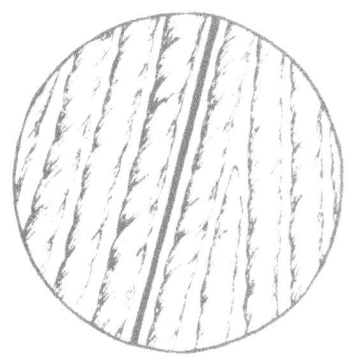

215. An added warp end

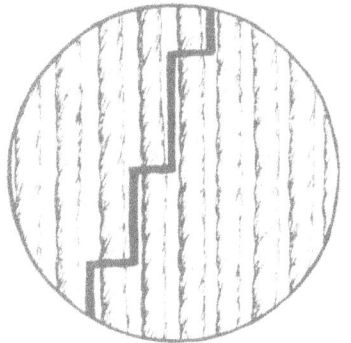

216. A stepped interlock

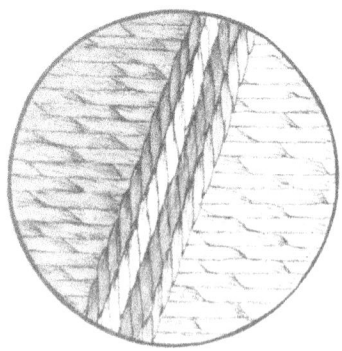

217. The appearance of the joins in figures 215 and 216 on the front of the weaving

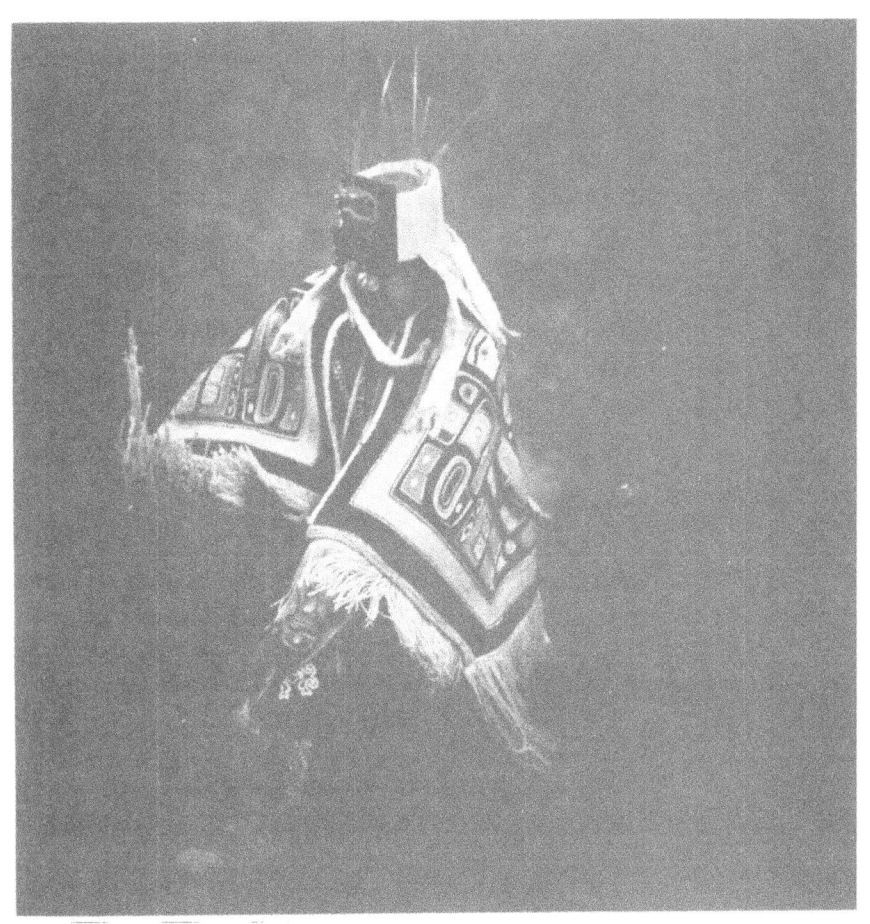

PART

WEAVING
A DANCING
BLANKET

IV

THE WOMAN WHO
WOVE IN THE WILDERNESS

Generations ago, in a time when weaving was not commonly practiced among the peoples of the coast, there lived a beautiful young woman whose greatest desire was to perfect the art of weaving. Her beauty was so great that she had hosts of admirers among the men of her tribe and she found it difficult to find time enough for her work. Consequently, she decided on a life of seclusion and chose to live far away by the side of an unknown lake in the great northern wilderness.

The stream which flowed from the small mountain lake twisted and tumbled, turning into a great river as it made its way to the sea. Certain salmon swam in this river and soon they heard of the woman's presence. Stimulated by curiosity, they journeyed through the swiftly flowing currents until they came at last to the place where the woman lived. When she saw them, she was concerned for her safety. "Come and live with me in my house," she beseeched. "Do not return to the salt waters; I do not wish for my people to know where I am living." The salmon did not heed her pleas. Their curiosity satisfied, they chose instead to make the easy journey back to the sea. Here they told the tribes of the beautiful woman who lived and wove in the wilderness.

One day, as the woman was bathing in the cool waters of the lake, she was startled by the sudden appearance of two strangers. She demanded to know who they were and on what business they had come. One of the men stepped forward and proclaimed that he was a great chief, come from the coast to tell her how the people mourned her absence. He related that after many fruitless inquiries as to her whereabouts, they had finally been told by their friends the salmon where they could find her. The journey to the lake had been a difficult one, but now that they were there, he wished to offer his son to her in marriage. "My son is a mighty hunter," said the chief. "He offers his heart for yours."

After considering a while, the woman accepted his proposal on the condition that they promise to live an isolated life until her death. The two men consented, and taking the chief's son as her husband, the young woman showed them the way to her house. It was built of strong timbers and was massive in proportion. The entrance was through an opening in the roof and they descended by means of a ladder. Inside, the men saw beautiful panels inlaid with white wood and a wonderful array of weavings. There were blankets, capes, leggings, aprons, and beautiful ceremonial robes. The men felt the soft wool of one of the finest robes and asked where she had obtained the material to weave it. She told them it was the inner coat of the goat who lived on the summit of the mountain. The chief's son volunteered to hunt the goat on the following day, if she would go with him.

Now these beings, whom the woman believed to be worthy of her love and confidence, were in reality Raven and Marten masquerading in the form of men. While the woman slept, they made their plans. During the hunting trip, Marten was to learn all he could of the art of weaving while Raven would stay behind to take an inventory of the house.

With the rising of the sun, the "men" set forth to carry out their mischief. The day was long and successful; by nightfall they had accomplished all they set out to do. Under cover of darkness, when the woman once more slept, the swift Raven and strong Marten carried off all of her woven goods. They flew with them to the peoples of the coast and distributed them as free gifts. As a result of this, weaving became common among all of the tribes. The most wonderful woolen robes, unique in design and exquisite in color, were reserved by the Chilkat chiefs for their ceremonies and for the dance.

To Sing the Song of a Woman

Florence Shotridge in her 1913 article, "The Life of a Chilkat Indian Girl," described the seclusion which accompanied the first months of a young girl's maturing. She claimed that, "A girl who goes through this training can, when entrusted with anything, whether great or small, be relied upon to see it properly."

When a young girl first showed signs of her coming womanhood, she was taken by her mother to a special room in the house in which she lived. Here she would remain for a season if she was a commoner, four seasons if a daughter of nobility. The time that she spent in seclusion was a time of learning in preparation for her life as a woman.

Her first four days were ones of fasting, drinking only fresh water which her mother provided. On the fifth day, she would eat a meal which was typical of those she would receive through the following months: dried fish, meat, and berries, softened by the pungent eulachon oil. She was allowed nothing fresh to eat; the cool, clear water which she sipped through a hollow bird's bone was a refreshing treat.

Strictly following the tribal taboos, her fingers were laced together and she would neither wash nor comb her own hair during the days of the fast. Only her mother was there to attend her and to provide the first instruction on how to accustom herself to her new life. Later, her girl friends and her aunts would come to visit, to talk quietly, and to share in her achievements. She was not allowed to go out in the daylight. At night, shrouded by the cover of darkness and wearing a fiber hood, she might walk with her mother or aunt to the nearby shore, taking time to breathe the salt-scented air and to stretch her growing limbs.

This time of isolation was a time of learning. Until now, all that she had learned of women's ways had come to her through watching and helping the older women as they worked; she had played with the warp ends of their weavings and padded behind as they gathered fresh fruits in their baskets. Now she was encouraged to weave baskets of her own, to tan hides, to make snowshoes, and to sing the songs of the women. Her mother, her grandmother, and her aunts would impart to her all the knowledge they could that would help her in the coming years of womanhood.

While the days of her learning seemed long, they were filled with the excitement of her increasing skills. Clumsy fingers became deft. Large baskets grew out of small ones, and if she was so destined, the art of weaving with mountain goat wool was shown to her. Perhaps at first she was shown how to measure and wind the side fringes for the Dancing Blankets. She watched as her grandmother handled the carved fringe-winder with easy dexterity and then copied each movement until her hands felt at home with the task. As her skills grew, she was introduced to the art of wool twining, working first on horizontal bands and finally attempting the curvilinear shapes which comprised the designs. She might weave a sample Dancing Blanket, no more than forty centimeters wide, which contained all of the basic parts of a full-sized blanket. One day, she would be asked to do a weaving for a very famous dancer. . . .

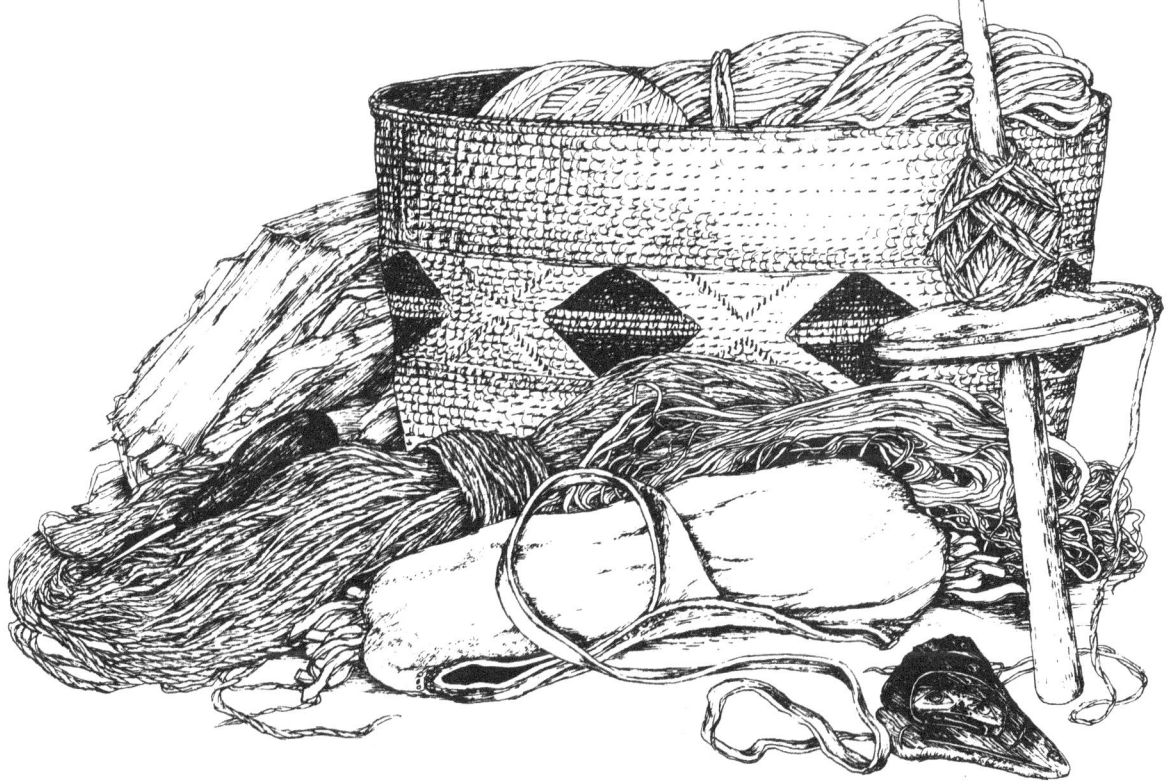

Mrs. Shotridge comments that "after the arrival of the mission-aries many people became Christians, while others preferred to keep the old-fashioned beliefs and ways of living. With the conversion, ancient customs faded away. Until a few years ago the custom of seclusion of young girls for a prescribed period just prior to entering upon the life of woman-hood was strictly observed. It may be doubted whether the missionaries understood its real significance when they opposed the practice."

THE LOOM

Most of the men on the coast were carvers. A weaver's husband might prepare any of the pieces of equipment that she would need: the loom, warping stick, fringe-winder, small spindle, and awl. The woman treasured these tools hewn by her man, for the motion of his hands created them and the motions of hers would, with their help, create a Dancing Blanket. In time, these tools would gather into them-selves the history of all her weaving.

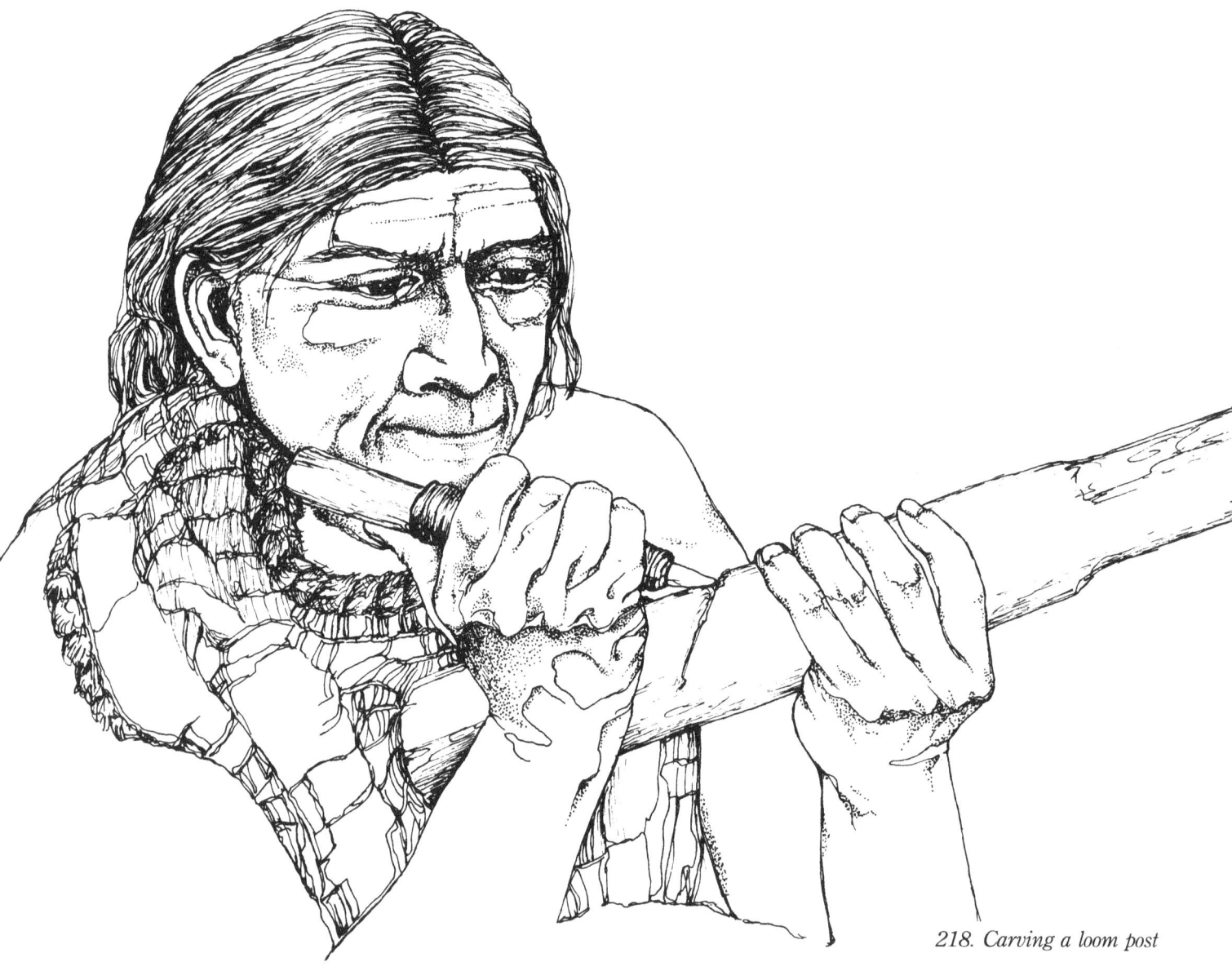

218. Carving a loom post

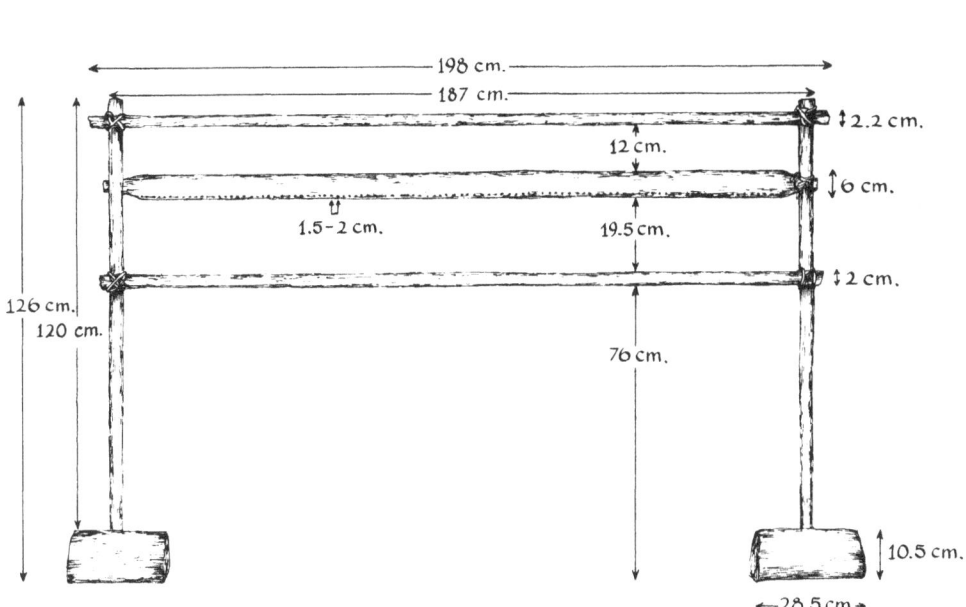

219. *Measurements taken from the loom in the Field Museum of Natural History, Chicago*

The loom was a very simple apparatus, consisting primarily of two upright posts and a broad crossbeam in which a series of holes was drilled along the lower edge. From this beam the warp would hang freely, as the technique used in weaving did not require that it be held under tension. Two thin slats were lashed across the loom to the upright posts with spruce root or sinew cord, one above the main beam to keep the uprights from spreading and one across the body of the weaving to support the tails of the braids while the weaving was in progress. The uprights were made of maple or alder, and each one was shaved at the bottom into a stake which fitted easily into a hole in the halved hardwood rounds which served as a base. The upper third of the post was often flattened to a rectangle and carved with the totemic designs of the weaver's clan. On the sides of this rectangle, one to three slits were carved which would support the crossbeam. The beam itself was narrowed at the ends so that it could slip into these slits and then be temporarily lashed to the posts. The weaver would start with the beam in the lowest slits and move it up as the weaving grew. When it reached the top set of slits, she would then rotate the beam, rolling the finished part of the weaving around it so that the working line of the twining would lie within easy reach of her hands.

The single-beam loom used by the Chilkat weavers was a simple one. When the seasons changed and the family moved to their summer camp, it could be easily dismantled. The weaving was rolled carefully around the beam in an intestine sheet and the two upright poles were bound to it for easy transport. The hemlock shoes were left behind; new ones were quickly fashioned at the new location.

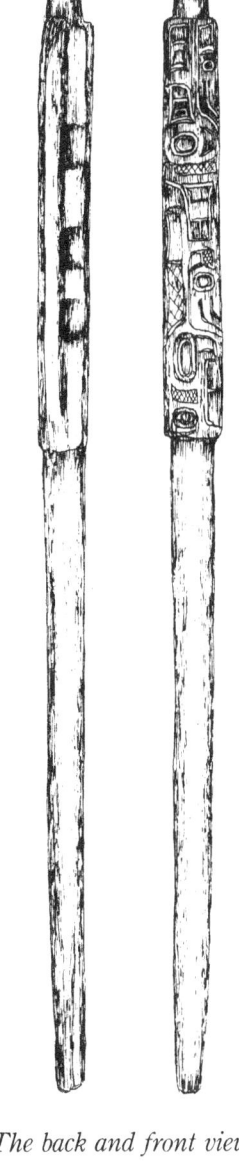

220. *The back and front views of a loom post*

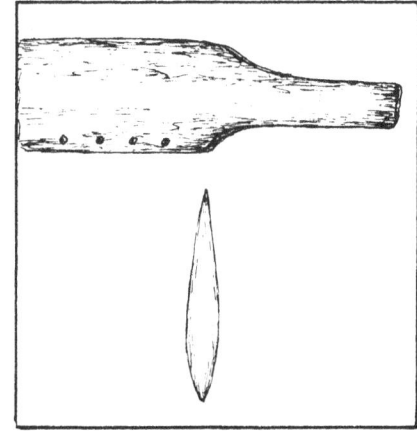

221. *A detail of the end of the beam, and a cross-section of the beam*

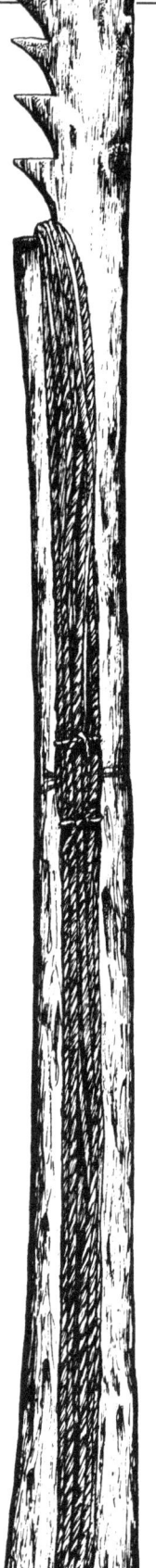

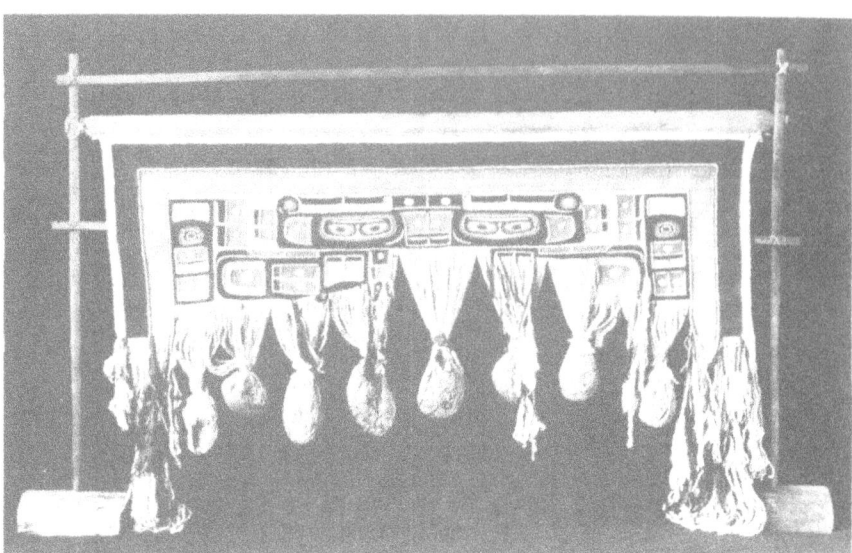

223. *A Dancing Blanket hanging on a loom and in the process of being woven. In this photograph, the cross-slat has been placed to the back to show off the design of the blanket. (Courtesy of the Field Museum, Chicago)*

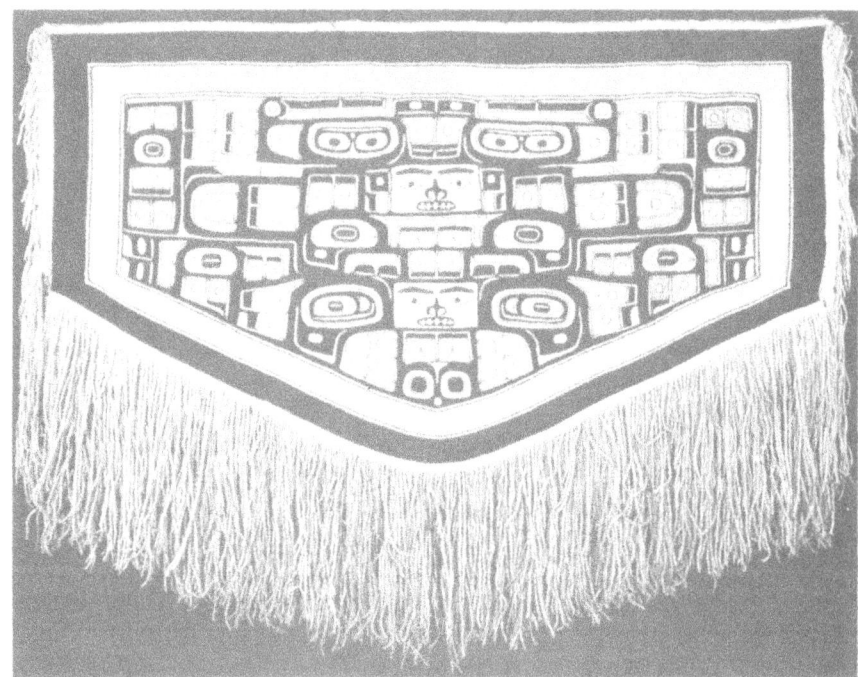

224. *A Dancing Blanket of the same pattern as the one on the loom in figure 223. (Courtesy of the Hudson Bay Company)*

WARPING THE LOOM

The warp of a Dancing Blanket consisted of two elements: the main body of warp strands and narrow sections on each side of this main body which formed the side braids. Both were spun of mountain goat wool with a yellow cedar bark core, the side braid strands often being half the size of the warp yarn.

The warp of a Dancing Blanket was shaped at the bottom in a

222. A warping stick with warp wound around the first notch

broad, shallow, stepped curve. To avoid wasting materials and spinning time, a warping stick was employed to measure the warp in different lengths. This stick, which was approximately 144 centimeters in length, sported a series of notches at one end which were about 5 centimeters apart. It was broad and flat on the other end. Different lengths of warp could be measured by wrapping yarn a specified number of times from a notch to the flat end. The bundle of warps was then tied in the middle of the stick in two places and cut between the ties. All warps so measured were doubled and hung over the heading cord; each half was considered to be a single warp "end."

Warping the loom was a very simple process, giving no hint of the complexity of the weaving that was to follow. Initially, a heading cord was measured, usually a rawhide strip .5 centimeters wide and a little longer than the length of the broad crossbeam of the loom. This cord would be tied to the loom beam at both ends with an easy overhand knot and then laced to it with a strong cord. Sometimes, a heavy two-ply cord of wool and bark was substituted for the leather, and after contact with traders, thick white cotton seine twine was often used.

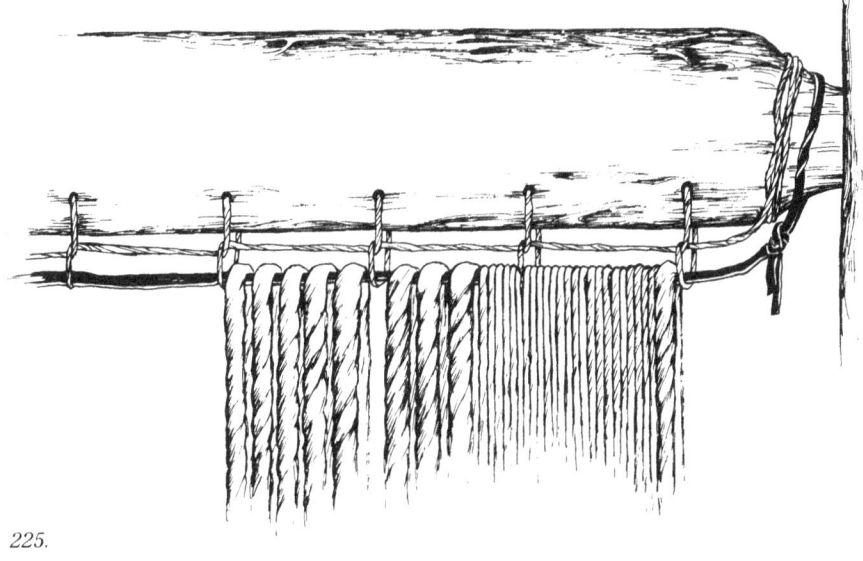

225.

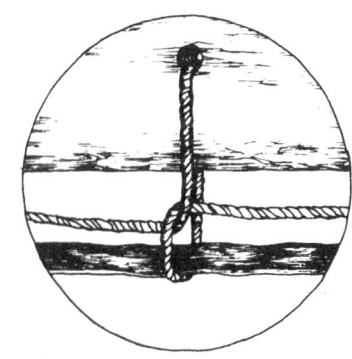

225. The beginning of the warping process, with the side braid strands and a few warp ends hung on the heading cord

226. The lacing cord was tied around the shoulder of the beam and then laced through the holes and tightened snugly around the heading cord in a hitched loop.

THE SIDE BRAID STRANDS

In warping the loom, the weaver would first measure and cut the yarn prepared for the side braids. Starting at a mark in the middle of the shaft of the warping stick, she would wrap the yarn around both ends of the stick and back to the mark again. This length would allow for take-up in the braiding and would constitute one doubled strand, or two single braid strands. To make a braid which was woven of forty-eight single strands, the weaver would have to wind the yarn around the stick twenty-four times. When this was done, she would tie the bundle on either side of the central mark and cut through the strands. These would then be hung over the leather heading cord starting at one side of the beam. They would spread about three centimeters, with one large doubled strand hung at the very edge.

THE WARP

Having measured, cut, and hung the strands for the side braids, the weaver proceeded with the main body of the warp. An average blanket would have been about 165 centimeters wide and had 4 warp ends to the centimeter. This would require 660 single warp ends, or 330 doubled lengths. The warps were measured and cut in even numbered bundles on the warping stick; when hung, they formed a series of steps which defined the shallow curve of the fringe. Four, five, or six steps were used, depending on the will of the weaver.

If a warp were to be hung with 660 warp ends in the heading, and if it was to be stepped five times, 66 single warp ends or 33 doubled strands would be needed for each step. The middle section contained a double quantity, helping to make the fringe line a curve rather than a V. The weaver would wind thirty-three times around the second notch on the warping stick, cut the strands, hang them over the heading cord, and lace them to the beam. Holes in the crossbeam which were 2.5 centimeters apart would call for 5 doubled strands to be hung between every lacing loop. This process would be repeated until all the warp ends and side braid strands were measured, cut, and hung on the loom.

THE GUT BAGS

Once the warp was hung on the loom, the ends were divided into sections, inserted into bags, and tied securely. The bags hung about twenty-five centimeters from the ground and were made of the bladder of a mountain goat. When a freshly killed goat was brought into camp, the deflated bladder was blown up with the aid of a straw, tied to prevent the air from escaping, and hung to dry. Once thoroughly dried, it would be cut neatly around the top and a leather collar was sewed to it. These bags could be made in varying sizes: tiny ones for the side braids, larger ones for the main warp. The strands of wool and cedar bark would curl easily into them and when tied with a leather thong around their collars, they formed a very durable protective covering. The warps would be kept quite clean inside these bags while the weaving was in progress and when the loom was being moved to another location. They also served to keep the warp ends from tangling and unspinning during the weaving process.

Figure 228 shows a loom in the process of being warped. Gut bags hang from the warp ends to keep them clean and orderly. On the left, the steps in the warp made by the measuring stick can be seen. The longest step is for the side braids, the next three are part of the main body of the warp. The central portion of the warp would drag on the ground if it were not held in pouches.

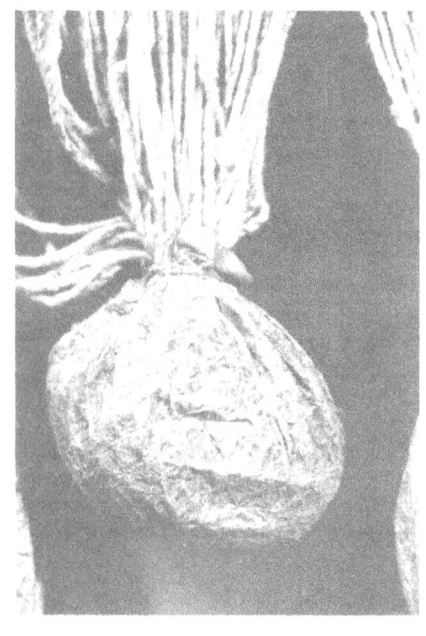

227. A gut bag enclosing a group of warp ends (Courtesy of the Field Museum, Chicago: CS)

TABBY VERSUS TWINING

The single-beam loom used by the Chilkat women to weave the Dancing Blanket has often been mistaken for a warp-weighted loom. This error can be understood as the misinterpretation of an early writer who, having seen a photograph of a Chilkat loom with its warp tied in bags, thought that these bags were rocks hung from the warp ends in order to put tension on them. A knowledge of the weaving

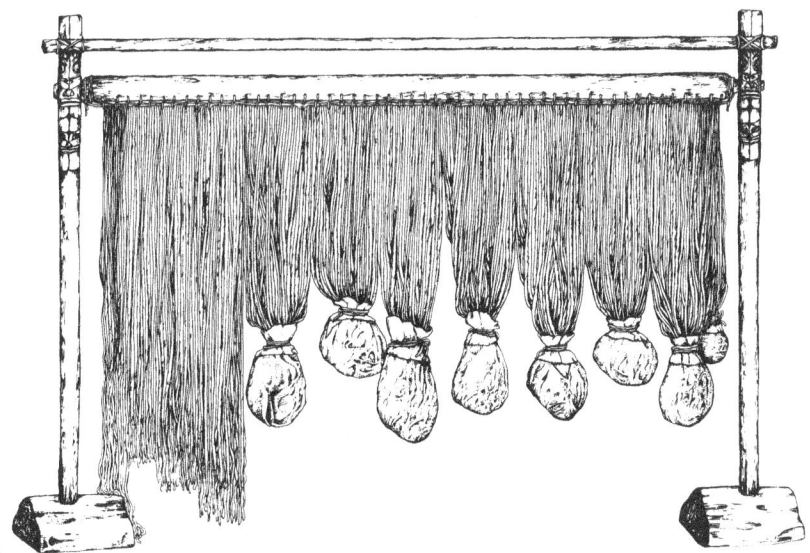

228.

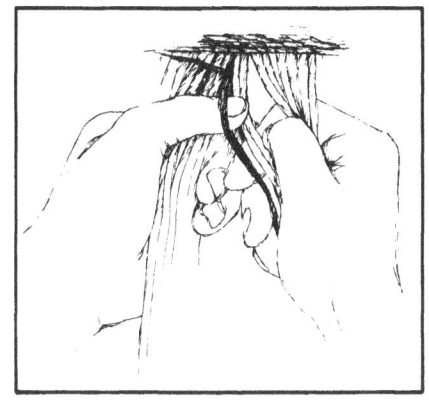

228. A Chilkat loom with gut bags protecting the warp

229. Chilkat twining is a finger weaving technique and does not need a warp under tension.

processes instantly shows that they are not equivalent: a warp-weighted loom such as that used by the Scandinavians produced a tabby cloth with a single weft traveling over and under every other warp end. On the single-beam loom of the Chilkat Indians, a twined cloth was produced, with two wefts encircling pairs of warp ends.

The twined cloth of the single-beam loom is produced by twisting two strands of weft around paired warp ends. The warp ends remain hanging in a vertical plane. No warp tension is needed, as the weft strands are manipulated entirely by the fingers.

The tabby cloth of a warp-weighted loom is woven with the aid of a harness, or stick, threaded through string loops which are attached to alternate warp ends. When the harness is raised, one-half of the warp ends are lifted and a weft can be passed through the opening or "shed." When the harness is returned to a resting position against the slanting loom posts, the weights pull the warp ends down, forming the opposite shed.

230. The operation of a warp-weighted loom requires tension.

231. A Scandinavian loom with weights hanging from the warp

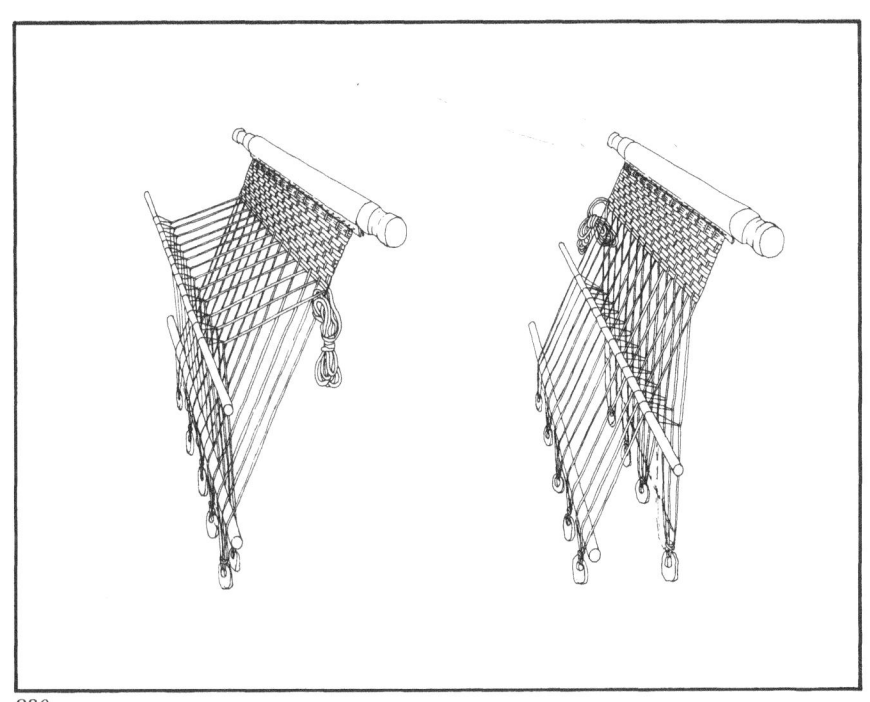

230.

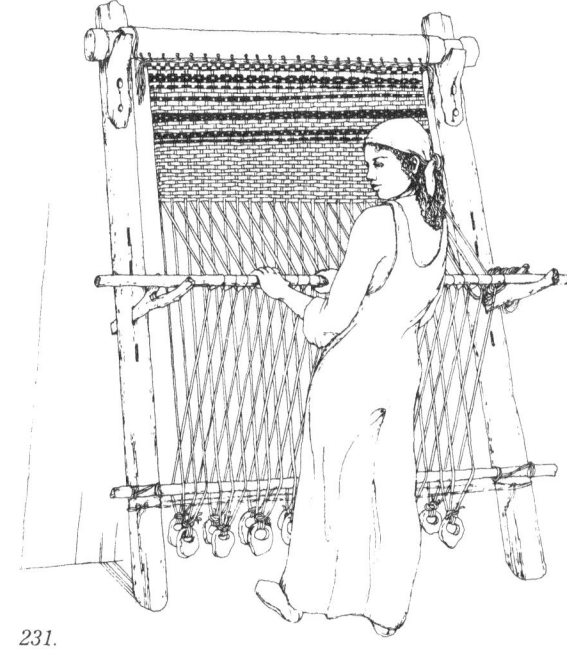

231.

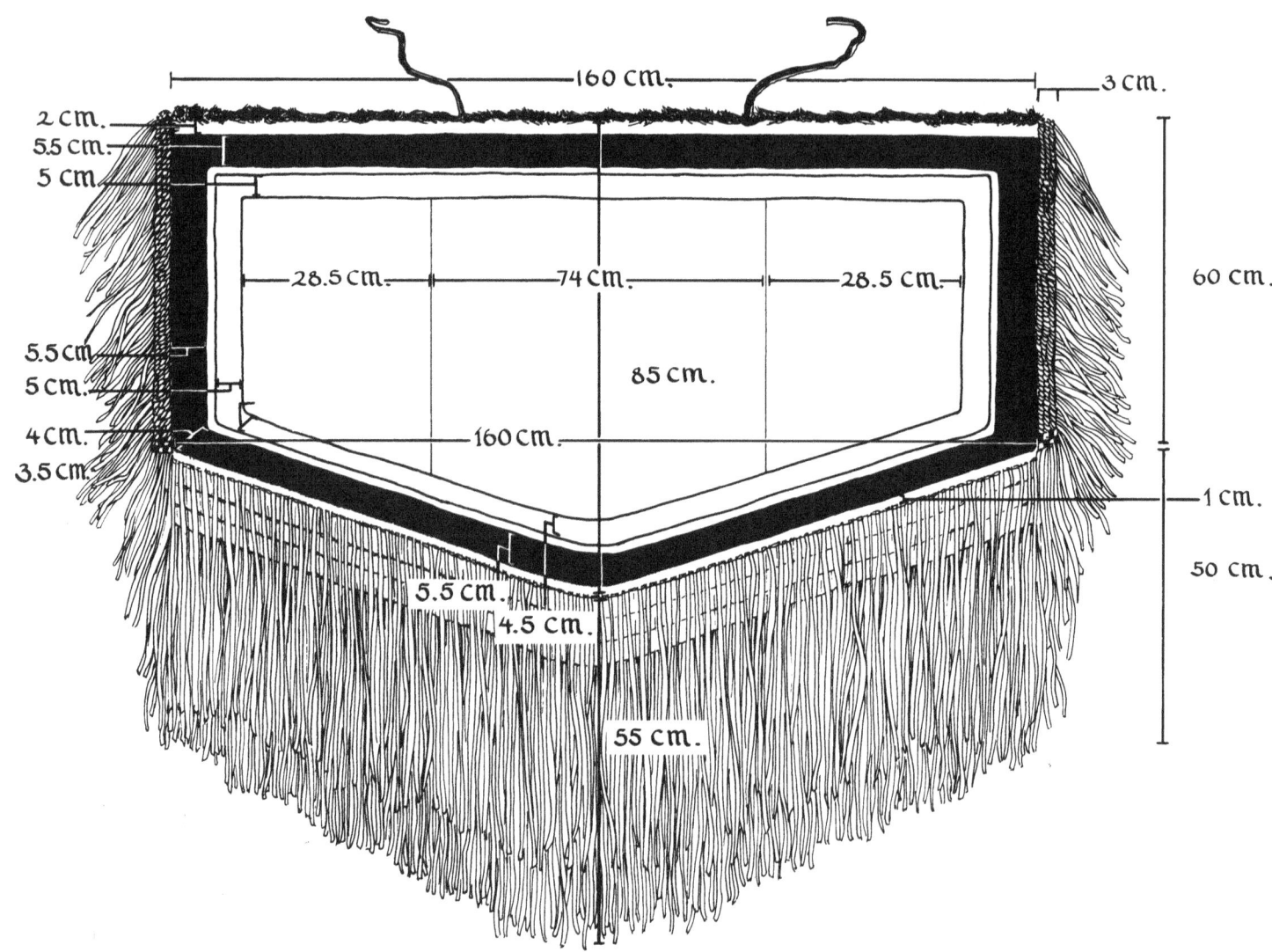

232. *The measurements of an average Dancing Blanket*

THE HEADING

After the warp is hung on the loom and the weaver has gathered the ends into gut bags, the heading is woven. The first rows of the heading arrange and secure the warp ends in position for the main weaving.

There were two methods for weaving the heading which differ only in the spacing between the rows and the treatment of the side braids. Method I seems to have been used on the older Dancing Blankets; Method II was used in the majority of blankets.

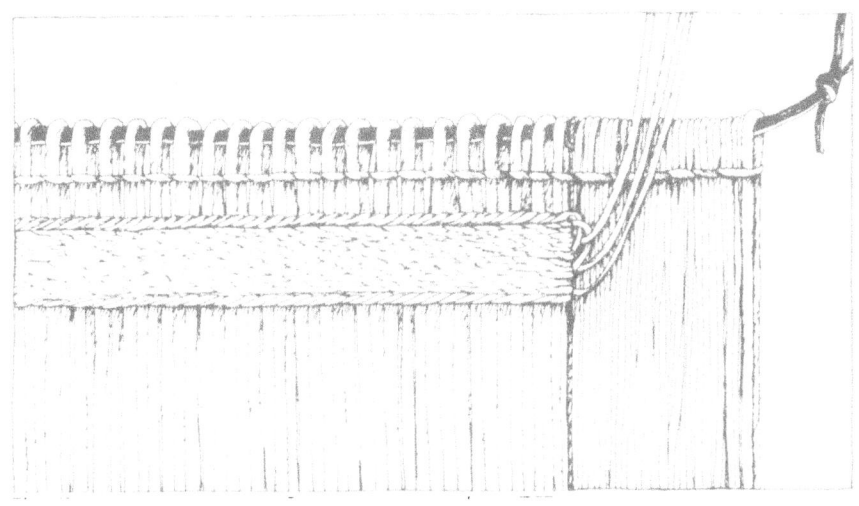

233. The heading, Method I

THE HEADING: METHOD I

The first row of white two-strand twining is inserted about half a centimeter below the heading cord. To start this row, the weaver must first twine around the ends of the side braid. These ends are bundled together, many more ends being included in one weft segment than is regularly found in two-strand twining.

To twine in the side braids, the weft is inserted around the thick

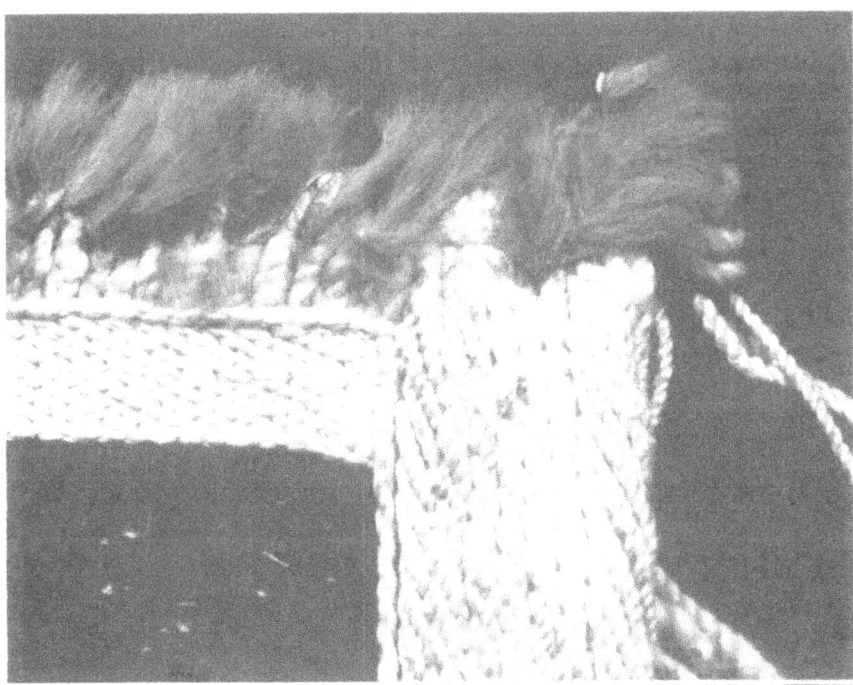

234. The heading, Method I (CS)

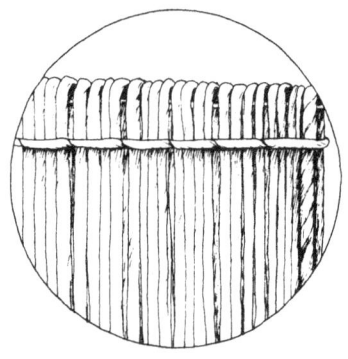

235. The first row of side braid twining

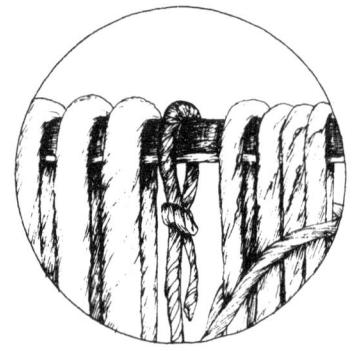

236. A drawstring attached to the heading cord

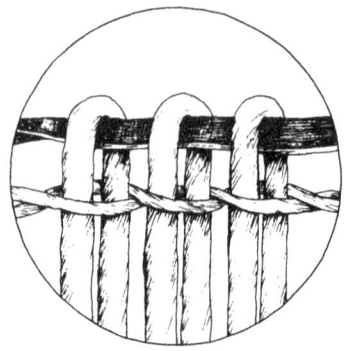

237. The first row of twining

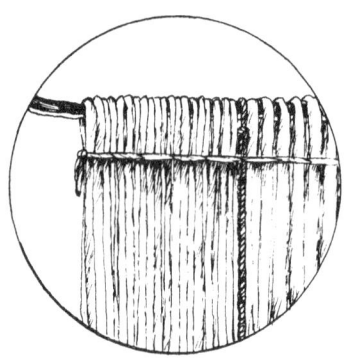

238. The left side of the first row of twining

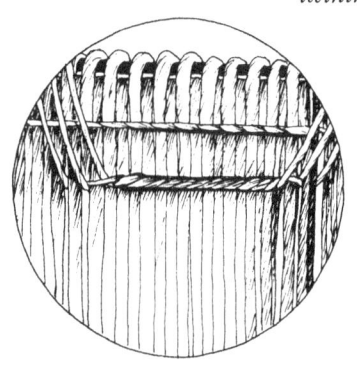

239. The first row of braided twining

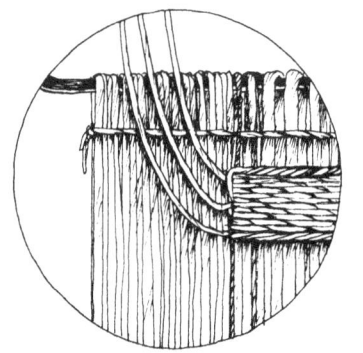

240. The left side of the heading, completed

warp end and around the next four doubled warp ends. The weaver then twists the wefts, twining around four doubled warp ends five more times, as in figure 235.

Before continuing to twine the main body of the warp, a drawstring is tied to the heading cord and dropped between the last warp end of the side braid and the first one of the blanket warp (fig. 236). This drawstring is woven into the outside edge of the black border and used to attach the side braid to the blanket.

One row of two-strand twining is now worked in the main body of the warp. Care is taken to arrange the warp ends in a symmetrical order, the back strand of each warp end preceding the front strand (fig. 237). The two sides of a doubled strand are included in one weft segment. The first row of twining arranges the warp ends and establishes their number per centimeter. This row is not twined too tightly; it must be very easy to push the weft segments up into position.

When the main body of the warp has been twined, a drawstring is inserted between it and the left side braid (fig. 238). The side braid strands are twined in the same manner as on the right side. The twining strands are tied securely around the thick warp end and cut off close to the knot.

After the first row of twining has been inserted, a space of half a centimeter is left free in Method I. A row of white braiding is then worked under this space (fig. 239). This row of braiding will round the top corners and then travel down around the entire perimeter of the blanket. Care must be taken, when braiding this row, not to miss warp ends; a constant check on the back is necessary.

One centimeter of white two-strand twining over alternate warp ends is worked underneath the first row of braiding. The corners of the braid are caught in the first three weft turns, and the drawstrings are inserted every other turn (fig. 240). One strand of the white braid and the drawstring must be caught in the last weft turn on each side of the heading. A white row of braiding is then worked underneath the weft twining. This row is entered on the right side and braided to the left, where its strands drop down next to the warp ends.

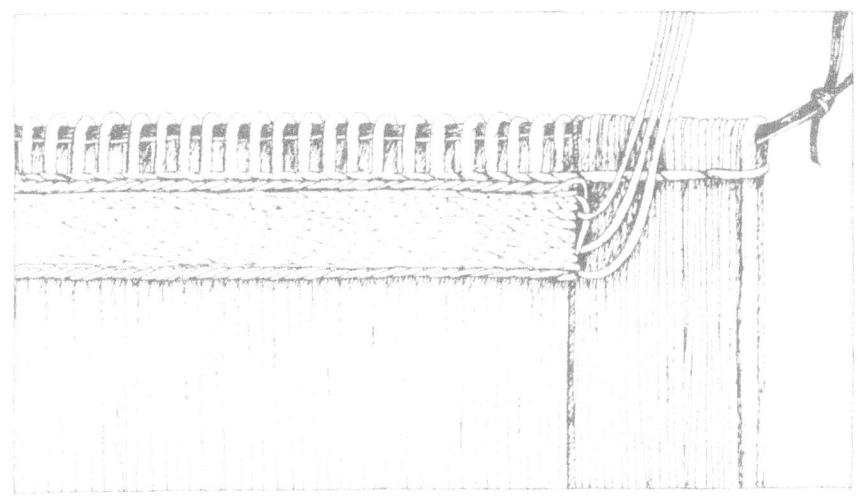

241. The heading, Method II

THE HEADING: METHOD II

The first row of twining in Method II bunches the side braid strands together in even greater numbers. Starting from the right, the white weft is inserted around the thick warp end and around the next six doubled warp ends. Three more bundles of six doubled warp ends are twined, making a total of four segments. Occasionally, the side braid strands will be twined into three or even two weft segments. The weaving of this heading is very similar to that of Method I, with the exception that there is no space between the first row of twining and the first row of braiding.

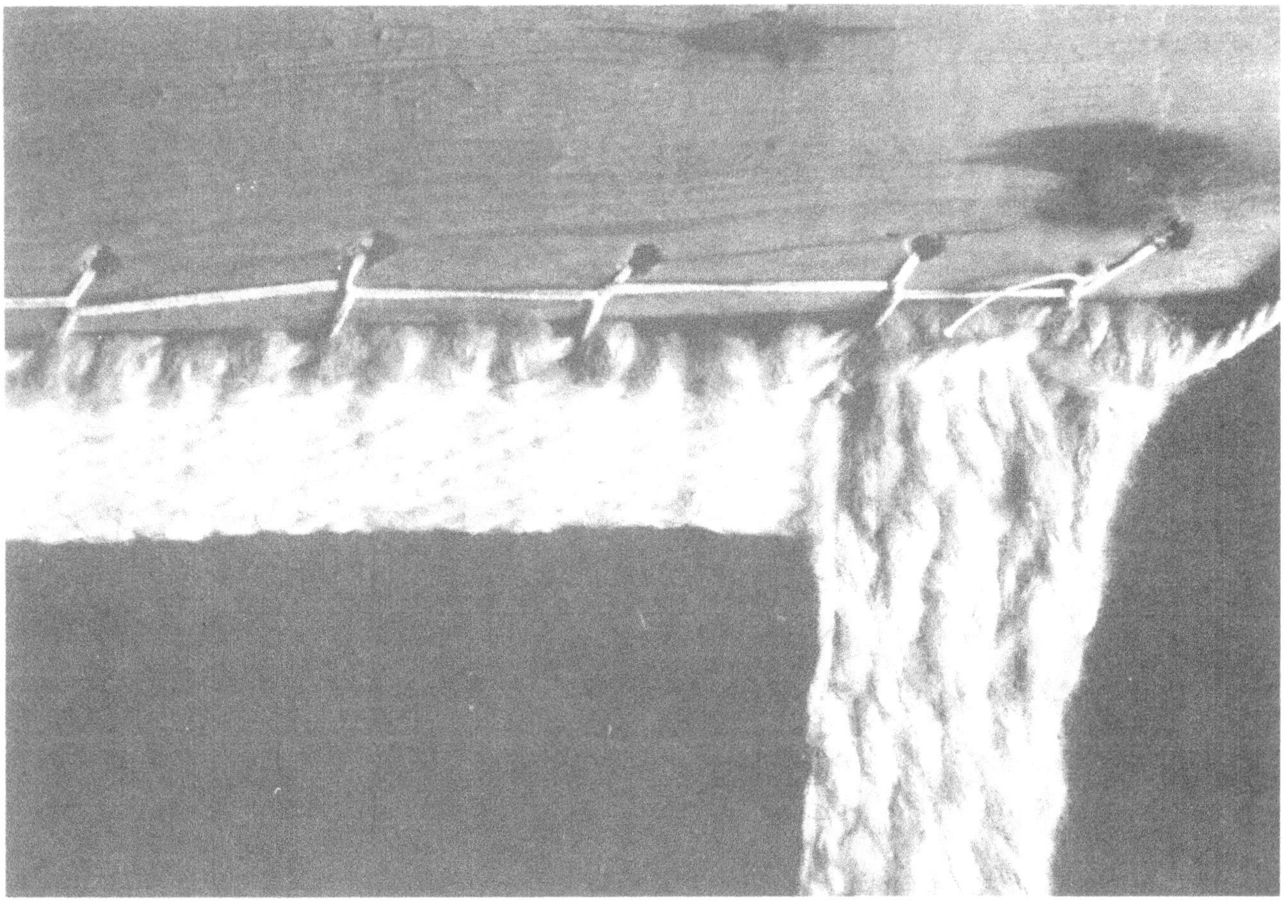

242. The side braid in this Method II heading, which is still on the loom, is caught in only two bundles. (CS)

THE SIDE BRAIDS

The folded plait which runs down each side of the Dancing Blanket is the only part of the garment which is not twined. It is composed of thin warp yarns which are braided in an over-one-under-two twill pattern. This pattern forms very distinct vertical ridges which appear on the outside of the braid and not on the inside.

The working strands of the side braid move from the outer edges to the center, where they are dropped through the drawstring which runs down the edge of the black border. At this point, they become part of the center strands of the other half of the braid. The fold in some braids is directly in the middle, producing two halves of equal widths. Other braids are folded slightly off center, the front being wider than the back. The working strands on each half of the braid turn around a thick core yarn, forming a beautifully rolled edge. All side braids are closed at the top over the heading cord and bound at the bottom with a special little weave called a tie-off.

243. Elements of a side braid

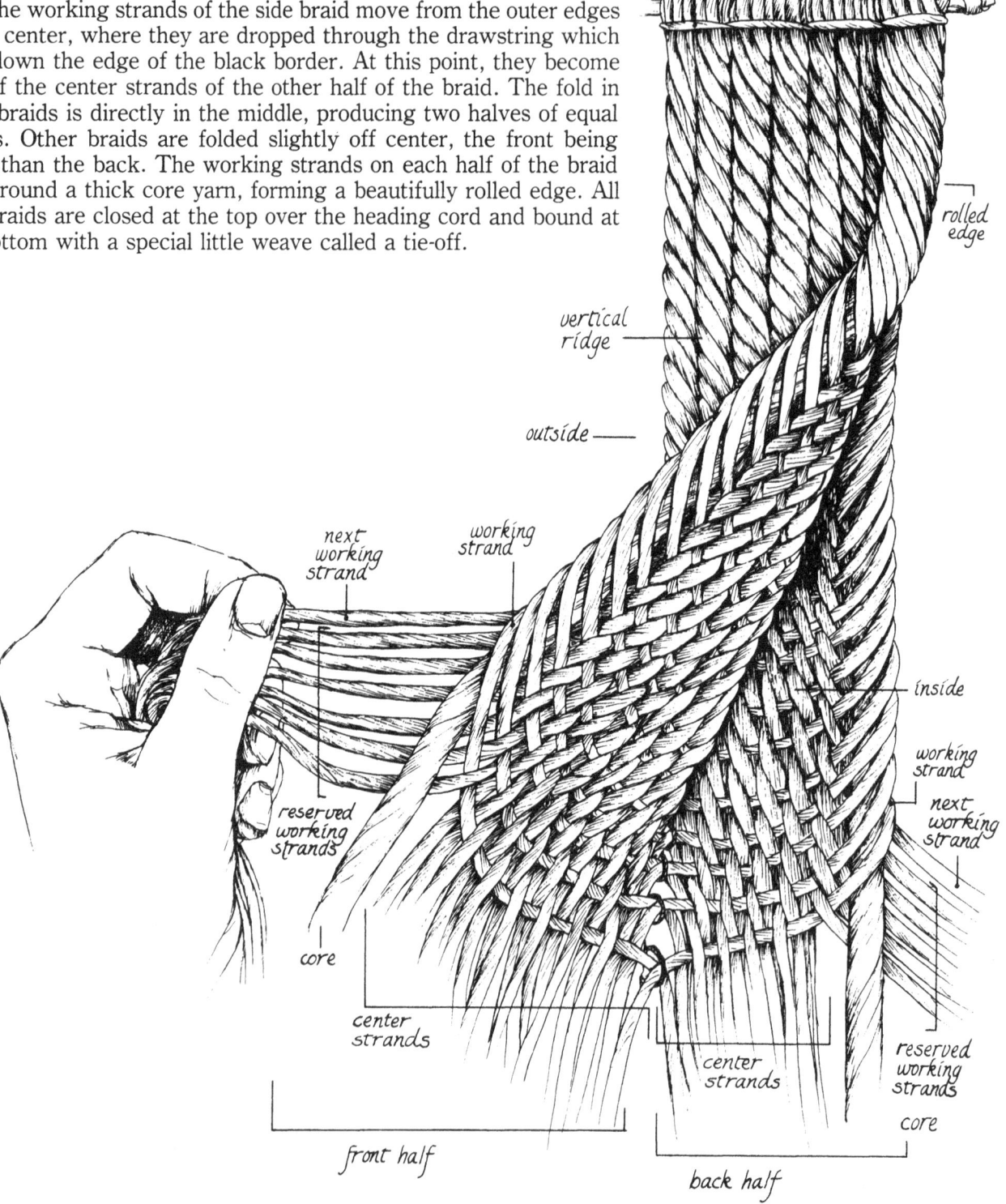

twining

heading cord

rolled edge

vertical ridge

outside

inside

working strand

next working strand

next working strand

working strand

reserved working strands

core

center strands

center strands

reserved working strands

core

front half

back half

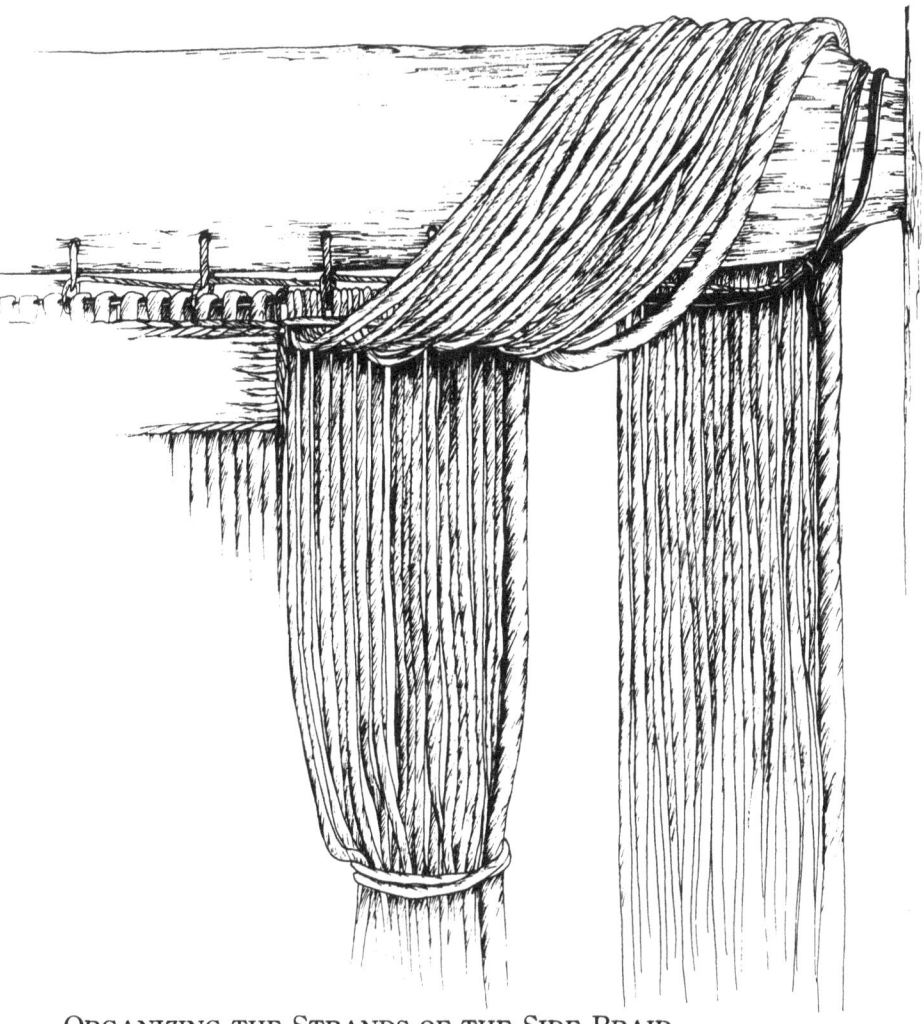

ORGANIZING THE STRANDS OF THE SIDE BRAID

To begin a side braid, the thin warp strands which are doubled over the heading cord have to be divided. A row of two-strand twining, which was entered when the heading was worked, holds them together in bundled groups. The strands in each group are divided evenly between front and back, the front ones being placed over the loom beam. One additional strand is selected from the inside edge of the hanging strands and is also placed over the loom beam. The strands which are over the beam will form the front half of the braid, those which remain hanging will form the back half. The thick core yarn is also divided between the front and the back halves of the braid. A tie is made around the strands of the back half to keep them separate while the front half is organized.

The strands which form the front half of the braid are removed from their position over the loom beam. Starting from the inside edge, which is next to the weaving, these strands are counted off in groups of three until five, six, or seven strands remain. This latter number forms the "reserved working strands" which create the side roll of the braid. The center strands of the front half of the braid must be divided in even groups of three; therefore, if two strands are left over, the last group of three is added to it to make five reserved working strands. If one strand is left over, the last two groups are added to it to make seven. If no strands are left over, the last two groups are used which equal six.

12 center strands

| | |-| | |-| | |-| | |-| | |-| |

5 reserved working strands

12 center strands

| | |-| | |-| | |-| | |-| | |-| | |-|

7 reserved working strands

9 center strands

| | |-| | |-| | |-| | |-| | |

6 reserved working strands

Once the reserved working strands are determined for the front half of the braid, they are marked off with a tie. All of the front strands are then repositioned over the loom beam.

On the back half of the braid, the reserved working strands equal *one less* than the number used on the front half. For example, if five are used on the front, four will be used on the back. The remaining strands will automatically be the correct number for the center strands of the back half of the braid.

The weaver may wish to make a braid which is divided off center, the front half being larger than the back. At this point, she would select three strands at equal intervals from the strands of the back half and place them over the loom beam with the strands of the front half.

The side braid on the following pages is composed of forty-eight strands and is folded off center. The following is a list of the steps used in organizing a side braid, with examples given for a braid of forty-eight strands:

1. Total number of strands must be an even number: forty-eight
2. Divide this number in half over the loom beam: twenty-four up, twenty-four down
3. Put one extra strand over the loom beam: twenty-five up, twenty-three down
4. Count the center strands of the front half off in threes:
   | | |-| | |-| | |-| | |-| | |-| | |-| | |-| | |-|
5. Reserve five, six, or seven strands: seven

   center strands: eighteen

   | | |-| | |-| | |-| | |-| | |-| | |-| | |-| | |-|

   reserved working
   strands: seven
6. On the back half of the braid, the reserved strands are one less than the front: seven less one = six
7. To fold the braid off center, select three strands from the back half to add to the front: front/center = eighteen + three or twenty-one strands

Side braids can be worked with or without a core yarn, although the edge roll is more firm when the core is present. This core yarn is a constant and must not be counted when organizing the side braid strands. The minimum total number of strands which make up a satisfactory side braid is twenty-four.

The weaver sits in front of the loom and works the braid in its folded position. This means that she works the front half of the braid from the outside and the back half from the inside. The outside, or ridge side, of the braid is executed in an over-one-under-two pattern. The reverse of this weave, which is found on the inside of the braid, is an under-one-over-two sequence.

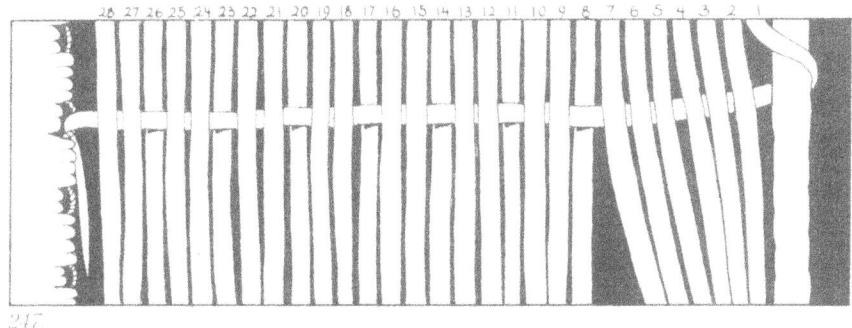

THE FRONT HALF: ROW ONE

STEP 1: The working strand, (1), which is the closest strand to the thick warp end, goes around the thick one and then under the reserved working strands, (2) through (7) (fig. 245).

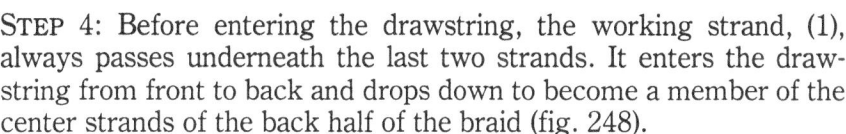

STEP 2: Working strand (1) then travels over strand (8) and under strands (9) and (10) (fig. 246).

STEP 3: The action of *over-one-and-under-two* is repeated until strand (1) has passed through all of the strands set aside for the front braid. It is then ready to drop into the drawstring (fig. 247).

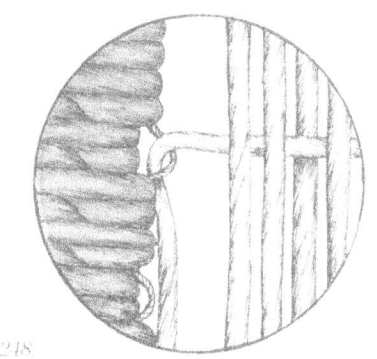

STEP 4: Before entering the drawstring, the working strand, (1), always passes underneath the last two strands. It enters the drawstring from front to back and drops down to become a member of the center strands of the back half of the braid (fig. 248).

It is important, in beginning a side braid, to keep the strands in order. This is difficult, as they are established in their positions as much by eye as by the method of plaiting. In figure 249, a sequence of over-one-under-two occurs in the horizontal direction on the front half of the braid (row 1), while the vertical direction on this half is over-two-under-one (row A). In starting the braid, the vertical sequence has to be watched carefully so that the strands are placed in their proper positions and none are left out.

249. *The twill pattern on the outside of the side braid: under-two-over-one*

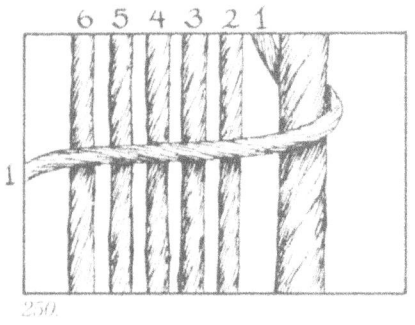

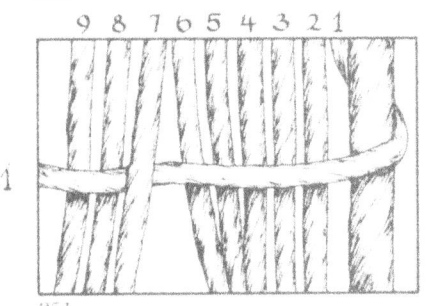

THE BACK HALF: ROW ONE

STEP 1: The working strand, (1), which is the closest strand to the thick warp end, goes behind this thick one and then over it and over the reserved working strands, (2) through (6) (fig. 250).

STEP 2: Working strand (1) then travels under strand (7) and over strands (8) and (9) (fig. 251).

STEP 3: The action of *under-one-and-over-two* is repeated until strand (1) has passed through all of the strands set aside for the back braid. It is then ready to drop into the drawstring (fig. 252).

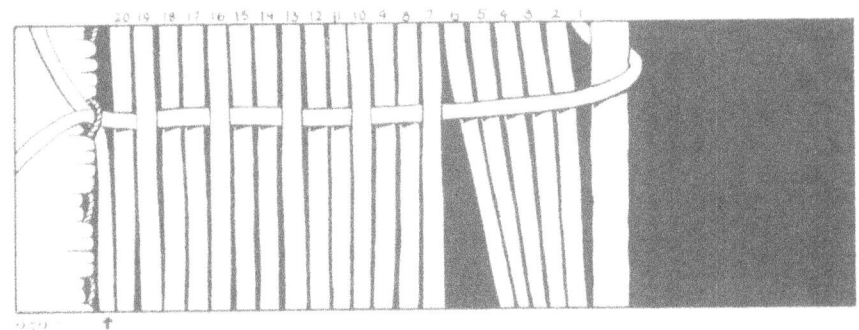

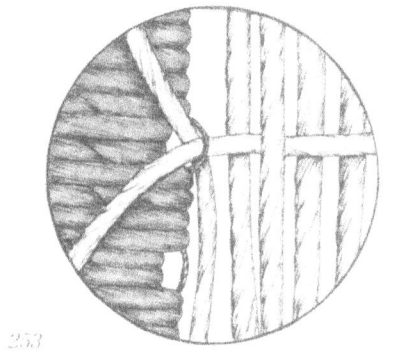

STEP 4: Before entering the drawstring, the working strand, (1), always passes under one strand and over two strands, the second strand of these latter two being the working strand which entered the drawstring from the front half. Strand (1) then enters the drawstring from back to front and drops down to become a member of the center strands of the front half of the braid (fig. 253).

The back half of the braid, because it is viewed from the inside by the weaver as she works, has the opposite strand sequence from the front half. In figure 254, a horizontal sequence of under-one-over-two (row 1) is balanced by a vertical sequence of under-two-over-one (row A). Once again, it is important to be aware of the vertical sequence while establishing the braid so that all of the strands will take their proper position.

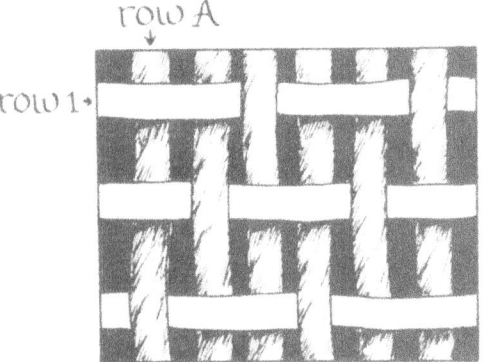

254. The twill pattern on the inside of a side braid: over-two-under-one

THE FRONT HALF: ROW TWO

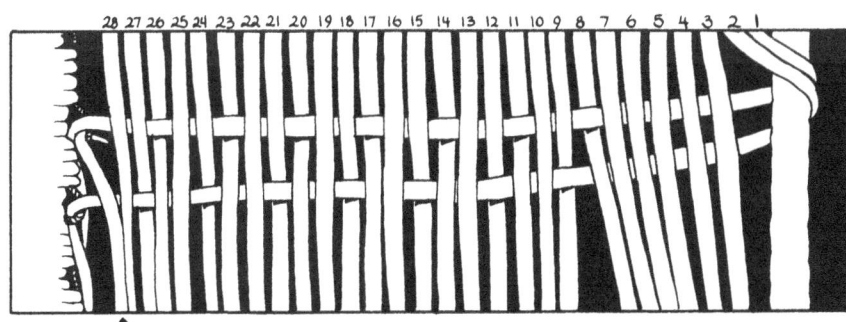

255. The second row of the front half

In the second row of plaiting (fig. 255), the working strand, (2), travels over the thick warp end and then under it and under the next six strands before it begins its over-one-under-two pattern. Note that strand (8) has now become one of the first six reserved working strands and that strand (2) starts its twill pattern with strand (9). When strand (2) has passed through all of the strands set aside for the front of the braid, strand (1) from the first row of the back half of the braid becomes the last strand under which it passes before it drops into the drawstring.

THE BACK HALF: ROW TWO

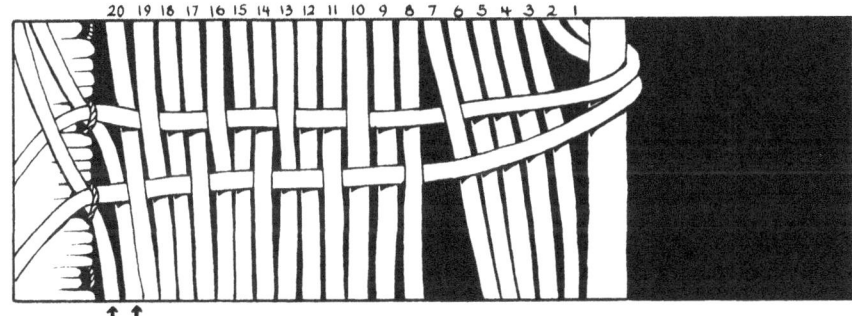

256. The second row of the back half

In the second row of plaiting (fig. 256), the working strand, (2), travels under the thick warp end and then over it and over the next five strands before it begins its under-one-over-two pattern. Note that strand (7) has now become one of the first five reserved working strands and that strand (2) starts its twill pattern with strand (8). When strand (2) has passed through all of the strands set aside for the back half of the braid, strand (2) from the second row of the front half of the braid becomes the last strand over which it travels before entering the drawstring.

THE FRONT HALF: ROW THREE

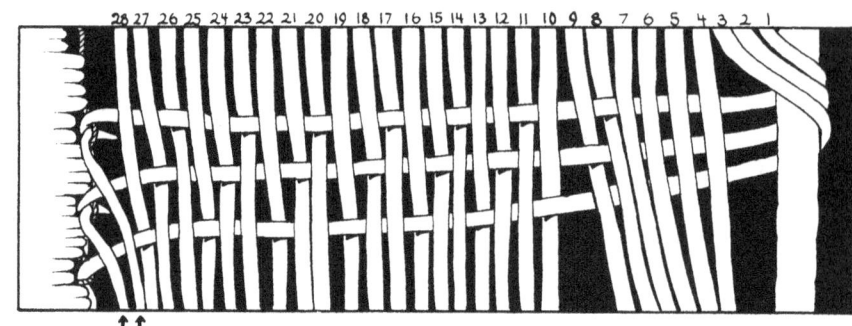

257. The third row of the front half

In the third row of plaiting (fig. 257), strand (3) is the working strand, strand (9) joins the first six reserved working strands, and strands (1) and (2) from the back half of the braid are the last two strands under which strand (3) passes before entering the drawstring.

THE BACK HALF: ROW THREE

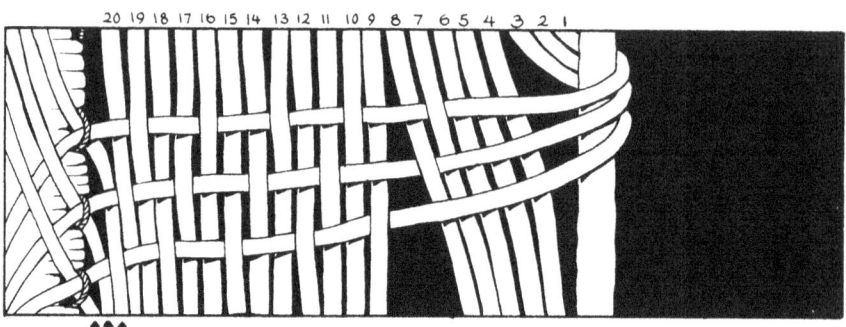

258. The third row of the back half

In the third row of plaiting (fig. 258), strand (3) is the working strand, strand (8) joins the first five reserved working strands, and strand (3) from the front half of the braid is the last strand over which the working strand passes before entering the drawstring.

THE BLACK AND YELLOW BORDERS

The Dancing Blanket is usually woven with a broad black border surrounding the entire weaving and a broad yellow border lying directly inside it. These borders come after the heading and are framed on the outside edges by the side braids.

THE BLACK BORDER

In weaving the top black border (fig. 259), a row of braided twining is first inserted in exactly the same way as the first row of white braided twining in the heading. It will travel along the top of the band and then join the white braid as it journeys around the perimeter of the weaving.

Five to six centimeters of two-strand twining follow this black braid. The first row of twining (fig. 260) must include the first strand of the corner of the black braid (a), as well as catch a vertical white braid strand from the heading (b) and the drawstring (c). This row will not go all the way across the weaving, but will be interrupted by a lazy line.

LAZY LINES

When weaving the horizontal portion of the black and yellow bands which border the design field, the weaver utilizes the diagonal join called a "lazy line." This join allows her to complete one side of the band from a single seated position and then move to the other side to finish the band. Two, and sometimes three, divisions are made in the border in this way without affecting its overall appearance.

The weaver twines sides (A) of the black border first (fig. 261). A steep diagonal is formed by retreating one warp end every turn; a more shallow angle is created by retreating two warp ends with each weft

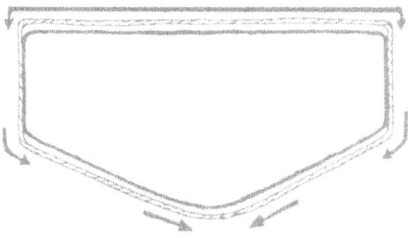

259. Braids around the perimeter of the woven field

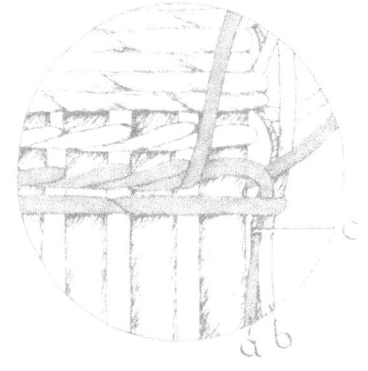

260. The first row of black two-strand twining

B   A

261. Lazy lines in the black and yellow borders

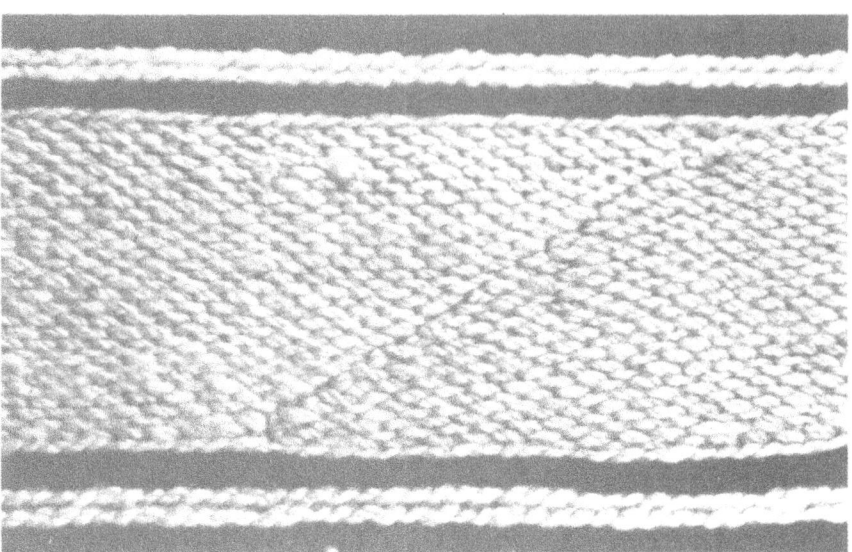

262. A lazy line in the yellow border which moves over one warp end in each succeeding row (CS)

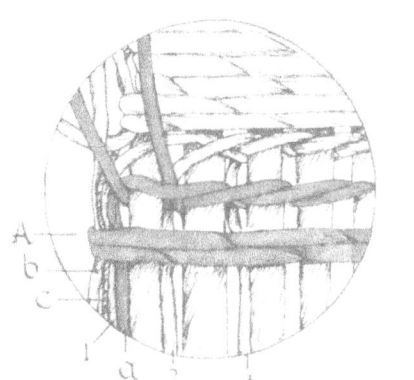

263. The first weft turn on the left side of the warp in the black border

turn. The first row of twining on side (B) is started from the middle, next to the diagonal, insuring that the proper sequence of paired warp ends will be maintained. In the yellow border, side (B) would be twined before side (A) due to the angle of the lazy line. The side of the angle which retreats must be twined before the side which advances.

When the weaver reaches the left side of the warp (fig. 263), the tails (1, 2, and 3) of the bottom row of white braiding from the heading must be twined in with the warp ends. This continues for a centimeter or so, when they can be cut off. The weft turn between the first and second rows of twining (A) must catch the first corner strand of black braiding (a), along with a white braid strand (b) and the drawstring (c).

The drawstring will continue to be caught every other weft turn for the entire length of the side of the blanket. Although the side braid is worked along with the borders, it is convenient to keep the twining a few rows ahead of this plait.

THE YELLOW BORDER

The yellow border can begin when five to six centimeters of black twining have been completed on both sides of the lazy line and the drawstring and strands from both the white and black vertical braids have been caught in the last weft turns on both sides of the weaving. Six rows of braiding separate the yellow from the black border. The first of these rows is black, as it is needed to enclose the black border. Two white braids are inserted, followed by two black ones; the white braids are the background, the black ones form an outline which separates the black and yellow borders. A final yellow braid completes the sequence and is needed to surround the yellow border.

ENTERING THE SIX HORIZONTAL BRAIDS

The vertical black borders on the sides of the blanket are also between five and six centimeters wide. The weaver measures the desired width on the right side of the warp, counts the number of warp ends included in this width, and then counts an equal number on the left side. These are marked with a loose tie. The braids are then entered and worked from right to left, a black braid and two white ones starting at the outside edge of the yellow border. Moving in one warp

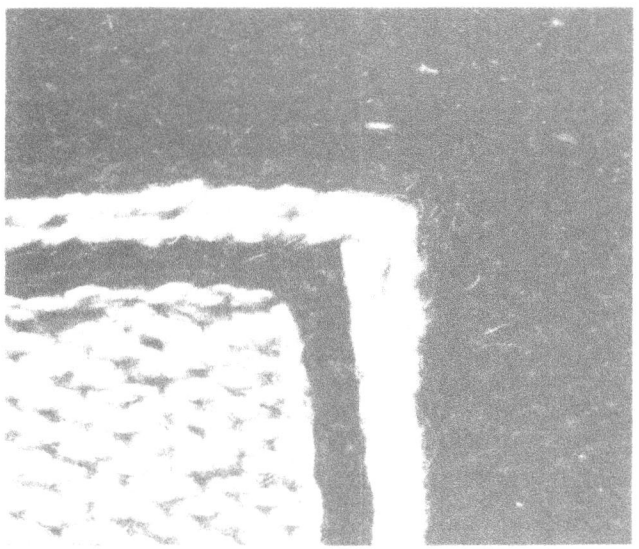

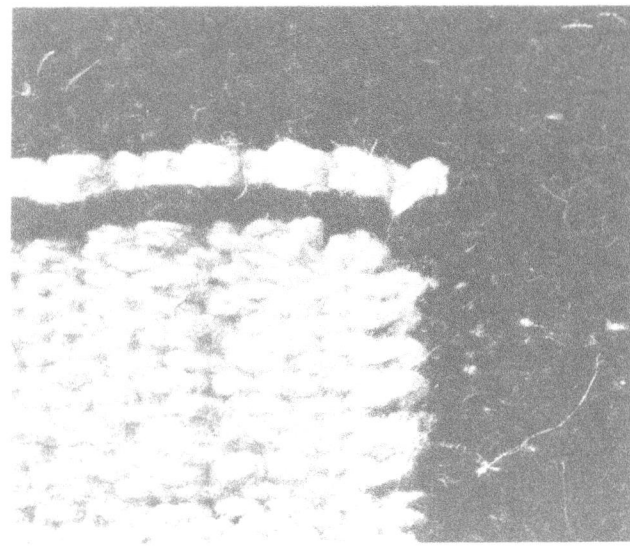

264. The top right corner between the black and yellow borders (CS)

265. The reverse side of the top right corner (CS)

end toward the center of the weaving, two black braids and one yellow one are entered and also worked to the left, stopping one warp end inside the preceding braids. The tails of all the braids are left in position to go around the corners in the first rows of twining.

Figure 266 illustrates the organization of the warp and weft between the black and yellow borders and the side braid. Section A indicates the side braid strands. Section B shows a tie around the warp ends to be used in the vertical black border. Section C notes the placement of braids between the black and yellow horizontal borders. Because there are so many braids, their entry is staggered to allow the outside braids to turn the corner before the inside ones do. If these six braided twining rows were all to turn the corner at once, they would bunch up and make an awkward, rounding turn.

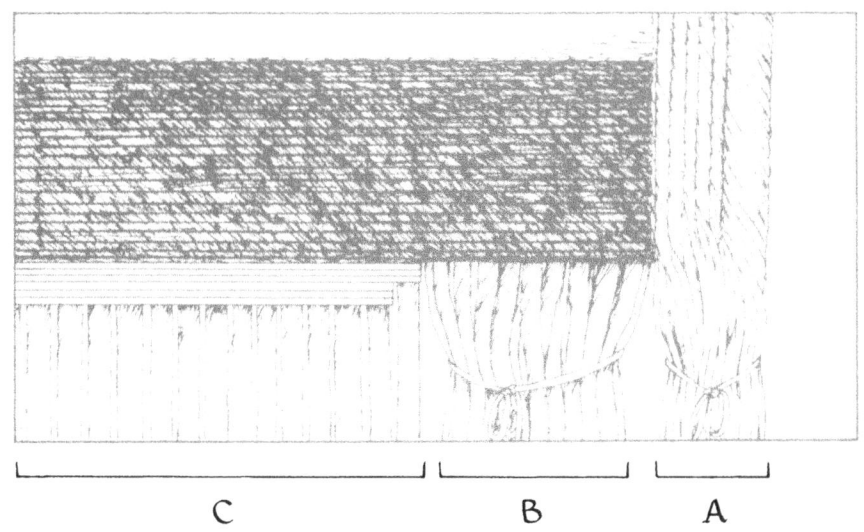

C   B   A

266. Organization of the warp and weft between the black and yellow borders and the side braid

The Dovetail Join

The join between the black and yellow vertical borders starts as an interlock and then becomes a dovetail join. There were weavers who used a straight interlock join for the entire vertical border. When the dovetail pattern was used, a symmetrical pattern was not always maintained; variations along its path frequently occurred (see fig. 117, p. 94). These variations were generally found, somewhat symmetrically, on both sides of the blanket. All of the six braids' strands cover the join on the front side of the weaving.

The Horizontal Yellow Border

The yellow border is usually the same width as the black border along the top and slightly narrower as it travels vertically. When five to six centimeters of yellow weft twining are completed, six more braided twining rows are inserted to set this border off from the main design field. These are first a yellow braid, then two black and two white braids, and finally a black braid. These braids are inserted in the same manner as the braids between the black and yellow borders. A drawstring is attached along the inside of the yellow border on both sides of the weaving. This drawstring is worked into the yellow border, being caught twice and freed once in a repeated pattern.

Added Warp Ends

The process of adding warp ends in order to increase the number of warp ends in the blanket begins immediately. If a weaver knows that she wants a total of from thirty to one hundred more warp ends at the bottom than were hung at the top on the heading cord, she must start adding them in the top horizontal borders. Eight to ten warp ends may be added, spaced evenly across the width of the design field.

WARP MARKERS

Upon completion of the top yellow border and its subsequent six braids, the weaver is ready to begin weaving the central design field. To prepare for this, she first finds the middle two warp ends of the entire warp and inserts a marker between them. The markers are made of white warp yarns plied with a black weft which spirals around every second twist. The warp end and the black weft are spun together down the leg in the manner of the single-ply warp yarns. Although this action untwists their plies, when released by the left hand, they instantly re-ply themselves, twisting together in a black-white-white spiral.

The warp markers, being made of warp yarn, are knotted and inserted into the warp in the same manner as added warps. If the central design field is divided into three panels, drawstrings which are placed at the panel lines will serve as markers for the general division of the warp. If the design field is not divided in this way, two warp markers might be placed where panel lines would normally be in order to help the weaver in placing the designs.

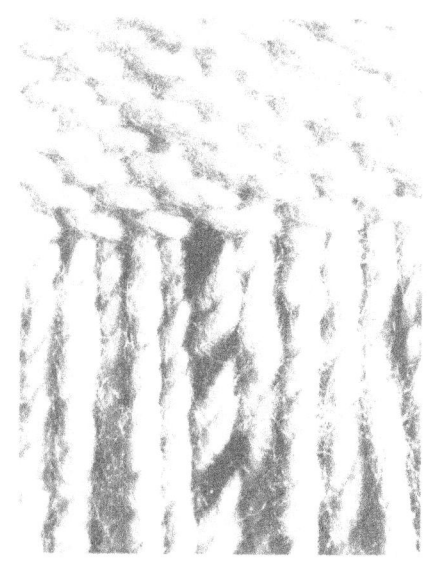

267. A black and white warp marker (CS)

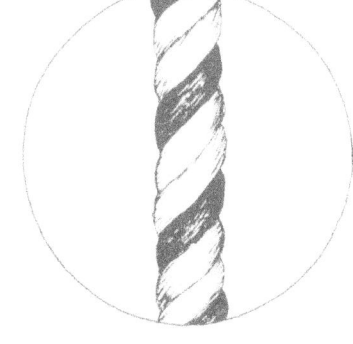

268. Close-up of a warp marker

INTESTINE SHEET

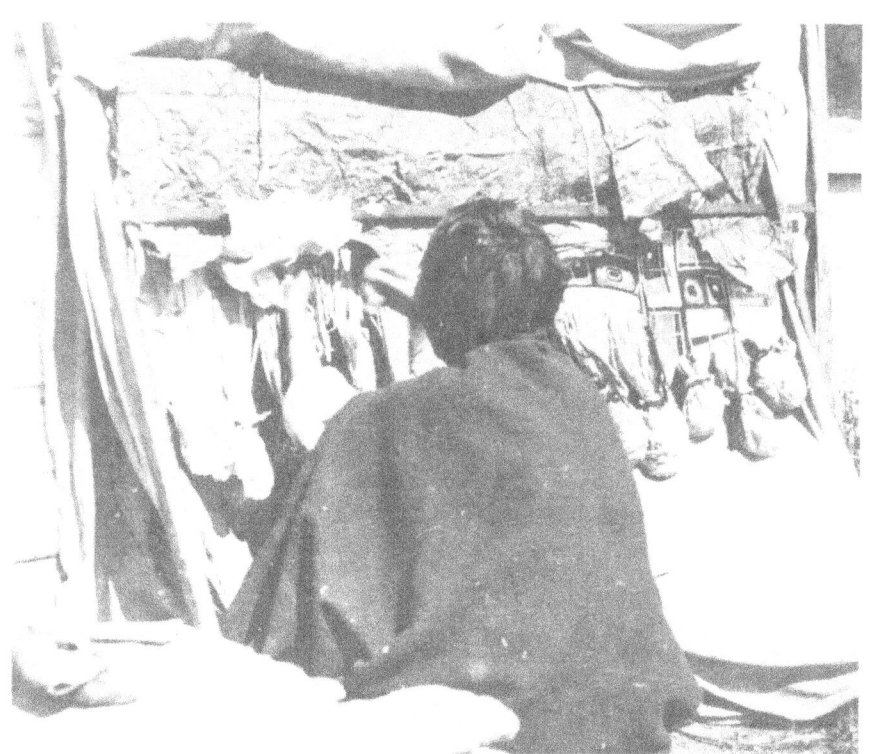

269. An intestine sheet protects the top of the weaving. (Courtesy of the American Museum of Natural History)

The actual weaving of a Dancing Blanket took as long as six months to complete. During this time, a protective sheet was hung over the loom beam and tied in position to the loom posts. The sheet was made of intestine which had been slit lengthwise, opened up and dried, and then carefully sewn together in lengths of the needed size. This intestine sheet was very durable, weatherproof, and provided excellent protection from wind, rain, and dirt or sand. As the weaving progressed and the top beam was rolled, the intestine sheet covered the roll and fell to the back of the loom.

WEAVING THE DESIGN FIELD

Once the weaver has finished the black and yellow horizontal borders, she can begin to weave the central design field. First she establishes the position of her initial drawstrings, and then she starts to weave the forms which lie between them.

It is easy, when concentrating on weaving a single shape, to become so involved in the shape itself that the formlines become "background" in the weaver's mind. *It must always be remembered that the figures being woven are composed of the primary formlines.* A good weaver is aware of the formline figures she is producing. She works her shapes so that their edges create these formlines, widening and diminishing them in their graceful curvilinear fashion.

The pattern board is placed close to the weaver's side; she uses a piece of inner cedar bark as a measuring stick to transfer the pattern dimensions from the board to the warp. To duplicate the shapes exactly on the other side of the weaving, she might work two sections simultaneously, measuring one shape and counting an equal number of warp ends for the same shape on the other side. As the number of weft rows woven determines the length of a shape, she is able to duplicate one shape exactly on the other side by weaving an equivalent number of rows. The design field, being symmetrical, has to be woven equally so that the formlines flow smoothly around the figures.

In weaving the forms, the weaver combines a knowledge of the techniques of her art with a certain amount of creative invention. Everything she does is directed toward creating beautiful, clean forms. The weaving itself employs a multitude of strands of yarn. If she discovers an easy means of reusing strands, she does not hesitate to use it provided the end result is a perfect form. The Dancing Blankets exhibit many ingenious answers to the challenge of the designs.

The following examination of the weaving techniques gives instruction on how the forms of the design field are woven. These techniques will vary depending on the size of the materials used and the shapes of the designs. As in the old days, weavers today must use ingenuity to make their weavings perfect.

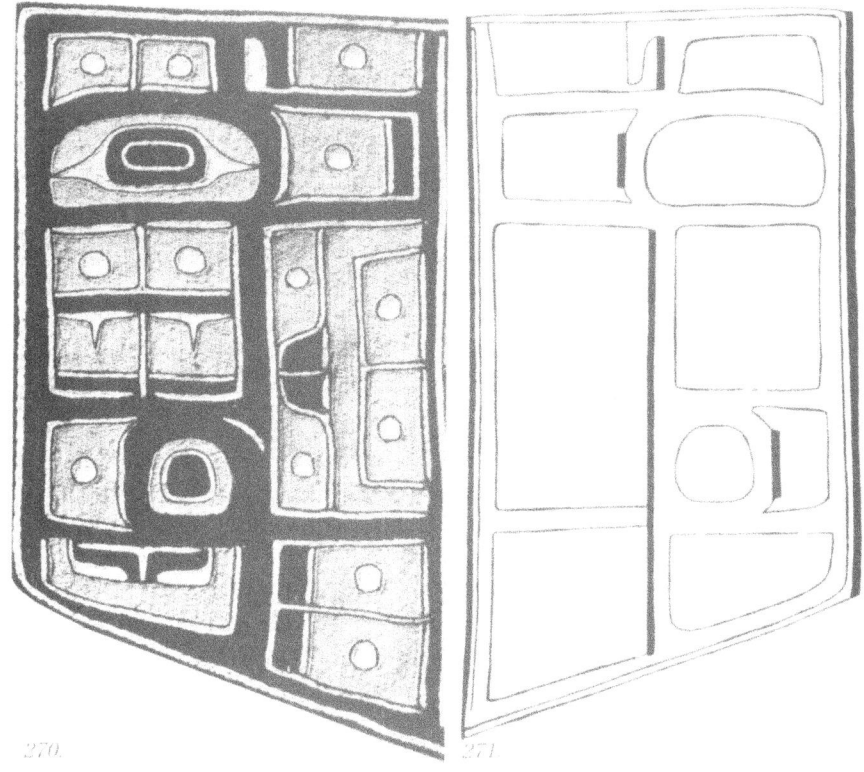

270. A woven side panel (CS)

271. Distribution of drawstrings in the side panel in figure 270. The heavy line indicates the placement of a drawstring.

DISTRIBUTION OF DRAWSTRINGS

Drawstrings were used to connect the black and yellow borders to the design field and to connect the three design panels. They were also used within the design field, underneath any obviously straight vertical line. Surprisingly, they also occurred for short distances under curved lines. This especially happened between the eye and the nose of the headlike shapes, the drawstring lying under the outside edge of the nose crescent. Placement here allowed the weaver to work the formline ovoid and its eye first, then to join the nose to it. Through frequent use of drawstrings, the weaver could concentrate on separate formline sections of the design, perfecting them without the complications of adjacent forms.

272. A woven central design panel (CS)

273. Distribution of the drawstrings in the central design panel in figure 272. The heavy lines indicate placement of the drawstrings. The numbered areas indicate the sequence in which they might have been woven.

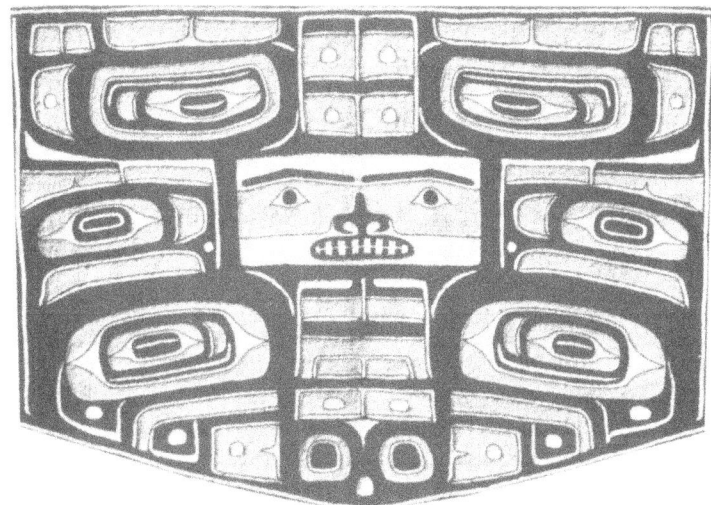

272.

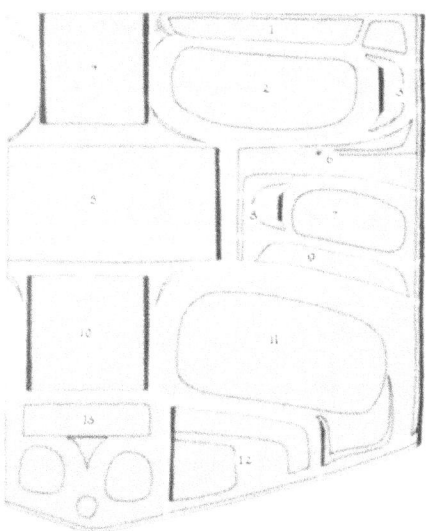

273.

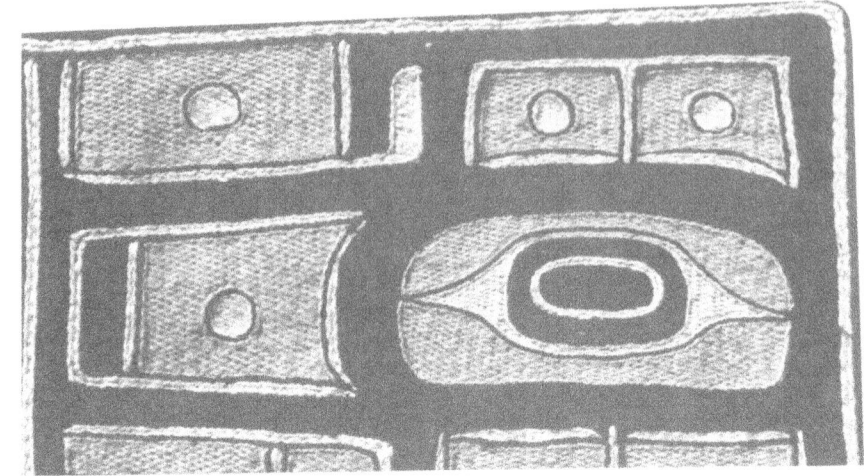

274. A woven upper portion of a side panel (CS)

WEAVING THE PRIMARY FORMLINE OVOIDS

A combination of lazy line techniques and drawstrings enables the weaver to weave the major formline ovoids as shapes, even though they merge with surrounding formline areas. The fact that these shapes were woven as units encourages the weaver to consider them as major forms rather than as background. The twining of primary formlines greatly benefits the visual flow of the total design.

To weave the primary formlines, the weaver first identifies them from the pattern board. She mentally curves the lines where they merge and decides from this where she will make her joins. In figure 276, a drawstring will be placed at (1), allowing the weaver to complete first the ear, (A), and then the adjacent ∪ shape, (B). A second drawstring will be placed at (2); the weaver will twine the eye shape, (C), and then connect it to the nose, (D). Because this is the top of a side panel, drawstrings run down both sides, (3) and (4).

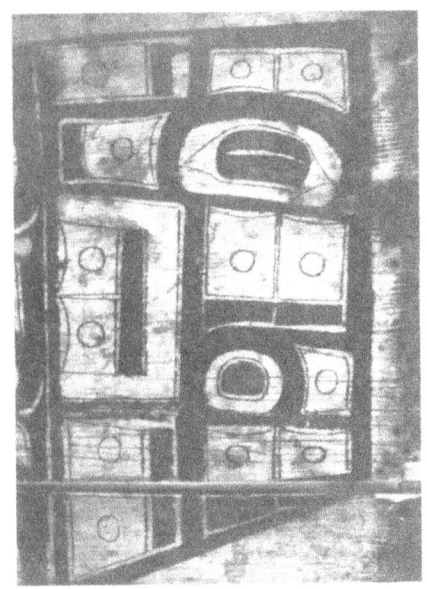

275. The side panel painted on a pattern board (Courtesy of the Field Museum, Chicago: CS)

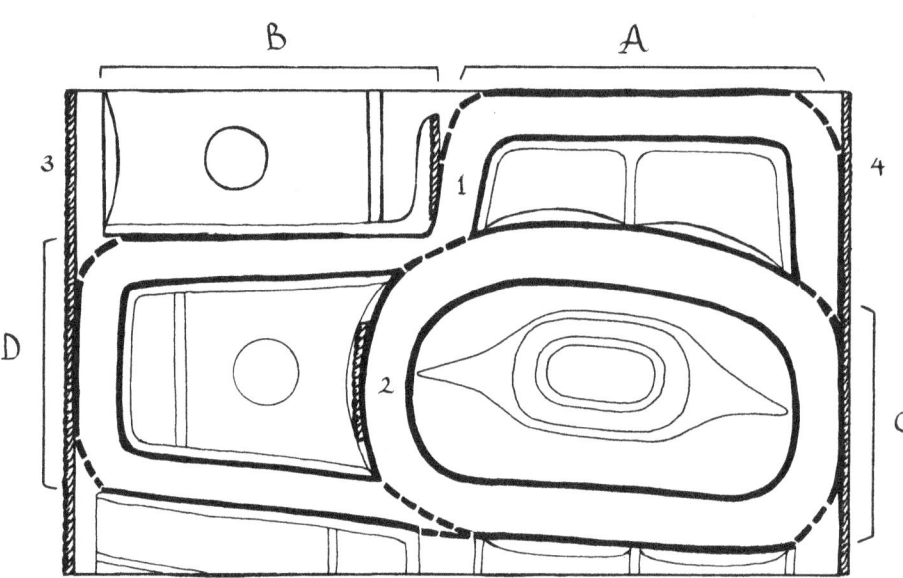

276. Placement of drawstrings

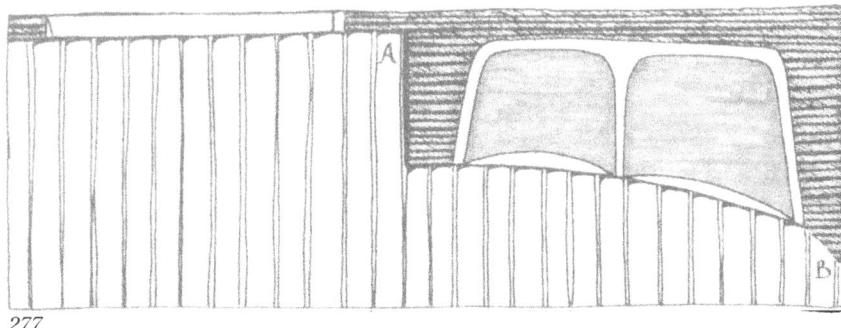

277.

STEP 1: The formline ∪ with its paired ∪ shapes is woven first. It is not necessary to curve the top right corner, as the connecting line on the right is a drawstring. On the left, the top of the adjacent ∪ shape is started and woven down to the point where the drawstring is entered, (A). The paired ∪ shapes are then twined, curving the bottom to define the upper edge of the formline ovoid. On the lower right, the ovoid is defined by the black weft of the formline ∪ (fig. 277).

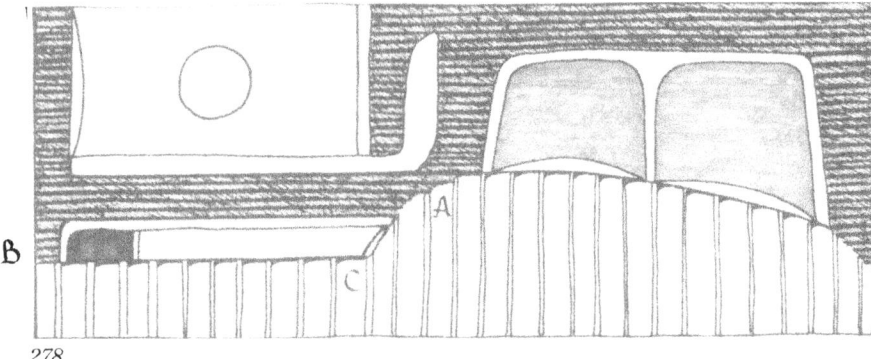

278.

STEP 2: The adjacent ∪ shape is woven next. It is connected to the drawstring and once completed, the black weft of the formline ∪ is twined, defining the curve of the adjacent ovoid on the right, (A), and weaving to the drawstring on the left, (B). The beginning of the inner ∪ shape is started in order to complete the curve of the ovoid to where it meets the drawstring which will lie to the right of the inner ∪ shape's crescent, (C) (fig. 278).

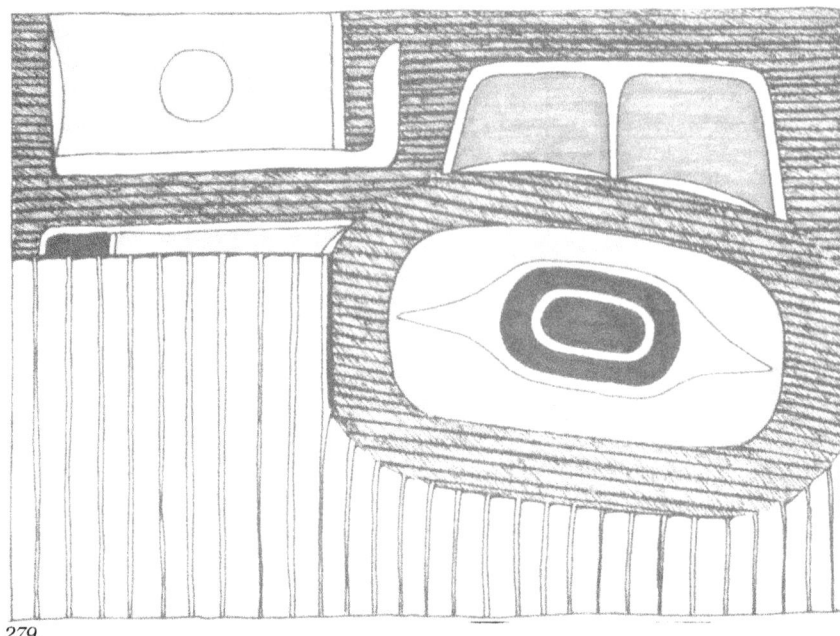

279.

STEP 3: The eye, comprised of the formline ovoid and its socket and eyelid line, can now be woven. The twining of the formline ovoid turns to follow the shape of the ovoid itself, meeting the formline Us of the ear and the nose, and working down the drawstrings on either side. The socket is then completed and the formline ovoid is twined underneath them. Here the weft follows the bottom of the shape, retreating one warp end each row to form the curve (fig. 279).

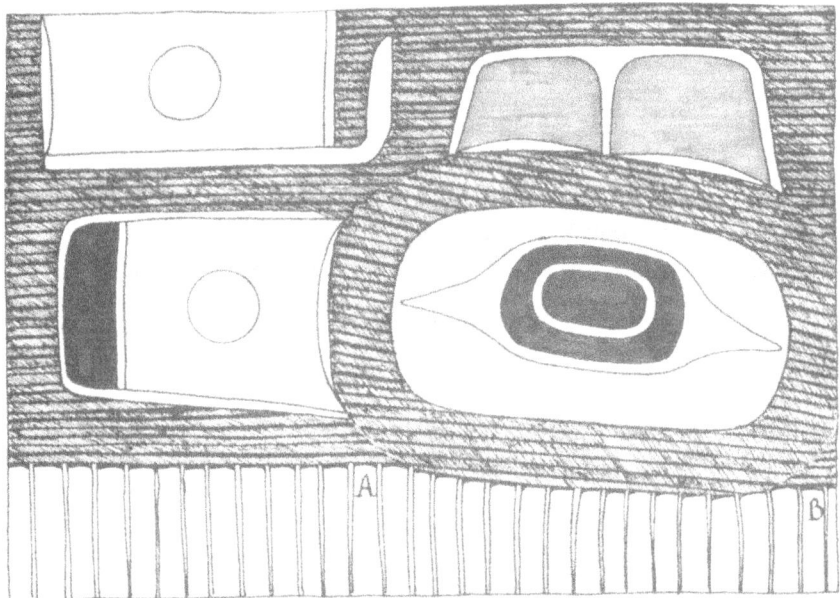

280.

STEP 4: Finishing the U shape adjacent to the eye completes this headlike shape. It is worked to the drawstring on the formline ovoid, creating the center portion of the inner U shape's crescent. The points of this crescent are completed as the shape moves into the warp under the ovoid, (A). The final side of the formline U is twined to meet the bottom of the formline ovoid. On the far right, a few rows of twining are entered to bring the line of weaving down in preparation for the next shapes, (B) (fig. 280).

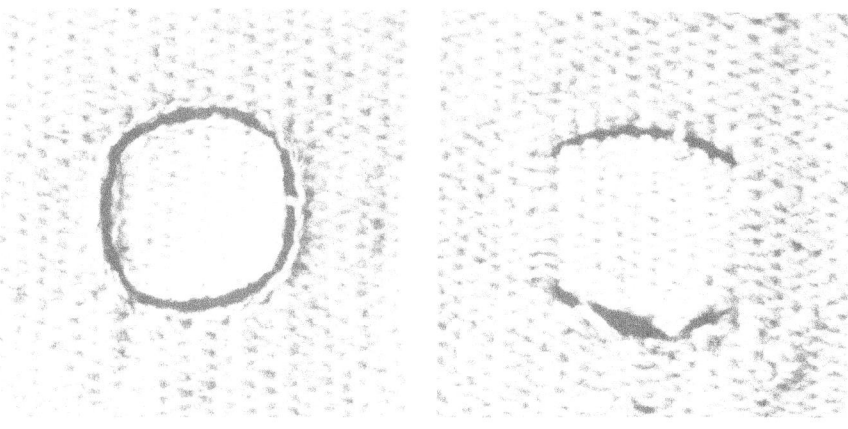

281. *A circle (CS)*   282. *The back of a circle (CS)*

A CIRCLE

In the weft, a circle is comprised of a top crescent, a rectangle, and a lower crescent (fig. 283). These are theoretical divisions which can be imagined when looking at the back of the weaving. On the front, the braids round these elements into a perfect circle; traveling in the warp around the top crescent, they move into the weft over the interlock join of the rectangle, then go once more into the warp around the bottom of the lower crescent. The trail of the braids curves the sides of the rectangle, outlining a circle on the front of the fabric.

Circles, woven of very fine weft yarns, were most commonly twined over alternate warp ends. In some of the oldest Dancing Blankets and Aprons, however, it is not uncommon to find them twined over single warp ends, an effect which is subtle and very striking.

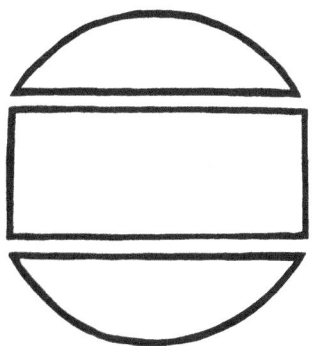

283. *The division of a circle*

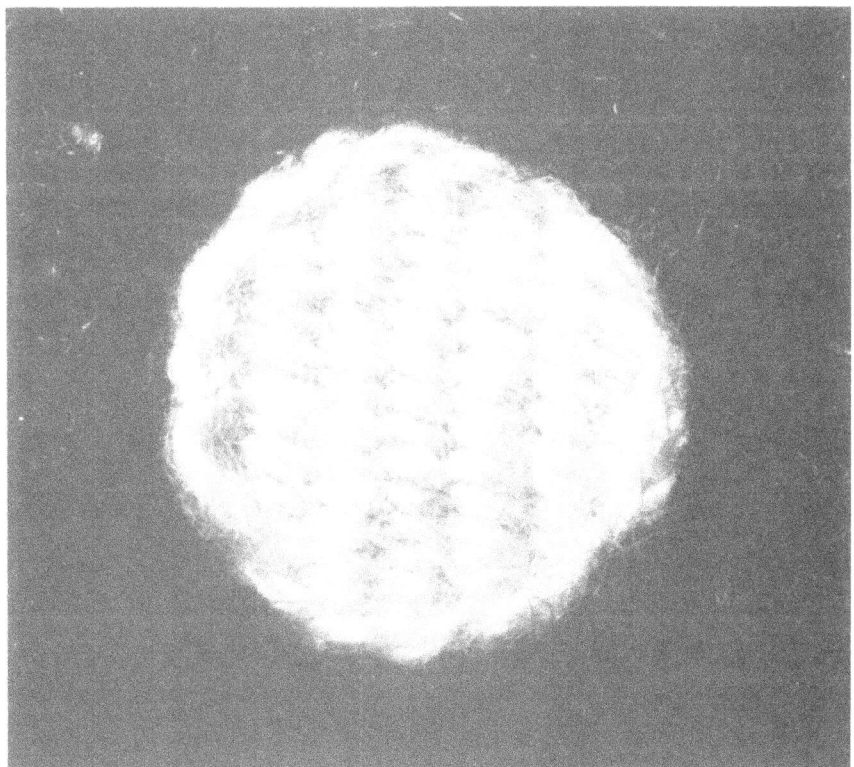

284. *A circle, twined over single warp ends (CS)*

STEP 1: The size of the circle to be woven is taken directly from the pattern board. The weaver plans this circle on her warp and marks the middle warp end with a small bow knot of scrap yarn. It is preferable to have an uneven number of warp ends in the circle; if the space allowed does not contain an odd number, a warp end can be added in the middle. Very small circles are woven on four warp ends (fig. 285).

STEP 2: The exterior of the circle is twined in the same color of the shape which surrounds it. At least three warp ends are left free in the middle. Two wefts are used, one being a continuation of the previous twining and the other a new piece which is added two warps over from the center (fig. 286).

STEP 3: When the top third is defined, braids are inserted. The circle illustrated here is a white one which relieves two dark formlines; therefore, it has a black braid and a white braid surrounding it. Circles in ∪ shapes generally have three braids: one yellow or blue, one black, and one white. All braids are entered in exactly the same position, starting on the right side around the warp which lies inside the last row of twining and finishing on the left side around the warp which precedes the last twined row (fig. 287).

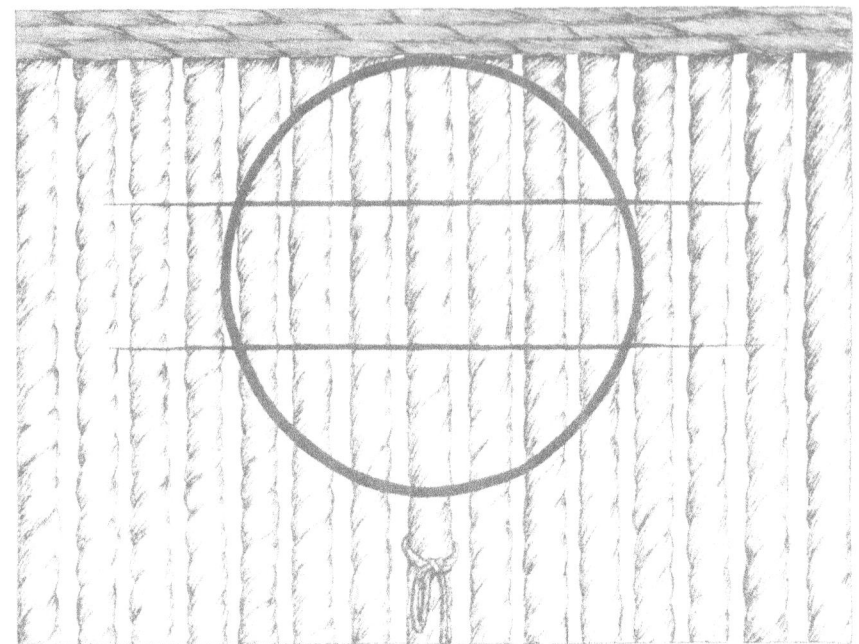
285.

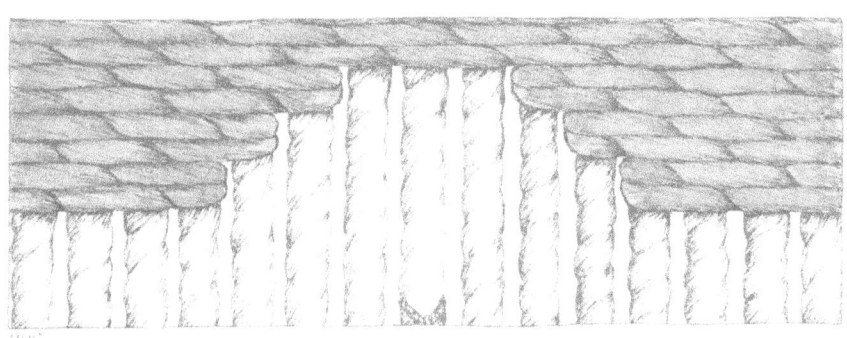
286.

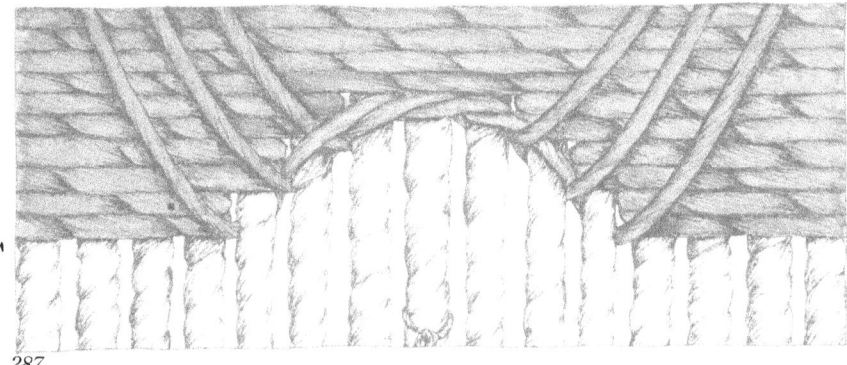
287.

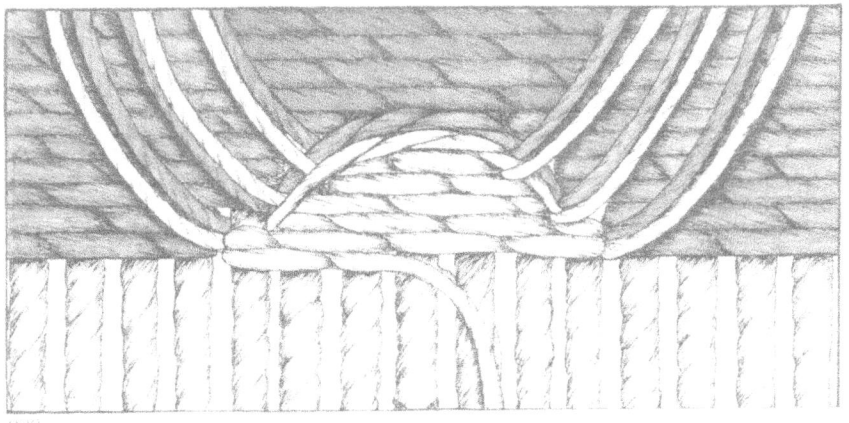

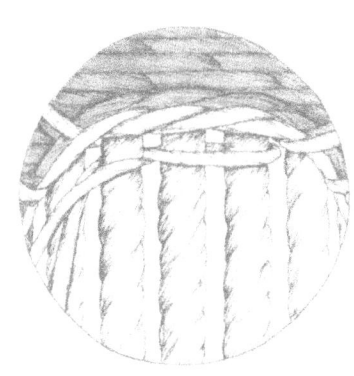

STEP 4: The top crescent is twined, either over alternate warp pairs or over single warp ends. This decision is left to the weaver. The twining is started at the top on the right and worked to the left, turning on the third warp end (fig. 289). The number of rows twined depends on the size of the circle, the number of braids already inserted, and the size of the weft yarn. The bottom row of twining should lie even with the bottom row of exterior twining. This is often accomplished within four or five rows (fig. 288).

289. The first row of twining underneath the circle braids

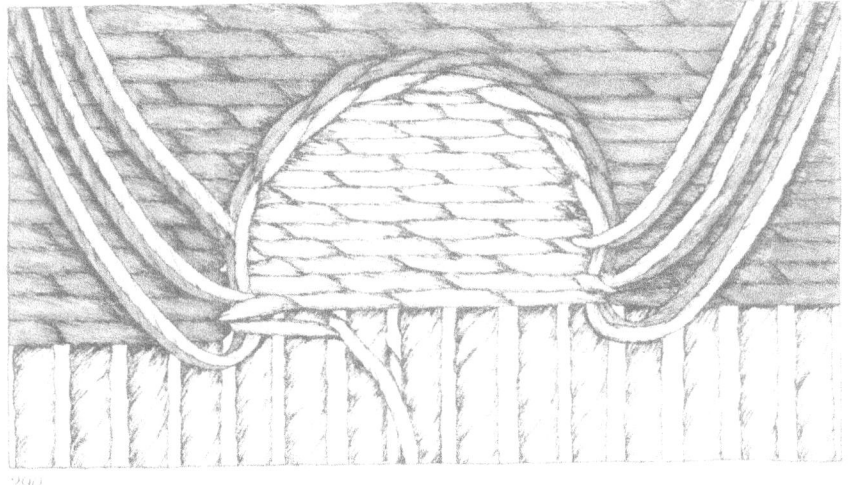

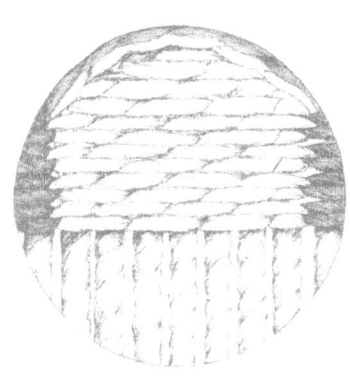

STEP 5: In order to weave the rectangle which forms the middle section, an interlock join is worked between the exterior wefts and the circle wefts. This join must always occur between the same two warp ends on each side (fig. 291). The braids are worked into each interlock. To keep the interlock from showing, it is best to split the braids, placing one on the outside and the others on the circle side of this join. They are caught each time the side is interlocked; because the circle is so small, no free rows are possible in the vertical braiding (fig. 290).

291. The interlock join shown on the back of a circle

STEP 6: The bottom crescent of the circle is then twined, free of braiding. The number of rows twined here should equal the number of rows twined in the top crescent. The tails of the twining strands are dropped beside the warp. The tension is adjusted in the braids around the edges of the rectangle before they are finished under the bottom crescent (fig. 292).

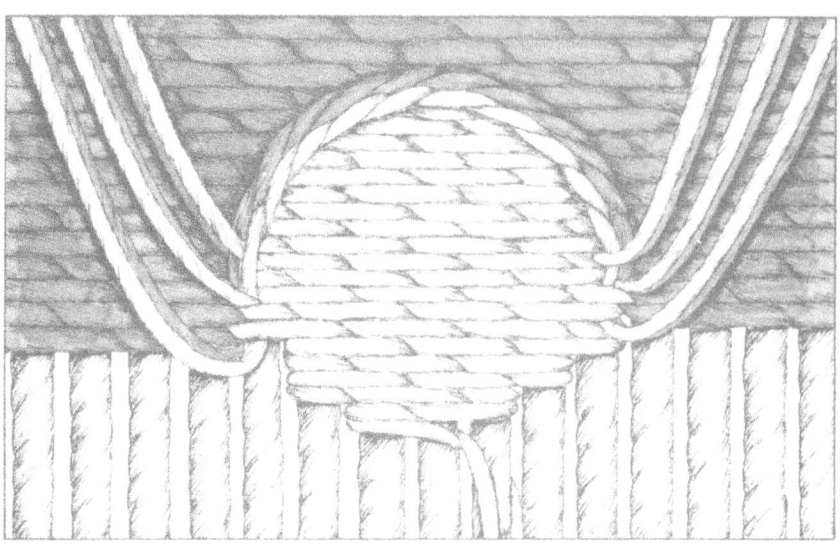

STEP 7: In this circle, the black braid is completed first and then the white braid. To splice each braid, one strand from the left side is dropped to the right of warp end #2, the next one to the right of warp end #3, and the final one around warp end #4 (fig. 294). The tails of the right side will splice, ending first to the left of #6, next to the left of #5, and finally to the left of #4. All tails are pushed to the back of the weaving (fig. 293).

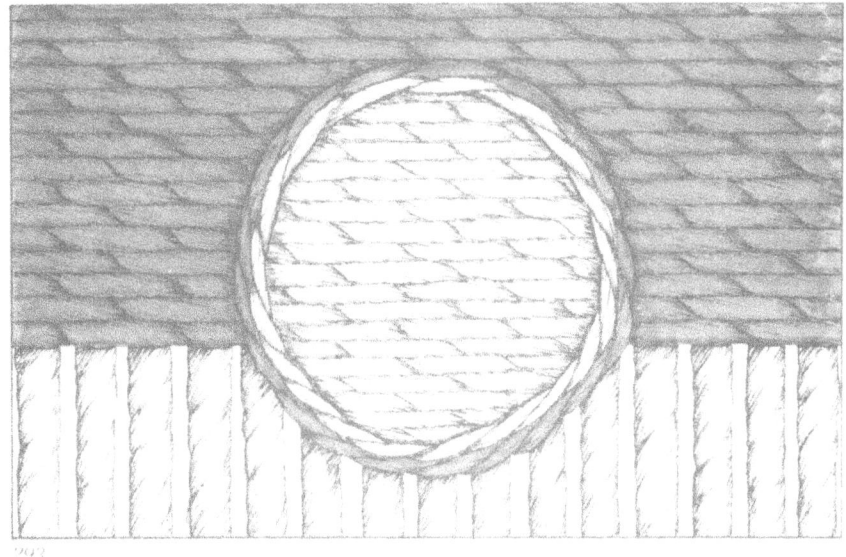

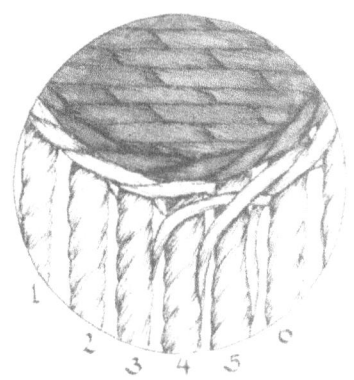

294. Finishing the braids of a circle

STEP 8: To complete the circle, the exterior weft is worked on each side down to the bottom of the circle underneath the braids. One weft is then dropped and the other continues to twine across the entire shape. The braid ends are either worked in later with a needle or dropped down alongside the warp, twined into the weft for approximately one centimeter, and then cut off at the back (fig. 295).

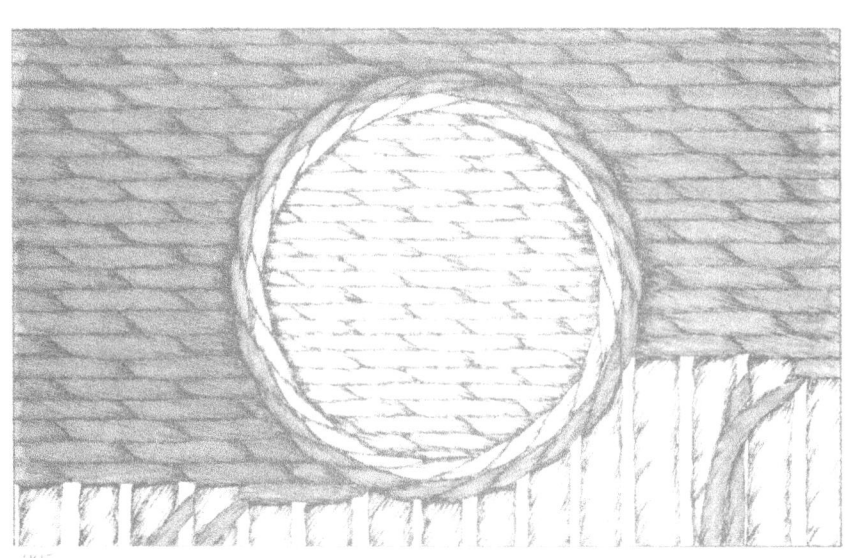

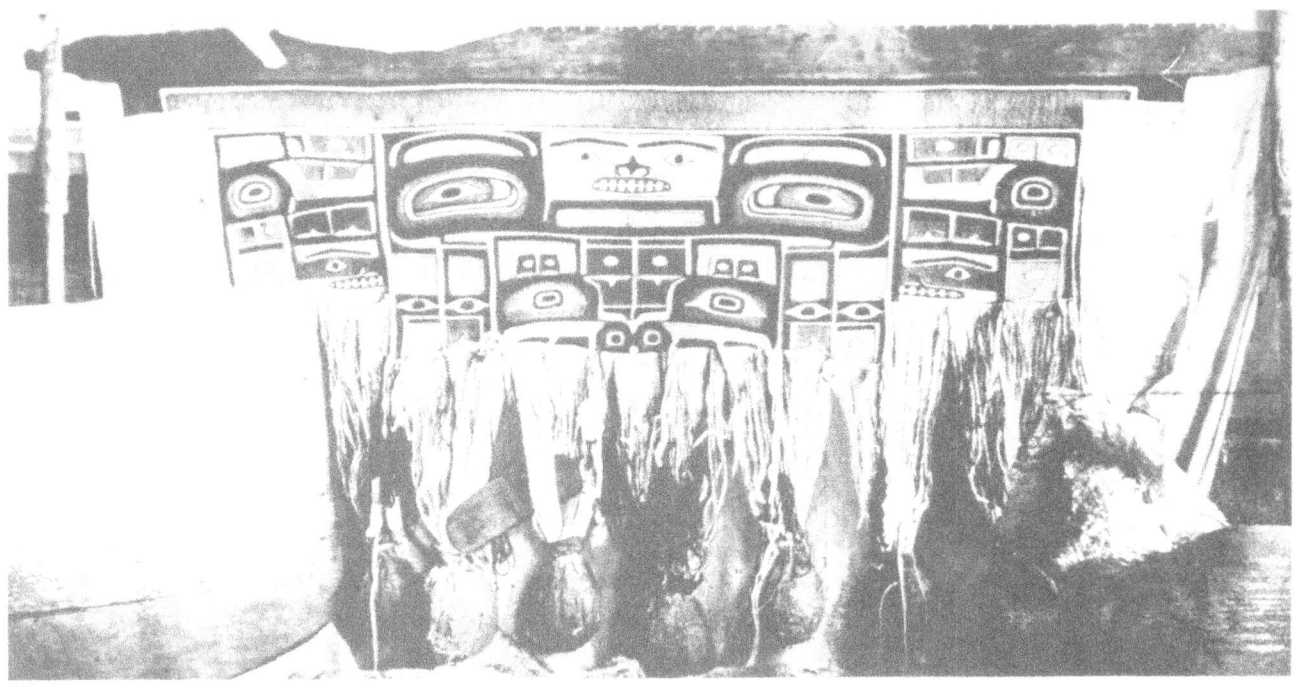

SOCKETS WITH EYELID LINES

To create the graceful curves of the eyelid lines, the fell of the weft turns to follow the shape of the figure. The braids which define the outlines can then be worked against smooth, perfectly formed curves. The diagram in figure 297 illustrates the direction of the black, yellow, and white wefts as they model the eyelid shape.

Within the weft, the warp ends move as they accommodate the action of the twining. Consequently, they bend toward the center of the eye, moving in from the top and out at the bottom. The spaces between the warp ends at the sides of the figure indicate that new warp strands will need to be added (fig. 298).

296. A loom with a weaving in progress. In the center of the warp, a template can be seen above the gut bags. Protective sheets are sewn to the black and yellow borders to keep them clean. In many old black and white photographs, the yellow areas registered darker than the blue. The colors in this blanket have not been reversed, but appear so due to the photographic problem. (Courtesy of the British Columbia Provincial Museum)

297. Direction of the weft

298. Direction of the warp

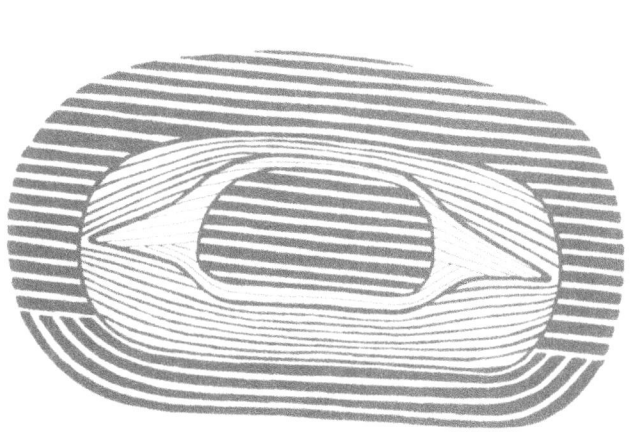

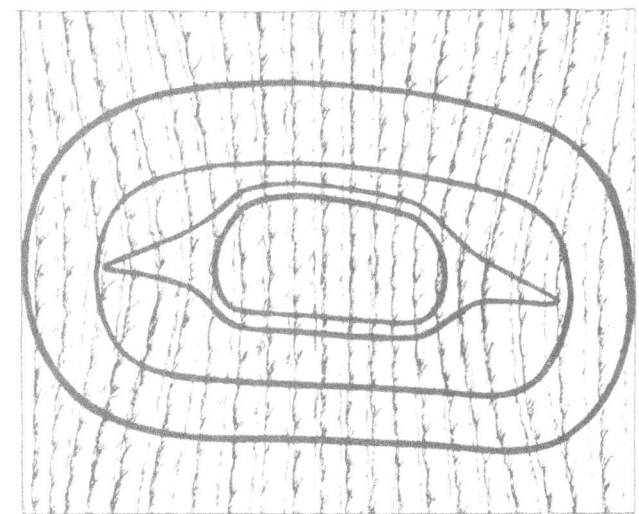

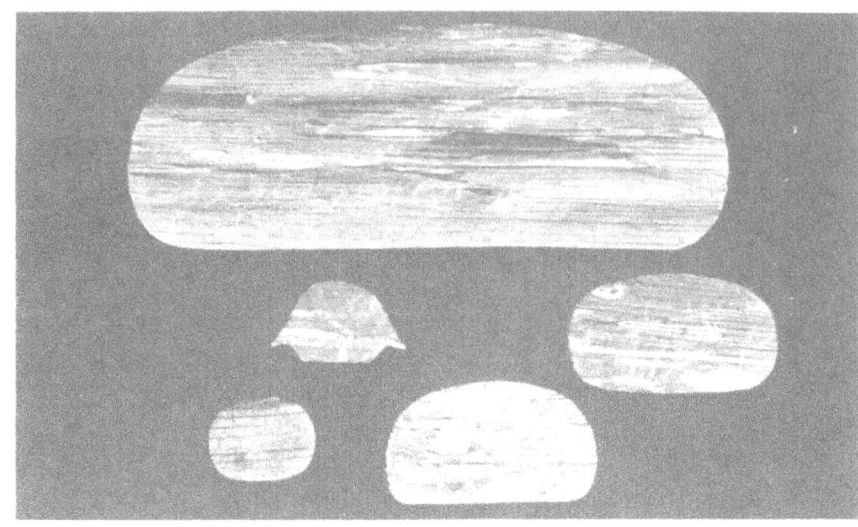

299. Cedar bark templates (Courtesy of the Burke Museum, University of Washington: CS)

To aid in creating the curves of the ovoids, the weaver might use the cedar bark templates which the artist used in painting the pattern board. She would hold them next to the warp as she gauged the curves.

Sockets, Eyelid Lines, and Inner Ovoids

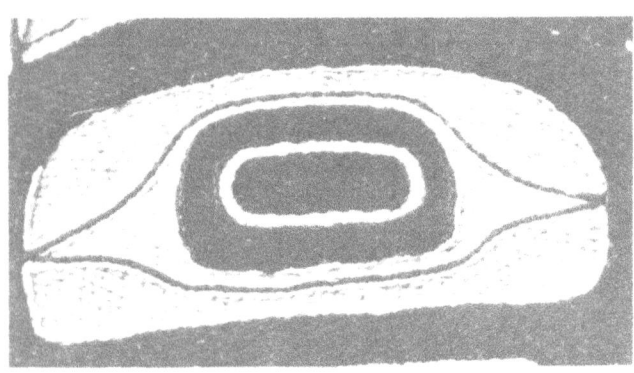

300. A socket and eyelid line with its inner ovoid (CS)

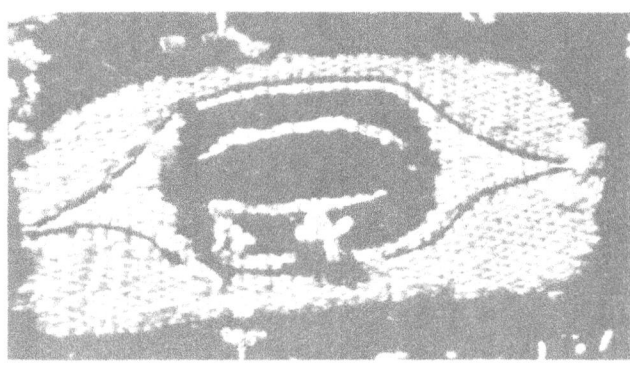

301. The back of the socket and eyelid line (CS)

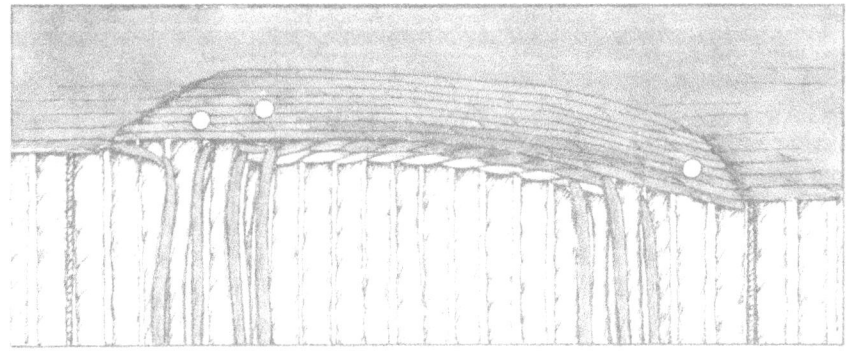

STEP 1: The black formline ovoid is twined first, adding warp ends as needed within the curves. These added warp ends are indicated by the white circles. One black and one yellow braid are inserted on the inside curve. In the design field, the ovoid will probably have a drawstring quite nearby on each side (fig. 302).

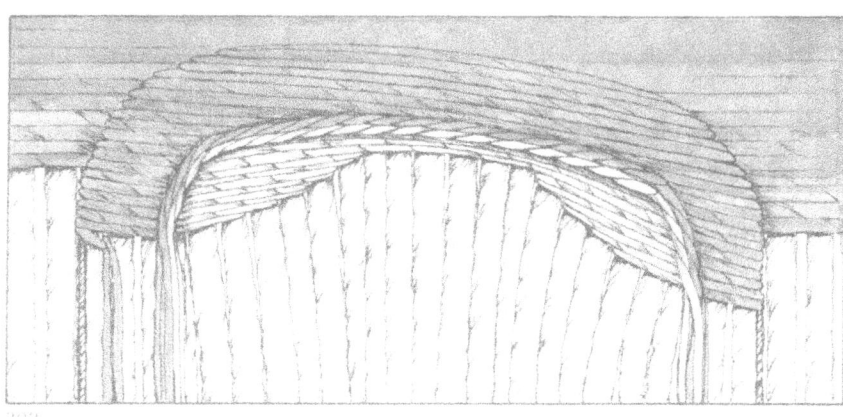

STEP 2: The yellow weft is twined, establishing the shape of the eyelid line within the yellow socket. The yellow weft interlocks to the black weft on the outside edges, the black and yellow braids being split between the two sides of the interlock (fig. 303).

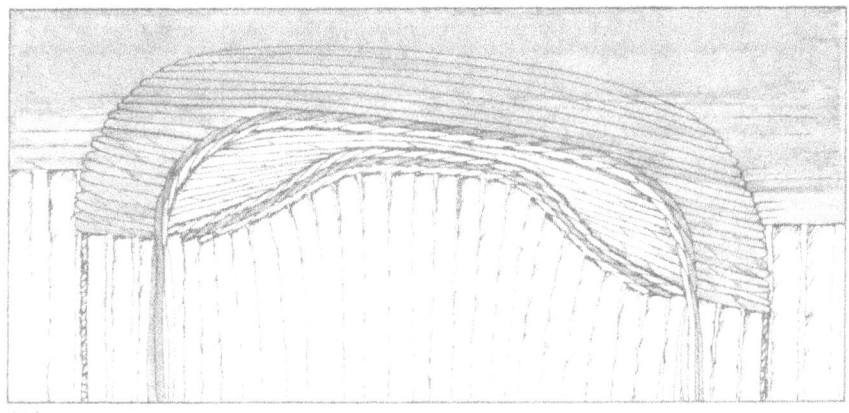

STEP 3: The braids which form the eyelid line are inserted. The yellow braid will touch the braid of the yellow ovoid, followed by a black braid which ends one warp end in from the yellow braid, and a white braid ending one warp end in from the black braid (fig. 304).

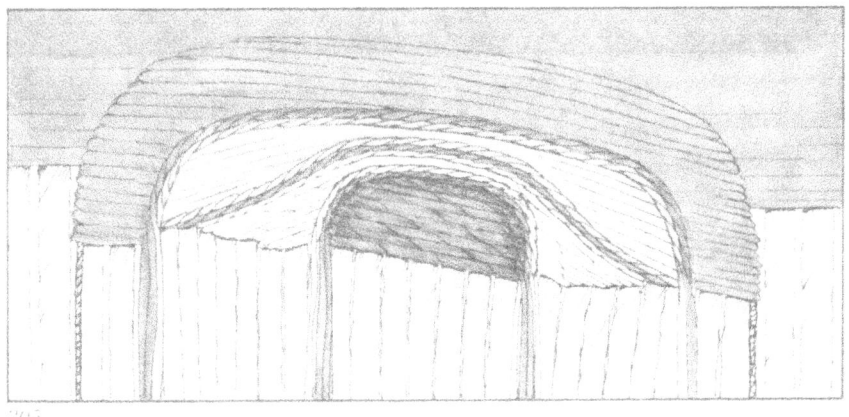

STEP 4: The white of the eye and the iris are twined, inserting a black, a white, and a black braid around the iris and interlocking the white and black wefts. The white weft will follow the line of the eyelid and fill in the shape to a horizontal line (fig. 305).

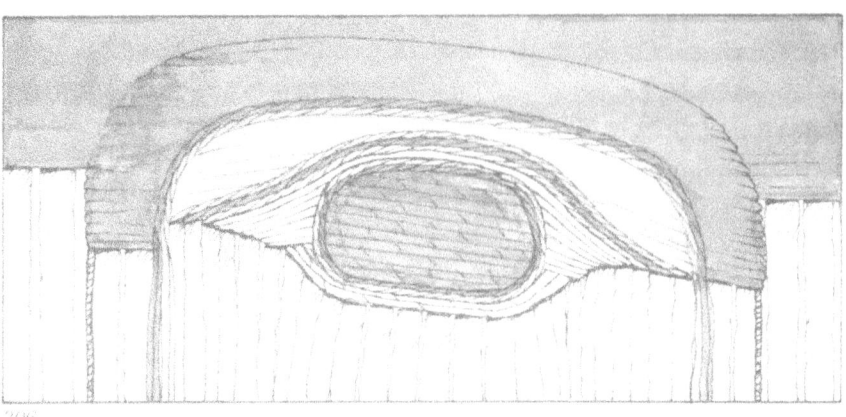

STEP 5: The iris is completed by finishing its black and white braids underneath it. Two white weft rows are twined under the iris (fig. 306).

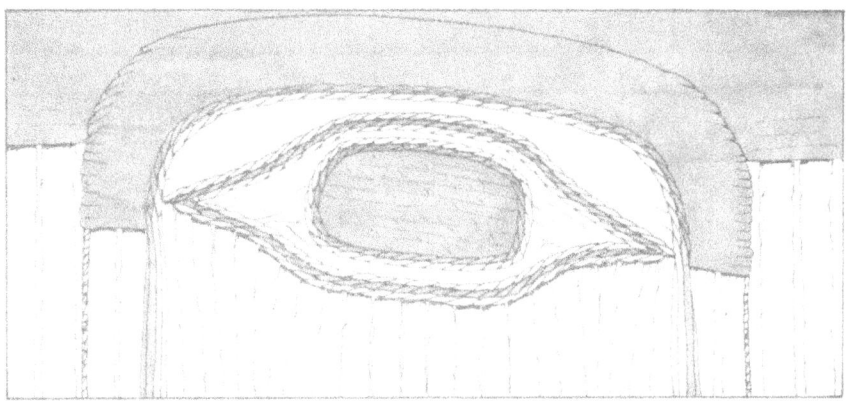

STEP 6: The bottom braids of the eyelid line are finished: first the white, then the black, and then the yellow one. Each braid should be staggered one warp in from its mate to create a fine point (fig. 307).

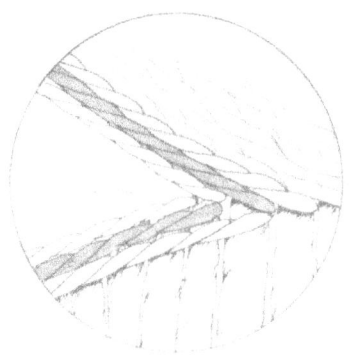

308. A detail of the points of an eyelid line showing how the braids are staggered

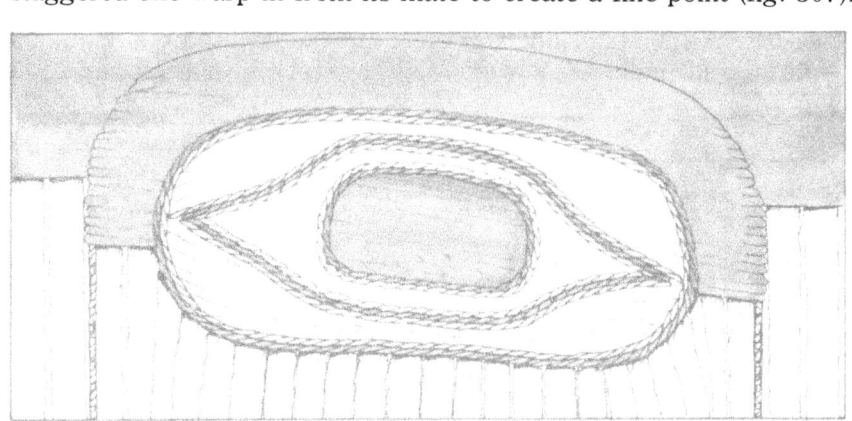

STEP 7: In order to twine the bottom of the yellow socket, rows must first be worked underneath the points of the eyelid shape to fill out the bottom curve. More rows are twined to complete the curve. The yellow and black braids which surround the socket are finished underneath this twining (fig. 309).

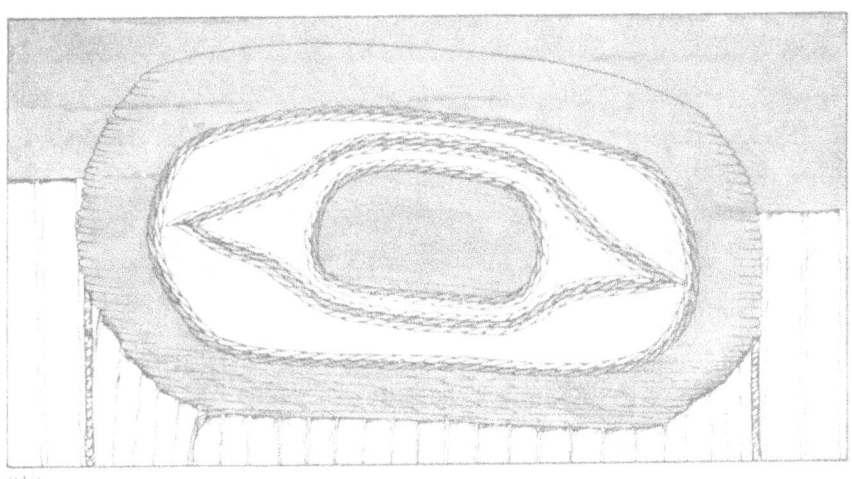

STEP 8: The twining of the black formline ovoid is completed underneath the bottom braids of the socket. As the warp ends change their angle, it may be necessary to remove some of them in the bottom curve if they bunch together too much. This will depend, in part, on the surrounding forms (fig. 310).

PAIRED U SHAPES OF THE SAME COLOR

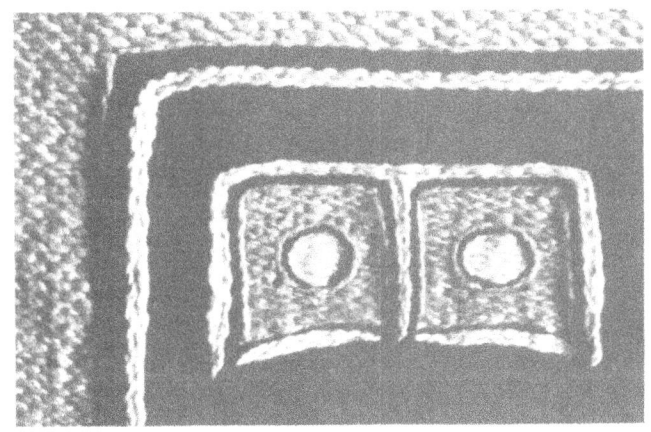

311. A pair of inner U shapes (CS)

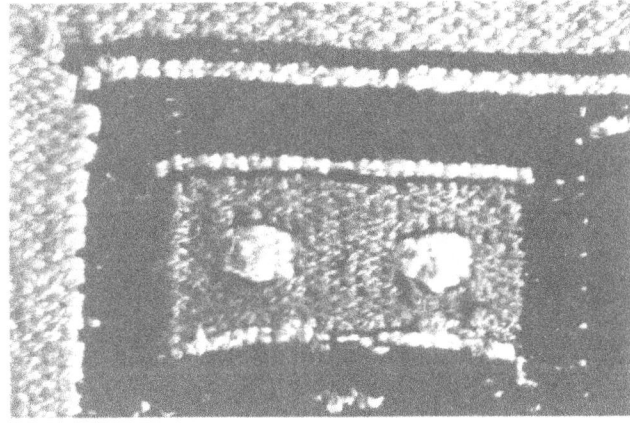

312. The back of the inner U shapes (CS)

Paired inner U shapes of the same color need not be woven with a weft join between them. Because braids can travel vertically at any point, the braids which outline and divide the two U shapes turn and travel through the center of the weft which twines across the width of both shapes.

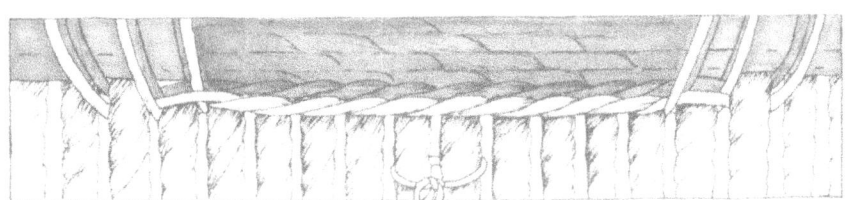

313.

STEP 1: A row of black braiding and then one of white are twined across both shapes. The middle two warps are marked with a small bow (fig. 313).

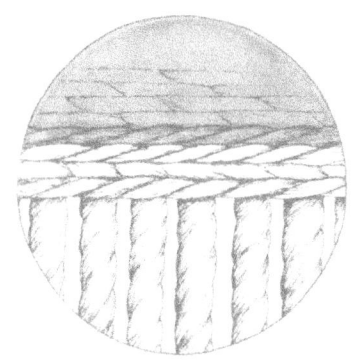

314. Sometimes two white braids are used, with a row of two-strand twining over single warp ends between them.

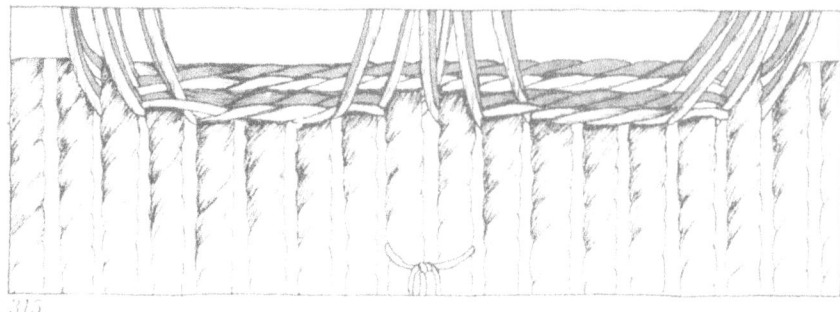

STEP 2: Two black braids are entered underneath the white one, one starting on the right and ending between the middle two warp ends, the other starting between the middle two warp ends and ending on the left. Two yellow braids are entered in exactly the same position (fig. 315).

STEP 3: Two white braids are entered vertically between the middle warp ends. To secure these closely to the horizontal white braid, the first doubled strands can be inserted into the back of the white braid. The third strands of these braids will be entered in the first row of weft twining (fig. 316).

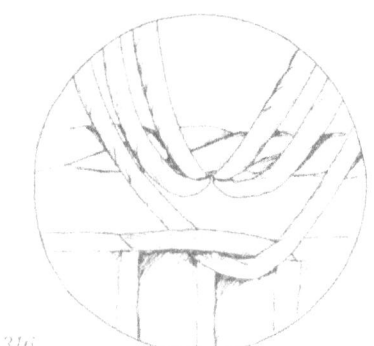

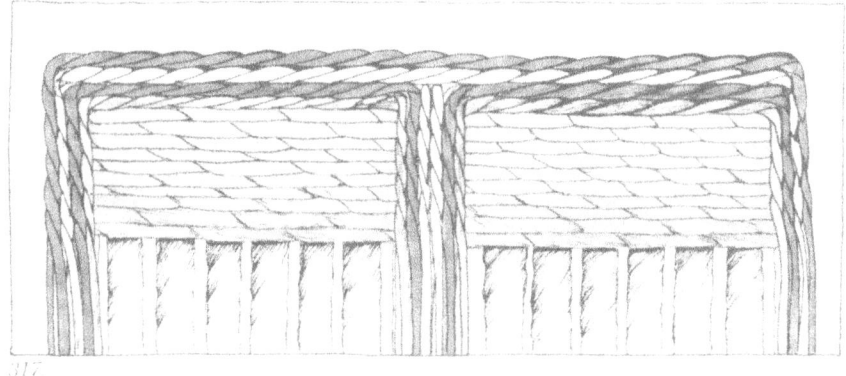

STEP 4: In the first weft rows, top corners are turned in the inner black and yellow braids. The entire shape is twined with a yellow weft, the braids catching vertically in the appropriate row; this must be a row which includes both marked warp ends (fig. 317).

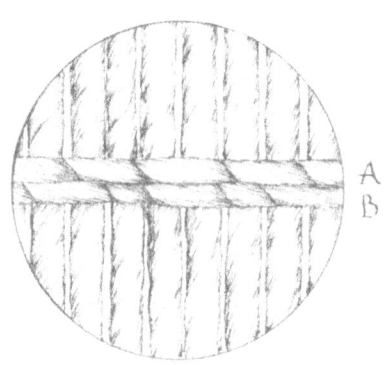

318. Paired warp ends underneath vertical braids

Some weavers use a special trick which allows them to catch the braids in any row they desire (fig. 318). This method includes two alternating rows of twining: (A), a normal row twined over pairs of warp ends and (B), a second row which twines over alternate warp pairs until it reaches the middle of the shape. It then twines over a single warp end before the two marked warp ends. Then these two are twined together, followed by the enclosure of another single warp end. When this pattern is completed, the weft resumes its alternate warp end twining. These two rows are repeated for the entire length of the shape.

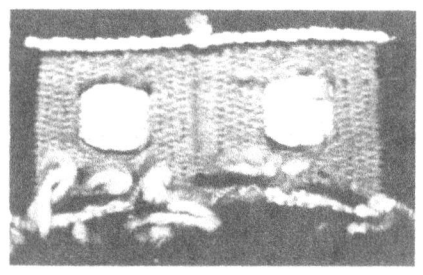

319. The back of paired ∪ shapes in which the weaver has twined over paired warp ends near the center (Courtesy of the Field Museum, Chicago: CS)

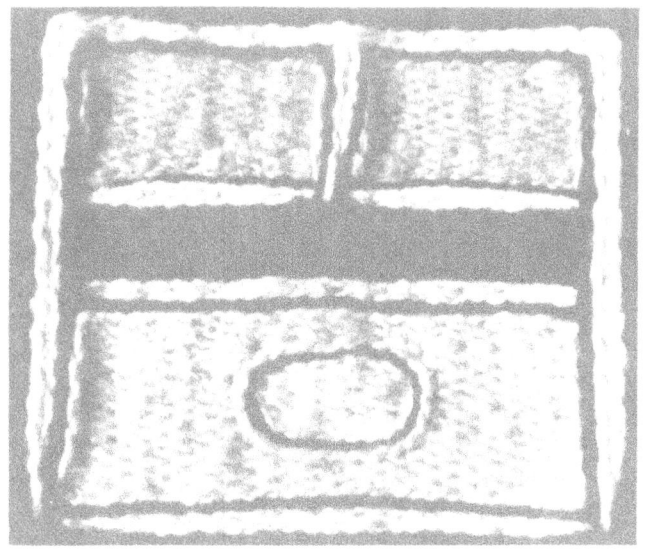

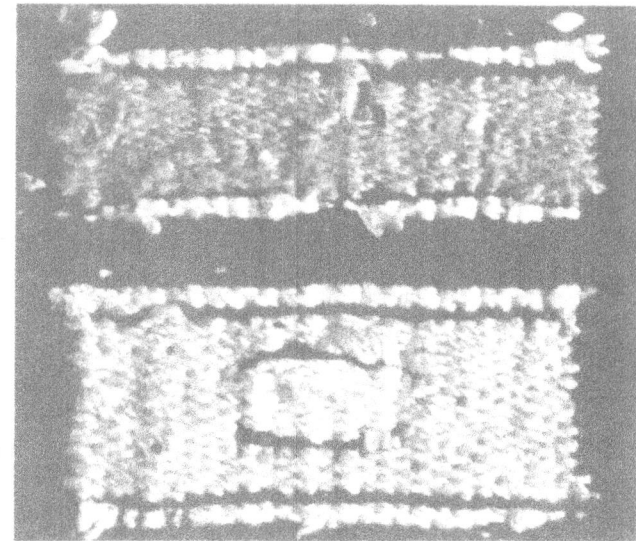

320. An upside down ∪ shape (CS)

321. The back of the ∪ shape (CS)

HORIZONTAL CRESCENTS IN UPSIDE DOWN ∪ SHAPES

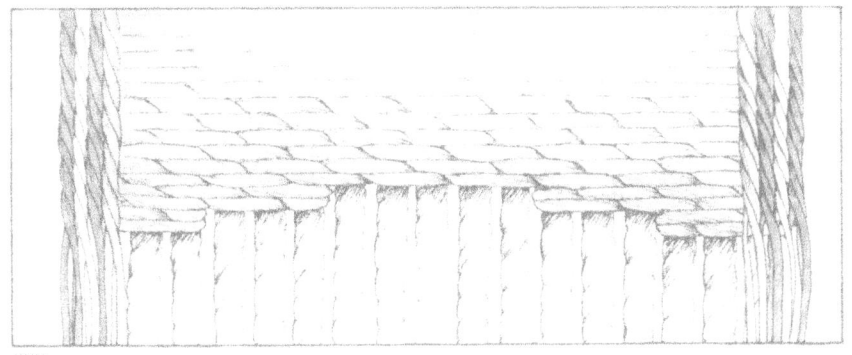

STEP 1: To weave a horizontal crescent in an upside down ∪ shape, the weaver must first imagine the outline of the crescent on the warp. She then weaves down on each side of the form, creating this shape in the weft. The weft strands on one side continue from the weft of the main body of the ∪ shape; on the other side, a new weft must be added. Very few rows are needed to form the crescent; the vertical braids on the sides are caught in each turn of the wefts. When the crescent shape has been established, the vertical braids can be braided free from the weft for about one centimeter (fig. 323). This will order and secure them and, due to the great number of strands, make them easier to work with (fig. 322).

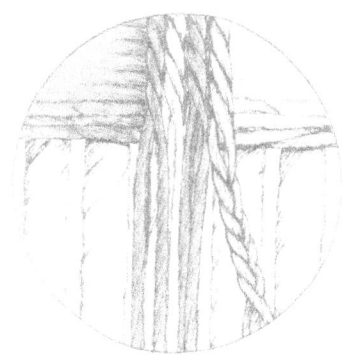

323. The ends of a vertical braid worked without the weft

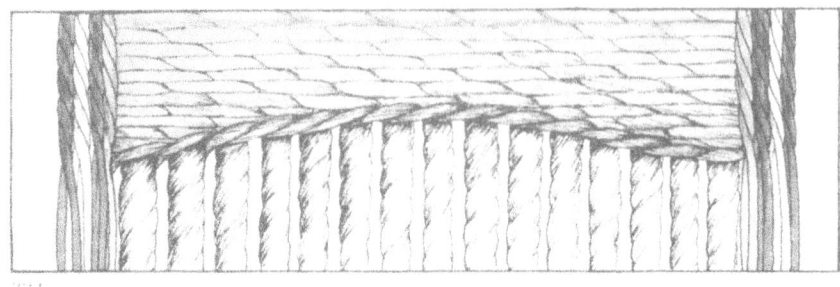

STEP 2: The weaver then braids across from the right to the left with the yellow or blue yarn of the U shape (fig. 324).

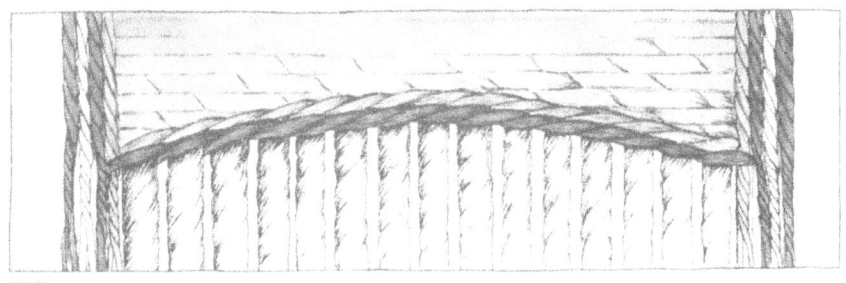

STEP 3: The second braid, a black one, is entered on the left and braided to the right. It should enclose the strands of the vertical blue or yellow braid. By starting successive horizontal braid rows on first one side of the shape and then the other, their tails are divided between the two sides of the shape and a buildup is not created on only one side (fig. 325).

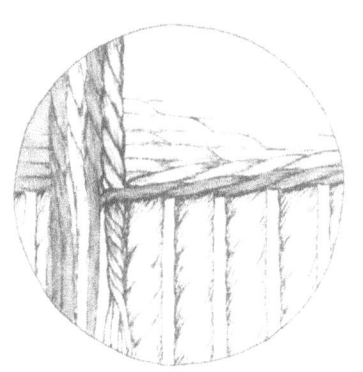

326. The vertical yellow braid is enclosed by the horizontal black outline braid.

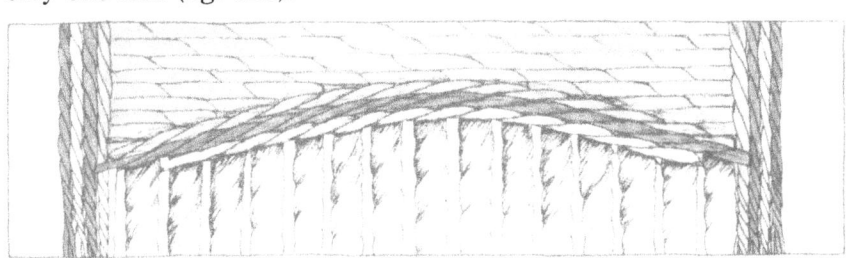

STEP 4: The first white braid of the crescent is inserted. It should be worked from right to left and should start and finish one warp end inside the horizontal black braid (fig. 327).

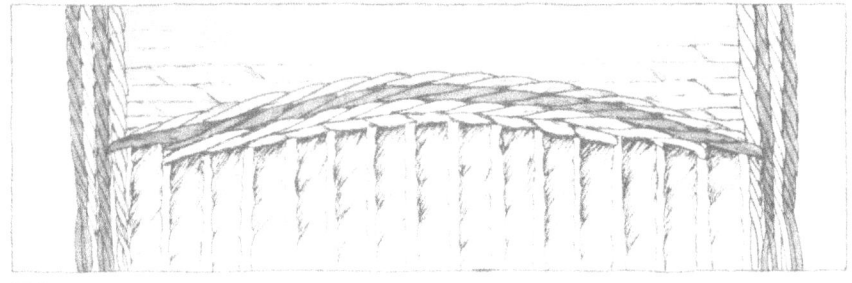

STEP 5: One row of weft twining is worked under the white braid. It can be worked over single warp ends as shown, or over paired warp ends. It should start and finish two warp ends inside the white braid (fig. 328).

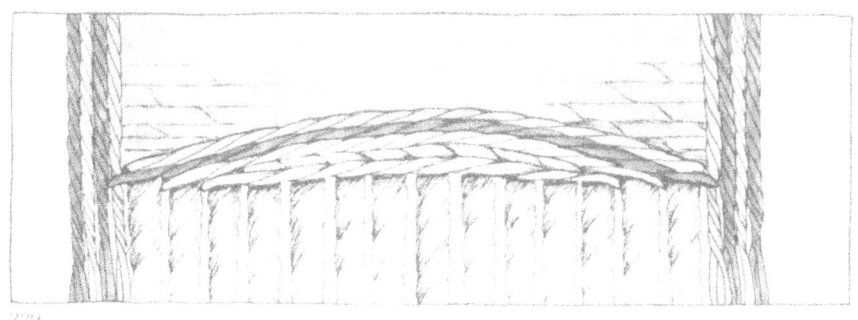

STEP 6: Another row of white braiding finishes the crescent. It starts and stops one warp end inside the first white braid (fig. 329).

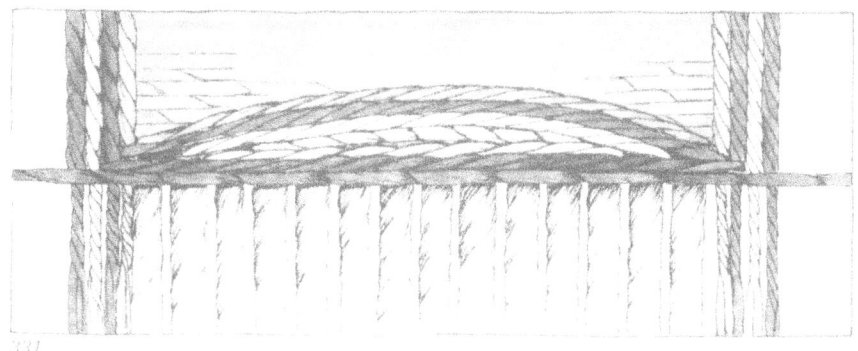

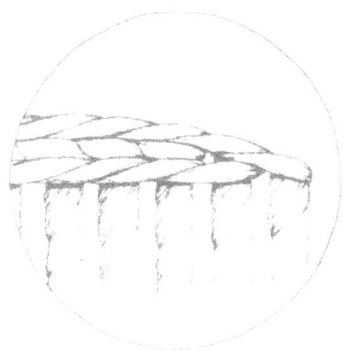

330. In order to make a very sharp point, the two white braids and the inner twining must be staggered in their entry.

STEP 7: To complete the ∪ shape, one row of black braiding is worked under the crescent from left to right. It should include the inside black vertical braid on either side of the ∪ shape.

The two-strand twining of the black formline is then worked underneath the crescent, all of the braid ends being caught for one centimeter and then cut off. The bottom line of the crescent should conform to the outside edge of the primary formline (fig. 331).

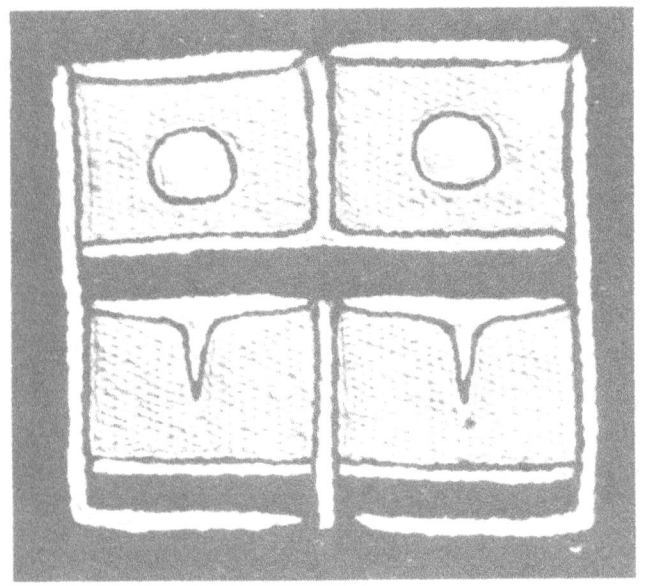 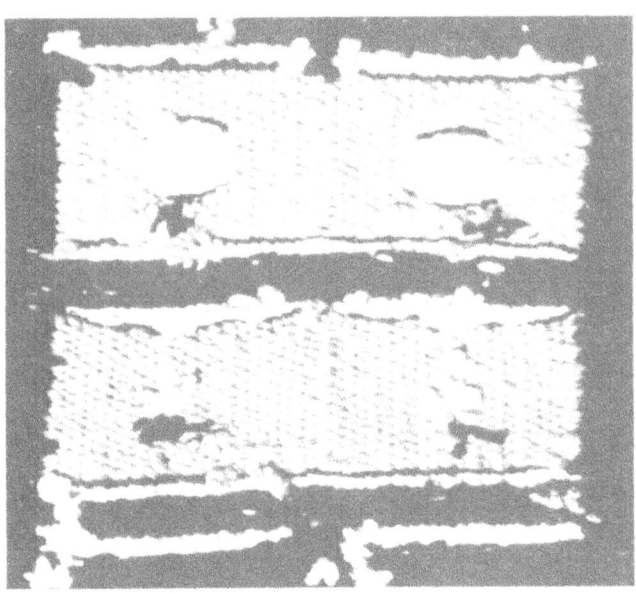

332. Crescents in paired upright ∪ shapes (CS)   *333. The back of the ∪ shapes (CS)*

CRESCENTS IN
PAIRED UPRIGHT ∪ SHAPES

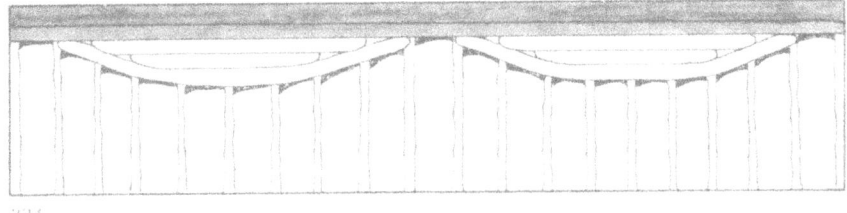

STEP 1: A black row of braiding is worked across the entire form under the formline. Vertical braids are entered on the outside edges of the shape. Two white crescents are inserted, each one starting one warp in from the outside edge and finishing before the middle two warp ends (fig. 334).

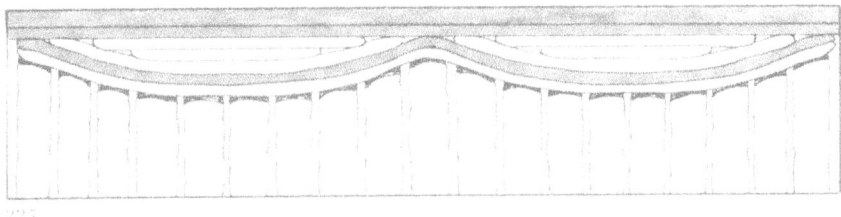

STEP 2: A black braid is worked across the entire form, starting adjacent to the vertical braids on the sides and curving up in the middle to meet the first braid. A yellow braid is entered and worked in the same manner (fig. 335).

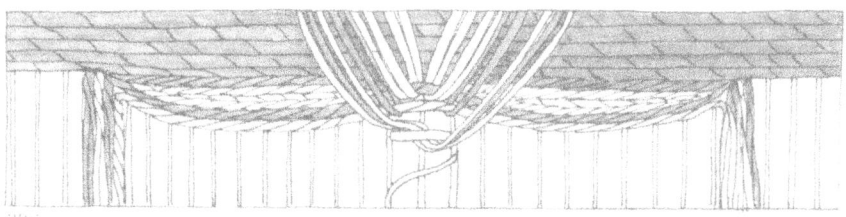

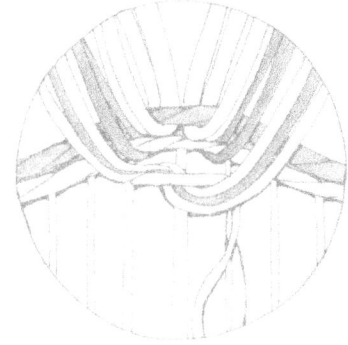

STEP 3: The vertical braids are inserted between the two crescents. A double strand of the black-white-white-black braids is entered in the curved black braid. Two yellow braids are entered in the row of yellow braiding, and the third strand of all six braids is entered in the first row of weft twining (figs. 336 and 337).

337. A detail of the insertion of the central vertical braids

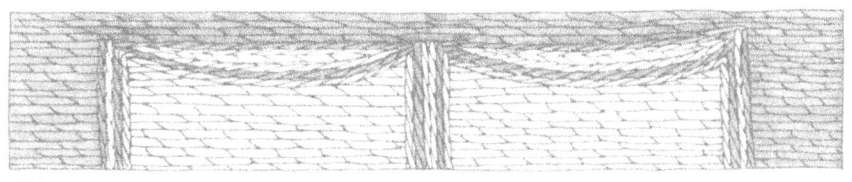

STEP 4: The weft is twined underneath the crescents until it can be woven in a straight line across the form. The braids are worked vertically and are caught in the appropriate weft rows (fig. 338).

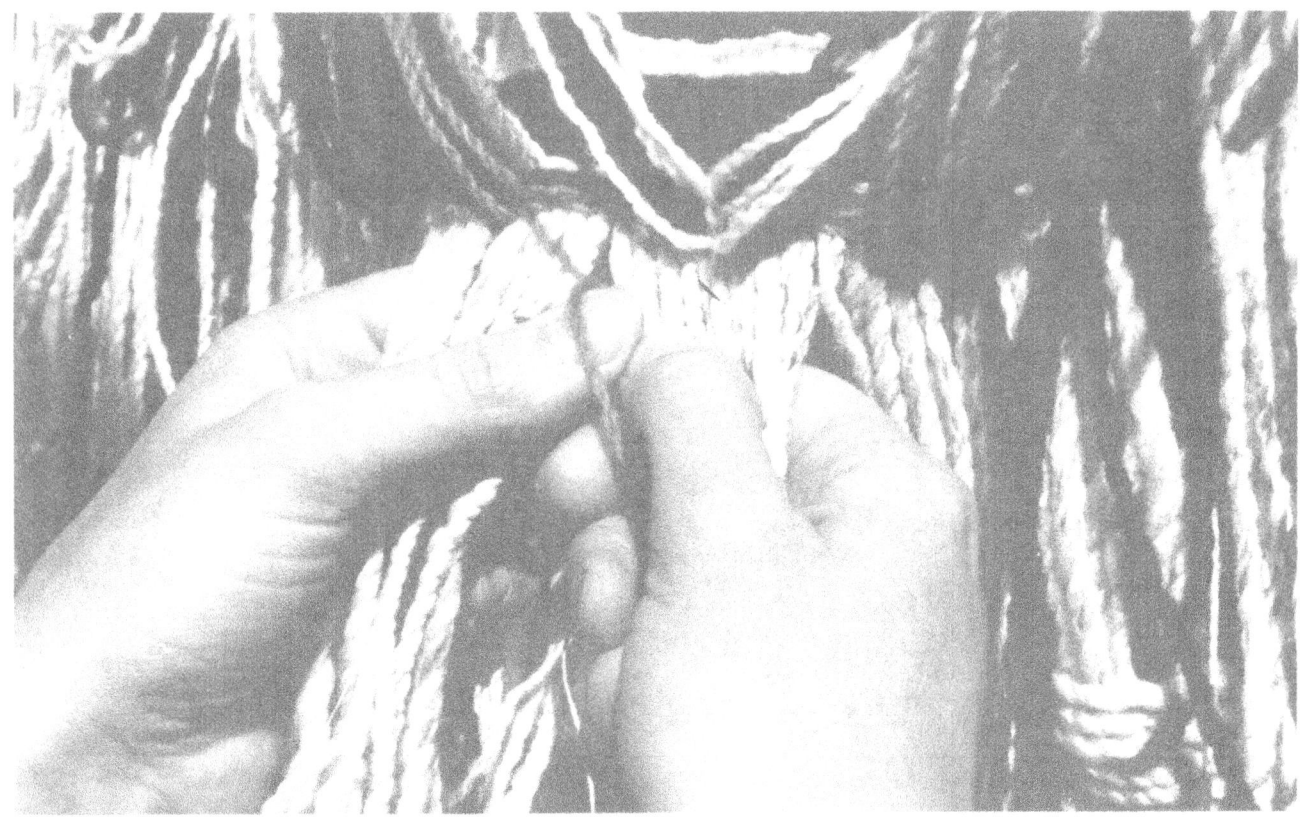

339. Twining across upright paired U shapes (Weaver: Cheryl Samuel)

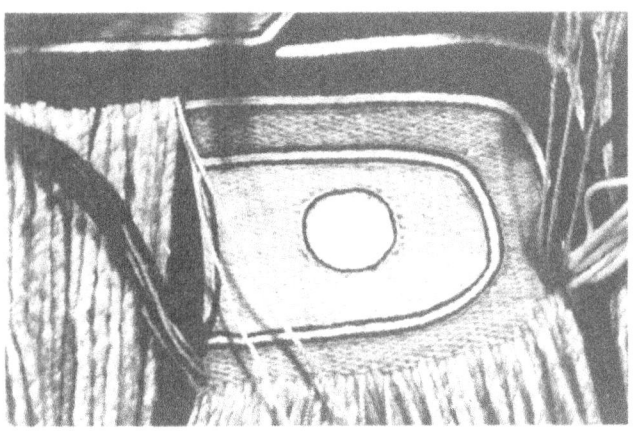

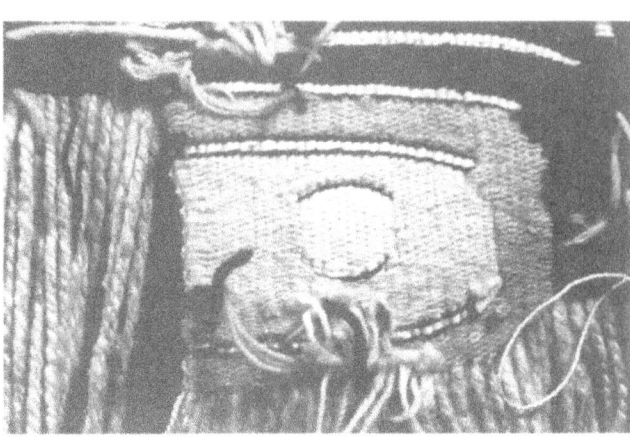

340. A vertical crescent being worked in a ∪ shape. Note the loop of the drawstring. (Courtesy of the Field Museum, Chicago: CS)

341. The back of the ∪ shape in figure 340. Note the loop of another drawstring. (Courtesy of the Field Museum, Chicago: CS)

VERTICAL CRESCENTS IN SIDEWAYS ∪ SHAPES

The ∪ shapes which lie on their sides in the design field have crescents which run vertically. They are entered in the weft in a staggered manner to create a point and are worked only in the weft.

CRESCENTS IN UPSIDE DOWN PAIRED ∪ SHAPES

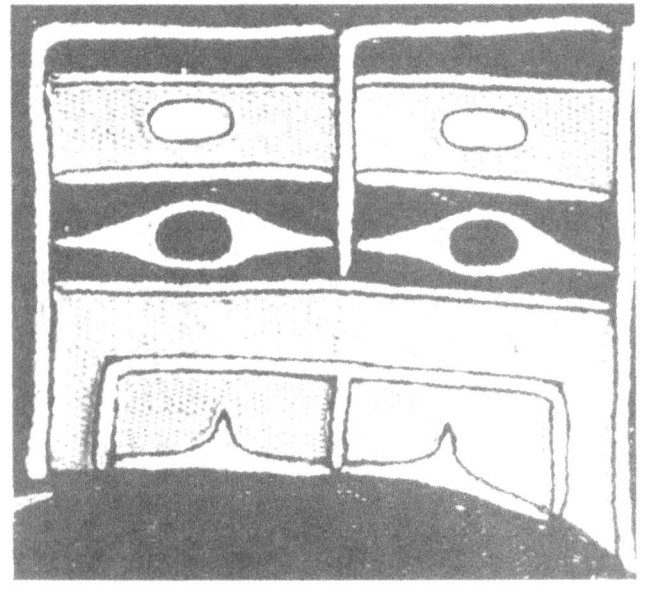

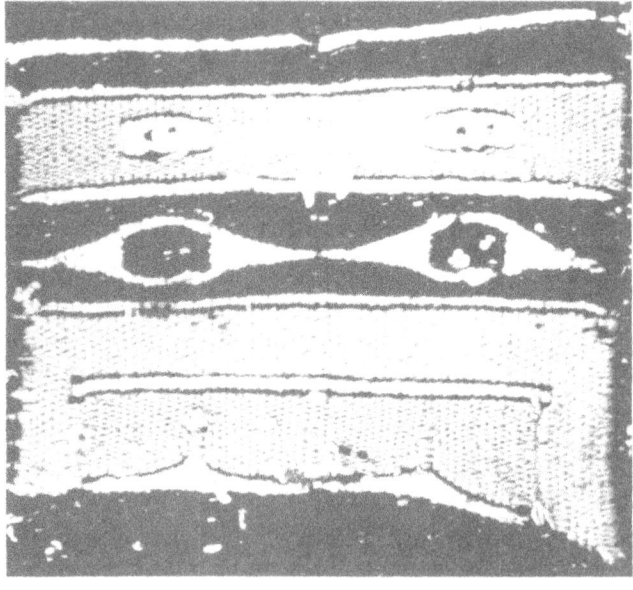

342. A pair of ∪ shapes with crescents which face downward (CS)

343. The back of the ∪ shapes (CS)

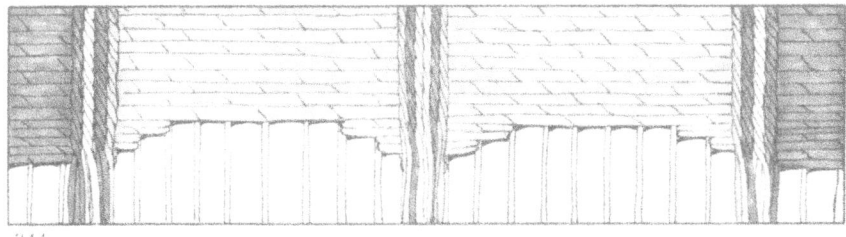

STEP 1: The yellow or blue weft is twined to define the shapes (fig. 344).

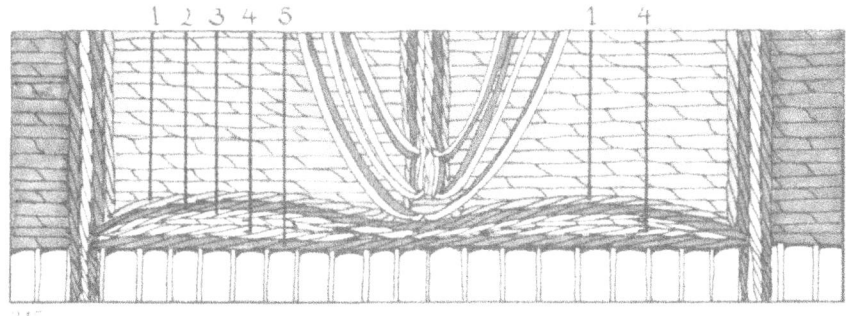

STEP 2: Two separate yellow or blue rows of braiding, (1), are worked across the shape under the twining. They meet the inside vertical braids at the sides and leave two warp ends free in the middle. All of the vertical yellow or blue braids are worked, free of the weft, for about one centimeter and are then dropped beside the warp ends.

A black row of braiding, (2), is worked across from left to right following the curve. This is repeated by a white braid, (3). A row of white twining and the bottom white braids of each crescent are worked individually, (4). A final black braid, (5), runs under the entire figure (fig. 345).

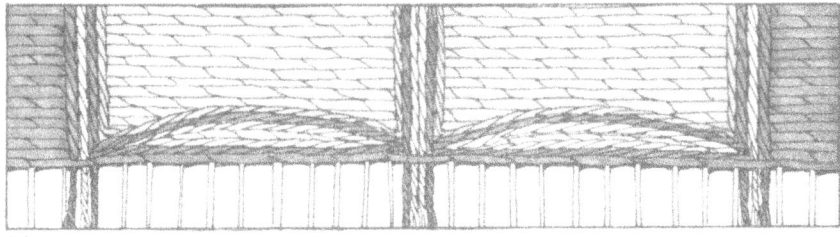

STEP 3: The vertical braids in the center and the three remaining vertical braids on either side of the shape are worked free of the weft for approximately one centimeter and then dropped beside the warp ends. They are caught in the weft twining for one centimeter and are then cut off (fig. 346).

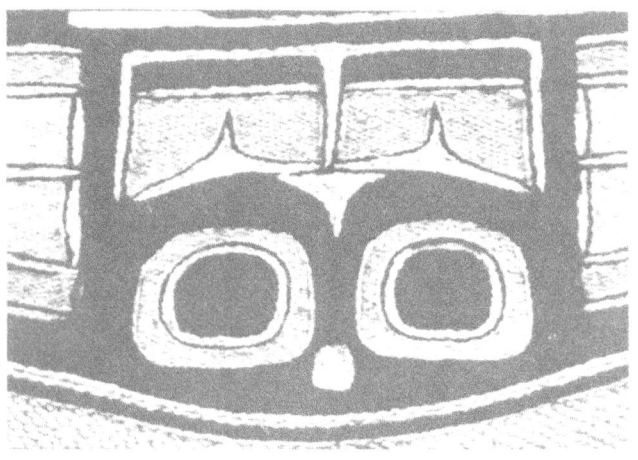 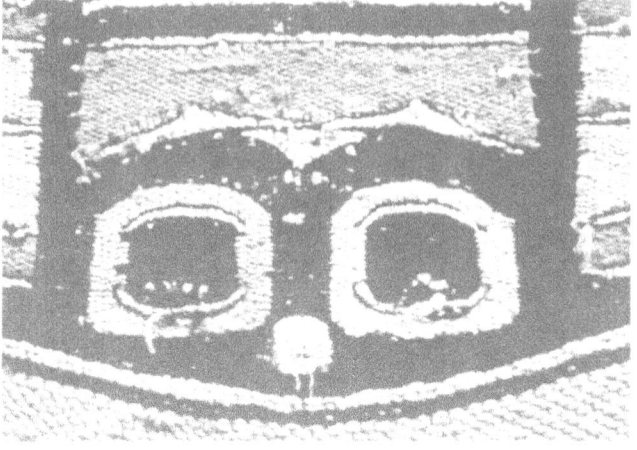

347. A pair of ∪ shapes with T-shaped crescents. They are placed above two formline ovoids. (CS)

348. The back of the ∪ shapes with T-shaped crescents (CS)

T-Shaped Crescents in Upright Split ∪ Shapes

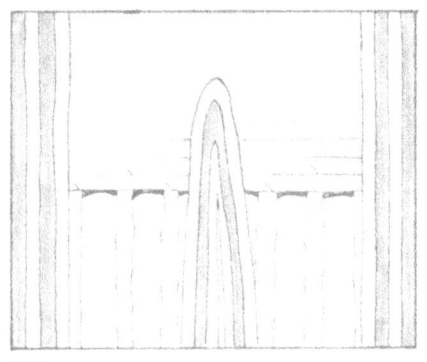 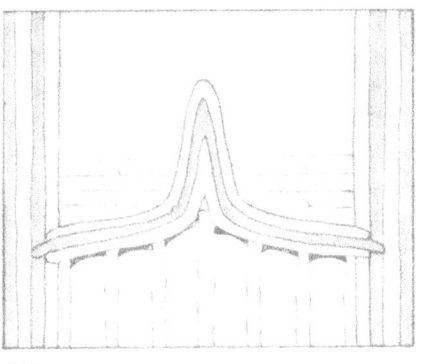 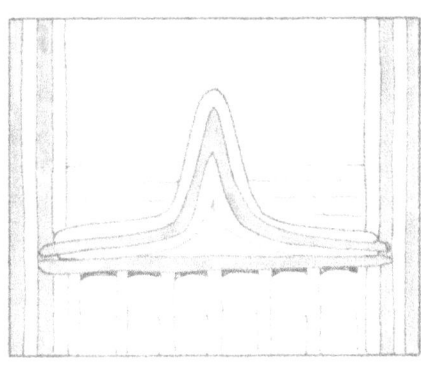

STEP 1: The point of the T-shaped crescent is entered in the weft in the center of the form (fig. 349). It consists of two yellow braids, two black, and two white braids. The white braids are staggered to make a fine point. The weft continues across the form from side to side underneath these braids.

STEP 2: The yellow weft is worked down to create the shape of the crescent (fig. 350).

STEP 3: The braids from the point are completed around the crescent. White two-strand twining fills in the shape, either over single warp ends or over alternate warp pairs. The bottom of the crescent is completed underneath this twining (fig. 351).

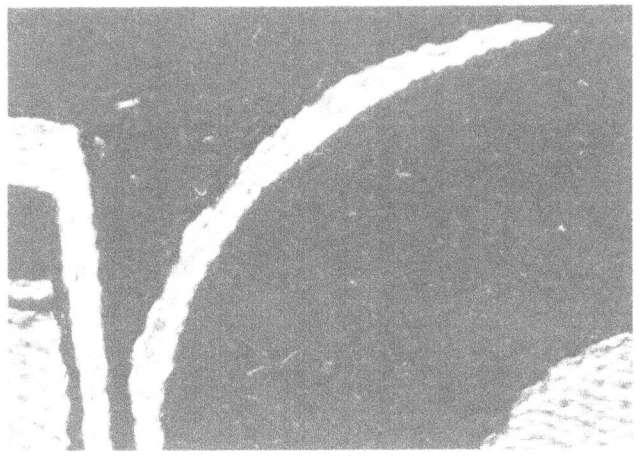

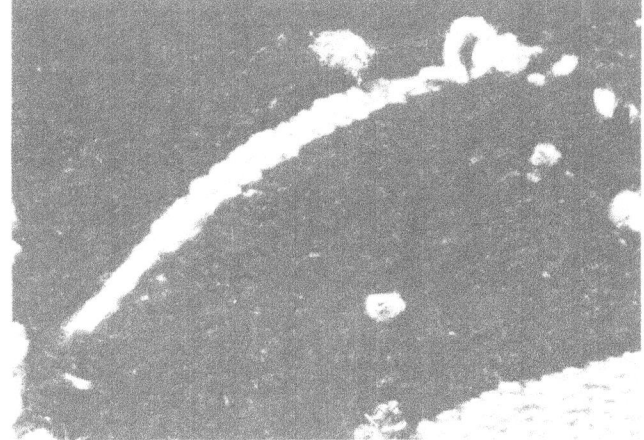

352. A crescent which defines a primary formline ovoid (CS)

353. The back of the crescent (CS)

RESULTANT FORMS

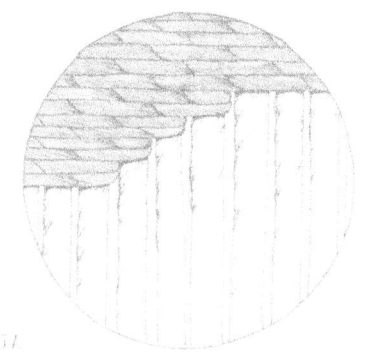

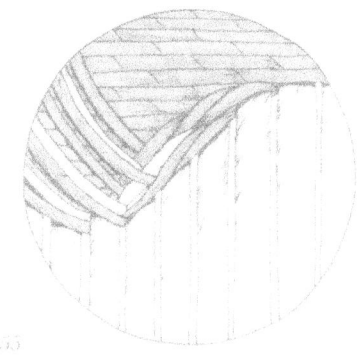

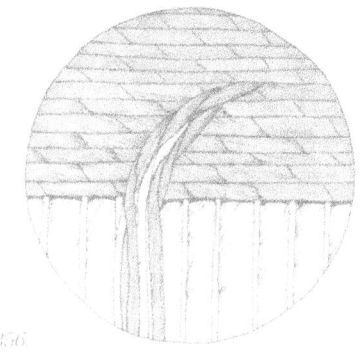

STEP 1: The top of the crescent is defined with the black formline weft (fig. 354).

STEP 2: A black braid, a white braid, and a black braid are inserted in the warp in a staggered fashion (fig. 355).

STEP 3: The adjacent black formline weft is twined until it meets the fell of the first weft. Twining is continued underneath the crescent and the braids are caught in the appropriate weft rows. A second white braid is inserted in the wefts on the inside of the crescent to give it width. Twining continues for the length of the crescent, minus six rows for finishing (fig. 356).

The bottom of a crescent must be finished in a staggered manner in order to create points. The inner white braid is dropped first, the outer white braid next, followed by the inner black braid, and finally the outer black braid. It takes six rows to finish four braids. One strand of each braid is dropped alongside the warp into succeeding weft rows until all three strands no longer appear on the surface. In the six weft rows, strands from the braids are dropped in the following sequence:

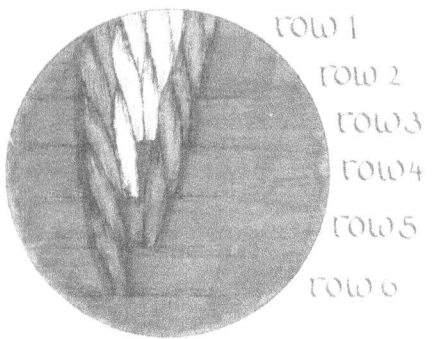

row 1
row 2
row 3
row 4
row 5
row 6

1. One strand from the inner white braid
2. One strand each from the inner and outer white braids
3. One strand each from the inner and outer white braids and the inner black braid
4. One strand each from the outer white braid and the inner and outer black braids
5. One strand each from the inner and outer black braids
6. One strand from the outer black braid

357. Finishing the point of a crescent

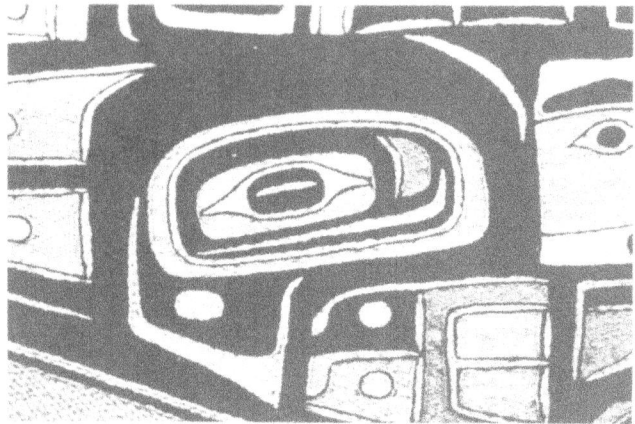

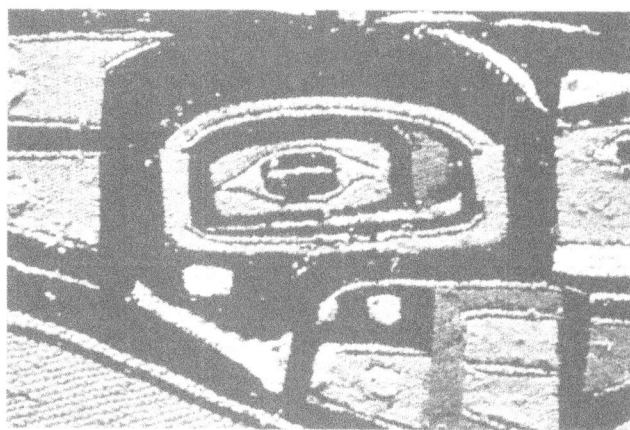

358. A form resulting from adjacent formlines (CS)

359. The back of the weaving showing the bottom of the white resultant form (CS)

STEP 1: To weave this resultant form, two crescents are inserted in the weft, the crescent on the left being thicker than that on the right due to the addition of a single row of vertical two-strand twining between the two white braids. The black weft is twined to the shape of the form (fig. 360).

STEP 2: The top braids are finished, the black and white braids from the left crescent moving over to meet the black and white braids of the right crescent at an angle. A small number of rows of white two-strand twining are inserted to widen the form. These can be done over alternate warp pairs or over single warp ends. The form is then completed by bringing the braids from the left underneath the twining and ending them perpendicular to the braids of the right crescent (fig. 361).

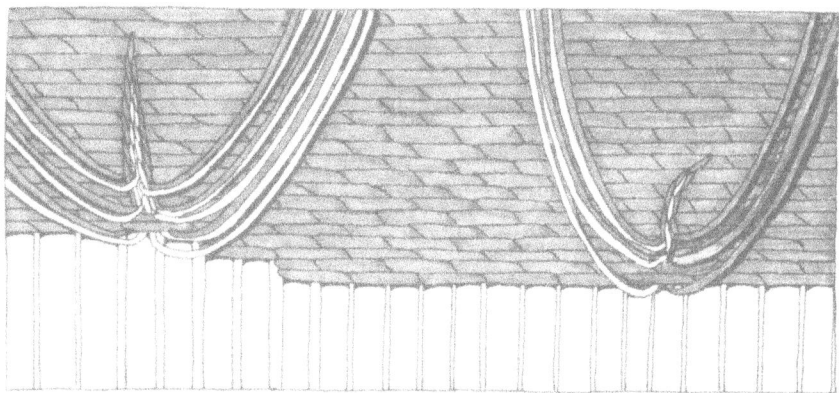

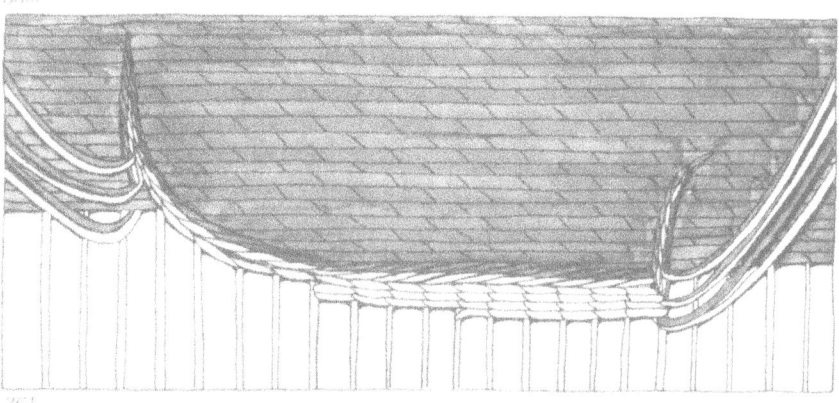

THE FACE SHAPE

Faces appear on almost all Dancing Blankets. They consist of eyebrows, eyes, a nose, a mouth and may be a frontal view or a profile. They are most commonly found in a rectangle, although occasionally they are rounded. They also may have a mask of yellow or blue which is outlined by a black line.

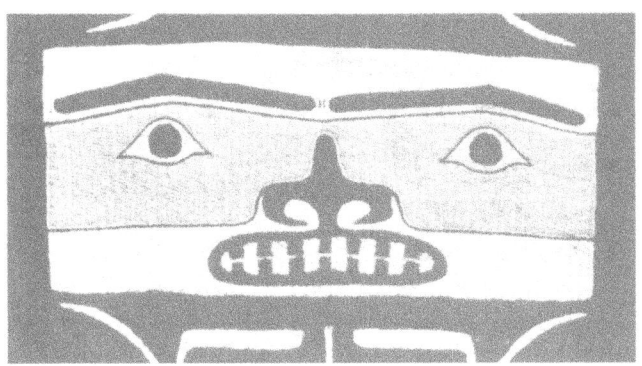

362. A face shape (CS)

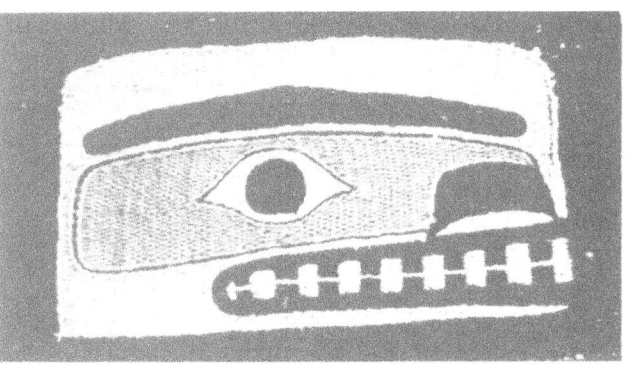

363. A face shape in profile (Courtesy of the British Columbia Provincial Museum: CS)

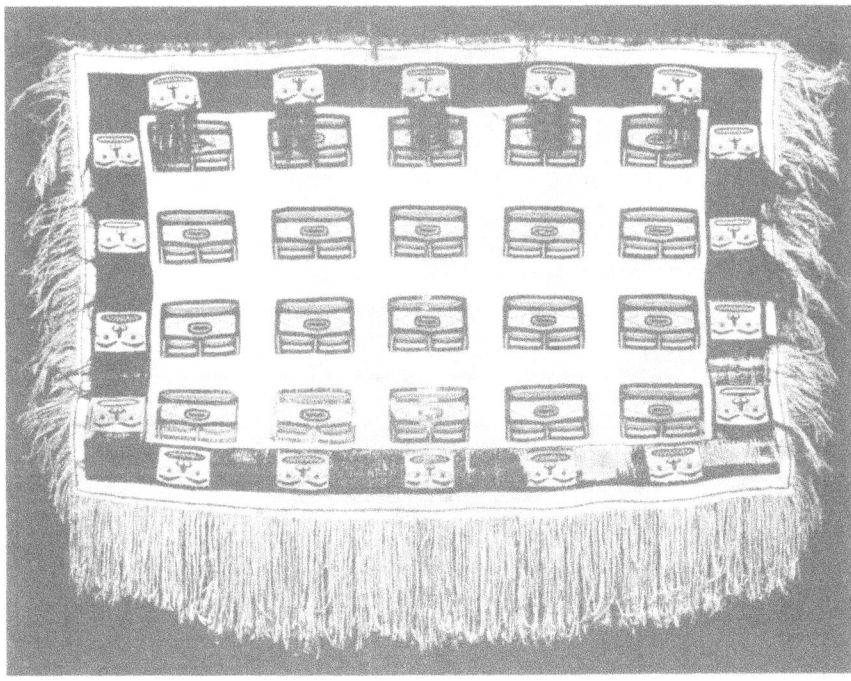

364. A fine old blanket which combines the geometric tradition with formline weaving. An extraordinary border of faces surrounds the design field. The entire white ground is woven in self-patterned twining. (Courtesy of the Royal Ontario Museum, Toronto)

A ghost face, which is another type of small face shape, is often found upside down on the backs of tunics (fig. 365). Sometimes it is placed on leggings or medicine pouches. This little face usually has round wide eyes, a mouth without teeth, and a nose without a bridge.

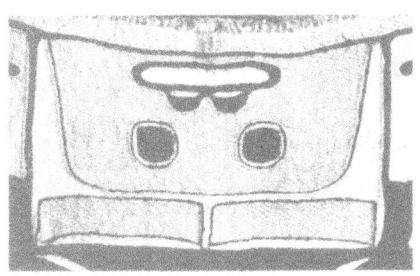

365. A ghost face (Courtesy of the British Columbia Provincial Museum: CS)

EYEBROWS AND FOREHEADS

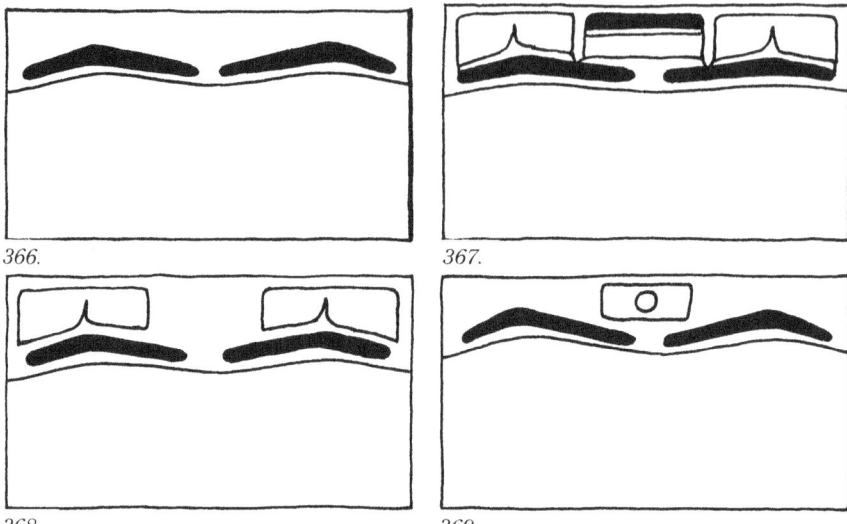

366.

367.

366. through 369. Styles of eyebrows and foreheads

368.

369.

The eyebrows are two long, thick, inverted shallow Vs which are above the eyes and the mask line (fig. 366). They are always colored black. Many faces have nothing above the eyebrows. The forehead is always white.

In some faces, shapes are found above the eyebrows (fig. 367). Split Us often occur in this space, sometimes with a square between them. In the face shape illustrated here, the black outlines of all the shapes touch the eyebrows.

Figure 368 shows a variation in which there is no square between the split Us. Furthermore, the outlines of the U shapes do not touch the eyebrows.

Another alternative to the shapes found above the eyebrows places a square in the center of the forehead (fig. 369).

MASKS

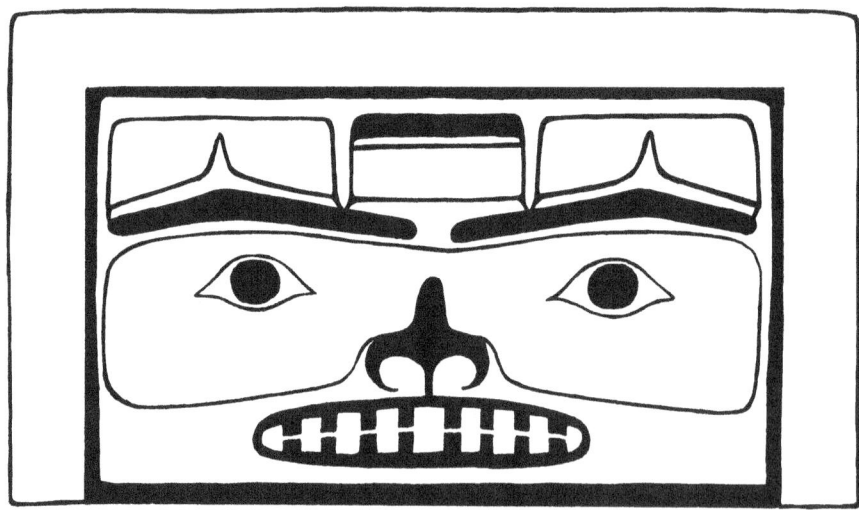

370. A face shape with a mask

Usually, but not always, a mask surrounds the eyes and the upper part of the nose (fig. 370). The mask is most often yellow; in a small minority of blankets it is blue. The upper three sides of the face shape are often surrounded by a border which is usually blue.

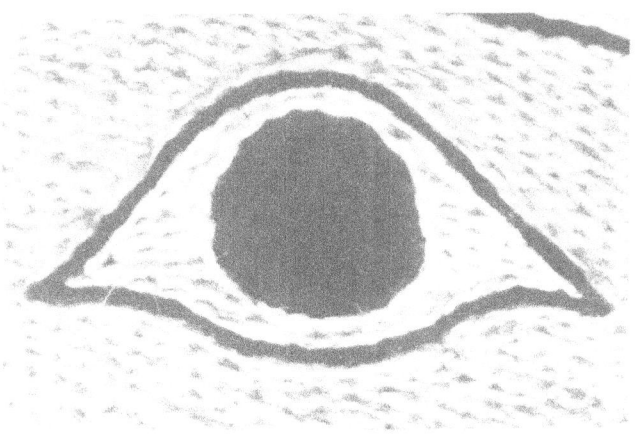

371. An eye (CS)

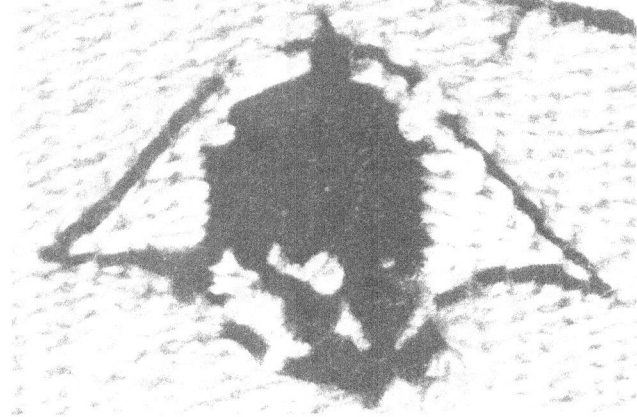

372. The back of the eye (CS)

EYES

The eye in a face shape is small and beautifully proportioned. A black eyelid line delineates the form; the black iris within it is a perfect circle. The eye is small and because of its size, the wefts do not change their angle of weave within the eye, but run horizontally through the form. In some blankets, very tiny white wefts are used to twine the white of this eye.

NOSES

Noses are formed in two parts: the bridge and the nostrils. There are two methods for weaving the bridge of the nose and three methods for weaving the nostrils. The shape which appears on the front of the weaving looks exactly the same regardless of which of these methods is used.

The Bridge of the Nose: Method I, Added Warp Ends. . . One or two warp ends are added after the bridge has been started (fig. 374). The shape expands while the vertical interlock between the bridge and the face mask continues to fall between the same two warp ends.

The Bridge of the Nose: Method II, Stepped Interlock. . . The bridge in Method II is created through the use of a stepped interlock (fig. 375). As the angle is very steep, only two steps are necessary to widen the shape slightly. The braids which travel over this line on the front of the weaving smooth it, creating a perfectly angled line.

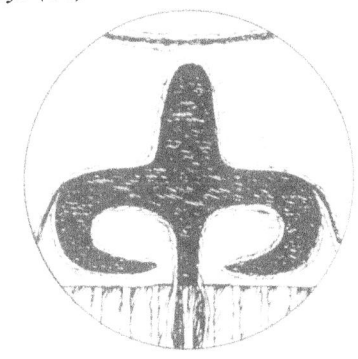

373. A nose from the front of the weaving

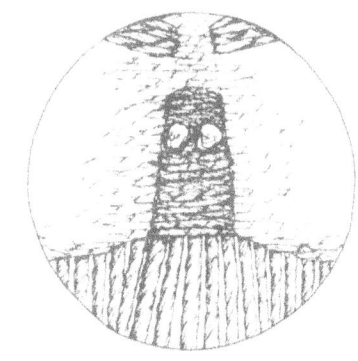

374. The bridge of the nose, Method I

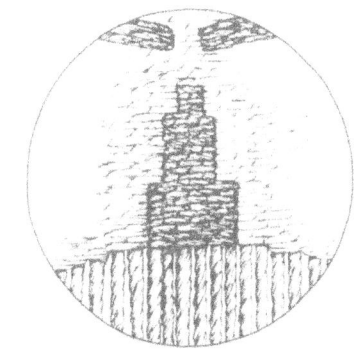

375. The bridge of the nose, Method II

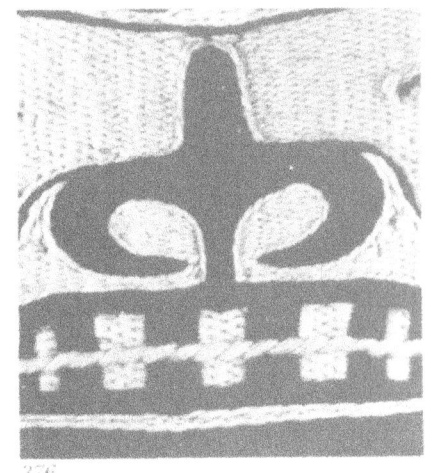
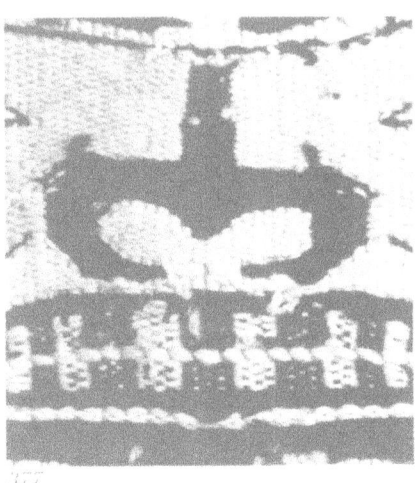

376. The nostrils, Method I (CS)

377. The back of the nostrils, Method I (CS)

The points of the nostrils are twined as crescents. The line between the nostrils is formed by one of the following three methods:

The Nostrils: Method I, Vertical Braids . . . The central line of the nostril is not twined, but is created on a white ground by black and white braids on the front of the weaving. This method allows the weaver to make a very narrow line. Note the use of commercial yarn for the line between the teeth (fig. 376).

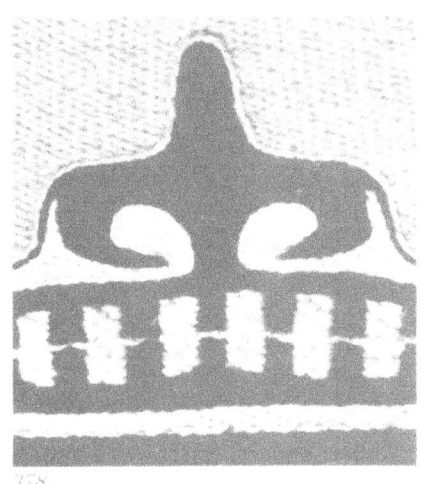
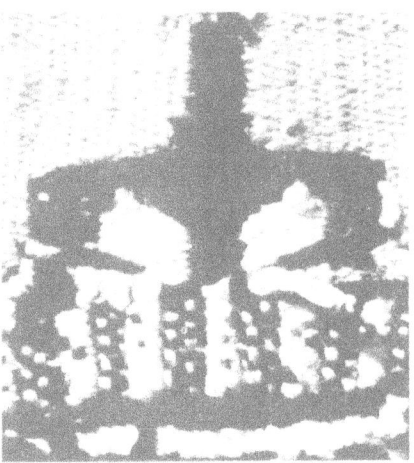

378. The nostrils, Method II (CS)

379. The back of the nostrils, Method II (CS)

The Nostrils: Method II, Interlock Join . . . The central line is twined over two warp ends and interlocked to the white ground (fig. 378). The division between the nostrils is wide.

The Nostrils: Method III, Stepped Interlock . . . In some instances, the black weft of the line between the nostrils starts over three warp ends and narrows to one before it reaches the mouth (fig. 380).

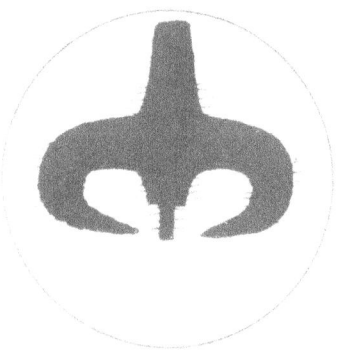

380. The nostrils, Method III

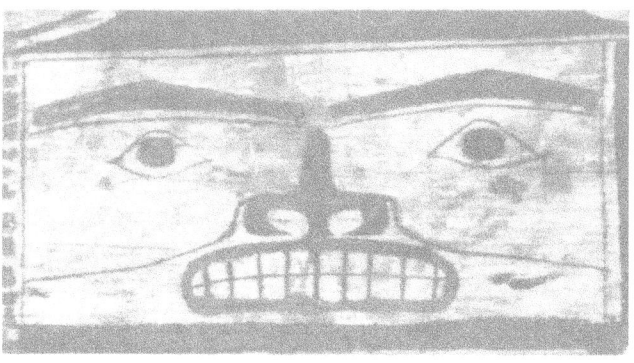

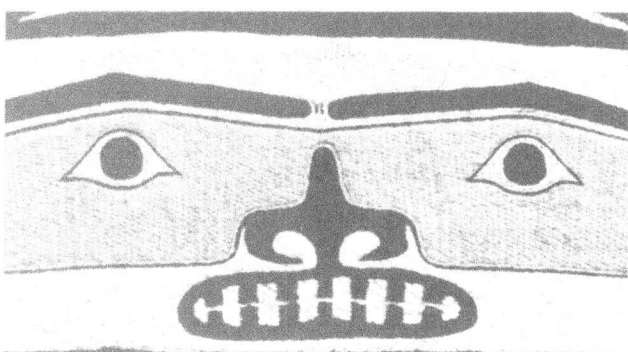

381. *A painting of a face shape on a pattern board. The teeth are formed in the painting style. (Courtesy of the Field Museum, Chicago: CS)*

382. *A woven face. The teeth are formed in weaving style. (CS)*

MOUTHS

The painting of the mouth on the pattern board indicates the shape of the lips and the number of teeth to be woven. The shape on the pattern board, however, is in the style of the painted art, with thin black lines separating the teeth. This seems to be an area where the weaver could change the painted pattern, for most of the teeth in Dancing Blankets are woven as thick black bars alternating with equally thick white ones. Sometimes these bars are staggered in a checkerboard pattern. A number of different methods exist for the weaving of teeth, some of them reminiscent of the earlier geometric techniques. It is the only place in the design field where two colors of weft are used simultaneously. The tie-off in the side braid is the only other area in the blanket which incorporates the use of two colors of weft.

383. *A detail of the nostrils and mouth showing the braids which connect them (CS)*

LIPS

The lips of the mouth are usually connected to the center line of the nostrils. The black and white braids from this line are continued around the top of the mouth.

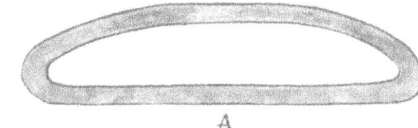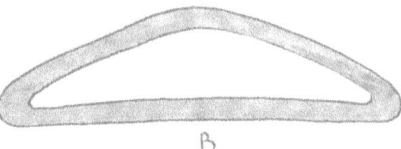

384. Lip shapes

A   B

The lips form either an elongated oval, (A), or an oval which angles upward toward the nose, (B) (fig. 384). They are always black, the teeth black and white, and the area which surrounds the mouth white. A very subtle coloring treatment was used by some expert weavers for the lips and the teeth. The lips themselves were woven with black yarn and the dark spaces between the teeth with a brown yarn. The mouth looks black and white from a distance; the subtlety of the two tones is discovered only upon close inspection. This treatment was also used in the blue shapes of a very few blankets. In these, one tone of blue would be used for the weft twining and a much greener tone for the braiding.

TEETH

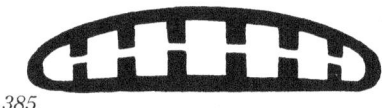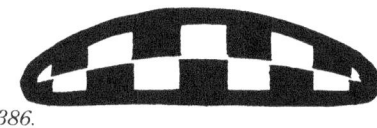

385. and 386. Styles of teeth

385.   386.

Seven, nine, or eleven teeth are usually found within the mouth. They either form vertical bars (fig. 385) or a checkerboard pattern (fig. 386). A white braided line divides the top teeth from the bottom ones. The teeth themselves are rectangular, the central teeth being slightly wider than the side teeth. The two teeth at the corners of the mouth appear as stubby crescents due to the rounding of the lips by the outline braids. The four different methods of teeth constrution discussed here introduce weaving techniques which are not found in the main body of the blanket. In all methods, the curve of the upper lip is defined with the white twining wefts (fig. 387). The white and black braids from the central line of the nostrils are worked under this curve. A narrow band of black is twined underneath these braids, followed by another black braid which lies under the inside curve of the lip.

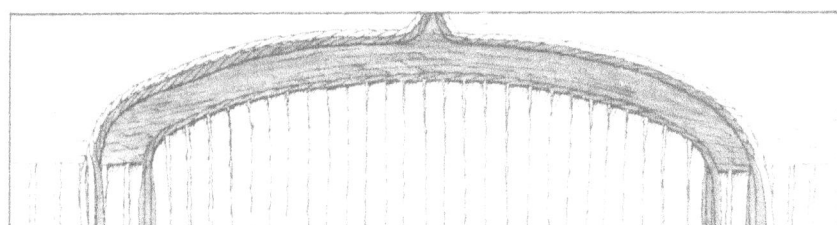

387. The upper lip

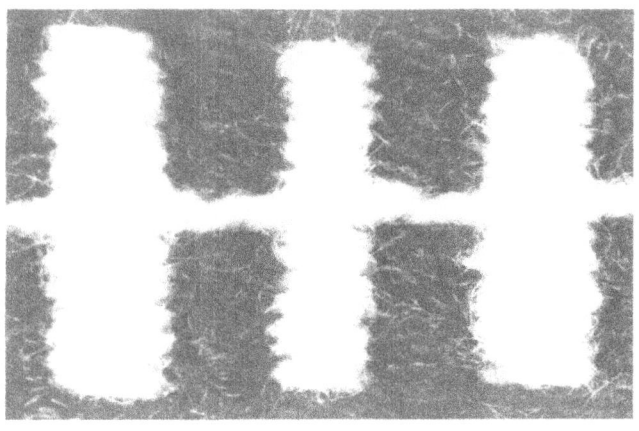

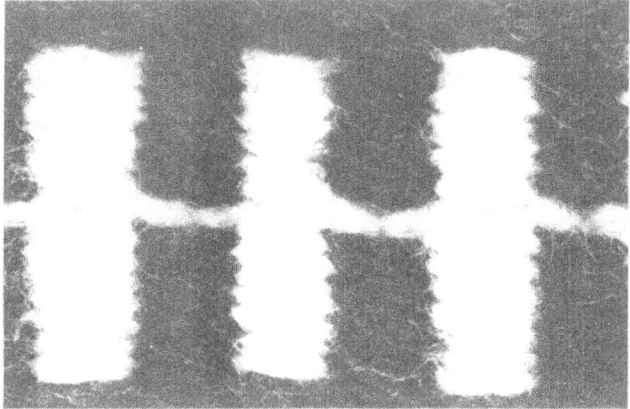

388. A detail of teeth woven over paired warp ends (CS)

389. The back of the teeth (CS)

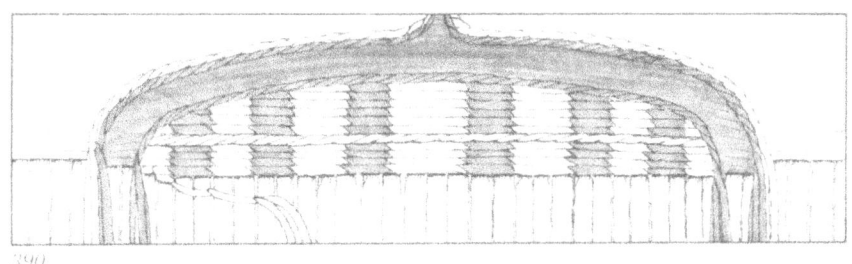

390. Teeth formed by paired warp ends

Method I, Paired Warp Ends... The top teeth are twined, using a black and white weft over paired warp ends (fig. 390). The first row is started on the right under the curve of the upper lip and one warp end in from the side of the mouth. It is twined to within one warp end from the left side, and then the twining turns for the second row. When the edge of the form is reached, the strands are twisted twice so that the bar on the front remains white. The twining continues over the same pairs of warp ends as in the first row (fig. 392). The second turn on both sides incorporates all warp ends. The weft of the teeth is interlocked to the sides of the lips and the lips are interlocked to the white face. Braids continue around the lips, covering the joins. To expand the middle teeth, the white strand of the weft is twined over three warp ends, while the black segment continues over two.

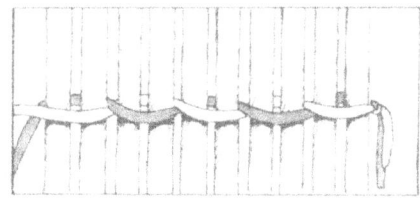

391. Black and white strands of yarn are tied together to form the two strands of the weft.

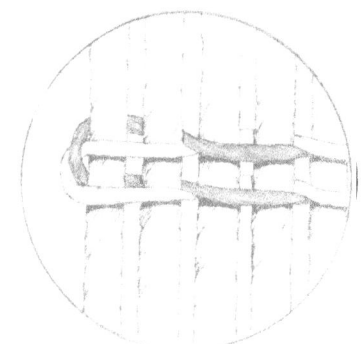

392. A weft turn using black and white yarns

When the upper teeth are completed (fig. 393), a white braid is inserted and then the lower teeth are twined in the same paired manner, curving the corners of the mouth. If checkerboard teeth are twined, the black and white bars are switched underneath the white braid; in this case, the teeth are all the same width. In all methods of teeth twining, the black braid is finished underneath the teeth and the lower lip is twined. The black and white braids which encircle the mouth are completed, after which the lower white portion of the face is finished.

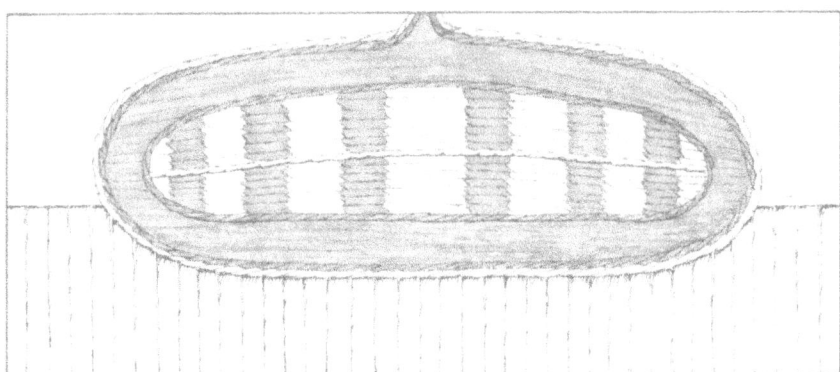

393. Finishing the mouth

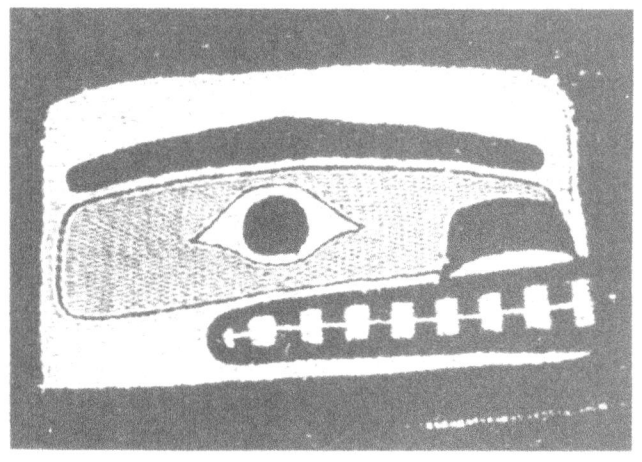

394. A profile face with teeth which are twined over alternate warp ends (Courtesy of the British Columbia Provincial Museum: CS)

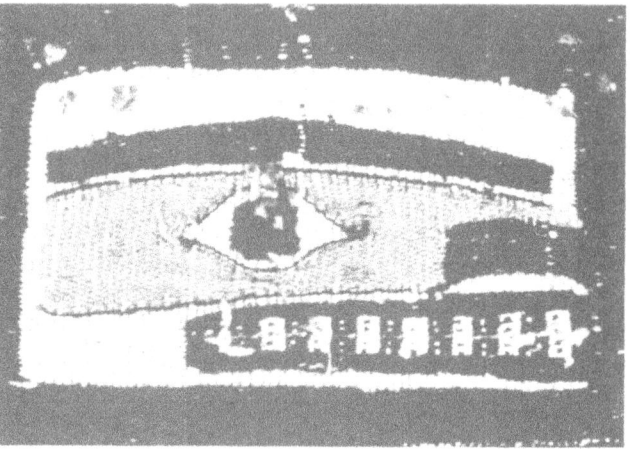

395. The back of the profile face (Courtesy of the British Columbia Provincial Museum: CS)

Method II, Alternate Warp Pairs. . . A two-colored black and white weft is used to twine over alternate warp ends. The twining proceeds as it does in the main body of the blanket, splitting the warp pairs in each successive row. In order to keep the bars of the teeth black and white, the weft must be given a full twist so that the appropriate color comes to the front when it is needed. The strand in the back travels in a straight line, pulling the binding point of the two yarns to the back (fig. 396). The weft has to travel over one warp end at the sides of each bar in order to keep the edges straight (fig. 397). When the other color is desired, the wefts twine in the simple half-twist of the two-strand twining.

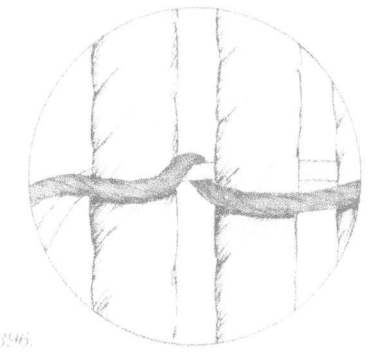

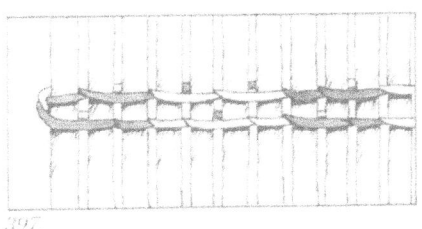

396. Two rows of black and white twining over alternate warp pairs

397. A close-up of a double twist

Method III, Single Warp Ends... This method of weaving teeth is found on a beautiful medicine bag woven in the shape of a ghost face. The top teeth are twined over alternate warp pairs with thin black lines between them (fig. 398). A narrow band crosses between the upper and lower teeth. The lower teeth are delicately patterned over single warp ends with white and black rows of braiding separating them from the lips. This unique treatment comes the closest to a faithful representation of the painted pattern.

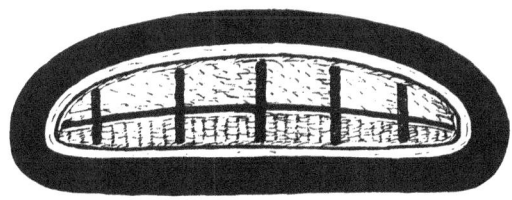

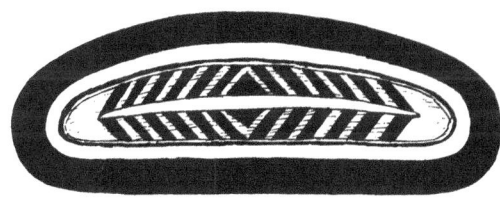

398. Teeth which match the painting on the pattern board

399. Diagonally twined teeth

Method IV, Diagonal Geometric Twining... A reconstruction of a very old and beautiful legging with a ghost face shows that the teeth were woven as diagonal lines (fig. 399). In this method, which utilizes a technique of the geometric style of weaving, a white and a black weft are used to twine over alternate warp pairs (fig. 400). A double twist is used when necessary to maintain a color area. The natural progression of twining over alternate warp pairs produces the diagonal lines.

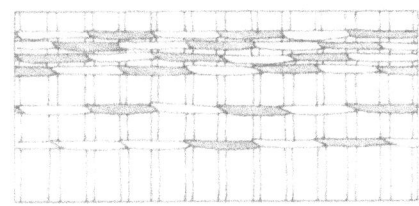

400. Diagonal lines produced by twining over alternate warp pairs with a two-colored weft

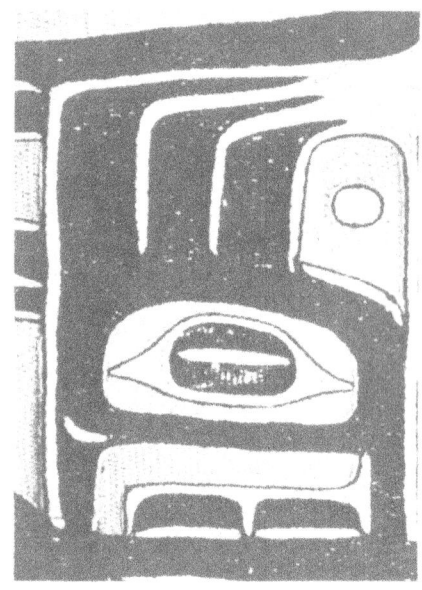

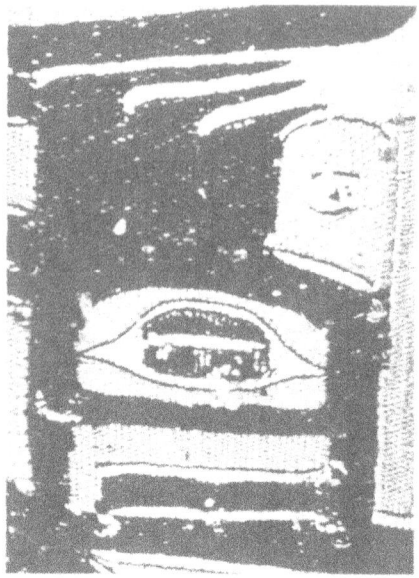

401. A claw with a thumb (CS)   *402. The back of the claw (CS)*

CLAWS

Technically, the claws are a combination of the various techniques used to weave the other forms of the design field. Fine points are inserted at the tips, a ∪ shape might be woven for the "thumb," and a formline ovoid with a socket and inner ovoid fills the palm.

The photograph in figure 403 shows a Dancing Blanket expertly woven by a very fine weaver. Two such blankets, woven by the same weaver, are now in the National Museum of Man, Ottawa. The creature in the central design field is sitting with his feet up and his claws surrounding the face shape in the body. Three more face shapes, with teeth which are woven with black and brown wefts, are seen at the top of the design field.

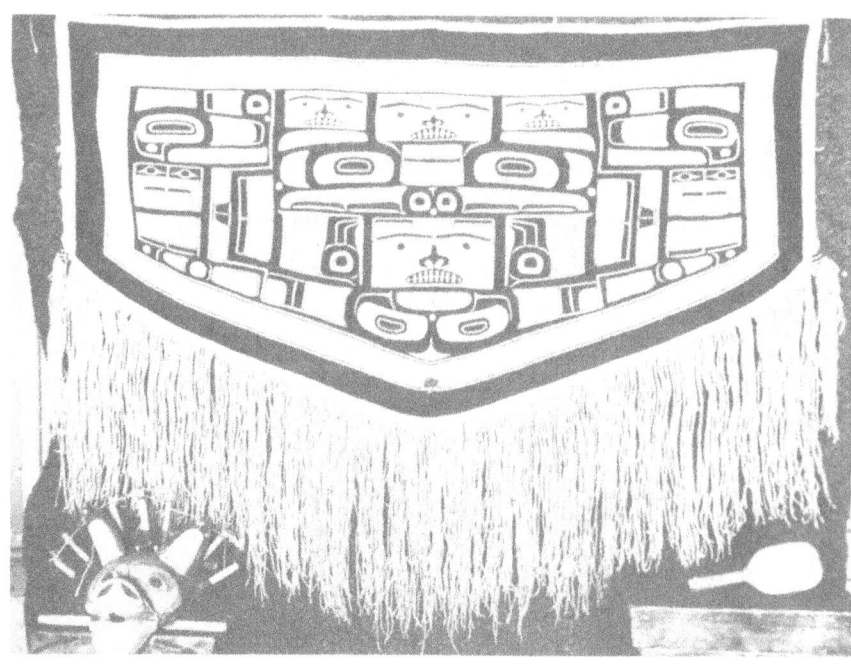

403. (Courtesy of the British Columbia Provincial Museum)

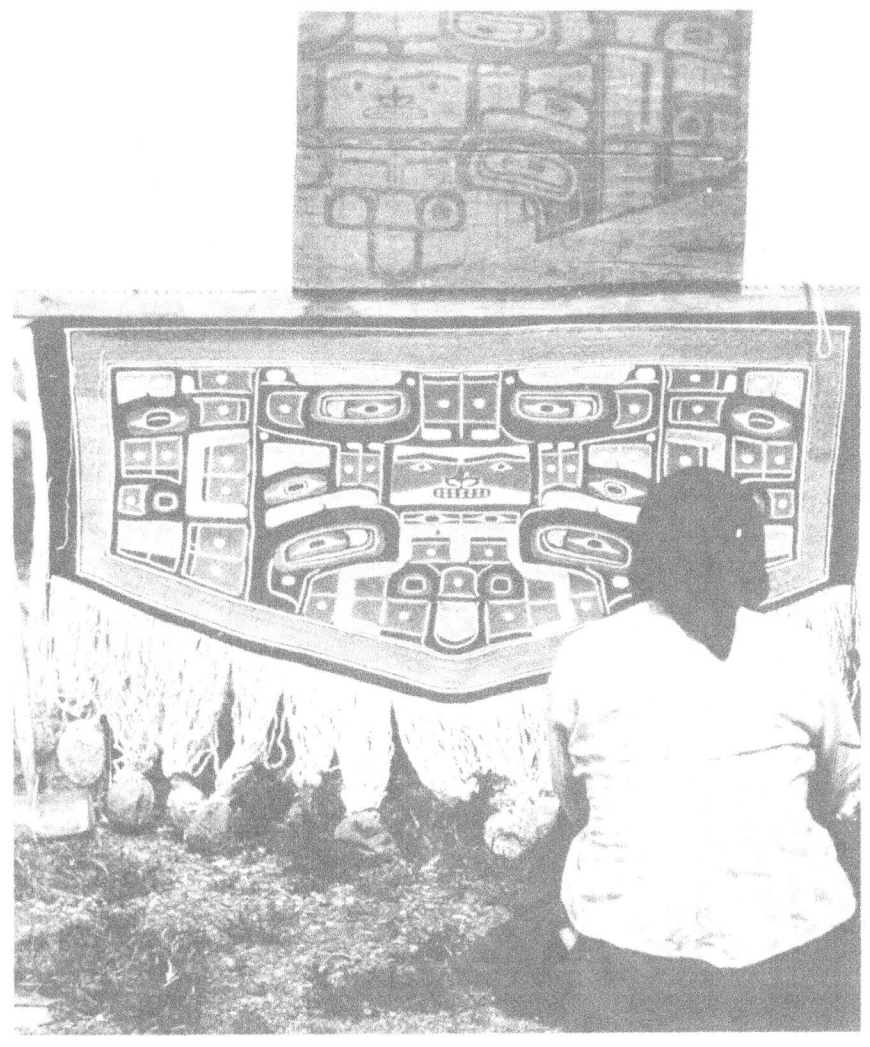

404. (Courtesy of the British Columbia Provincial Museum)

COMPLETING THE
BLACK AND YELLOW BORDERS

The Dancing Blanket on the loom in figure 404 is almost finished. The design field has been completed and the yellow border twined underneath it. The weaver is working on the black border which surrounds the entire blanket. She knows that the remaining steps are easy, compared with the obstacle course of shapes and strands over which she has just claimed victory. She knows that the day of the dance is near.

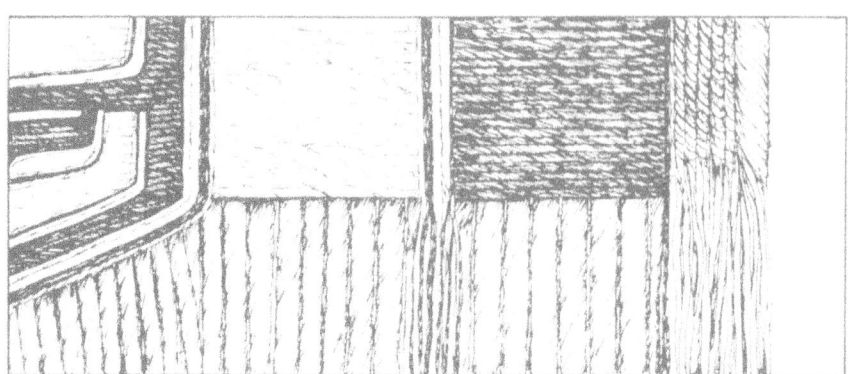

405. *The black and yellow borders before they turn the bottom corner*

The black and yellow vertical borders are twined to a horizontal line which is even with the corner of the design field (fig. 405). Six braids run directly underneath the design field. These black, white, white, black, black, and yellow braids are a continuation of the braids which have traveled along the upper edge and down the sides of this field. The left side of each braid is worked toward the center; the right side is then braided to meet and splice with it.

Having completed the braids under the design field, the weaver then begins the bottom yellow border. The weft turns to travel with the angle of the border, necessitating the addition of warp ends in the center of the V. Two lazy lines are placed near the center so that the weaver can twine one side at a time.

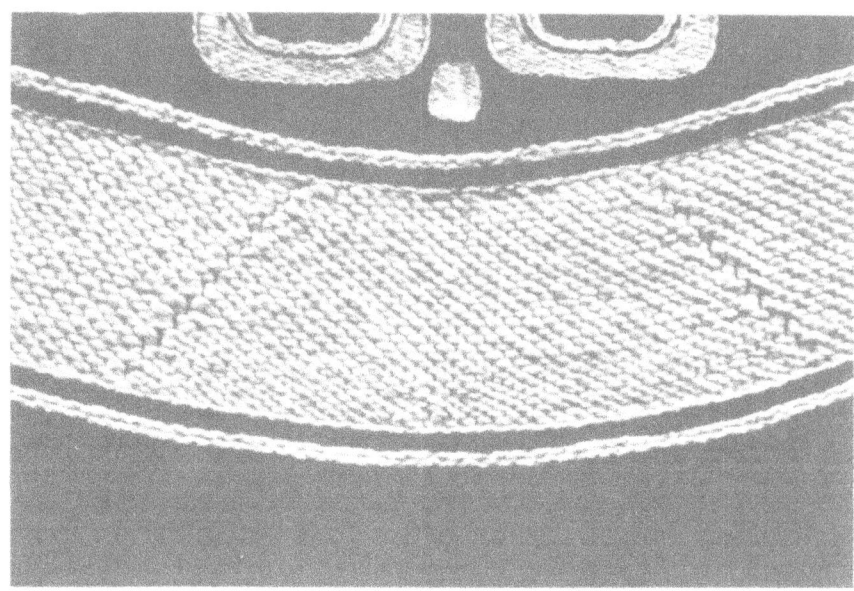

406. *Lazy lines inserted in the bottom yellow border (CS)*

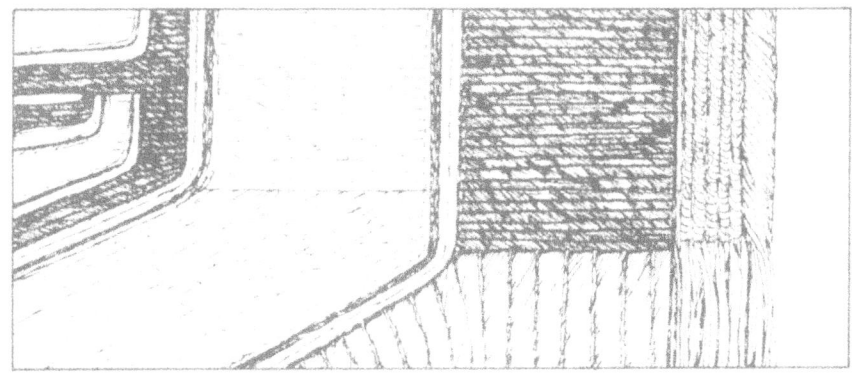

407. The yellow border has turned the corner.

Due to the direction of the wefts, the yellow and black bottom borders meet the vertical borders at an oblique angle (fig. 407). The yellow border is between four and six centimeters wide. When it has been woven, the braids which separate the two borders are worked underneath it, being spliced together somewhere near the center of the curve. The black border itself is then twined in the same manner as the yellow one. The black braid which travels down the very outside edge of the blanket is completed underneath it.

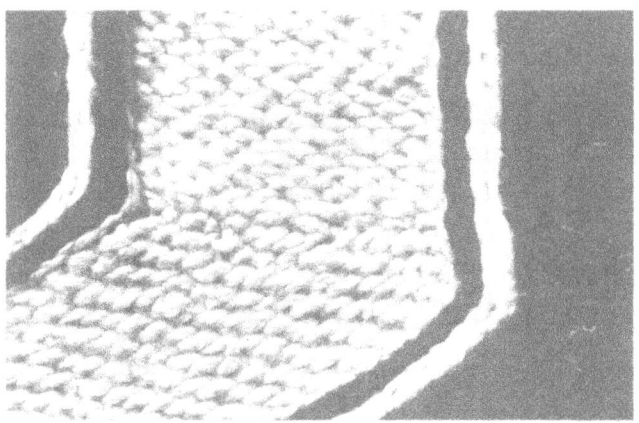

408. The diagonal weft join in the yellow border (CS)

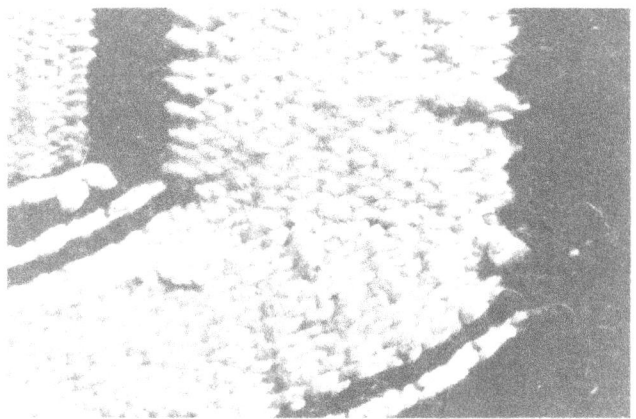

409. The back of the join (CS)

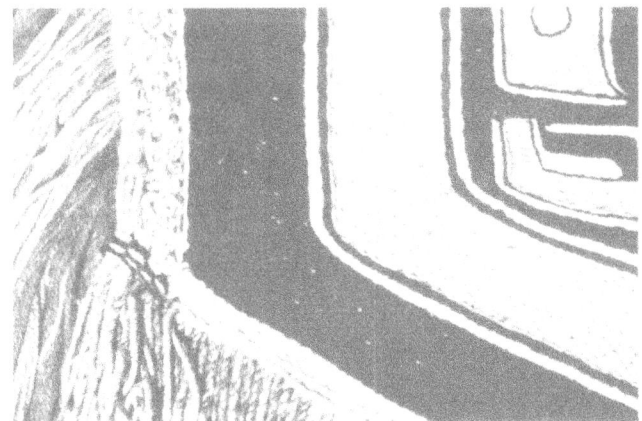

410. The bottom corner (CS)

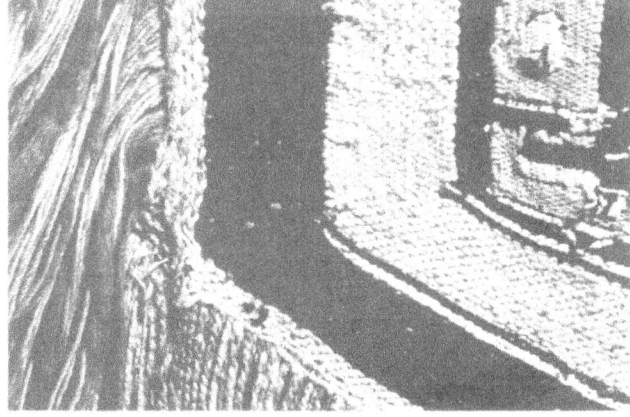

411. The back of the corner (CS)

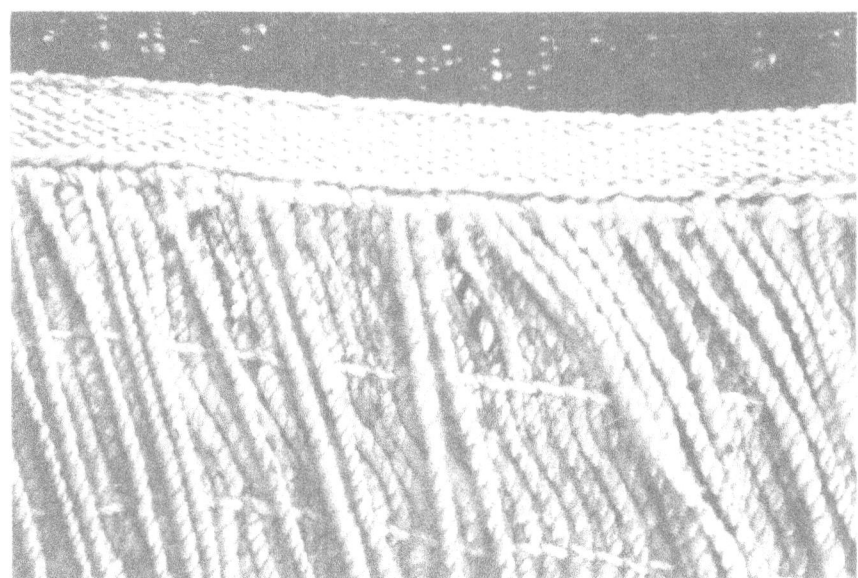

412. The footing and fringe of a blanket. The tail of a warp marker shows just under the footing. (CS)

THE FOOTING

A white footing, similar to the heading, is woven underneath the black border. A white braid is entered on the right and worked to the left. This is followed by six to eight rows of weft twining. The outermost white braid, which has traveled around the top and sides of the weaving, turns from its position between the side braid and the black border and completes the braiding under the footing.

THE OVERLAY FRINGE

The warp of the Dancing Blanket hangs from beneath the footing, becoming the great fringe. An additional fringe is added to it. These strands, called the "overlay fringe," are white mountain goat weft yarns which are slightly shorter in length than the warp fringe. They hang over the top of the main fringe.

To attach the overlay fringe, a single row of two-strand twining is entered under the final white braid and the strands are inserted in it. Two different methods are used for inserting these fringe yarns, Method I being the most common.

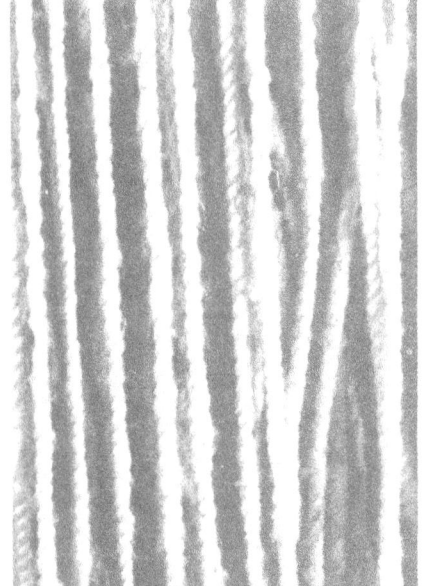

413. The overlay fringe (CS)

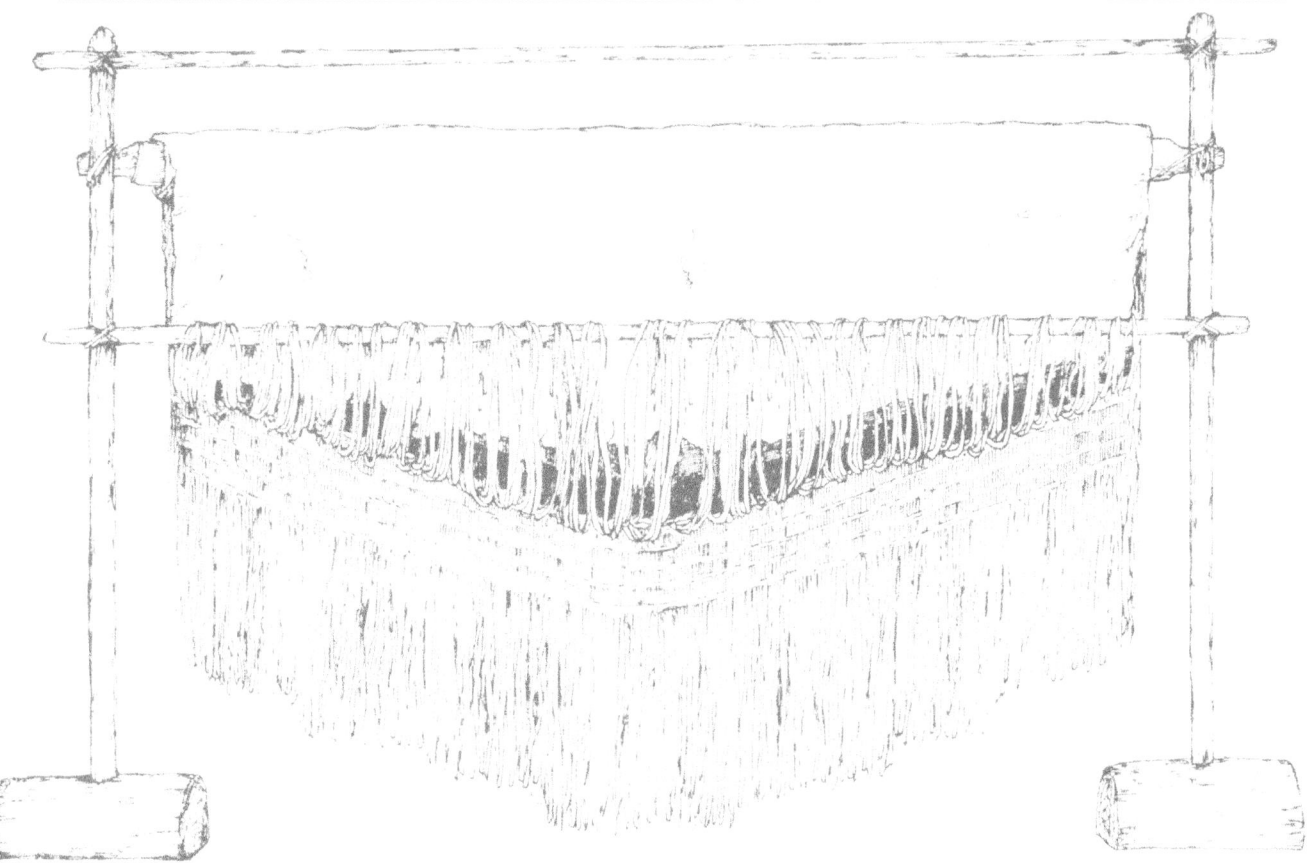

414. A completed weaving before it is taken from the loom. The warp fringe twining has just been inserted and the gut bags removed. The steps in the warp, due to the measuring stick, show at the bottom of the fringe.

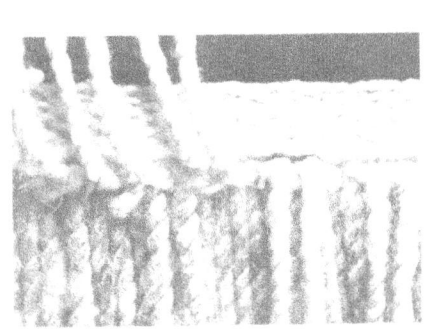

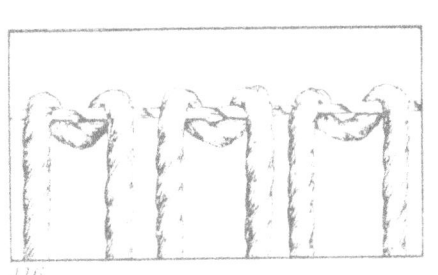

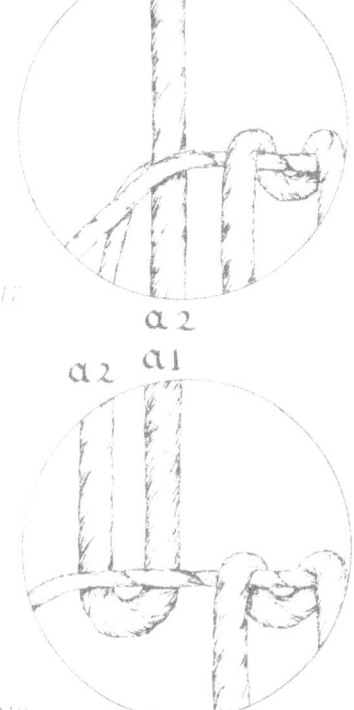

415. and 416. The overlay fringe, Method I (CS)

In Method I a number of thick, doubled weft strands, slightly shorter than the fringe of the blanket, are measured and then cut. One end of a doubled strand is inserted in one segment of the weft twining, its tail, (a1), hanging over the top of the cross-slat to keep it out of the way (fig. 417).

The bottom tail of the doubled strand, (a2), is then raised and inserted in the next weft segment (fig. 418). It, too, is placed over the cross-slat. All of the overlay fringe strands will stay up and out of the way until the warp fringe twining is completed.

417. and 418. The overlay fringe, Method I

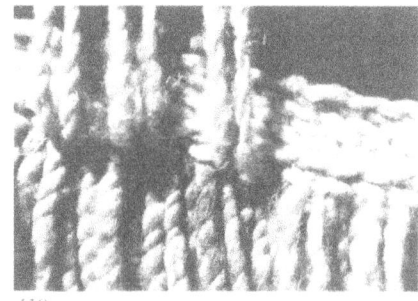

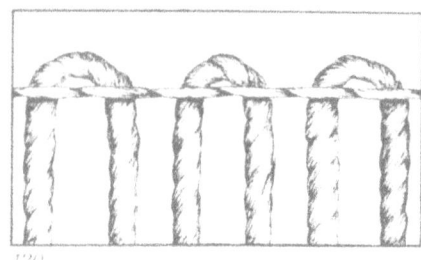

419. and 420. The overlay fringe, Method II (CS)

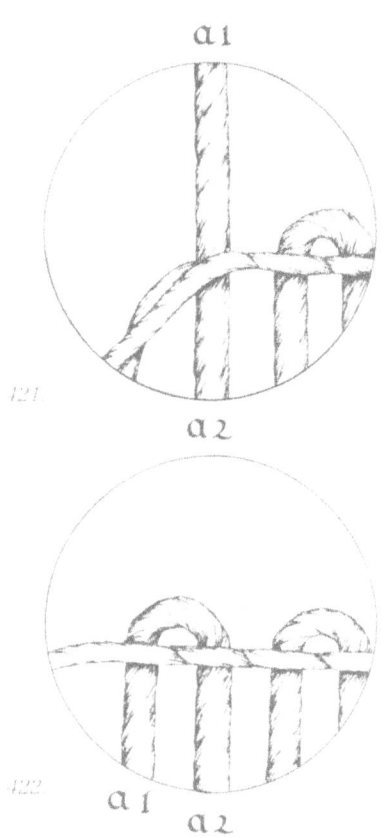

421. and 422. The overlay fringe,
Method II

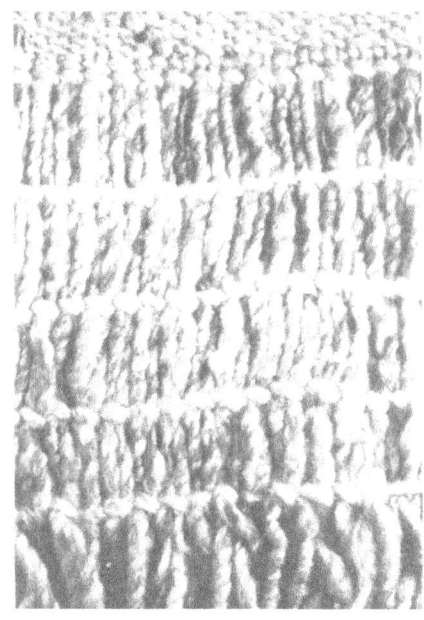

423. The warp fringe twining (CS)

In Method II, the strands of the overlay fringe are measured and cut in the same manner as in Method I. One end of a doubled strand is inserted in one segment of the weft twining, its tail, (a1), hanging over the top of the cross-slat (fig. 421).

When the next segment of the weft is twined, (a1) is lowered and caught into it (fig. 422). All of the overlay fringes, once completed, are placed over the cross-slat in order to keep them out of the way while the warp fringe is twined.

Sometimes, in either method, a sparse overlay fringe was necessary. This was probably due to a limited supply of mountain goat yarn. If this was the case, a segment of the twining was left free between additions of fringe, or the weft twining encircled three warp ends instead of two.

THE WARP FRINGE TWINING

The fringe of the Dancing Blanket hangs from beneath the footing. It contains many more warp ends than were originally hung on the loom due to the addition of warp ends during the weaving process. To control and order the fringe below the footing, four to six widely spaced rows of two-strand twining are inserted. These rows are generally white, although on occasions yellow, blue, or even multicolored wefts were used. They are evenly spaced, covering a distance from five to fifteen centimeters below the footing. Sometimes they are twined over paired warp ends, sometimes over alternate warp pairs. The weaver's personal sense of perfection and completion governed her placement of these rows.

REMOVING THE WEAVING FROM THE LOOM

When the warp fringe twining was completed, it was time to take the Dancing Blanket off the loom. First, each gut bag was removed from the warp. The loom beam was then unrolled until the entire blanket could be seen. The sinew lacing cord, which fastened the heading cord to the loom, was unlaced. The weaving was now completely free from the loom. The heading cord remained in the weaving and to it were attached the leather thongs which served as ties to hold the Dancing Blanket on the dancer. A strip of fur was wound around the heading cord, the side fringes attached, and finally the tie-off was twined. The Dancing Blanket was ready for the dance.

The Fur

A strip of sea otter fur was wound around the heading cord after the blanket was removed from the loom. More than one strip would be needed to wind the entire length of the heading cord. These strips were thin, usually no more than one-half a centimeter in width. The winding would begin on the right side of the blanket. One strip of fur was entered from the front side of the weaving, under the heading cord and between two warp ends. The strip would then be wound, between every two warp ends and around the heading cord, always entering from the front. Once the strips were wound, the fur had to be fluffed with the tip of an awl.

The Side Fringe

A short additional fringe was added along the sides of the blanket between the layers of the side braids. It was made of strands of mountain goat wool which might have been measured and cut on the shuttlelike implement in figure 425. These "winders," as Emmons called them, are about twenty-eight centimeters long and have a number of knife cuts crossing the middle section. The side fringes of the Dancing Blankets range between twenty-five and thirty centimeters in length. Mountain goat wool could have been wound around the winders and then cut in the middle to form the strands of these fringes. The side fringe was generally white, although a few blankets are found which have a blue and white banded fringe. In fringes of this type, the bands of alternating colors were six to ten centimeters wide.

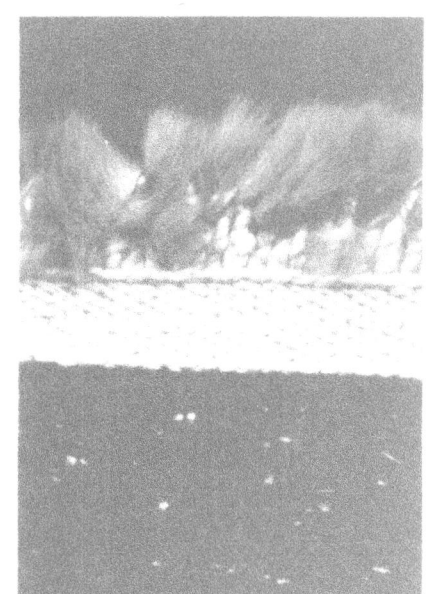

424. The heading, with a strip of sea otter fur wound round the cord (CS)

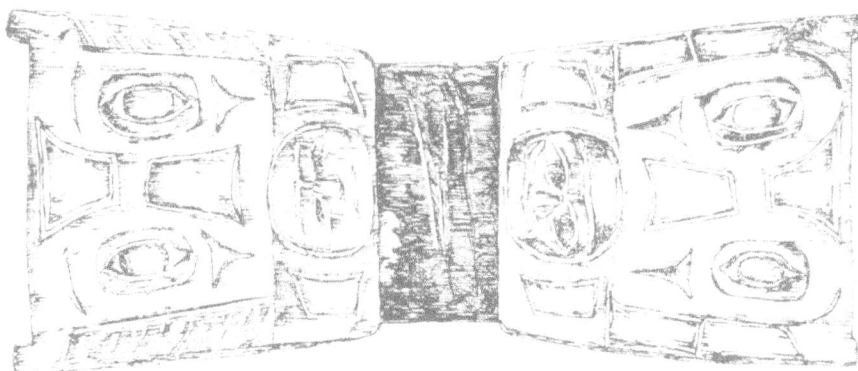

425. A yarn winder

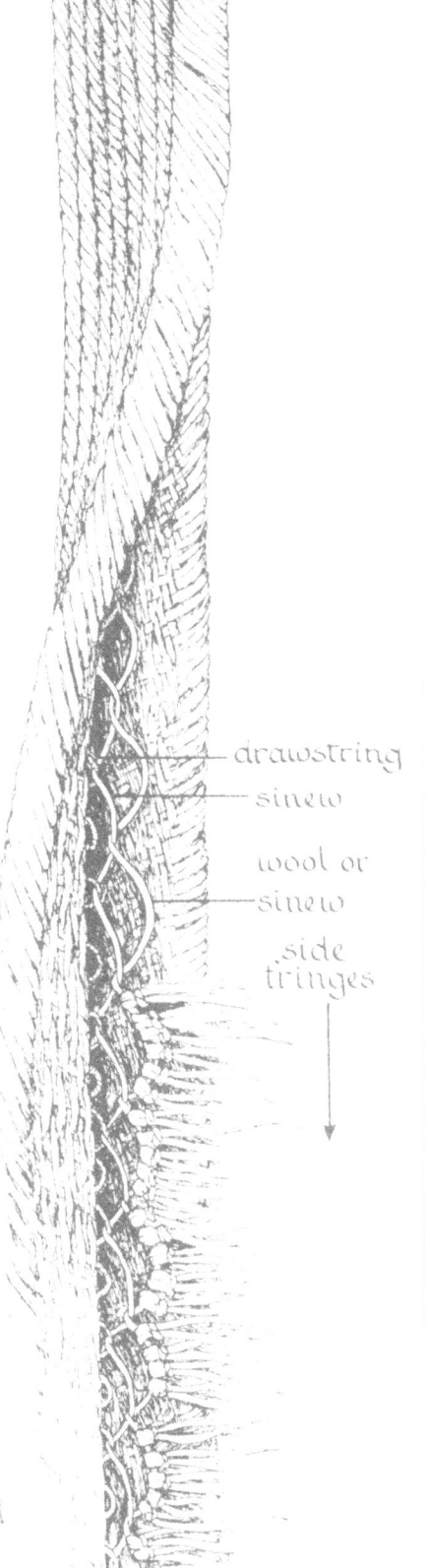

ATTACHING THE SIDE FRINGE

The side fringe is attached to a cord which is laced to the blanket in the middle of the side braid. First, a two-ply sinew strand is stitched into every other loop of the drawstring. Into this another strand is laced, either of sinew or wool. The fringes themselves are hitched to this outer strand. The oldest blankets have wool, sinew, or wool and cedar bark strands which attach the fringe to the blanket edge. After contact with white men, cotton seine twine became available and the weavers used this almost exclusively.

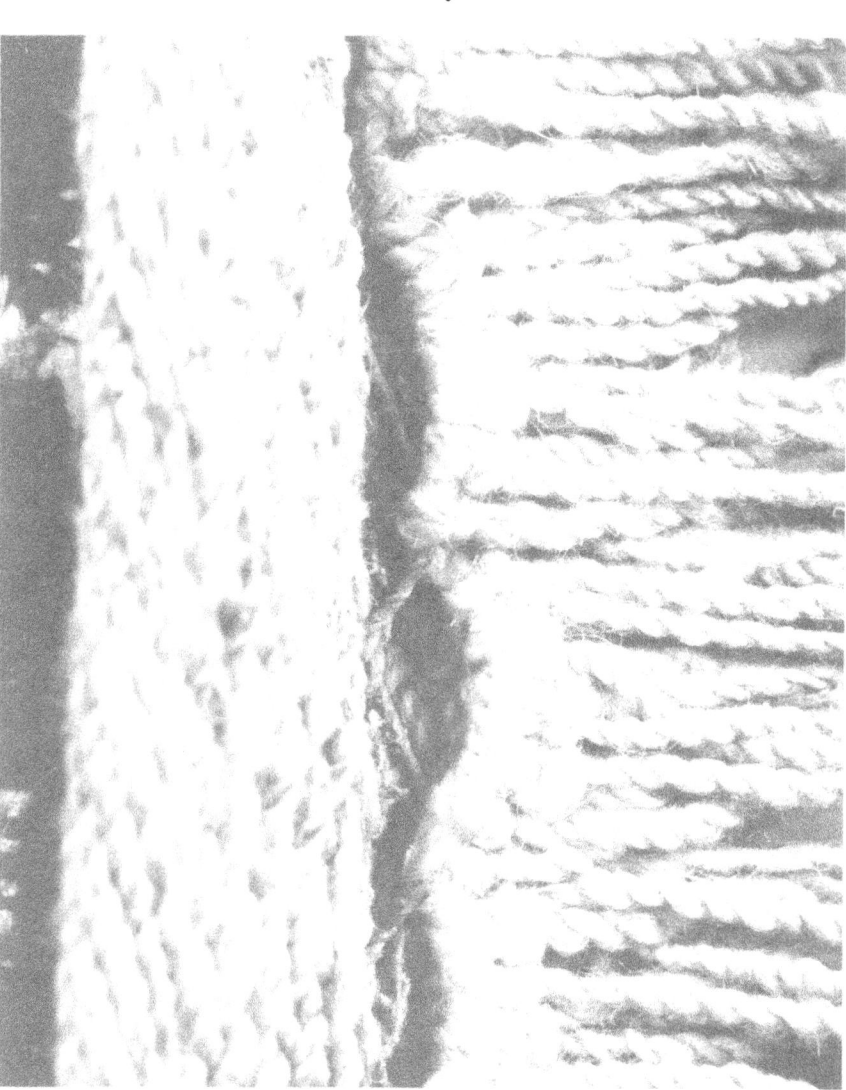

427. Four to six side fringes were hitched to one loop of the wool or sinew strand. (CS)

426. Entering the side fringe

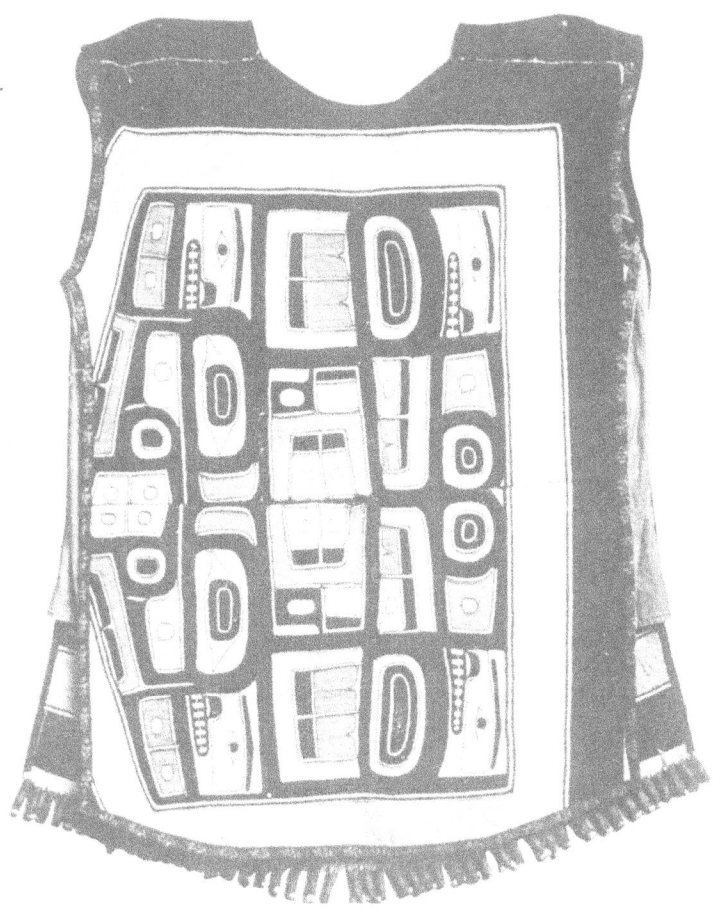

428. A potlatch tunic (Courtesy of the British Columbia Provincial Museum)

WARP WRAPPING

Warp wrapping was a technique which was used to finish the bottoms of the tunics and was occasionally used in the tie-offs at the corners of a Dancing Blanket. The photograph in figure 428 shows a potlatch tunic in which the warp ends of the back side have been wrapped. The warp-wrapped bundles are very dirty; therefore, their black-yellow-black pattern is indistinct. Figures D and E show this patterning clearly (Color Plate Section). On the outer edges a glimpse can be had of the small sticks which serve to fatten the bundles. The design here is made up of the side panels of one Dancing Blanket seamed together. It is unusual that care has been taken to match the two panels. Careful note of the profile faces will show how they have been designed to fit around the primary formlines which they border.

429. Warp wrapping at the bottom of a tunic

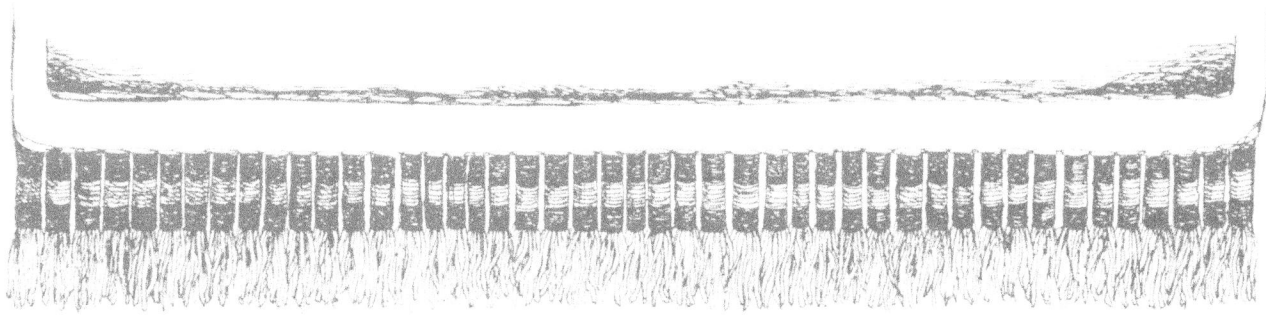

A   B   C

430. The technique of warp wrapping

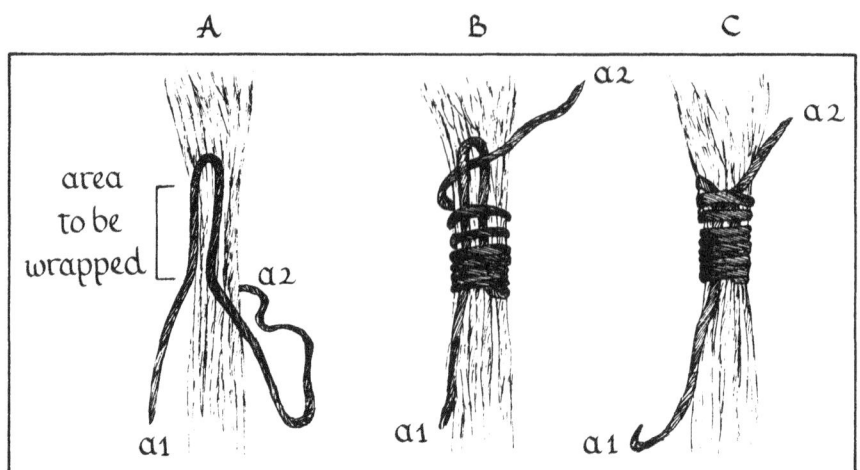

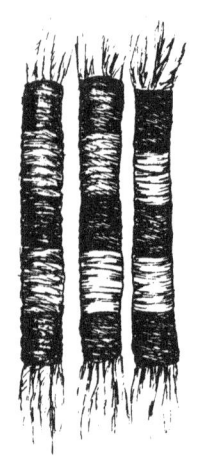

431. A warp-wrapped tie-off

To wrap a bundle of strands so that a knot need not be tied, a short length of yarn is cut and doubled over the area to be covered (A) (fig. 430). A short tail, (a1), extends to the left. The longer tail, (a2), is wrapped tightly around the bundle of warp ends and the doubled part of the yarn. When the top of the loop is reached, (a2) is inserted through it (B). Tail (a1) is then pulled until (a2) disappears into the middle of the bundle, (C). Both ends of the wrapping yarn can be cut off flush without any fear of the wrapping coming loose.

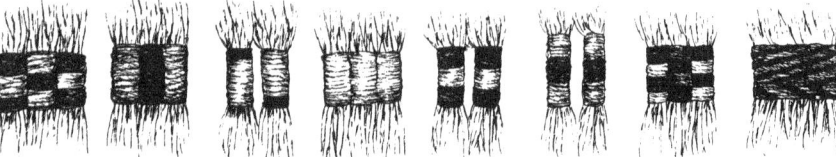

432. A variety of tie-offs

THE TIE-OFF

To complete the side braids, the weaver created a tiny pattern at their bases in colors of her own choosing. Each individual was free to design this pattern as she wished. The variety of tie-offs on Dancing Blankets is great. They range from checkerboard styles in yellow, blue, and black to bars of single colors. Many of the older blankets have diagonally patterned tie-offs reminiscent of the geometric style of weaving. The majority of these personal marks are variations of a black and yellow checkerboard pattern.

The tie-offs at the bottom of each side braid were almost always a mirror image of each other. The tie-off, if patterned in two colors, was twined with a two-color weft. It is quite likely that a woman would have used the same pattern, or at least a pattern of similar colors and design, on each blanket she wove. Certain blankets which were woven by the same weaver, as determined through technical and artistic similarities, have been identified and their tie-offs are similar, if not identical.

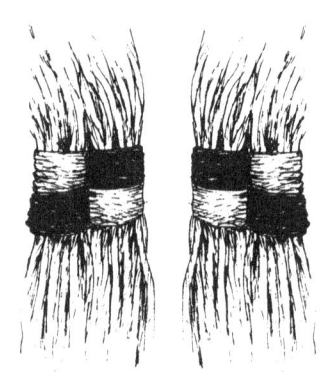

433. The two tie-offs of one blanket

Two very unusual tie-offs are worth noting. Both are on very old blankets. One is composed of two layers, each geometrically patterned in a yellow and black diagonal. Each half of the side braid on both sides of this blanket was given its own tie-off. The blanket is called the "Kane" Blanket and is in the Manitoba Museum of Man and Nature, Winnipeg. The other tie-off is on the Killer Whale Blanket illustrated on p. 40. It is composed of a bundle of shredded cedar bark wrapped tightly with black and yellow yarns. The wrapped bundle is quite fat, having a circumference of five centimeters.

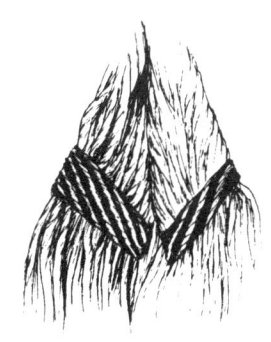

434. The Kane Blanket tie-off

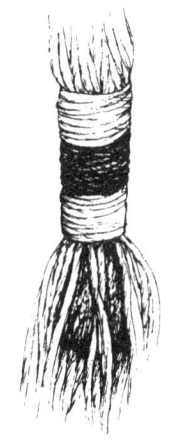

435. The Killer Whale Blanket tie-off

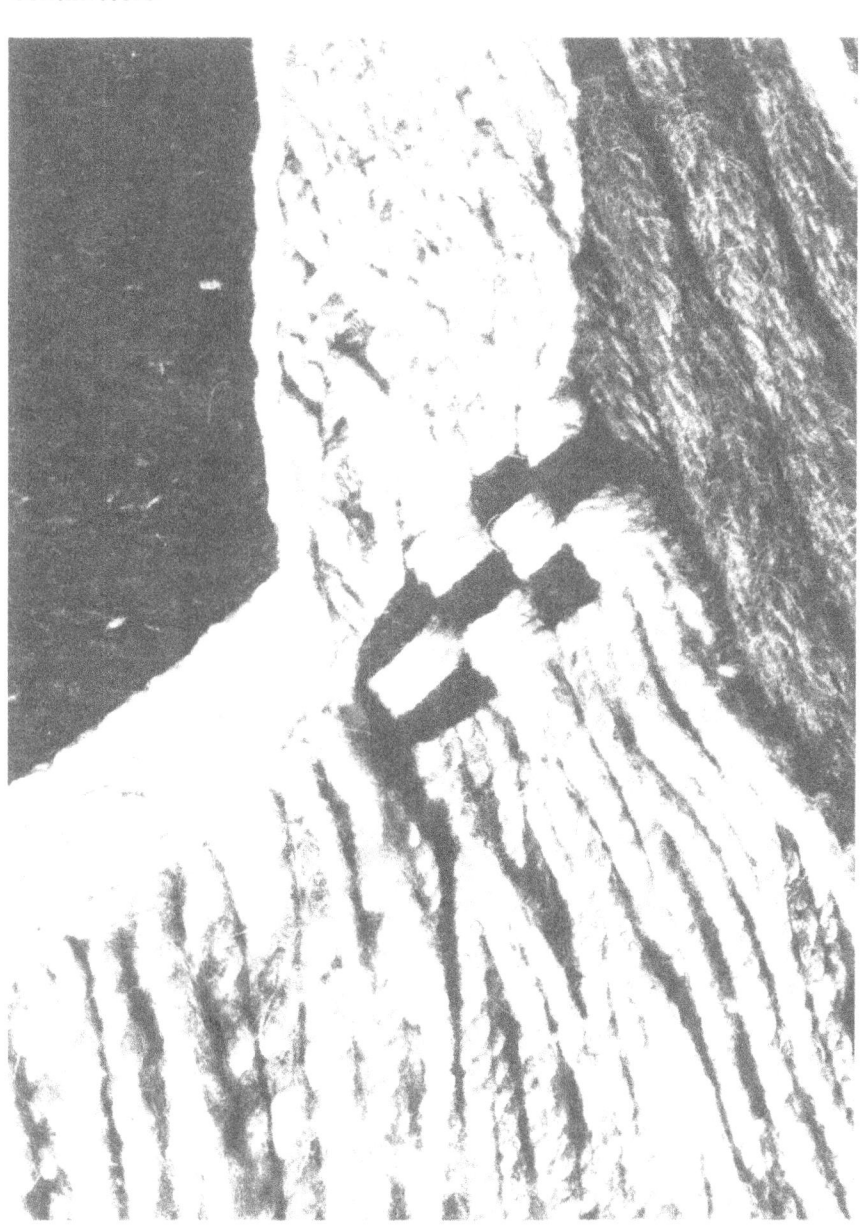

436. (Private Collection: CS)

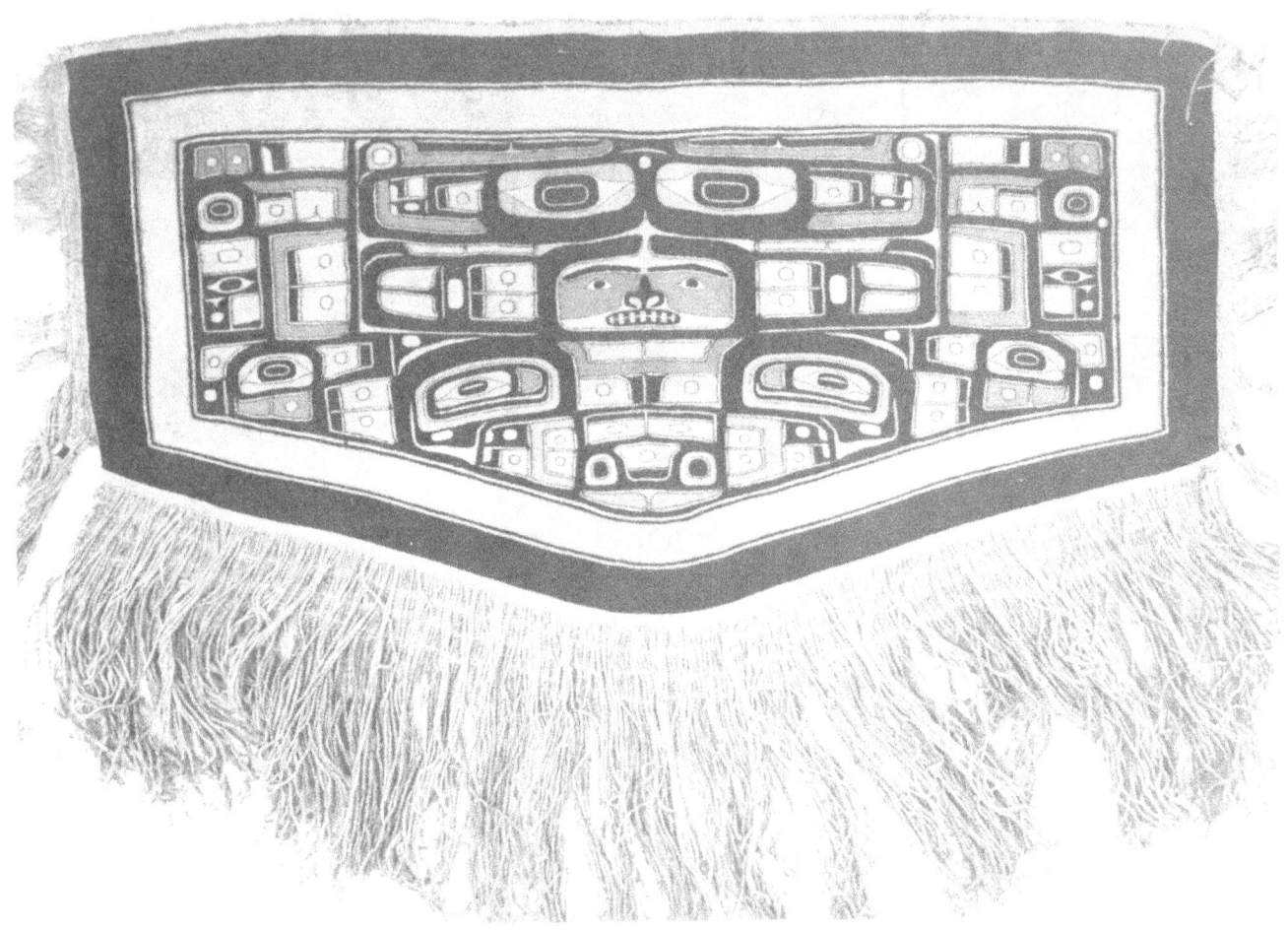

437. A Dancing Blanket with a whale as the main figure in the central design panel. The face shape in the body has a round head and may represent the blowhole. A careful comparison with the back of this blanket clearly shows how the use of the braids helps to define the shapes in the design. (Courtesy of the National Museum of Natural History, Smithsonian Institution)

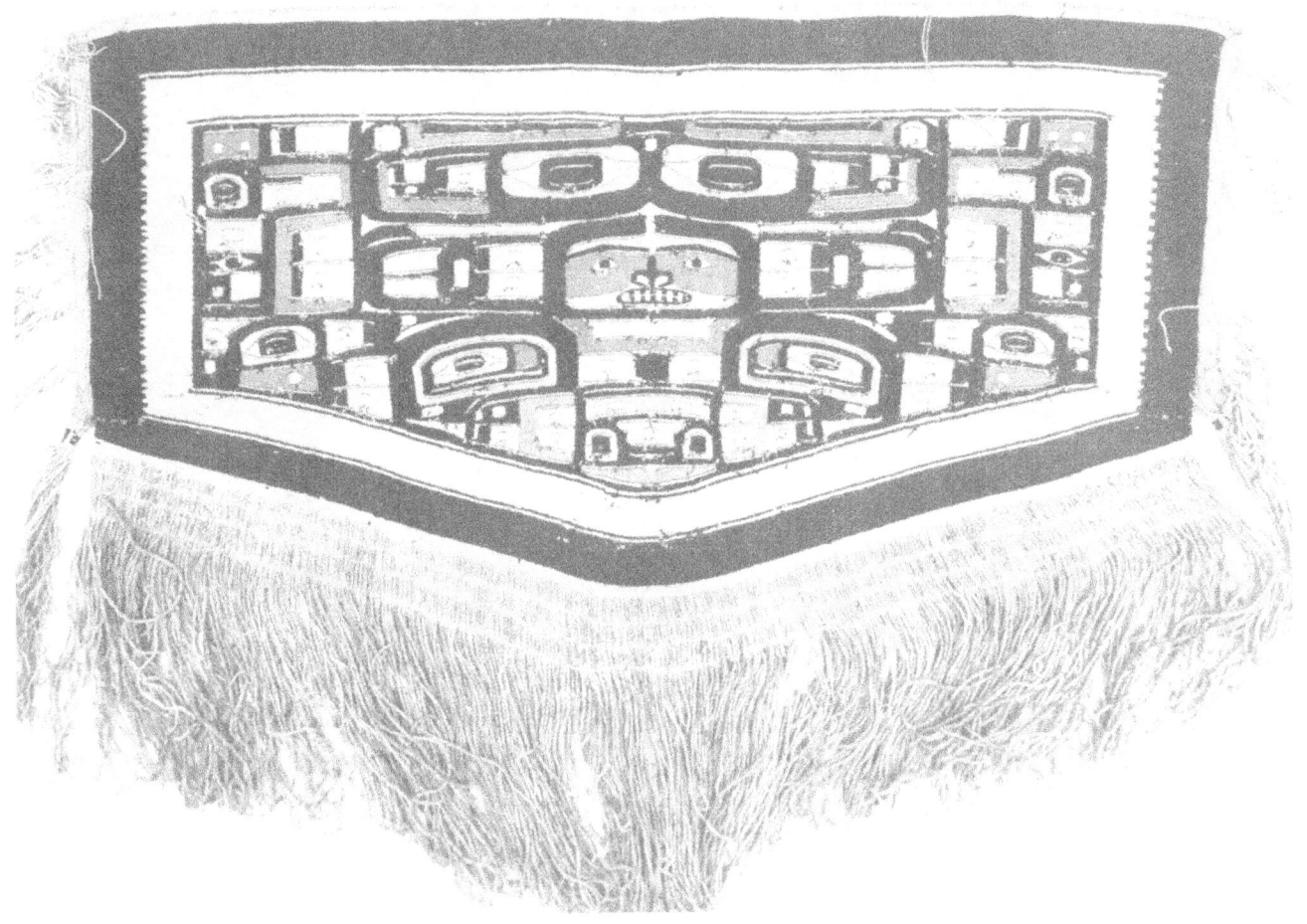

438. *The back of the Dancing Blanket on the preceding page. Many of the technical features of the weaving can be seen in this photograph. The dovetail join between the black and yellow border varies in its patterning, the vertical braids do not appear on this surface, and the tails of the weft and braid strands are cut off. (Courtesy of the National Museum of Natural History, Smithsonian Institution)*

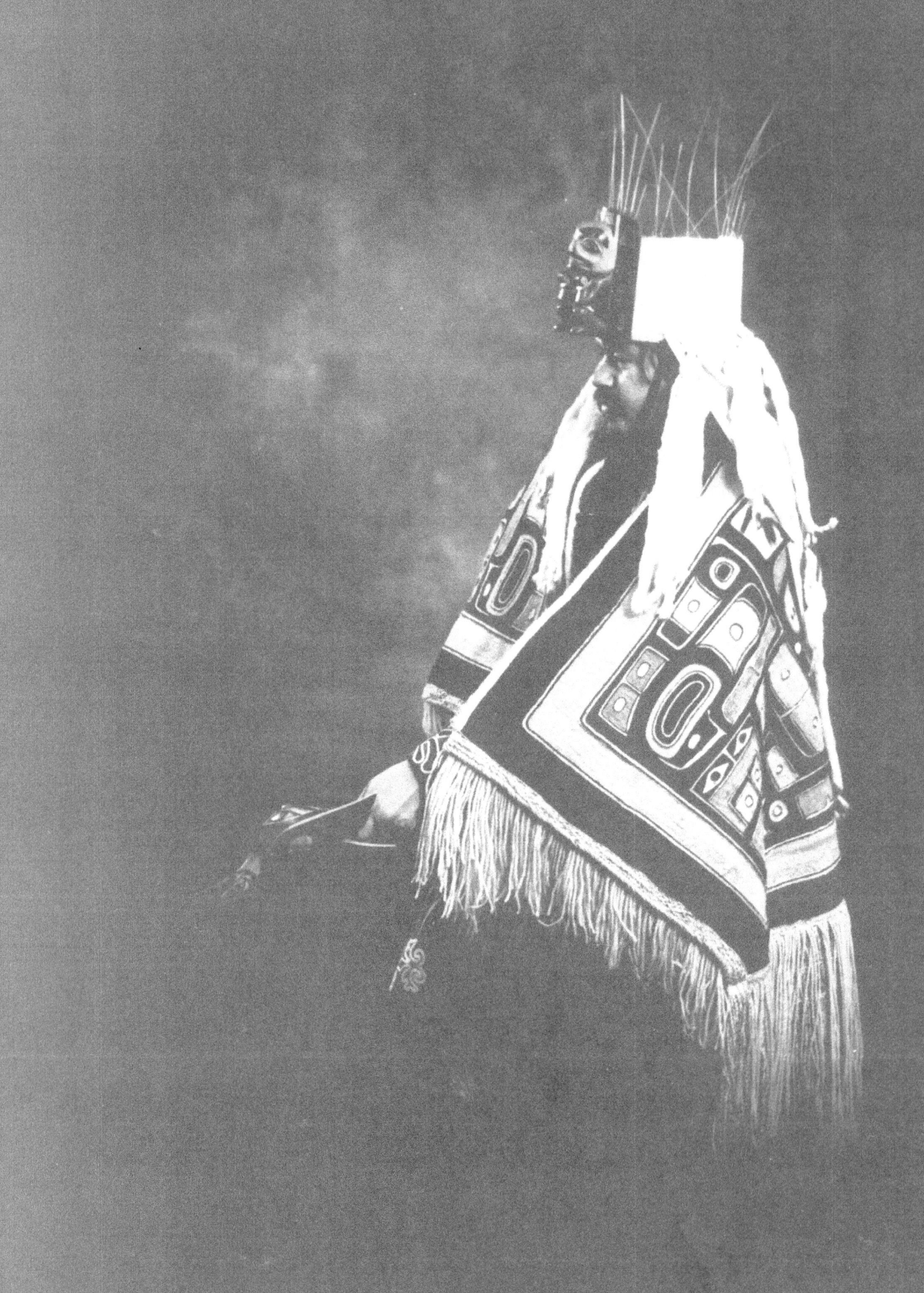

A NEW DAWN

Chilkat weavings were once the glory of the coast. Magnificent in design, spectacular in performance, they gave pride and esteem both to the people who wore them and to the women who wove them.

After contact with white men, the lives of the people of the coast changed very rapidly. An initial impact of the exchange between the Indians and the explorers and traders was to vastly increase the production of native art. Men and women artists quickly appreciated the advantages the new culture had to offer them. They realized that with steel knives, with axe blades, with wool that was already spun, the amount of time which they had to spend on their work was greatly reduced. They were willing to experiment, to try new methods and ideas. Because of their intellectual curiosity and open-mindedness, their art flourished.

During the period of trading, contact with the white culture continued to stimulate artistic production. Traders and collectors wanted works of art, and thus a new market was opened. In return for their carved masks and Dancing Blankets, the people wanted western clothing which was much easier to wear and to make than the native leather and bark clothes. They wanted blankets, metal, guns, and ammunition. As in all societies which have experienced "westernization," the machine-made goods of an industrialized society were considered extremely valuable. They were more convenient, they were time saving, and they were *new*.

When the pioneers eventually settled on the land, when they set up canneries and farms and built their towns and cities, the lives of the Indians changed to an even greater degree. A new religion challenged the old ways. Money arrived, and with it came jobs. The social values of prestige and esteem were still important, but the goods which bought that prestige changed. If a woman could get a job in a cannery and earn one hundred dollars in a year, this was of much greater value than to spend an equal amount of time weaving a Dancing Blanket which might sell for twenty-five dollars. With the money, she could purchase a far greater number of trade blankets to add to the family esteem.

Values changed, and so did life-styles. The native people adopted new ways, not realizing that by doing so their entire culture would change. Many times this change was forced on them by overzealous missionaries or government officials who consciously sought to destroy the native traditions. The potlatch was forbidden, the winter ceremonials ceased. New diseases took a heavy toll.

But the peoples of the coast were rich, not only in natural resources but also in the spirit of their traditions. For a time, this spirit receded into the backdrop of forest and sea to lie dormant until a more tolerant age. Its strength, power, and vitality, instilled in the hearts, minds, and souls of continued generations, has been given a new life in the last twenty years. Today, carvers, painters, and basket makers create art works in the tradition of their forefathers. It is a new art, born of a people who have westernized *and* retained the essential

439. Dancer: Tony Hunt

spirit of the old ways. New tools are still being tried, new media explored. With the inquisitive minds of creative perfectionists, the artists retain or discard these new ideas depending on their success. In the old days, paper was not used to paint on. Today, silkscreen printing has proven to be an excellent medium for design expression. The conventions of the art, established generations ago, play a vital role in the creation of the new designs. Great works of art are produced by inspired, creative artists who have a fluent control of convention and technique.

The Chilkat Dancing Blanket was, and still is, a glorious thing. In today's world it retains its position of esteem. With the revival of the potlatch, it can once more be seen in its dancing role as Nahkeen. It also hangs in pride of place in museums and in the homes of art collectors and lovers of beauty.

Chilkat weaving will revive more slowly than the other art forms. Perhaps this is due to time, for in the late twentieth century time has presented a new face. "How long does it take to weave a circle?" "How many meters can be spun in an hour?" These questions, at the forefront of peoples' minds today, probably had little significance to the Chilkat weaver of the 1800s. To weave, one simply must have time.

Time—and technique. The technique of Chilkat weaving slipped into the recesses of peoples' minds as westernization took hold. Over the last fifty years only a handful of people have been interested in drawing these techniques out of the past. They are difficult techniques, born of a complex design form which demanded that flowing, curvilinear lines be accomplished on a vertical grid. Paint will flow easily over a surface of wood or leather. Wool does not flow, but needs to be manipulated strand by strand in order to "paint" a picture. The brilliance of the women who developed techniques which coped with the problems presented by the designs is remarkable. Today's weavers, challenged by the technique and having a profound respect for the conventions of the art, can repeat this achievement.

Raven, through one legend or another, took the technique of weaving and gave it to the people. Raven was a mighty trickster, yet he had at heart the good of all mankind. Is it possible that Raven will, once again, disguise himself in order to renew this gift?

440. Katherine Thompson, four years old, wearing a child's Dancing Blanket. Katherine is the daughter of Arthur and Polly Thompson.

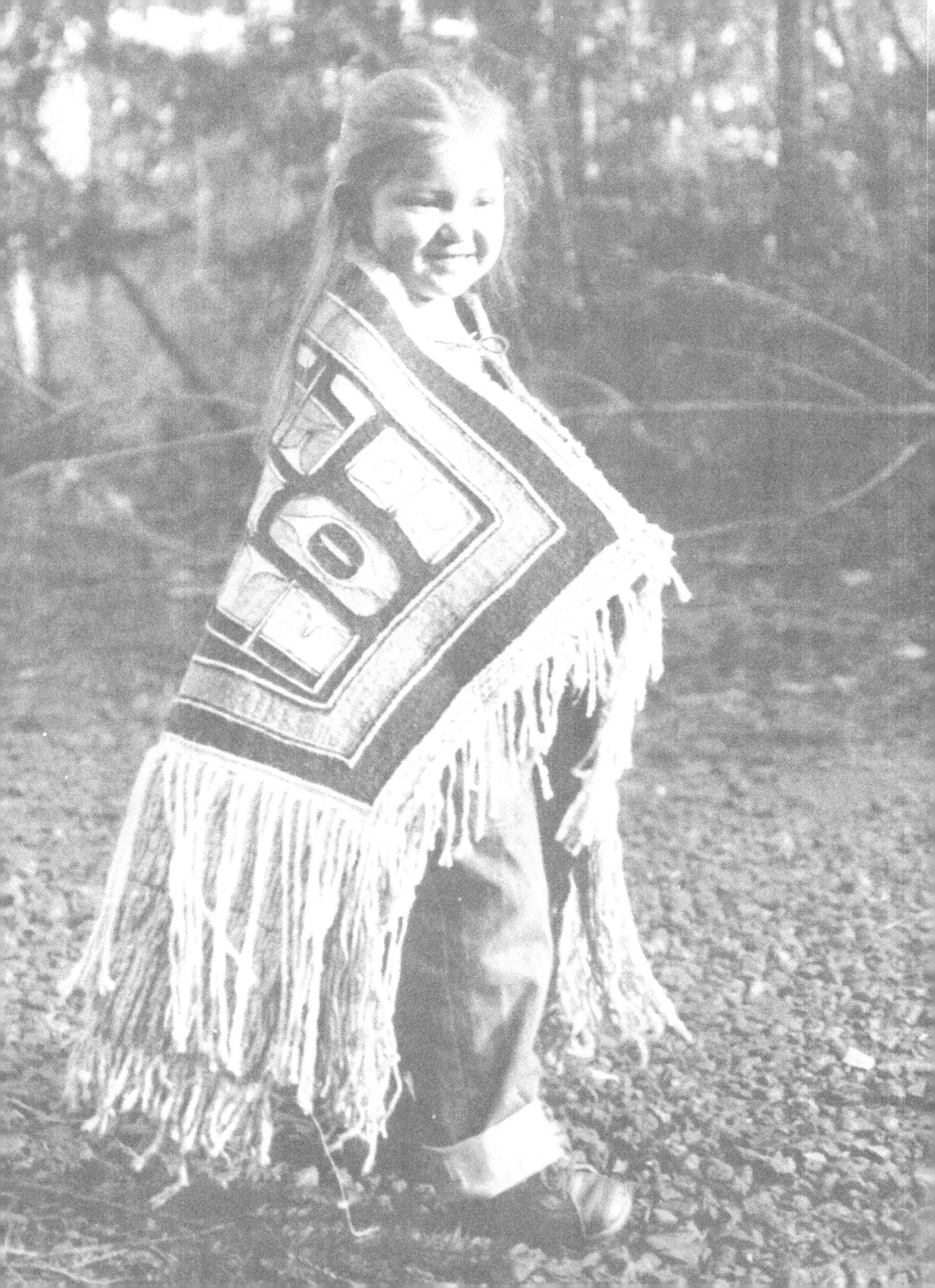

Map of Major Tribes of the Northern Northwest Coast

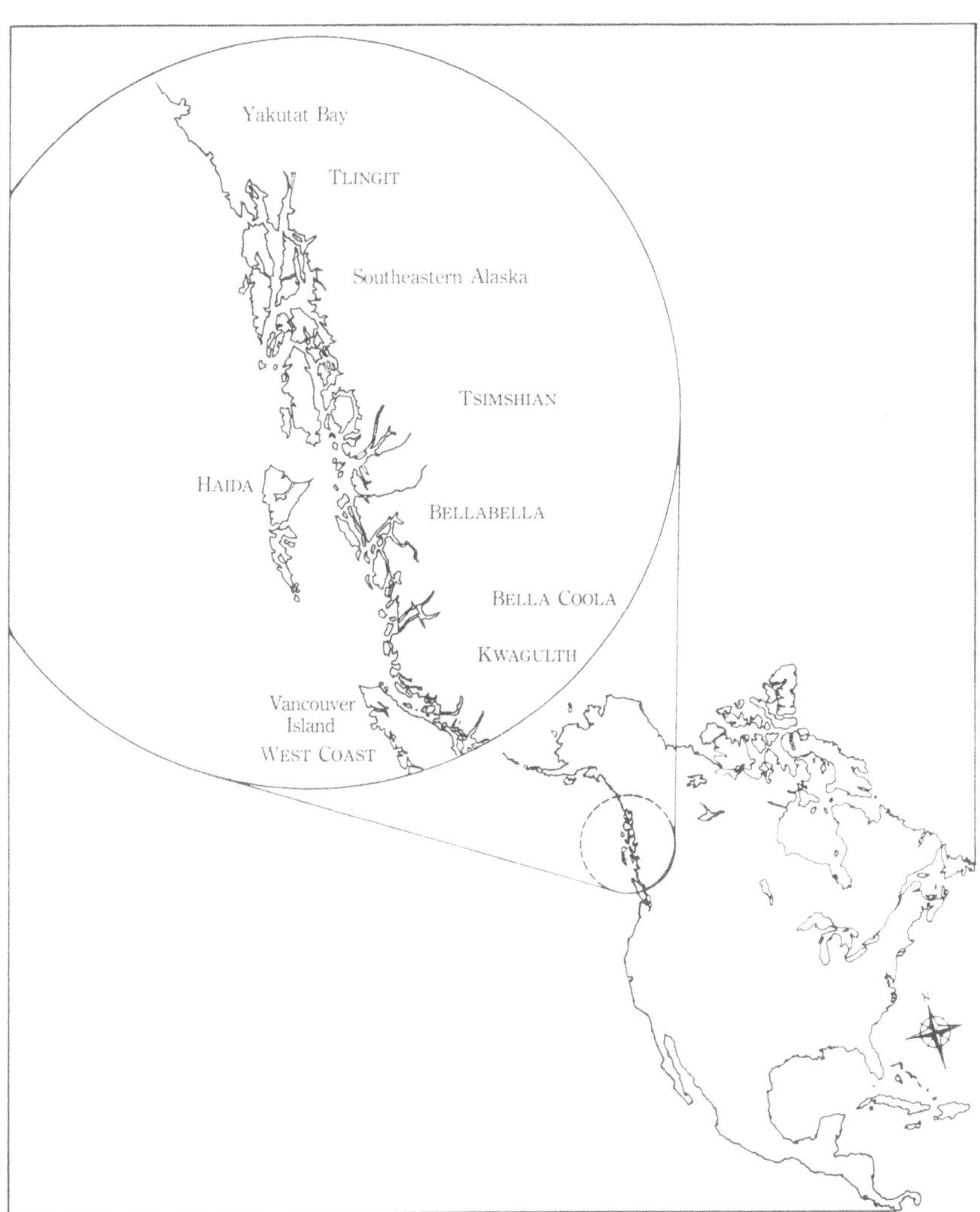

Yakutat Bay

TLINGIT

Southeastern Alaska

TSIMSHIAN

HAIDA

BELLABELLA

BELLA COOLA

KWAGULTH

Vancouver
Island
WEST COAST

The following recipes have been produced by professional dyer Judith MacKenzie of Victoria, British Columbia. They use dye powders from the Ciba Superwash Dye Series, are colorfast, and if used accurately will produce colors which are in the range of the Chilkat yarns.

THE PROCESS

These recipes are designed to dye thirty gram skeins of wool, dry weight. The amount of water used is not critical; enough should be placed in the dye pot so that the skeins will move freely. The critical aspect of these dyes is the ratio of dye to dry weight of wool. To get an accurate color, the dyebath should be allowed to exhaust. This means that the skeins of wool are left in the dye until no pigment is left in the water and it appears clear. The recipes use household strength white vinegar. If there is a problem in exhausting the bath after twenty minutes at a simmer, a bit more vinegar may be added. The dyebath should be placed in a stainless steel or enamel pot which does not have any eroded spots. To prepare a dyebath, the stock solutions, in the ratio and dilutions required, are added to enough cold water for the skeins to move easily. The vinegar is added to the dyebath. The skeins of yarn are first evenly saturated in cold water and then settled into the dyebath. The dyebath is brought to a simmer and kept at this temperature until all the color has been absorbed by the wool. For an even dye, the skeins should be turned over gently every few minutes. When the dye has been exhausted, the skeins are then cooled and rinsed.

THE MEASURING EQUIPMENT

Care must be taken when measuring the dyes because they are very strong. In these recipes, twenty grams of dry dye powder has been used as the basis for the stock solution as this seems to be the most common amount on the market in a premeasured amount. As the dyes have various volumes, it is not possible to measure them by the teaspoon. If it is necessary to weigh the dye powder, a gram scale that will weigh accurately to at least five grams should be used. For measuring the stock solutions, a graduated cylinder that measures down to five milliliters is needed. A hypodermic syringe is an excellent device for measuring individual milliliters. One should be obtained for each stock solution, which will save time and eliminate the possibility of contaminating the dyes. It should be noted that cc's and ml's are equivalent.

Equivalents:
1 ounce = 28.35 grams
1 cc = 1 milliliter

THE STOCK SOLUTIONS

Each recipe uses Ciba *Superwash Dye Series* dyes mixed in a stock solution. For accuracy of color, it is important to use this series of Ciba Dye. To make the stock solution, take twenty grams of dye powder and mix with a small amount of cold water to form a paste. In a stainless steel or enamel pot, mix this paste with approximately 500 milliliters of cold water. Bring to a simmer, stirring occasionally, and keep at a simmer for ten minutes. Let this mixture cool, add enough water to make 1000 milliliters and store. Shake well before using. The dye powders needed are: canary yellow, khaki golden, red red, orange, turquoise, and black.

THE DYEBATH

The yellow and blue recipes call for portions of *dilute solutions*. With the exception of the red red dye, all of the stock solutions should be treated as follows:

Dilute 15 milliliters stock solution with 180 milliliters water. Reserve this dye for use when the recipes call for *dilute* solutions.

THE YELLOW DYE *(similar to wolf moss yellow)*

In the dye pot place:
     15 ml of the *dilute* khaki golden solution
     15 ml of the canary stock solution
     8 ml of the *dilute* orange stock solution

Add 90 ml white vinegar and enough cold water to cover the wool. Simmer until the dyebath is exhausted. Cool and rinse.

THE BLUE-GREEN DYE *(similar to trade blanket blue with a wolf moss overdye)*

In the dye pot place:
     15 ml of the *dilute* turquoise solution
     7 ml of the *dilute* canary solution
     1.5 ml of the *dilute* khaki golden solution
     7 ml of the *dilute* black solution

Add 90 ml white vinegar and enough cold water to cover the wool. Simmer until the dyebath is exhausted. Cool and rinse.

THE RICH BLACK DYE *(similar to hemlock bark brown with an overdye of copper and urine)*

In the dye pot place:
     9 ml of the red red stock solution
     45 ml of the orange stock solution
     34 ml of the black stock solution

Add 90 ml white vinegar and enough cold water to cover the wool. Simmer until the dyebath is exhausted. Cool and rinse. It should be noted that this dye takes quite a long time to exhaust, and vinegar should be added after twenty minutes.

AN ALTERNATIVE BLACK DYE

This recipe is provided in case it is difficult to obtain the Ciba Superwash Series black dye powder. The color produced is very accurate.

In 500 ml (or approximately two cups) of cold water, dissolve one package of RIT Dark Brown 25.

Add 500 ml cold water. Add 30 grams (or approximately one ounce) of dry wool which has been saturated in cold water. Simmer gently for forty-five minutes, turning skeins often to keep the dye even. Remove, cool and rinse until the dye stops bleeding.

Coloring Guidelines

441. All the areas painted black on the pattern board are woven with black wool. The pattern board shown here is the reverse side of the board shown in figure 36. (Courtesy of the British Columbia Provincial Museum)

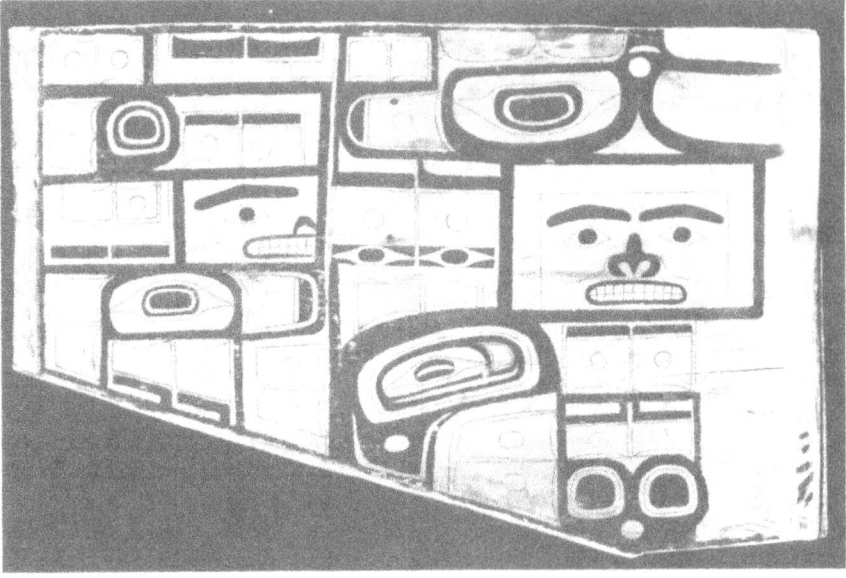

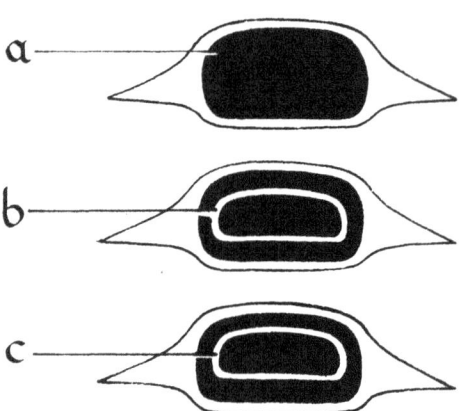

442. The iris, or inner ovoid, within the eyelid line

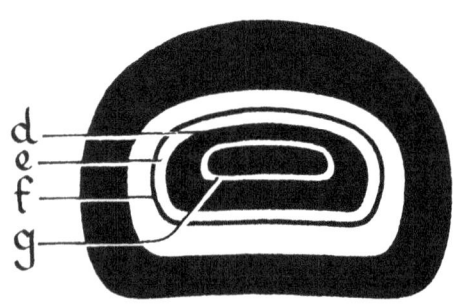

443. A rounded eye socket

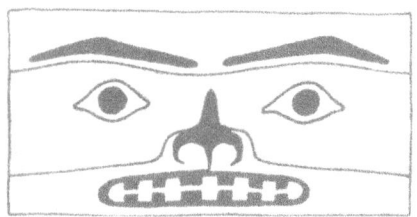

444. The black in a face shape

In the older Dancing Blankets, a yellow-green color was used in place of the blue-green found in the majority of newer ones. In a few blankets, red is substituted for some of the blue areas. As these three colors fill the same color function, ''blue'' will be used to represent all of them.

BLACK

All primary formlines are black. Every inner shape of the design field is surrounded in some way by black. If the shape lies adjacent to a primary formline, the black is automatically present. If, as in the circles and eyelids, the forms are surrounded by blue or yellow, a thin black line always defines each shape. These lines are all present on the pattern board.

The iris, or inner ovoid, within the eyelid line is always black (fig. 442, a). It may be relieved by a thin white ground line which is either concentric or nonconcentric (fig. 442, b and c). Black inner ovoids are also found within the more rounded eye sockets (fig. 443, d). A black outline and a white ground line always surround these inner ovoids (fig. 443, e and f). They also may be relieved with a thin white line (fig. 443, g).

In the face shape, the eyebrows, eyes, nose, and lips are always black. The teeth are always white (fig. 444).

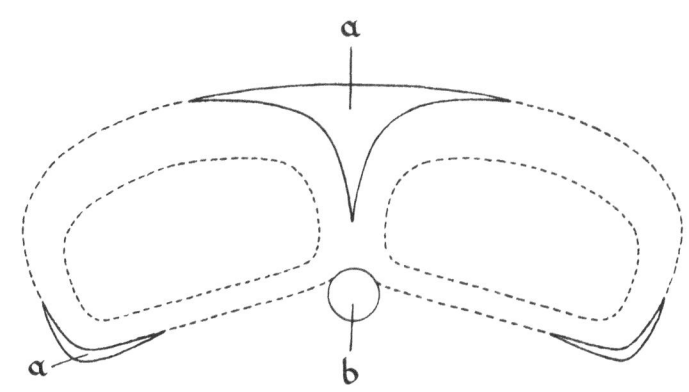

445. Resultant forms

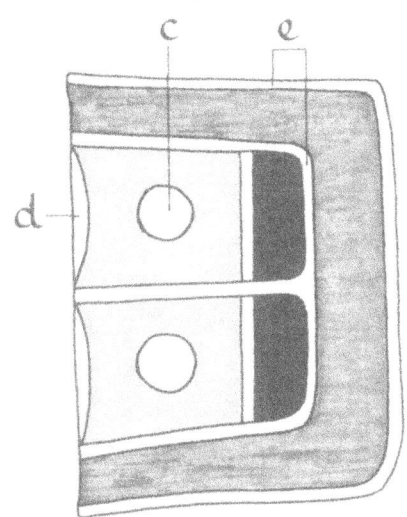

446. Inner ∪ shapes

WHITE

All resultant forms are white (fig. 445, a).

All small perfect circles, except those found within the eyelid line of a face shape, are white. These may occur between two primary formline ovoids (fig. 445, b), or within the blue and yellow inner ∪ shapes (fig. 446, c and fig. 447, c).

The crescents which relieve the inner ∪ shapes are always white (fig, 446, d and fig. 447, d).

Thin white lines set off the black outlines which surround the colored forms. On the pattern board, they are the spaces resulting from the addition of the outlines. These thin spaces are always white (fig. 446, e and fig. 447, e).

The S shapes found at the base of some ∪ shapes are always white (fig. 446, f).

Slits within an iris ovoid are white, as are the "whites" of the eye (fig. 448, g).

447. Inner ∪ shapes

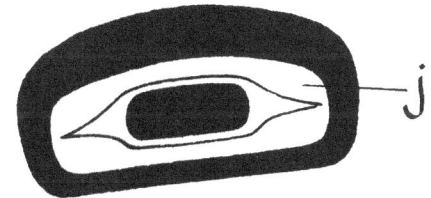

448. An eye

449. A "salmon-trout's head"

BLUE

Whenever a small ∪ shape falls within a "salmon-trout's head," it is always blue (fig. 449, i). Emmons gave this name to the figure; it does not necessarily mean that the form is a head or even a fish.

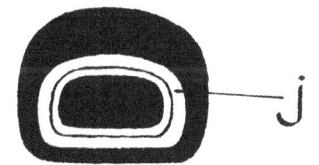

YELLOW

The sockets of eyes and joints are always yellow (fig. 449, j and fig. 450, j).

450. Sockets

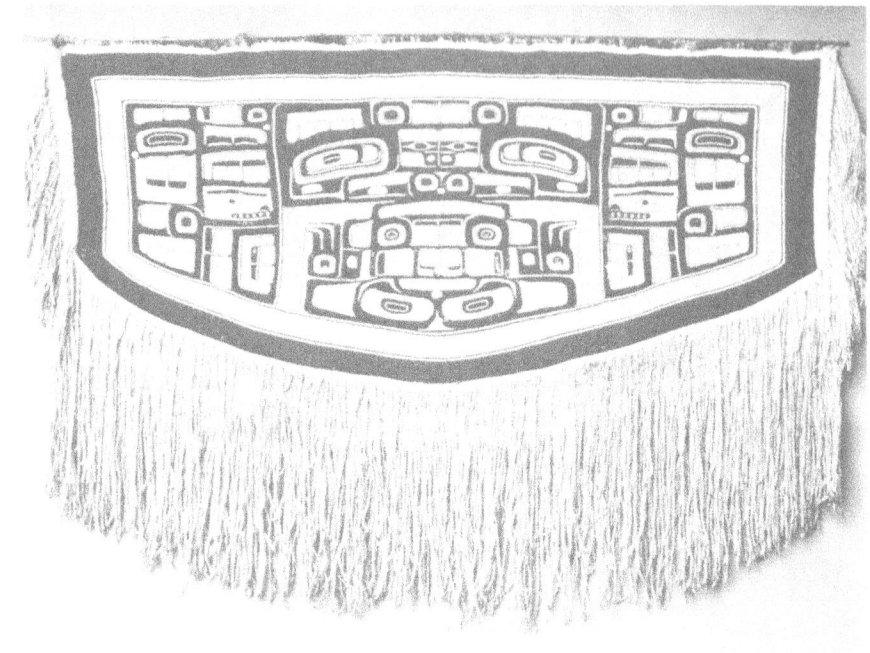

451. *The headlike shapes in figures 452 to 455 are found in this Dancing Blanket. (Courtesy of the Field Museum, Chicago)*

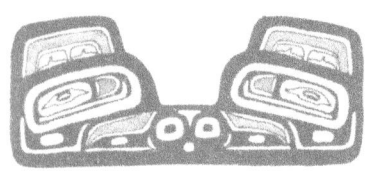

452. *Found in the central design field: the head of the figure*

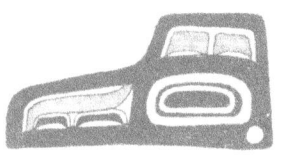

453. *Found in the central design field: the tail of the crest figure. It is upside down and splayed.*

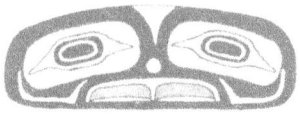

454. *Found in the upper left and right corners of the side panels. Perhaps this is the head of a figure.*

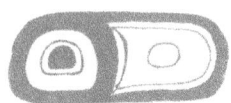

455. *Found in the lower left and right corners of the side panels. The identity of this form is hard to determine.*

HEADLIKE SHAPES

When coloring the remaining figures of the design field, "headlike shapes," composed of eye-ear-nose-mouth units, can be identified which govern the placement of the yellow and the blue. These headlike shapes are found within all areas of the design, regardless of whether the area represents the head, tail, wing, or flipper of the major figure. They will be upside down or right side up, depending on their function in the overall design, and are either profiles or frontal views.

The major component on a headlike shape is the eye unit. The eye can exist with only an ear, only a nose (fig. 455), only a nose and ear (fig. 453), or only a mouth (fig. 454).

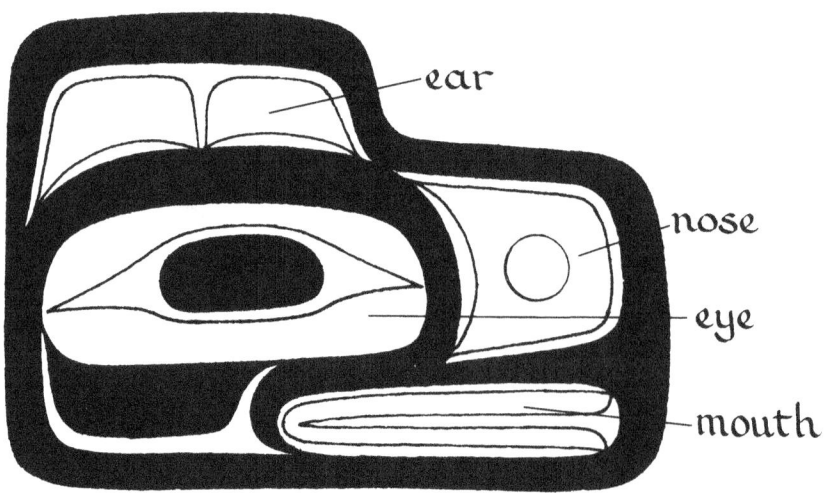

456. *A headlike shape*

COLORING THE COMPONENTS OF THE HEADLIKE SHAPES: THE EYE, THE NOSE, THE EAR

The eye socket of a headlike shape is always yellow.
The nose unit of a headlike shape is usually yellow.
The ear unit of a headlike shape is usually blue.

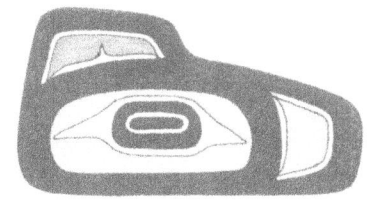

457. A headlike shape composed of an eye, nose, and ear

MOUTHS

The mouths of the headlike shapes are almost always blue.

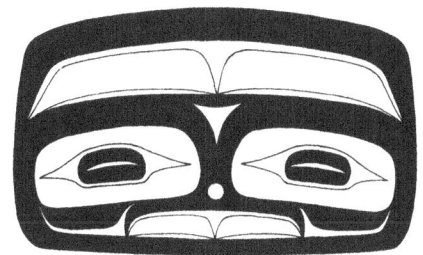

458. The mouth can be shared between two large eyes in a frontal view.

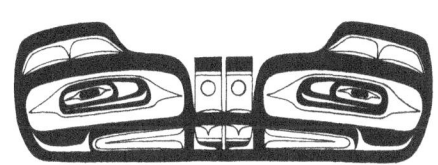

459. The mouth can lie underneath a double eye, separated by ∪ shapes.

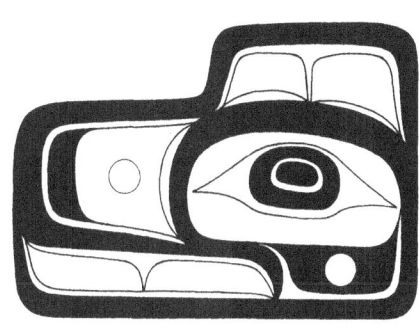

460. The mouth can lie underneath a profile eye and nose.

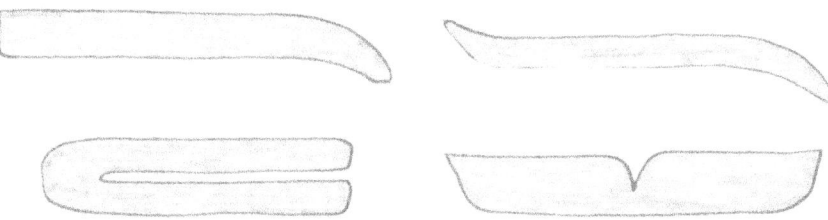

461. Mouth shapes are elongated forms in the figure of an S or a ∪.

FURTHER GUIDELINES FOR COLORING OTHER SHAPES

Squared ∟ and ∪ shapes are usually blue (fig. 462, a).
The long ∟ shape which contains small white circles is always yellow (fig. 462, b).

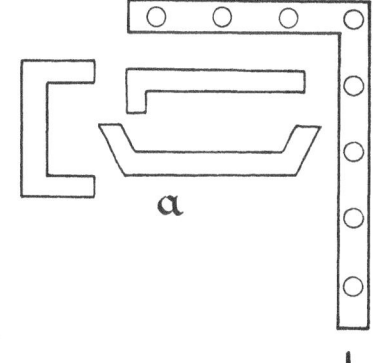

462. Squared ∟ and ∪ shapes

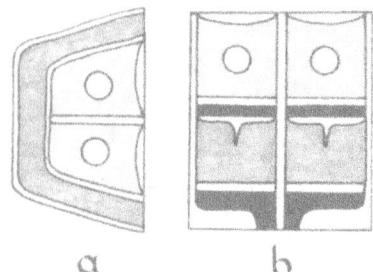

463. Inner ∪ shapes

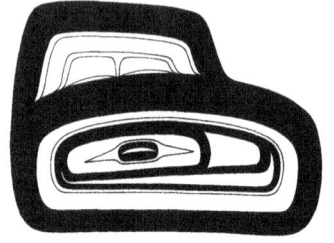

464. Inner ∪ shapes in the ear of a
headlike shape

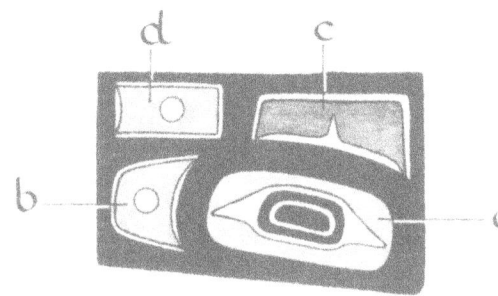

465. The shapes in this illustration
are colored according to the following
guidelines: (a) yellow: an eye unit; (b)
yellow: a nose unit; (c) blue: an ear
unit; (d) blue: blue shapes do not lie
next to each other.

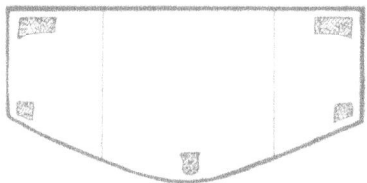

466. Shapes in the corners of the
design field

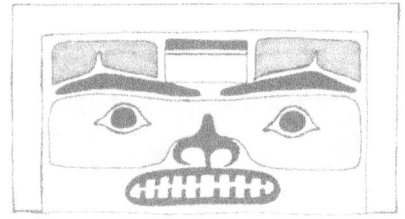

467. The yellow and blue in a face
shape

Blue shapes are never surrounded by other blue shapes. Because the squared L and ∪ shapes are usually blue, any ∪s near them must be yellow (fig. 463, a). In a block of paired ∪s, two are usually blue and two yellow (fig. 463, b).

Paired ∪ shapes are usually the same color. When a squared ∪ is found over an eye unit, it forms an ear. As it should be blue, the interior ∪ shapes must be yellow. If the weaver has thought of the ∪ shapes as the ear unit and colored them blue, the squared ∪ must then be yellow (fig. 464).

Two blue shapes do not usually lie next to each other, even if separated by a black primary formline (fig. 465). Paired ∪s should be treated as a single unit.

The shapes in the four outside corners of the design field are usually blue (fig. 466). This is probably a result of the placement of the crest figures being depicted. However, it should be noted that a yellow shape, if placed in the top corners, would tend to round the design field visually, as it would be placed next to the yellow border. Very often the point of the shallow V of the design panel also contains a blue form.

In the face shape, the mask is usually, but not always, yellow (fig. 467). The ∪ shapes above the eyebrows are usually blue. The square between them would then be yellow. If the central square exists without the ∪s, and if the mask is yellow, the square will be blue.

The technical information in this volume was obtained primarily from the weavings themselves. In all, approximately 250 weavings and 50 pieces of equipment were examined between 1979 and 1981. Documentation was done on analysis sheets (see sample at end of "Notes") and photographs were taken of every piece. A short form of the analysis sheets was used when time or material demanded. Equipment was sketched, measured, weighed where applicable, and photographed.

In the following notes, weavings and equipment which are excellent examples of various points in the text have been noted. These entries are listed under subject, abbreviation of museum, and catalog number. (Wherever possible, pieces have been selected which can be obtained, through photograph, from the museum collections.) All notes are organized to correspond to the order in which the subject matter appears in the text.

The legends have been paraphrased from the sources which are noted. The stories themselves have not been changed; they have only been edited and retold in order to present a unified style. As the majority of them are from Emmons' sources, an attempt has been made to follow his versions and style very closely. It is hoped that through illustration and retelling they give a vibrant picture of the life of the people of the northwest coast.

MUSEUM ABBREVIATIONS

NORTH AMERICAN MUSEUMS

AMNH — American Museum of Natural History
79th and Central Park West
New York, New York 10024

BCPM — British Columbia Provincial Museum
675 Belleville
Victoria, British Columbia

Burke — Burke Museum
University of Washington
Seattle, Washington 98195

CCI — Canadian Conservation Institute
National Museums of Canada
1030 Innes Road
Ottawa, Ontario K1A 0M8

CFM — Field Museum of Natural History
Roosevelt Drive at Lakeshore
Chicago, Illinois 60605

G — Glenbow
9th Avenue and 1st Street, Southeast
Calgary, Alberta T2G 0P3

HP — Peabody Museum, Harvard University
11 Divinity Avenue
Cambridge, Massachusetts 02138

LACMNH — Los Angeles County Museum of Natural History
Exposition Park
900 Exposition Boulevard
Los Angeles, California 90007

MAI — Museum of the American Indian
Heye Foundation
Broadway at 155th Street
New York, New York 10032

MMMN — Manitoba Museum of Man and Nature
190 Rupert Avenue
Winnipeg, Manitoba R3B 0N2

NMM — National Museum of Man
National Museums of Canada
Canadian Ethnology Service
Esplanade Laurier
300 Laurier Avenue, West
Ottawa, Ontario K1A 0M8

PAM — Portland Art Museum
1219 Southwest Park Avenue
Portland, Oregon 97205

ROM — Royal Ontario Museum
100 Queen's Park
Toronto, Ontario M5S 2C6

Smith — National Museum of Natural History
Washington, D. C. 20560

SP — Salem Peabody
161 Essex Street
Salem, Massachusetts 01970

SIM — Southwest Indian Museum
234 Museum Drive
Los Angeles, California 90065

EUROPEAN MUSEUMS

MAE	Museum of Anthropology and Ethnography Universitetskaya nab. 3 Leningrad B-164 USSR		NMD	National Museum of Denmark Department of Ethnography 10, Ny Vestergade DK - 1471 Copenhagen K Denmark
MAG	Museum and Art Gallery George Street, Perth Scotland PH1 5LB		NMI	National Museum of Ireland Kildare Street Dublin 2 EIRE
BM	Museum of Mankind, British Museum Burlington Gardens London England W1X 2EX		PR	Pitt Rivers Museum University of Oxford Parks Road Oxford England OX1 3PP
MV	Museum für Völkerkunde A-1014 Wien, Neue Hofberg Austria			

PAGE

Prologue
12–13   Dawn of the Dancing Blanket
            Emmons, *The Chilkat Blanket,* pp. 329–30
            Additional information on wild celery and spruce
                root cords: de Laguna, *Under Mt. St. Elias,* p. 407
                and p. 427

Part I
18–19   Raven Gives the Dancing Blanket to Women to Unravel
                and Reweave
            Emmons, *The Chilkat Blanket,* p. 330

20–21   The First Dancing Apron
            Emmons, *The Chilkat Blanket,* pp. 345–46

22   Tsimshian to Tlingit
            Native names and their definitions: Emmons, *The Chilkat
                Blanket,* p. 329. "Chilkat," before westernization, was
                phonetically spelled "Djiłqat" by J.R. Swanton in
                "Contributions to the Ethnology of the Haida,"
                legend number four, p. 239. Emmons translates it as
                "the salmon storehouse" from the wealth of fish that
                crowds the river in the spring and summer: Emmons,
                "The Chilkat Tlingit," an unfinished essay in the
                BCPM Archives, folder #11. See also Drucker,
                Indians of the Northwest Coast, pp. 84–86.

23–25   The Element of Time
            Quotation: Reid, *Out of the Silence,* p. 80
            Length of time to spin and weave: Emmons, *The Chilkat
                Blanket,* p. 344
            Spinner and weaver as different people: Drucker,
                Culture Element Distributions, p. 264; and personal
                experience

26–31   A Ceremonial Costume
            Quotation: Reid, *Indian Art of the Northwest Coast of*

North America, p. 156

Position of Dancing Blanket on body: personal communication, Bill Holm. For similar style of wearing a cedar
bark robe, see Curtis, *The North American Indians,*
p. 71.

Leggings: *rectangular*—Smith cat. no. T–663 (fig. F)
This one is rare as it was woven as a legging. Most
leggings in collections were once pieces of Dancing
Blankets. *fishtail*—Smith cat. no. 341202 (fig. G)

Hat: Smith cat. no. 204776 (fig. 7)

Bear's ears: AMNH cat. no. 19–978 (fig. 7)

Ghost face medicine bag: SIM (fig. 7)

Cartridge pouch: Smith cat. no. 75443 (fig. 7)

Manufacture of aprons: Emmons, *The Chilkat
Blanket,* pp. 345–46

Figure 9: Oberg, *The Social Economy of the Tlingit
Indians,* first photograph following p. 44

Beaver Apron: Smith cat. no. 341202 (fig. 8)

Puffin beaks: MAI cat. no. 1/4281—beautiful rows of
puffin beaks sewn to the fringe

Feathers in puffin beaks: AMNH cat. no. E 2602

Tunic woven together on one side with a drawstring:
Smith cat. no. 229789 (figs. D and E)

Tunic with sleeves: NMM cat. no. VII–C–2099

Raven rattle: Holm and Reid, *Indian Art of the Northwest Coast of North America,* p. 192. Position of
holding rattle: personal communication, Bill Holm

34–37   Symbols of Wealth

Potlatch blankets: Emmons, *The Chilkat Blanket,* p. 345

Potlatch apron: Smith cat. no. 341202

Potlatch tunic: MAI cat. no. 3 9273

Potlatch leggings: Smith cat. no. 341202 (fig. G)
MAI cat. no. 7070
AMNH cat. no. 16.1 1613 A-D

Cremation: Emmons, "The Tlingit," Ch. VI, pp. 16–19;
Swanton, *Tlingit Myths and Texts,* p. 82; Krause, *The
Tlingit Indians,* pp. 157-59

Grave house photograph (fig. 17): The design is repre-
sentative of the design which was woven most often,
and is the same as that in figure 35 (BCPM photo
CPN 6630).

38–44   The Designs on a Dancing Blanket

Quotation: Emmons, *The Chilkat Blanket,* p. 347

Relief carvings painted first and then carved: Holm,
Analysis of Form, p. 33

House post board with gussets: Bancroft-Hunt and
Forman, *People of the Totem,* p. 44

Interpretation of designs: Emmons, *The Chilkat Blanket,*
pp. 386-89; Boas, *Primitive Art,* pp. 213–17

Categories of design: Holm, *An Analysis of Form,* pp. 11–13

Formlines: Holm, *An Analysis of Form,* p. 29

45   How the Design is Affected by the Weaving

Paintings similar to weavings in design: Wardwell, *Objects
of Bright Pride,* p. 97—painting on the Haida coffin;
University of Pennsylvania Museum Journal, Vol. 5,
No. 3, Fig. 83, p. 97—the painted screens and house
posts

45   The Pattern Board
      Pattern boards which are *almost* identical: Smith cat. no.
       209581; ROM cat. no. HN 1292; PAM Rasmussen
       Collection cat. no. 127; BCPM cat. no. CPN 14655,
       view 1

47–48   The Forms of the Design
      For a comprehensive discussion, read Holm, *An Analysis
       of Form.*

      Part II
50–51   The Spirit of the Goat
      Emmons, *The Chilkat Blanket,* pp. 333–34

52–53   Mountain Goats
      Wool as the major material used: verified by CCI
       research on Chilkat fibers, 1980
      Discussion of mountain goats: Chadwick, *National
       Geographic* August 1978, pp. 284-89

53–54   Mountain Goat Wool
      Goat hunters: Emmons, *The Chilkat Blanket,* p. 333
      Preparation of the fleece: Emmons, "The Tlingit," p. 55;
       Emmons, unpublished notes, BCPM Archives folder
       #19
      Clay and beater: Burnham, unpublished notes, NMM,
       p. 50; verification of presence of clay: CCI research
       on Chilkat fibers, 1980 and research by Mary Lou
       Florian, BCPM, 1980
      Compared with merino: Lisianskii, *Voyage Round the
       World,* p. 238

55   The Warp
      Yellow cedar: identified absolutely by Mary Lou Florian,
       BCPM, 1980. Botanical name: Chamaecyparis
       nootkatensis
      Size of warp yarns: a Dancing Blanket with small warp
       yarns, BCPM cat. no. 16511; a Dancing Blanket with
       large warp yarns, NMM cat. no. 76/76/81

56–57   Collecting the Cedar Bark
      Emmons, *The Chilkat Blanket,* p. 335
      Steltzer, *Indian Artists at Work,* pp. 34–36
      Drying of bark, preparation of bark strips, and thickness
       of bark: personal experience

58–60   Spinning the Warp
      This has been primarily determined by personal
       experience and descriptions by Emmons, *The Chilkat
       Blanket,* pp. 334–36, and Emmons, unpublished notes,
       BCPM Archives folder #12, and Drucker, *Culture
       Element Distributions,* p. 264.
      Speed of spinning: personal communication, Alena
       Samuel

62   The Weft
      Size of weft: a Dancing Blanket with fine weft yarns,
       AMNH cat. no. 16.1 1842 (fig. 26); a Dancing
       Blanket with thicker weft yarns, NMM cat. no. VII–
       C–259
      Commercial yarns: Emmons, *The Chilkat Blanket,*
       pp. 336–37

62–63   Spindles and Whorls
    Spinning: Emmons, *The Chilkat Blanket,* pp. 334–35
    Difficulty in spinning weft on the leg: personal experience
    Spindle collected from the Tlingit: MAI cat. no. 1/8923
        (fig. 61, right)
    Spindle collected from the Chilkat Tlingit: MAI cat. no.
        5/3510 (fig. 6, left)
    Whorls: MAI cat. no. 2/2118 (fig. 64)
    Spinning nettle and cedar bark with wool on a spindle:
        Boas, *The Kwakiutl,* pp. 372, 374–77

63–64   Spinning the Weft
    Description of spinning with a spindle: Boas, *The*
        Kwakiutl, pp. 373–77
    Description of the position of women when working:
        Emmons, "The Tlingit," no page number

64–65   Spinning Sinew
    Splitting sinew: de Laguna, *Under Mt. St. Elias,* Part I,
        p. 425
    Spinning sinew: Emmons, "The Tlingit," no page number,
        and Emmons, unpublished notes, BCPM Archives
        folder #19

65   The Sewing Pouch
    Examples: AMNH cat. no. 16.1 1196 and MAI cat. no.
        5/9699 (fig. 66)
    Use of bear's tooth: Paul, *Spruce Root Basketry of the*
        Alaskan Tlingit, p. 20

66   Dyeing the Weft
    Examples of black, white, and yellow robes: BM cat. no.
        NWC 51 and AMNH cat. no. 16.1 932 G (fig. 75)
    A Dancing Blanket with yellow-green yarn: AMNH cat.
        no. 16.952 (fig. B)
    A Dancing Blanket with blue-green yarn: AMNH cat. no.
        16.1 869 (fig. K)
    Use of commercial dyes: Emmons, *The Chilkat Blanket,*
        p. 337

66–67   Black Dye
    Hemlock bark: Emmons, *The Chilkat Blanket,* p. 336
    Mud: Emmons and Gunther report the use of black
        mud to obtain the black dye. Emmons, *The Chilkat*
        Blanket, p. 336; Gunther, *Indian Life on the Northwest*
        Coast of North America, p. 256. (Experiments have
        totally disintegrated the yarn and have produced no
        color.)
    Iron: presence verified by CCI research on Chilkat fibers
        and dyes, 1980. Use of iron as a darkening agent:
        Grae, *Nature's Colors,* p. 53
    La Pérouse: *Voyage,* p. 163
    Presence of iron in Tlingit country: de Laguna, *Under*
        Mt. St. Elias, Part I, p. 113
    Dyeing process: personal experience. Use of strong urine:
        Emmons, *The Chilkat Blanket,* p. 336. Use of salt
        water: de Laguna, p. 429
    Twill pattern due to different dye lots: CFM cat. no. 1571
        (fig. 23)

67–68   Yellow Dye
    Dyeing time: personal experience

68–70   From Green Dye to Blue
                 Determination of absence of copper in blue yarns and its
                     presence in the yellow-green yarns: CCI research on
                     Chilkat fibers and dyes, 1980, and Arvid Lacis of the
                     Metallurgy Department of the University of British
                     Columbia, and Mary Lou Florian of the Archaeology
                     and Conservation Division of the BCPM
                 Boiling blue trade cloth: Emmons, unpublished notes,
                     BCPM Archives folder #12
                 Shades of blue-green dye: AMNH cat. no. E 627, blue-
                     green (See also figure C.); CFM cat. no. 78963
                     (weaving on the loom), greener blue-green (fig. 223)
                 Blue dye painted over yellow-green areas: AMNH cat. no.
                     16/952 (fig. 24)
                 Use of woad and indigo: Grae, *Nature's Colors,* pp. 8–9

PART III
72–73   Two Tlingit Women Unravel the Mysteries of a
             Tsimshian Dancing Blanket
                 Emmons, *The Chilkat Blanket,* pp. 342–43

74–75   Twined Baskets and Twined Garments
                 Twined Basketry: Paul, *Spruce Root Basketry of the
                     Alaskan Tlingit,* pp. 13–32
                 Emmons, "The Tlingit," Ch. VII, pp. 1–19
                 de Laguna, *Under Mt. St. Elias,* Part I, pp. 427–28
                 Emmons, "The Basketry of the Tlingit," Vol. 3, Part 2,
                     pp. 229–77
                 Self-patterned twining is found in the following geometric
                     robes: NMD cat. no. KC 119, ROM cat. no. HN 821
                     (fig. 362), MAE cat. no. 2520-7, HP cat. no.
                     09-8-10/76401 (fig. 79), and NMM cat. no. VII–X–55
                     (fig. 83)

75–77   Geometric Chief's Robes
                 Drucker, *Indians of the Northwest Coast,* pp. 86–87
                 For detailed descriptions of all existing geometric robes see
                     Samuel, *Geometric Styled Chief's Robes of the Tlingit*
                 Hair in warp determined by CCI research on Chilkat
                     fibers and dyes, 1980
                 Fur and wool blankets: MAE cat. no. 2520-4 and
                     2520-5 (figs. 76–78). These are the only two in
                     existence. See Gunther, *Indian Life on the North-
                     west Coast of North America,* p. 261; Kaeppler,
                     "Cook Voyage Artifacts," p. 265; and Shur and
                     Pierce, "Artists in Russian America," pp. 40–49
                 The Swift Blanket: Willoughby, "A New Type of
                     Ceremonial Blanket from the Northwest Coast,"
                     pp. 1–10
                 Kissel, "The Early Geometric Patterned Chilkat,"
                     pp. 116–20
                 Distribution of geometric robes in the 1700s: de Laguna,
                     Under Mt. St. Elias, Part I, pp. 431–32

77–78   Cedar Bark Robes
                 With geometric border and formline design: ROM cat. no.
                     HN 13
                 With geometric border: BM cat. no. NWC 54
                 With checkerboard border: NMI cat. no. "Gunther,
                     Ireland 2"

78–81   The Transition

The transitional weavings are: MV cat. no. 218 (fig. 82),
NMI cat. no. "Gunther, Ireland 4" and "Gunther,
Ireland 5" (See Gunther, *Indian Life on the Northwest
Coast of North America,* pp. 257–58.), BM cat. no.
7262, BM cat. no. NWC 2262
Geometric robes with formline design: NMM cat. no.
VII–X–55 along with MAI cat. no. 4177 A (fig. 83);
ROM cat. no. HN 821. (fig. 364). See also a
photograph in the Ketchikan, Alaska Library:
6 77 9.930 T.H.S.—75.5.11.5.

82–83   Anatomy of a Dancing Blanket
Tie-off: Emmons, *The Chilkat Blanket,* p. 341. See also
notes under The Tie-Off.

90–91   Slipknots
Length of strand: personal experience
Use of: Drucker, *Culture Element Distributions,* p. 264
Example: CFM cat. no. 78963—loom with unfinished
weaving (fig. 223)

95–96   Drawstring Join
Example of a small unfinished face with drawstring joins
on either side: MAI cat. no. 15–4377
Sinew drawstring: AMNH cat. no. 16.956—sinew on side
braid, sinew or cedar bark on central areas
Cotton drawstring: AMNH cat. no. 16.1 2502
Occasionally wool or wool and cedar bark drawstrings
were used: SP cat. no. E 3648 (the Coppers Blanket,
fig. 85)

99   Braided Twining or Three-Strand Twining?
Method of determining the difference: personal
communication, Dr. Charles Rozaire, LACMNH, 1980

99–100   The Cross-Slat
Loom with cross-slat: CFM cat. no. 78963 (fig. 223)

119   The Use of Braids
Commercial yarns used in braids: AMNH cat. no. 19
1048, NMM cat. no. VII–A–237. Use of red
commercial yarn: NMM cat. no. VII–C–2089 (fig. 11).
See also figure J.

121–22   Added Warp Ends
50 warp ends added: SIM cat. no. 609–6–643
100 warp ends added: SP cat. no. E 3648 (Coppers
Blanket, fig. 85)
200 warp ends added: AMNH cat. no. 16 351

        Part IV
126–27   The Woman Who Wove in the Wilderness
Landsberg, unpublished notes, BCPM Archives

128–30   To Sing the Song of a Woman
Shotridge, "The Life of a Chilkat Indian Girl," pp. 101–3
Emmons, "The Tlingit," Ch. VI, pp. 8–9
Krause, *The Tlingit Indians,* pp. 152–53
Sample Dancing Blankets: MAI cat. no. 19–8635, MAI
cat. no. 15–4378, MAI cat. no. 00–1094
Labrets: When a young girl finished her time of seclusion,
her lower lip was pierced and a small bone plug

inserted. This was the beginning of the labret, an ornament worn by all women of nobility.

130–32　The Loom

For examples of looms: CFM cat. no. 78963 (fig. 223); a loom on display, Smith cat. no. 209964; loom posts, CFM cat. no. 57835 (very beautifully carved), AMNH cat. no. 19 579, Burke cat. no. 2.5 651

Portability: Emmons, *The Chilkat Blanket,* p. 337

132–33　Warping the Loom

Warping stick: CFM cat. no. 57836. This one has cutting marks in the middle of the shaft.

Drucker, *Culture Element Distributions,* p. 264

Emmons, *The Chilkat Blanket,* pp. 337–38

134　The Gut Bags

Emmons, *The Chilkat Blanket,* pp. 338–39

Emmons, "The Tlingit," Ch. VII, p. 55

Examples: AMNH cat. No. E 2091 B and 16.1 356, Smith cat. no. 209964 (on display), MAI cat. no. 9/8016

Occasionally cloth bags were substituted for gut bags.

141–43　Organizing the Strands of the Side Braid

Mathematics on the side braids: personal communication, Amy Wooten, mathematics professor at Lancaster University, Lancaster, England and Andrew Spray, mathematics professor at Lester B. Pearson College of the Pacific, Victoria, British Columbia

147–48　Lazy Lines

Emery, *The Primary Structures of Fabrics,* p. 83

151　Warp Markers

Examples: BCPM cat. no. 16511 and CFM cat. no. 78963 (fig. 223)

151　Intestine Sheet

The loom with its weaving in figure 269 is now on permanent display in the Smithsonian, cat. no. 209964.

152　Weaving the Design Field

Bark measuring stick: Emmons, *The Chilkat Blanket,* p. 342 and Drucker, *Culture Element Distributions,* p. 264

177–78　The Face Shape

Rounded head: MAI cat no. 14/2220, AMNH cat. no. T 25542, Smith cat. no. 219504 (b)

Ghost face legging: Smith cat. no. T–663 (fig. F)

Ghost face tunic: Smith cat. no. 229789 (fig. E)

193　The Side Fringe

A blue and white side fringe: NMM cat. no. VII–C–259

The Denver Art Museum has a blanket with a blue and white *great fringe*: personal communication, Bill Holm.

196–97　The Tie-Off

Tie-offs by the same weaver: AMNH cat. no. 16. 1 869 (fig. K) and NMM cat. no. 76/76/81 (fig. 403). These are both blankets woven by the woman to whom this book is dedicated, and are of the same design. In a personal communication to Katie Pasco, Mildred Sparks, a Tlingit woman from Klukwan whose mother was a weaver, indicated that the weavers of each clan had a particular tie-off pattern.

201–2   A New Dawn
Desire for western clothing: Vancouver, *Voyage, 1794*, p. 257

#

ANALYSIS SHEET: CHILKAT WEAVING

DATE: ANALYST:

ITEM: OWNER:
HISTORY: ADDRESS:

SIZE:

a	j
b	k
c	l
d	m
e	n
f	o
g	p
h	q
i	r
	s
	t
	u

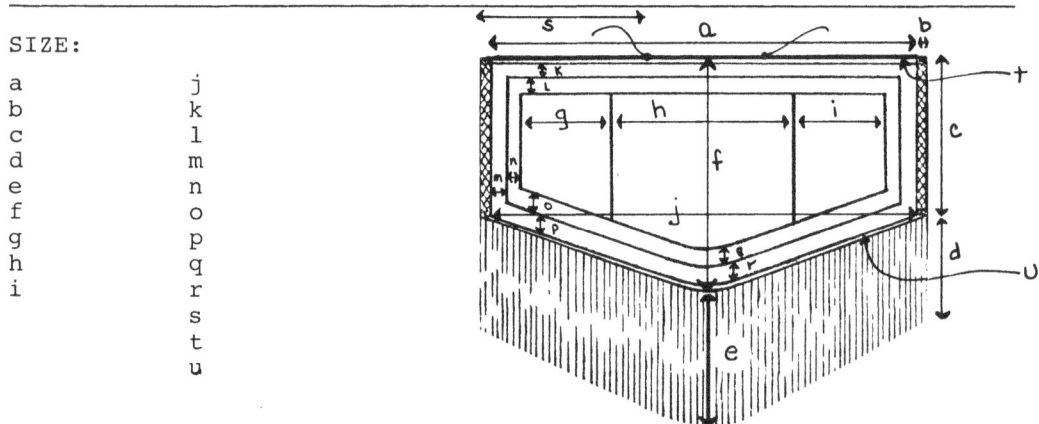

TIE OFF: (facing the weaving)

         left   right

MATERIALS: mountain goat wool yellow cedar bark
            commercial weft   sheep's wool in warp
            red cedar bark   twine substitute for cedar bark

DESIGN:

COLOURS: black   white   yellow   green   blue   red

BORDER COLOURS: (including braid rows, designated by a capital letter)

WARPS/CM: WEFTS/CM (large):   WEFTS/CM (small):

WARPS IN HEADING: #WARPS IN FRINGE:

PLIED TWIST OF YARNS: native warp   native weft
                          commercial warp   commercial weft

SLANT OF 3 STRAND BRAID: SLANT OF 2 STRAND TWINING:

HEADING: 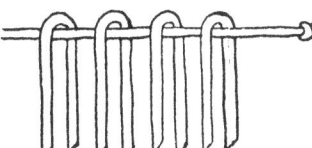

FUR:

TAPESTRY CONNECTIONS: (borders)   LAZY LINES:

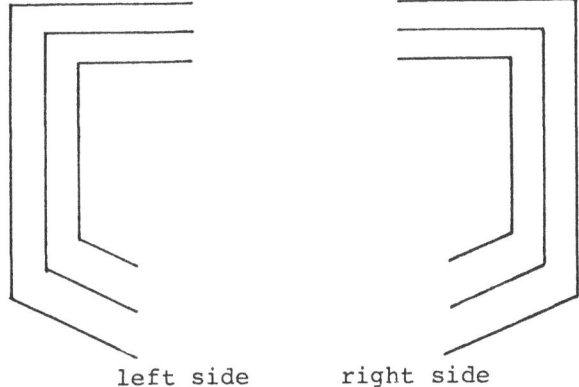

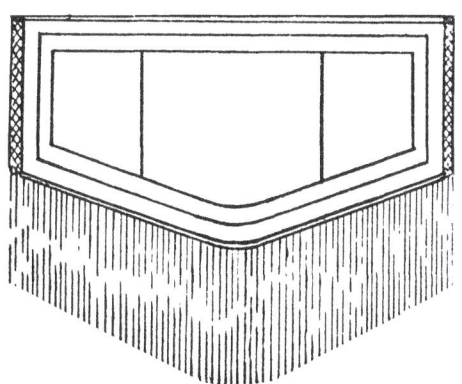

left side   right side

DRAWSTRING: material
               # of weft rows between inclusion of drawstring
               position of vertical braids over drawstring:
                   left   centered   right

TEETH: # of faces with teeth   full faces   side faces
         method of twining: a = alternate warp ends
                         b = paired warp ends
                         x = number of warp ends included in a stitch
                            (eg. "b3")

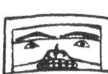

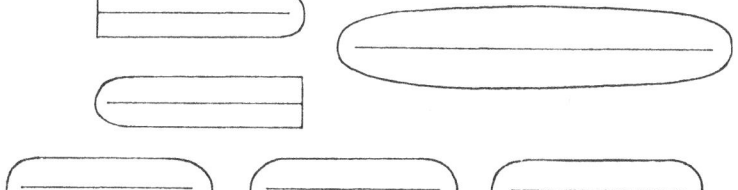

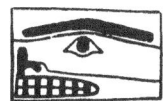

ADDED WARP ENDS: approximate # in top borders
                   approximate # in bottom borders
                   area where majority are added

METHOD OF SHAPING THE VERTICALLY SLANTED DESIGN ELEMENTS:
                   c = stepped   d = added warp ends
          nose   U shapes   ovoids

FRINGE: # of 2 strand rows   colour of 2 strand rows
          distance from white band:

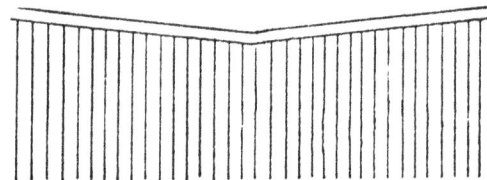

FALSE FRINGE: method of addition:

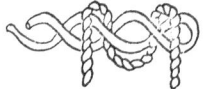   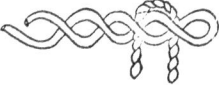

          frequency of addition
          weight of strands

SIDE BRAIDS: # of strands in left tie-off: right tie-off:
          method of attaching   method of attachment
          fringe insertion: to heading:

blanket
edge

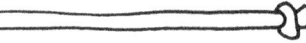

LOCATION OF COLOURS:

black = B
white = w
yellow = y
green = g
blue   = b
red   = r

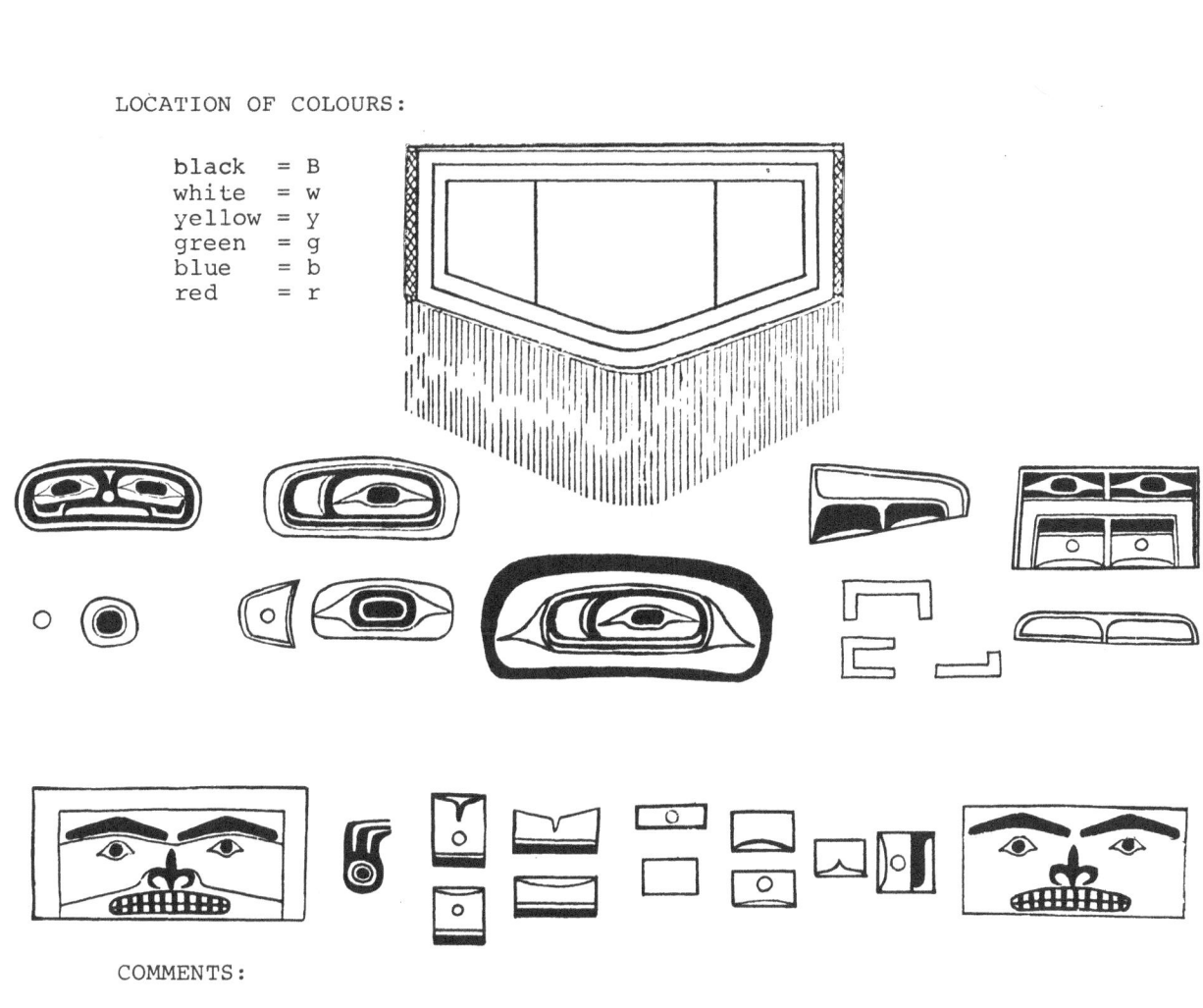

COMMENTS:

analysis sheets designed by Cheryl Samuel   September 1979

BIBLIOGRAPHY

Arts Canada. *Stones, Bones and Skin: Ritual and Shamanic Art.* Edited by
  Anne Trueblood Brodsky, Rose Danesewich, and Nick Johnson.
  Toronto: The Society for Art Publications, 1977.

Bancroft-Hunt, Norman, and Forman, Werner. *People of the Totem.*
  Toronto: Doubleday, 1979.

Bemis, Elijah. *The Dyer's Companion.* 1815. Reprint. Introduction by
  Rita J. Adrosko. New York: Dover, 1973.

Boas, Franz. *Second General Report on the Indians of British Columbia.*
  Report on the Northwestern Tribes of Canada, vol. 1, pp. 10–163.
  London: British Association for the Advancement of Science, 1890.

———. *The Kwakiutl of Vancouver Island.* Memoirs of the American
  Museum of Natural History, vol. V, part II, pp. 370–405. New York:
  American Museum of Natural History, 1909.

———. "Tsimshian Mythology." (Based on tapes recorded by Henry Tate)
  Washington, D.C.: 31st Annual Report of the Bureau of American
  Ethnology (1901–1910), 1916.

———. *Primitive Art.* 1927. Reprint. pp. 253–63, 283; plates X & XI.
  New York: Dover, 1955.

Burnham, Harold. "The Salish Weaving Complex" and notes entitled
  "Canadian Textiles," unpublished and held in the National Museum of
  Man, Ottawa.

Chadwick, Douglas. "Mountain Goats: Daring Guardians of the Heights."
  National Geographic August 1978: 284–89.

Crespi, Juan, and de la Peña, Fray Tomás. *The California Coast.* A
  bilingual edition of documents from the Sutro Collection. Translated
  and edited in 1891 by George Butler Griffin. Re-edited by Donald C.
  Cutter. Document 19, pp. 204–78. Norman, Oklahoma: University of
  Oklahoma Press, 1969.

Curtis, Edward S. *In a Sacred Manner We Live: Photographs of the North
  American Indian.* 1913. Reprint. Introduction by Don D. Fowler.
  New York: Weathervane, 1972.

———. *The North American Indians, A Selection of Photographs.*
  Introduction by Joseph Epes Brown. New York: Aperture, 1972.

De Laguna, Frederica. *Under Mount Saint Elias: The History and Culture
  of the Yakutat Tlingit.* Part I, pp. 412–44. Washington, D.C.:
  Smithsonian Institution Press, 1972.

De Laguna, Frederica; Ridell, Francis; McGeein, Donald F.; Lane,
  Kenneth; and Freed, J. Arthur. *Archaeology of the Yakutat Bay Area,
  Alaska.* Washington, D.C.: Bureau of American Ethnology, Bulletin
  192, 1964.

De Menil, Adelaide, and Reid, Bill. *Out of the Silence.* New York:
  Outerbridge and Dienstfrey, 1961.

Drucker, Philip. *Culture Element Distributions. XXVI, Northwest Coast,*
  Drucker, Anthropological Records, vol. 9, no. 3, pp. 259–66.
  Berkeley: University of California Press, 1950.

———. *The Indians of the Northwest Coast.* New York: McGraw-Hill, 1963.

———. *Cultures of the North Pacific Coast.* San Francisco: Chandler, 1965.

Emery, Irene. *The Primary Structures of Fabrics.* Washington, D.C.: The
  Textile Museum, 1966.

Emmons, George T. *The Basketry of the Tlingit.* Memoirs of the American
  Museum of Natural History, vol. III, part II, pp. 229–77. New York:
  American Museum of Natural History, 1903.

———. *The Chilkat Blanket.* With notes on the blanket designs by Franz
  Boas. Memoirs of the American Museum of Natural History, vol. III,
  part IV, pp. 329–401. New York: American Museum of Natural
  History, 1907.

———. "The Use of the Chilcat Blanket." *The American Museum Journal*
  8(1908):65–71.

——— "An Account of the Meeting between La Pérouse and the Tlingit."
  American Anthropologist 13(1911):294–98.

——. "The Tlingit." Unpublished manuscript held in the British Columbia Provincial Museum Ethnology Division Archives, Victoria.

——. Unpublished notes in the Newcombe Collection. Provincial Archives of British Columbia. Add. Mss 1077, Vol. 61: Folders 11–13, 19, 24.

Frame, Mary. "Tsimshian Blankets." Unpublished paper presented at the University of British Columbia, Vancouver, as part of a master's thesis course. 1979.

Grae, Ida. *Nature's Colors: Dyes from Plants.* New York: Macmillan Co., 1974.

Gunther, Erna. *Art in the Life of the Northwest Coast Indian.* pp. 69–89. Portland: Portland Art Museum Catalogue of the Rasmussen Collection, 1966.

——. *Indian Life on the Northwest Coast of North America.* Appendix 2, pp. 252–62. Chicago: University of Chicago Press, 1972.

Harvey, Virginia I., and Tidball, Harriet. *Weft Twining.* Monograph 28. Lansing, Michigan: Shuttle Craft Guild, 1969.

Hirabayashi, Joanne. "The Chilkat Weaving Complex." *Davidson Journal of Anthropology* 1(1953):43–61.

Holm, Bill. *Northwest Coast Indian Art: An Analysis of Form.* Seattle: University of Washington Press, 1965.

Holm, Bill, and Reid, Bill. *Indian Art of the Northwest Coast of North America.* Seattle: University of Washington Press, 1975.

James, George Wharton. *Indian Basketry: How to Make Baskets.* Glorieta, New Mexico: Rio Grande Press, 1903.

Kaeppler, Adrienne L. *Cook Voyage Artifacts in Leningrad, Berne, and Florence Museums.* Bernice P. Bishop Museum Special Publication 66. Honolulu: Bishop Museum Press, 1978.

Kissell, Mary Louise. "The Early Geometric Patterned Chilkat." *American Anthropologist* 30(1928):116–20.

Krause, Aurel. *The Tlingit Indians.* Translated by Erna Gunther. Seattle: University of Washington Press, 1956.

Landsberg, F. "Story of the Chilkat Blanket," unpublished notes held in the Provincial Archives of British Columbia, Manuscript Division. Add. Mss 1077, Vol. 44: Folder 25.

La Pérouse, Jean Francois Galup de. *The Voyage of La Pérouse Round the World, in the years 1785, 1786, 1787 and 1788.* Vol. 1. (Translated from the French in 2 vols.) Arranged by M.L.A. Milet Mureau. London: J. Stockdale, 1798.

Lisianskii, Iurii Fedorovich. *A Voyage Round the World in the Years 1803, 1804, 1805 and 1806.* Translated from the original Russian into English by Lisiansky. 1814. Reprint. Ridgewood, New Jersey: Gregg Press, 1968.

Niblack, Albert P. *The Coast Indians of South Eastern Alaska and Northern British Columbia.* Washington, D.C.: U.S. National Museum Report for 1888.

Oberg, Kalervo. *The Social Economy of the Tlingit Indians.* Seattle: University of Washington Press, 1973.

Olson, Ronald Le Ray. "The Possible Middle American Origin of N.W. Coast Weaving." *American Anthropologist* 31(1929):114–21.

Osborne, Carolyn, "The Yakutat Blanket." In *Archaeology of the Yakutat Bay Area, Alaska,* F. de Laguna et al. Washington, D.C.: Bureau of American Ethnology, Bulletin 192, 1964.

Paul, Frances. *Spruce Root Basketry of the Alaska Tlingit.* Edited by Willard W. Beatty. Washington, D.C.: U.S. Department of the Interior, Bureau of Indian Affairs, Division of Education, 1944.

Samuel, Cheryl. *Geometric Style Chief's Robes of the Tlingit.* Mercury Series Monograph. Ottawa: National Museums of Canada, forthcoming.

Shotridge, Florence. "The Life of a Chilkat Indian Girl." *The Museum Journal,* University of Pennsylvania 4(1913):101–3.

Shotridge, Louis, and Shotridge, Florence. "Indians of the Northwest." *The Museum Journal,* University of Pennsylvania 4(1913):69–99.

Shur, L.A., and Pierce, R.A. "Artists in Russian America: Mikhail Tikhanov (1818)." *Alaska Journal* Winter 1976:40–49.

Siebert, Erna, and Forman, Werner. *North American Indian Art.* London: Paul Hamlyn, 1967.

Steltzer, Ulli. *Indian Artists at Work.* Vancouver: J.J. Douglas, 1976.

Suría, Tomás de. *Journal of Tomás de Suría, of His Voyage with Malaspina to the Northwest Coast of America in 1791.* Translated and edited by Henry R. Wagner. pp. 254–57. Glendale, California: The Arthur H. Clark Co., 1936.

Swanton, John R. *Contributions to the Ethnology of the Haida.* The Jessup North Pacific Expedition, edited by Franz Boas. 1905. Reprint. pp. 1–300. New York: AMS Press, 1975.

———. *Tlingit Myths and Texts.* Bulletin no. 39 of the Bureau of American Ethnology. Smithsonian Institution, Washington, D.C.: Government Printing Office, 1909.

Vancouver, George. *A Voyage of Discovery to the North Pacific Ocean and Round the World, in the years 1790–1795.* 3 vols. 1798. Reprint. New York: N. Israel/Amsterdam and Da Capo Press, 1967.

Vanderberg, Joanne. "Chilkat and Salish Weaving." Master's thesis, University of Washington, 1953.

Wardwell, Allen. *Objects of Bright Pride: Northwest Coast Indian Art from the American Museum of Natural History.* New York: The Center for Inter-American Relations and the American Federation of the Arts, 1978.

Willoughby, Charles C. "A New Type of Ceremonial Blanket from the Northwest Coast." *American Anthropologist* 12(1910):1–10.

A C K N O W L E D G M E N T S

It is a great pleasure to be able to express my gratitude to the following people and the institutions they work for:

Burke Museum, University of Washington: Bill Holm
    Where would we be without the knowledge, enthusiasm, and generosity of Bill Holm? What would our work be without the standards he sets for himself and inspires in us?

Lieutenant G.T. Emmons: His vital interest in the Tlingit people and his observations of their weaving have left us with an invaluable record.

NORTH AMERICAN MUSEUMS

American Museum of Natural History: Dr. Phillip Gifford, Jr., Anibal Rodriquez, Dr. Junius Bird
British Columbia Provincial Museum: Dr. Peter McNair, Dan Savard, Liz Virolainen, Marilyn Chechik, Mary Lou Florian, Alan Hoover
Canadian Conservation Institute: Dr. J.M. Taylor and his team of scientists
Field Museum of Natural History, Chicago: Dr. Ron Weber, Phyllis Rabineau
Glenbow: Carol Sheehan, Julia Harrison
Heard Museum: Camile Tumolo
Museum of the American Indian, Heye Foundation: Brenda Holland
Los Angeles County Museum of Natural History: Nancy Blomberg, Dr. William Lee, Dr. Charles Rozaire
Manitoba Museum of Man and Nature: Katherine Pettipas
National Museum of Man: Annette McFadyen Clark, Dr. George MacDonald, Judy Hall
Peabody Museum, Harvard: Dr. Edwin Wade
Peabody Museum, Salem: John Grimes, Dr. Peter Fetchko
Portland Art Museum: Dr. William Chiego
Royal Ontario Museum: Kenneth Lister, Dr. H. Fuchs
Santa Barbara Museum of Natural History: Jan Timbrook, Dr. Travis Hudson
Smithsonian Institution: Barbara Stuckenrath, Dr. William Sturtevant
Southwest Indian Museum: Dee Ulrich
University of British Columbia, Metallurgy Department: Arvid Lacis

EUROPEAN MUSEUMS

Museum of Anthropology and Ethnography, Leningrad: Madame Rosa Lyapunova, Academician Julian Bromley
Museum and Art Gallery, Perth: Susan Payne
Museum of Mankind, British Museum, London: Dr. Jonathan King
Museum für Völkerkunde, Vienna: Dr. Christian Feest
National Museum of Denmark, Copenhagen: Else Østergård, Niels Erik Jehrbo
National Museum of Ireland, Dublin: Mary Cahill
Pitt Rivers Museum, Oxford: Lynn Williams, Birgitta Speake

The warmest thanks to all who have shared in this very remarkable, sometimes comical, and always rewarding experience:

Especially Ann Meerkerk, who encouraged me to write it all down

Katie Pasco, who stands behind the revival of Chilkat weaving with her knowledge, her passion, and her boundless support
Martha Cram, who shares my inner circle
Patty Oliver, who wove in that first circle of friends
Steve Brown, who painted my pattern board and sent me a box of deer toes

Bill Reid, whose words continue to inspire me

Christine Olsen, who tempered my travels with gentle intelligence

Jack Matthews, Director of Pearson College, who gave me time

I. Norman Smith, who bundled me in his confidence

Tony Hunt, who danced

Jorgen Svendsen, who caught the essence of the dance in his photographs

Kate Williams and David Bruce, who printed all of my photographs

Jill Mallett, who lettered the diagrams

Dorothy Burnham, who shared Harold Burnham's notes

Christopher Peet, who first saw the hair in the ROM blanket

Mike and Eileen Nesbitt, who share my love for the beautiful blankets

Duane Pasco, who painted the formline designs and gives me courage

Isabel Tipton, who gathered yellow cedar bark and tested the dyes

Amy Wooten and Andrew Spray, who worked on the math for the side braids

Esmé Davis and Elizabeth Anderson, who wove from the manuscript

Judith MacKenzie, who patiently worked out the dye recipes

Art and Polly Thompson, and Katherine, who share in the beginnings of a new dawn

Arthur and June Gallon, my parents, who have faith in me

Dean Samuel, who fashioned Tlingit tools and drew the map

Alena Samuel, who provided dye material and spins beautiful warp yarns

Silvina Samuel, who loves corners

Sara Porter, who shared a rainbow and the call of a raven

And especially Edgar Samuel, who has lived through and supported this project in so many ways and without whose confidence it could not have been done.

I N D E X

www.ingramcontent.com/pod-product-compliance
Lightning Source LLC
Chambersburg PA
CBHW080408290526
45791CB00008BA/2197